THE LAW
ON
THE MISUSE OF DRUGS
AND
DRUG TRAFFICKING OFFENCES

AUSTRALIA
The Law Book Company
Brisbane • Sydney • Melbourne • Perth

CANADA
Carswell
Ottawa • Toronto • Calgary • Montreal • Vancouver

AGENTS
Steimatzky's Agency Ltd., Tel Aviv
N.M Tripathi (Private) Ltd., Bombay
Eastern Law House (Private) Ltd., Calcutta
M.P.P. House, Bangalore
Universal Book Traders, Delhi
Aditya Books, Delhi
MacMillan Shuppan KK, Tokyo
Pakistan Law House, Karachi, Lahore

THE LAW
ON
THE MISUSE OF DRUGS
AND
DRUG TRAFFICKING OFFENCES

Second edition

I worked with this guy on a work-placement — a decent chap!

RUDI FORTSON LL.B. (LOND.)
of the Middle Temple,
Barrister

London
Sweet & Maxwell
1992

First edition 1988
Second edition 1992

Published in 1992 by
Sweet & Maxwell Ltd., of
South Quay Plaza, 183 Marsh Wall,
London, E14 9FT
Typeset by Tradespools Ltd., Frome
Printed and bound in Great Britain
by Butler & Tanner, Frome and London

**A CIP catalogue for this book is
available from the British Library**

ISBN 0-421-459-204

©
Rudi Fortson
1992

PREFACE

In the wake of rapid cultural changes (internationally) in respect of the use and misuse of drugs, the Misuse of Drugs Act 1971 was enacted with a view to controlling the importation, distribution and use of substances and products considered by the government of the day to be capable of having "harmful effects likely to constitute a social problem." However, the drug problem, far from being nearer to a solution, has increased considerably in complexity due, in part, to the popularity of so-called "designer drugs" some of which are dangerous "cocktails." It is too early to say whether the consumption of these drugs will wane as the "fashions" that they represent pass. Whereas by 1988 there was some evidence that the use of LSD was in decline, the drug soared in popularity during 1990, but slumped during 1991 as it competed with the consumption of other hallucinogenics such as "Ecstasy" (methylenedioxymethylamphetamine hydrochloride, *i.e.* M.D.M.A.) and M.D.A. (methylenedioxyamphetamine). Both M.D.M.A. and M.D.A. are Class A derivatives of amphetamine, the latter being a Class B drug. Two disturbing features have emerged in connection with M.D.M.A. abuse. The first is that the drug seems to be popular with a large group of persons who previously avoided, or even shunned, drug abuse. The second, and perhaps more disturbing feature, are the number of cases where a substance is passed off as M.D.M.A. when in fact it is a blend of amphetamine, LSD and ketamine.

Ketamine is itself growing in popularity. It is not yet controlled under the Misuse of Drugs Act 1971 but it is classified as an anaesthetic under the Medicines Act 1968.

Although it is the "designer drugs" which are currently hitting the headlines, the reality is that a considerable number of substances and medicinal products are currently being abused or made into drug "cocktails."

The courts have striven to give effect to the letter (and to the spirit) of the relevant legislation, but they have also endeavoured to balance various competing interests so as to control drug use on the one hand without unnecessarily making criminals out of people on the other. The upshot is that the law governing this field is becoming increasingly complex. Where drug trafficking is involved, the powers vested in the courts to seize the proceeds of such trafficking is utterly draconian.

At a time when many governments around the globe are taking sterner measures to curb drug abuse, the "legislation debate" is intensifying. This book does not involve itself in that debate. However, one point which is often overlooked by the debaters concerns the constitutional and political obstacles that face any government endeavouring to act unilaterally in contravention of any treaty to which that government was a signatory (*e.g.* the Single Convention on Narcotic Drugs (1961) or, more recently, the Convention against Illicit Traffic in Narcotic Drugs and Psychotropic Substances (1988)).

The object of this book is to guide the reader through the legal complexities of drug law – *not* by a cold citation of statutory provisions and authorities, but by attempting to analyse various problems and examining how the Legislature and the courts have approached each problem. Accordingly, even if the reader does not agree with the analysis (which is entirely my responsibility) it is intended and hoped that he or she will acquire a greater understanding of this area of the law and gain food for further thought.

Because the relevant statutes, statutory instruments and their respective Schedules are continually subject to amendment or modification, I have seen little value in blandly reproducing them in their original form. Instead the relevant provisions (as amended) are appropriately set out in the text.

If is often remarked that the publication of a book is a team effort that tests the patience of the team. I have come to learn just how true that statement is and I am sure that I have succeeded in testing the patience of my team to the limit. I am, therefore, extremely grateful to my publishers, and in particular the editorial staff, who have worked way beyond the call of duty in the preparation of this book. They have given me much support, advice and assistance. I would also like to thank the many colleagues who have given me food for thought – in particular, John Perry Q.C., Steven Kay Esq., and also Detective Constable Geoff Monaghan, for their very helpful comments, suggestions and information. Trawling through cases and materials is a tiresome task and in this regard I am very grateful to Edward Fitzpatrick Esq. who helped me considerably. I should also like to thank my wife Fiona for her unfailing patience and typing skills, my parents for their support, and last but not least, G. Benham Esq. who opened my eyes to the fact that a book of this nature was called for. Needless to say, any errors that exist are my responsibility.

Gray's Inn
London.
September, 1992   RUDI FORTSON

CONTENTS

TABLE OF CASES

A bold paragraph reference indicates that a summary of the relevant case is given.

TABLE OF STATUTES

FOREIGN STATUTES

UNITED STATES AND CANADIAN STATUTES

TABLE OF STATUTORY INSTRUMENTS

Chapter 1
Introduction

A. AN HISTORICAL SKETCH OF DRUG MISUSE

Until the early 1960s Britain did not have a major social narcotics problem. **1–01**
Today it is conservatively estimated that some five million people in Britain
regularly abuse drugs—from cannabis, amphetamines and barbiturates, to
cocaine and heroin. It is beyond the scope of this book to examine why drug-
taking should have such a wide appeal. The reasons are intensely complicated
and probably not fully understood but it should always be borne in mind that
not all drug abuse is rooted in delinquency; drugs are often unwittingly
abused as well. The familiar image of the physically sick addict ignores the
fact that many drugs produce harmful effects even if they are not proved to be
physically dangerous, *e.g.* psychological dependence or drug-related crime.

It is therefore with good reason that the legislature has moved away from
narrow terms such as "dangerous drugs" and "poisons" and speaks instead
of the "misuse" of drugs: hence the Misuse of Drugs Act 1971.

I. THE EMERGENCE OF A SOCIAL DRUG PROBLEM

Drug misuse is an ancient problem. It is easy to overlook the fact that prob- **1–02**
ably the oldest drug is alcohol, which has been used and abused on an international scale since time immemorial. In the Far East and in Africa, opium and
cannabis have been taken socially for thousands of years. The South Amer-
icans discovered that chewing coca-leaves stimulated the mind while the
Greeks and Aztecs used hallucinogenic herbs and plants in some of their religious ceremonies to create mystical effects. The Egyptians, too, compounded
many mind-altering potions.

With the advent of the Industrial Revolution (1760–1840), the skills of
chemistry and pharmacy were combined to form a powerful industry which
made available a host of new drugs to meet a host of new demands.

Opium was principally used for the purposes of stupefaction but no restric- **1–03**
tions were placed on its distribution and use until the Pharmacy Act 1868
regulated the sale of the drug. Nevertheless, the drug remained readily obtain-
able for many years thereafter. As early as 1803 morphine (an opiate) was
developed and soon became recognised as a most powerful pain reliever. It

1

was also highly addictive. Its widespread use to treat the wounded, both in war-time and in peace-time, unfortunately resulted in a large number of patients becoming opiate-dependent. Moreover, drugs such as opium and morphine found their way into many commercial substances and products which claimed to alleviate all kinds of ailments. Morphine, in turn, led to the discovery of another powerful drug—heroin—produced in London in 1874. Foolishly this drug was also used in many commercial preparations. It was thought not to be addictive. It is, and it follows from the above that many opiate users became unwillingly addicted.

There were, of course, substances and products which were wilfully (even fashionably) abused by the consumer.

Thus, cocaine, formerly a popular local anaesthetic, appealed to an eccentric, middle-aged circle of the Victorian middle class, as a stimulant. Sir Arthur Conan Doyle mirrored that fact in his portrayal of the fictional character Sherlock Holmes as an occasional user of the drug. Interest in cocaine waned until the 1920s when, once again, a relatively well-heeled set in America, and in Europe, abused it.

1–04 Similarly, amphetamine was used to treat depression and narcolepsy, but its ability to stimulate the mind has, for decades, prompted people to abuse it. Thus, Drinamyl attained notoriety in the 1960s when it was widely abused by delinquent teenagers, by students revising for examinations and by performers in the entertainment industry. Better known as the "Purple Heart" this product accelerated legislation to control amphetamines.

More recently, Ritalin has become popular with heroin addicts who use it to counteract some of the adverse effects experienced with heroin, *e.g.* depression.

Other products contained active constituents (*e.g.* morphine or amphetamine) the effects of which were not fully understood until the manifestations of abuse or side effects were realised.

It is sometimes said that major wars have contributed to the current drug problem but this superficial claim overlooks the fact that the majority of those currently abusing drugs have not seen National Service, let alone active service. Certainly major wars have significantly contributed to the development of new drugs and probably encouraged a much wider use of many dangerous substances such as morphine and other painkillers. Amphetamines, too, were regularly prescribed to servicemen, to keep them awake and alert during combat. Their use could not be sustained since they were addictive and capable of producing aggression, confusion and panic.

1–05 Significantly, in the West, relatively few drug abusers deliberately self-administered the first dose of a "hard drug," *e.g.* heroin, until the 1960s. By contrast, opium addiction in the Far East was a major concern of the world over 150 years ago.

Unfortunately, Britain played a major role in the highly profitable "opium trade" of the Far East. In 1830, Britain declined to allow China to put a ban on opium and 1842 saw Britain's victory in the so-called "opium war." The resulting widespread abuse of opium generated international alarm, with calls for positive action to eradicate the problem. A series of conferences and treaties followed. Britain honoured its commitment by ratifying several treaties. The Pharmacy Act 1868 regulated the use and preparation of opium. Between 1868 and 1925, three further statutes were passed restricting the use of a number of other substances. Significantly, the Dangerous Drugs Act 1920 codified a number of wartime regulations which outlawed the possession of opium and cocaine for personal consumption. Following the Geneva Convention in 1925, and after representations made by the Egyptian Delegation, the use of cannabis came in for strong condemnation. As a result the Dangerous Drugs Act 1925 regulated the possession and use of that substance. There is some evidence that, after 1925, drug abuse in the United Kingdom (as small as it was) was in decline. Of course domestic laws could have little effect on the drug problem overseas. Accordingly, the League of Nations, and later the United Nations, sought to prevent addiction and drug trafficking throughout the world. Their success has been limited and perhaps frustrated by a cumbersome bureaucratic method of control based on quantifying the amount of world production and consumption of dangerous drugs. "Taking stock" of drug production is largely dependant on relying on member states submitting estimates of their own production of the relevant drug. Inevitably the drug barons, carrying out illicit production and supplies, either furnish no particulars at all or falsify them. Member States whose "balance sheets" reveal a disturbing quantity of "lost drugs" may be asked to explain the loss, but efficiently policing drug production and supply, in this way and in accordance with international law, is virtually impossible.

For approximately 100 years between 1860 and 1960, the addict was seen as a person suffering from illness. In one sense such a perception is justified if one looks purely at the effects various drugs may have on both the body and the mind, but drug abuse cannot be regarded as a disease, as it certainly was regarded in 1926, when the Departmental Committee on Morphine and Heroin Addiction (the "Rolleston Committee") published its Report (HMSO, 1926). Medical thinking had not significantly changed when the first Report of the Interdepartmental Committee on Drug Addiction (the I.C.D.A.) was published in 1961. Again, the suggestion was that drug addicts were "sick"; suffering a form of mental illness.

However, in the wake of rapid cultural changes, narcotic abuse became fashionable on an international scale. The second Report of the I.C.D.A. (HMSO 1965) shows that the committee revised its thinking and directed its attack against the black market and doctors who over-prescribe.

In the treatment of addicts the role of doctors complicates the picture. A doctor might, for example, prescribe the hard drug itself, prescribe a substitute, e.g. methadone for heroin, or prescribe nothing at all and instead advise therapy. Often doctors prescribed heroin or cocaine privately. The pharmacist, likewise, often charged a fee for encashing the prescription. From the addict's point of view the cost was cheaper than buying on the black market, but, such a doctor was (and is) in danger of becoming an "easy touch," liable to attract many drug users. He would be encouraged to prescribe liberally, perhaps fearing that to turn users away empty-handed was forcing them to resort to the black market and probably to commit offences in order to pay the black market prices. The General Medical Council has considered many cases of doctors prescribing in this way. Some doctors were undoubtedly well-motivated while a few were unscrupulous and issued private prescriptions like confetti. Although the existence and enforcement of regulations may seriously reduce the range of drugs a doctor may administer, prescribe and supply, nevertheless they also serve to protect him from manipulative addicts.

1–07   The doctor was (and still is) liable to be the victim of another manipulation of the system, namely by unwittingly prescribing controlled drugs to a drug user who is already registered with another doctor. The practice of "double-scripting" is rife and not easy to detect. The addict having increased his supply of drugs through the comparatively cheap medium of the private or National Health Service might then sell his surplus stock on the black market at street level prices. The income would pay his doctors fees, allow him to buy other drugs and to pay the general household bills. It is partly with this practice in mind that the legislature has sought to enact a structured system of licensing, registration, recording and book-keeping in order to monitor the distribution of controlled drugs.

Much controversy has arisen concerning the "drugs problem" and how to deal with it. Views range between demands for stern penal sanctions on the one hand, to calls for no action at all on the other. The former school advocates the need to deter others; the latter advocates that left alone the "practice" will burn itself out. Between 1868 and 1971 Parliament's approach had been piecemeal. The Pharmacy Act 1868 was designed principally to regulate the use of opium. The Drugs (Prevention of Misuse) Act 1964 sought to restrict the use of amphetamines. Those restrictions were extended to the drug LSD by the Dangerous Drugs Act 1965. For over 100 years attention was focused on those drugs considered to be "dangerous." In truth, little was known about the medical and social effects of many popular drugs from aspirin and Librium, to cannabis and cocaine. To control the use of some drugs and not others was unpopular in principle because legislation was thereby demonstrated to be arbitrary in its approach. Parliament ultimately endeavoured to search for a method of control that would be open ended in its scope and reasonably subtle in its administration. The result was the Misuse of Drugs Act 1971.

1–08   The Misuse of Drugs Act 1971 (the "M.D.A.") can be summarised as setting up six main objectives. First, to control the use, production and distribution of all drugs recognised as being medically or socially harmful. Secondly, to create a body (the Advisory Council) comprising of experts in the fields of science and social science that would give to the government of the day sound professional advice. Thirdly, to promote a deeper understanding of the problem by undertaking research. Fourthly, to enforce the law by criminal sanctions if necessary. Fifthly, to facilitate the treatment of drug-dependants and finally to educate the public. Finally legislation has recently been enacted to recover the proceeds of drug trafficking, notably the Drug Trafficking Offences Act 1986 (or, in Scotland, the Criminal Justice (Scotland) Act 1967) and Part III of the Criminal Justice (International Co-operation) Act 1990. Although these statutes are not primarily directed at drug use, the Government clearly hopes that by stripping drug traffickers of their ill-gotten gains, others will be deterred from embarking upon drug trafficking.

B. DRUG CONTROL AND DRUG CLASSIFICATION

I. WHICH DRUGS ARE LIABLE TO CONTROL?

The *Oxford English Dictionary* defines a "drug" as being: 1–09

> "An original, simple, medicinal substance organic or inorganic, used by itself, or as an ingredient in medicine . . . a narcotic or opiate . . . ."

The word "narcotic," by contrast has a much narrower meaning:

> ". . . a substance which when swallowed, inhaled or injected into the system induces drowsiness, sleep, stupefaction or insensibility . . . ."

Oddly, the Misuse of Drugs Act 1971 does not define the word "drug," preferring instead to merely list those "substances" which are "controlled" in their use. Clearly all medicines are drugs but not all drugs are medicines. Scientists generally access a drug's level of safety by reference to its *therapeutic index*, being the ratio between the median *effective* dose as against the median *toxic* dose.

For present purposes drugs can be loosely grouped as follows:

(i) substances either organic or inorganic, which are used in medicines;
(ii) drugs present in naturally occurring substances, *e.g.* caffeine in tea and coffee, alcohol, nicotine in tobacco, T.H.C. in cannabis;
(iii) narcotics contained in substances not naturally occurring, *e.g.* in solvent glues, nail varnishes, butane fuels;
(iv) substances cultivated, extracted or created principally for narcotic abuse, *e.g.* LSD, psilocin (the "magic mushroom").

The Preamble to the M.D.A. reads as follows: 1–10

> "An Act to make provision with respect to dangerous or otherwise harmful drugs . . . ."

Hence certain drugs are "controlled" and listed as Class A, B or C type drugs depending on the magnitude of danger or harm attached to them: see section 2(1) M.D.A. While it is not difficult to predict substances which would fall into the dangerous drugs category, being dangerous to one's health, physically or mentally, it is apparent that Parliament had in mind yet another category of drug which it sought to control, namely, those drugs that are described by the M.D.A. as being *"otherwise harmful."* The problem is identifying those drugs which are liable to fall into this latter category. An indication is given in section 1(2) which imposes a duty on the Advisory Council to keep under review drugs "likely to be misused and of which the misuse is . . . capable of having *harmful effects* to constitute a *social problem* . . ." What then is meant by the phrase "a harmful effect" in the context of section 1(2) M.D.A.? Also what type of problem is a "social" one?

(a) Harmful effects = dangerous drugs + 'otherwise harmful'

1–11   The first point to note is that, unlike the Preamble to the Act, section 1(2) does not distinguish between "dangerous" drugs and those that are "otherwise harmful." Instead the legislature preferred to rely on the phrase "harmful effects" as being all-embracing. Secondly, Parliament clearly intended to include drugs that were not only capable of causing physical or mental "harm" to the user, directly or indirectly, but also drugs which are capable of producing harmful *results*, or *consequences*, amounting to a "social problem." Accordingly, in this wider context, the "harm" encompasses sociological "damage," *e.g.* delinquency, or the emergence of a social group of users who are in danger of acquiring no more than psychological dependence to a certain drug, *e.g.* barbiturates.

(b) Defining what is a social problem

1–12   Any *irregular activity* in the pattern of human behaviour in which some action is required to be carried out by and on behalf of the community in order to maintain harmonious co-existence, or to maintain the reciprocation of benefits, may be said to give rise to a social problem. Accordingly, drugs that cause an unacceptably high level of addiction and which place significant demands on the resources of the medical profession and the social sciences create a social problem. But suppose the taking of a certain drug does no more than mark adolescent rebellion and causes no physical or psychological harm at all. Such behaviour may be delinquent and therefore a "social problem" but it is also likely to be seen as a harmful effect of the drug misuse and the drug is liable to be controlled.

With the emphasis therefore being placed on the recognition of any drug-linked social problem (which need not be based on delinquency), it is evident that *all* drugs are capable of being controlled by the M.D.A. even if they may not produce any physical or psychological harm (medically speaking). The consequential sociological problem is, in itself, one "harmful effect" of the abuse.

The classes of controlled drugs are not closed, and consequently substances may be added to, or removed from Schedule 2 by an Order in Council: section 2(2). A draft of that order must be laid before Parliament and approved by a resolution of each House: section 2(5). This is designed to give Parliament the opportunity of vetting any proposed changes to the law. It is also the probable reason why any radical alteration to Schedule 2 is unlikely to occur lest it should spark off a politically-damaging response.

II. PRACTICAL CONSIDERATIONS OF DRUG CLASSIFICATION

(a) Flexibility

1–13   It is clearly desirable that the classes of controlled drugs should be kept open and that any alterations made to them are based on sound empirical research. Both the Advisory Council and the Secretary of State may initiate their own research to that end, but the Secretary of State cannot lay a draft order before Parliament without first consulting the Advisory Council: see section 2(5). Determining just how flexible the law really is can best be measured by noting the rate at which the law changes in response to the prevailing conditions and state of scientific opinion.

Since 1971 no less than ten "Modification Orders" have been approved, the latest being S.I. 1990 No. 2589. (See also S.I. 1973 No. 771, S.I. 1975 No. 421, S.I. 1977 No. 1243, S.I. 1979 No. 299, S.I. 1983 No. 765, S.I. 1984 No. 859, S.I. 1985 No. 1995, S.I. 1986 No. 2230, S.I. 1989 No. 1340.) In the majority of cases, the changes have not been particularly startling. But more sweeping changes have taken place in the last two years, including (after much pressure), controlling certain barbiturates and tranquillisers which have been deliberately abused or taken to excess for a considerable number of years. For the moment the trend is to select, with one hand, an increasing number of drugs for the purposes of classification so as to bring them within the scrutiny of the law but, using the other hand, to grant an extension of the general authority to possess and supply, a limited number of them; as well as making a number of other concessions. Laudable though it is for the law to be flexible, and to be seen to be so, three other factors must be put into the equation. First, the law must strive to be certain. From the moment of manufacture, until the moment of consumption, a drug will change hands countless times. It may be imported or exported. It will be used for different purposes. Different considerations will inevitably apply at different stages, but the manufacturer and every other party in the chain must make his arrangements in accordance with the law, and he can only do so if he knows where he stands. Secondly, the law does not exist to make criminals out of people unnecessarily. The wider the net of the M.D.A. is cast, the more likely it is that individuals and companies will fall foul of the law. Thirdly, consideration must also be given to the impact that such a restriction will have on innocent parties, including the drug manufacturers themselves who can suddenly experience much administrative inconvenience, loss of income and possible legal action. The manufacturer may also be forced to litigate, at much expense, and challenge the classification of his drug as a "controlled" drug.

(b) Classification should not be arbitrary

This is particularly important where drugs are controlled on the basis that   **1–14** their misuse may have harmful effects sufficient to constitute a social problem. Drugs may or may not be fashionable to misuse. Those which are fashionable and meet the criteria, one would expect to see added to the list, and those ceasing to be so, deleted. Furthermore, it was presumably not the intention of the legislature to control drugs that demonstrably appealed only to an eccentric few and was likely to remain so. In those circumstances the abuse is contained and limited to an isolated group and therefore not likely to constitute a social problem. If flexibility is not maintained so that drugs are classified in keeping with current social and scientific opinion, then the courts are placed at a considerable disadvantage, at least on the question of sentence, believing the drugs in question to be more or less harmful than they really are.

(c) Challenging the classifications

1–15   Most people recognise certain drugs by their "brand name" but the government designates a controlled drug by its chemical address, as it must do for clarity. Since drugs are controlled in this way it follows that many different brands can be affected even if it is, in truth, one brand name that seems to be the target of misuse. Furthermore, a drug which produces an effect *similar* to the misused drug might also find itself being controlled for that reason, even though the comparable substance is differently chemically constituted and has no history of having been misused at all. The drug may also be controlled, not because it is inherently dangerous, but because its harmful effect is said to be rooted in a social problem.

What, then, can a company do about it? Its only recourse is to attempt to go behind the making of the Order in Council by ascertaining that the Secretary of State acted *ultra vires* and the designation was made on a misconceived basis. It goes without saying that such a company sets itself a most formidable task.

III. EXERCISING CONTROL: MAPPING THE M.D.A. 1971

1–16   Since the M.D.A. is designed and intended to regulate the flow of drugs and their use, the following structure is enacted:

(i)   Certain drugs are specified as being "controlled": see Schedule 2.
(ii) As a *general rule* it is unlawful to:
    (*a*) import or export controlled drugs: section 3;
    (*b*) produce or supply controlled drugs: section 4;
    (*c*) possess controlled drugs: section 5;
    (*d*) cultivate the cannabis plant: section 6;
    (*e*) prepare or smoke opium: section 9;
    (*f*) permit premises to be used for the purposes listed above: section 8;
    (*g*) use utensils or allow others to use them in connection with the smoking of opium: section 9;
    (*h*) frequent opium "dens": section 9.
(iii) It is unlawful for a person in the United Kingdom to assist in or induce the commission of a "corresponding offence" abroad: section 20.
(iv) Companies may also be guilty of committing offences: section 21.
(v)   However, the government may create exceptions to the general rule and;
    (*a*) allow certain controlled drugs to be imported/exported, produced, supplied or possessed: section 7(1)(*a*);
    (*b*) allow certain persons to use controlled drugs under licence: section 7(1)(*b*) and section 7(2);
    (*c*) allow practitioners in the medical and veterinary professions to supply drugs: section 7(3)(*a*);
    (*d*) allow those practitioners to possess certain controlled drugs: section 7(3)(*b*);
But:(vi) The government may:

(a) restrict certain controlled drugs to reseach use only: section 7(4)(a);

(b) require medical practitioners, etc., to hold a licence before supplying or possessing certain controlled drugs: section 7(4)(b).

The M.D.A. provides the legal framework. However, it is the regulations   **1–17**
which seek to administer its objectives. The bulk of the regulations are to be found in the Misuse of Drugs Regulations 1985 (S.I. 1985 No. 2066) (the M.D.Regs.). The earlier Misuse of Drugs Regulations 1973 and its amending instruments have been revoked. Other regulations are considered separately in this work.

Many of the regulations and rules are designed to ensure that certain beneficial drugs remain in proper hands by requiring that drugs be kept secure; that documents are kept of drug transactions; that suitable records be maintained and furnished for possible inspection; that drugs are properly packed, labelled and safely transported; and that the issue of prescriptions be carefully regulated.

IV. CONTROLLING THE ACTIVITIES OF DOCTORS/PHARMACISTS, ETC.

Again, the M.D.A. seeks to provide a framework regulating the activities of   **1–18**
patients, doctors and pharmacists.

Put in simplified terms the basic framework is as follows:

(i)   A doctor may administer specified drugs: M.D. Regs. 7(2).

(ii)   Certain doctors may supply or offer to supply specified drugs to another: M.D. Regs. 8(4) and 9(4).

(iii)   Prescriptions must meet certain conditions: M.D. Regs. 15 and 16.

(iv)   A doctor who attends a person whom he suspects to be addicted to any drug must normally notify the Chief Medical Officer at the Home Office: section 10(h) M.D.A. 1971 and S.I. 1973 No. 799, reg. 3(1).

(v)   Only a licensed doctor may prescribe cocaine, heroin or dipipanone to addicts: S.I. 1973 No. 799, reg. 4(1)(b); M.D.A., s.10 and regulation 5 of the M.D. Regs.

(vi)   An addict lawfully entitled to drugs may administer them to himself and therefore be in possession of them: M.D.A., s.5(1) and M.D. Regs. 10(2).

(vii)   Such an addict must NOT "double-script": M.D. Regs. 10(2)(a).

(viii) Such an addict must not obtain a prescription by providing false particulars: M.D. Regs. 10(2)(b).

(ix)   Doctors convicted of certain offences may not be permitted to supply controlled drugs: M.D.A., s.12.

(x)   Doctors who act in breach of certain regulations may not be allowed to supply certain controlled drugs: M.D.A., ss.13 and 14. And—such doctors may also be committing criminal offences as a result: M.D.A., s.18.

Chapter 2
The Importation and Exportation of Controlled Drugs

A. THE IMPORTATION AND EXPORTATION OF CONTROLLED DRUGS

2–01   Of all narcotics appearing in Britain, the vast majority will have been imported—particularly those drugs which naturally subsist in plants and which cannot be successfully grown in this country. All heroin and cocaine must be imported. Cannabis can be home produced but only with varying degrees of success. The home grown plant tends to be less bushy than it would otherwise be if grown in warmer regions of the world. Indeed, in such regions, *e.g.* Morocco, Nigeria and Jamaica, the plant grows in such natural abundance that its harvesting, processing and exportation is a remarkably inexpensive exercise. The British domestic market, however, accounts for only a part of all drug-importations. Britain's geographical position makes it an ideal "staging post" for the onward transmission of narcotics to other countries. This is because many air routes converge in the United Kingdom making it one of the busiest "junctions" in the world. As we shall see, the movement of controlled drugs entering and leaving the country is heavily restricted or prohibited. It is therefore hardly surprising to discover that much court time is devoted to the disposal of cases involving the unlawful evasion of the prohibitions and/or the restrictions imposed.

2–02   The burden of "policing" the flow of imports and exports and prosecuting offenders, falls chiefly on the Commissioners of Customs and Excise whose existence, powers, rights and privileges are embodied in the Customs and Excise Management Act 1979 (the "C.E.M.A.") which describes the duties to be performed by the Commissioners as "assigned matters" (see s.1(1)). It is not clear whether any of the provisions of the Drug Trafficking Offences Act 1986 (the "D.T.O.A.") may be regarded as "assigned matters" for the purposes of the C.E.M.A. 1979, s.1. For reasons that are not entirely clear, the Home Office Working Party on Drug Trafficking appears to believe that the answer is in the negative. However, in *Stafford Magistrates' Court, ex p. Commissioners of Customs & Excise, The Times*, April 5, 1990, the Divisional Court accepted that an offence under section 24 of the D.T.O.A. (assisting a drug trafficker) should for all material purposes be regarded as an "assigned matter," being a matter in relation to which the commissioners were required in pursuance of an enactment to perform any duties: *per* Watkins L.J.

To increase resources, as circumstances demand, Parliament has imposed a duty on all constables, coast-guards and members of the armed forces, to assist in enforcing the law in respect of these matters; see section 11 of the C.E.M.A.

Every drug seized on the streets (and which must originally have been **2–03** unlawfully imported) is of interest to customs officers but, in practice, offences committed at this stage will normally be a matter for the police to investigate pursuant to their powers under the M.D.A. The police try to avoid charging individuals with offences under the C.E.M.A. since all proceedings under that Act should be instituted by order of the Commissioners (section 145). Conversely, the Commissioners of Customs and Excise prefer not to charge offenders with offences under the M.D.A. if they can bring a prosecution under the C.E.M.A. As a result, a defendant accused of drug-smuggling is likely to find that he faces very different charges depending on which law-enforcement agency is investigating the matter. Clearly, this is not a satisfactory state of affairs. For example, in the case of a smuggler who imports a quantity of heroin which is wholly inconsistent with personal use, the police (if they are investigating the matter) are likely to charge the accused with the unlawful possession of drugs with intent to supply them contrary to section 5(3) of the M.D.A. or, alternatively (if others are involved), with conspiracy to evade the prohibition on importation imposed by section 3(1) of the M.D.A. (see *Whitehead* [1982] Q.B. 1272). The Commissioners of Customs and Excise would, by contrast, charge the accused with an "importation/exportation offence" under the C.E.M.A., which is eminently more appropriate. It should also be borne in mind that defences available to an accused under one enactment will not always be available to him under another enactment. Thus, section 28 of the M.D.A. will not apply to offences brought under the C.E.M.A.

B. THE STATUTORY PROHIBITIONS

Section 3 of the M.D.A. 1971 reads: **2–04**

"(1) Subject to subsection (2) below—
  (*a*) the importation of a controlled drug; and
  (*b*) the exportation of a controlled drug,
are hereby prohibited.
(2) Subsection (1) above does not apply—
  (*a*) to the importation or exportation of a controlled drug which is for
    the time being excepted from paragraph (*a*) or, as the case may be,
    paragraph (*b*) of subsection (1) above by regulations under section
    7 of this Act; or
  (*b*) to the importation or exportation of a controlled drug under and
    in accordance with the terms of a licence issued by the Secretary of
    State and in compliance with any conditions attached thereto."

It will be seen that section 3(1) of the M.D.A. merely establishes the existence of two separate prohibitions—it does not, by itself, make it an offence to contravene either prohibition. The reason is that many enactments similarly prohibit or restrict the importation, exportation, or carriage coastwise, of many different goods, substances, or even wildlife. Accordingly, for the purposes of the C.E.M.A., the legislature aptly terms all such goods "prohibited or restricted goods" (see section 1(1) of the C.E.M.A.) and has created a mere handful of offences to punish an unlawful contravention of the relevant prohibition or restriction.

2–05   "Prohibited or restricted goods" must be carefully distinguished from "dutiable goods." Dutiable goods may be lawfully imported but, customs "duty" or "excise" is payable before the goods may be cleared. The importance of making this distinction will become apparent.

Given that section 3(1) of the M.D.A. only imposes a prohibition on the exportation or importation of controlled drugs, it is necessary to look to the C.E.M.A. to find the offences arising out of a contravention of section 3(1). Broadly speaking, there are three offences. Section 50 punishes unlawful importations; section 68 punishes unlawful exportations; and section 170 serves as a "mopping-up" provision, punishing ventures designed to evade the prohibitions. Each offence is widely drawn. Each section uses different language which inevitably creates problems of construction. In practice, offences under section 50 or section 68 are rarely charged whereas offences under section 170 are commonplace.

It follows that offences for the unlawful exportation or importation of controlled drugs arise by a combination of section 3(1) of the M.D.A. and an offence created under the C.E.M.A. As a matter of convenience the offence may be described, or even charged, as an offence under either or both enactments but the underlying offence undoubtedly exists under the C.E.M.A. Accordingly, no proceedings for an offence arising out of a contravention of section 3(1) of the M.D.A. may be instituted except by order of the Commissioners of Customs and Excise, unless they fall within section 145(6): see section 145(1) of the C.E.M.A., *Menocal* [1980] A.C. 598 and *Whitehead* [1982] Q.B. 1272.

I. INSTITUTING PROCEEDINGS

2–06   In the majority of cases, few problems are likely to be encountered, but the relevant provisions cannot always be applied literally. As a result some difficulties of construction arise.

The basic restriction on the institution of proceedings appears in section 145 of the C.E.M.A. (as amended by the Police and Criminal Evidence Act 1984, s.114) which reads as follows:

"(1) Subject to the following provisions of this section, no proceedings for an offence under the customs and excise Acts or for condemnation under Schedule 3 to this Act shall be instituted except by order of the

Commissioners.

(2) Subject to the following provisions of this section, any proceedings under the customs and excise Acts instituted in a magistrates' court, and any such proceedings instituted in a court of summary jurisdiction in Northern Ireland, shall be commenced in the name of an officer.

(3) Subsections (1) and (2) above shall not apply to proceedings on indictment in Scotland.

(4) In the case of the death, removal, discharge or absence of the officer in whose name any proceedings were commenced under subsection (2) above, those proceedings may be continued by any officer authorised on that behalf by the Commissioners.

(5) Nothing in the foregoing provisions of this section shall prevent the institution of proceedings for an offence under the customs and excise Acts by order and in the name of a law officer of the Crown in any case in which he thinks it proper that proceedings should be so instituted.

(6) Notwithstanding anything in the foregoing provisions of this section, where any person has been [arrested] for any offence for which he is liable to be detained under the customs and excise Acts, any court before which he is brought may proceed to deal with the case although the proceedings have not been instituted by order of the Commissioners or have not been commenced in the name of an officer."

There is a peculiar conflict—if it be a conflict—between the effect of sub- **2–07** section (1) and subsection (6). On the one hand, proceedings can only be instituted by order of the Commissioners (subsection (1)) but, on the other hand, no such order is required if the defendant is detained, or arrested, for a customs offence (subsection (6)). It is difficult to envisage many cases, involving the prosecution of a customs offence, which would not be satisfied by section 145(6), even if an order of the Commissioners is not obtained under subsection (1). One possible explanation for this curious state of affairs was given by Donaldson L.J. in *Whitehead* [1982] Q.B. 1272, when he said (at p.1282B):

"... the section is designed only to ensure that proceedings under [the C.E.M.A.] are not brought without the commissioners being aware of them. The commissioners will become aware of such proceedings if the proceedings are brought by their order. They should also become aware of them if the accused is detained by any offence under the Act."

In *Whitehead* [1982] Q.B. 1272 the appellants had been convicted of two **2–08** counts of conspiracy to evade the prohibition imposed by section 3(1) of the M.D.A. contrary to section 1(1) of the Criminal Law Act 1977. On appeal, it was contended that the proceedings were invalid on the grounds that: (*a*) section 3(1) merely imposed a prohibition on importation or exportation; (*b*) the offence of evading section 3(1) existed under section 304 of the Customs and Excise Act 1952 (now section 170 of the C.E.M.A.); (*c*) an order of the Commissioners was therefore required to institute proceedings under the Customs and Excise Acts (see section 145(1), formerly section 281(1) of the 1952 Act); (*d*) such an order was required for a conspiracy to commit the offence (see section 4(3) of the Criminal Law Act 1977); and (e) no such consent had in fact been obtained.

The Court of Appeal dismissed the appeals but only after a non-literal application of section 145(6) (formerly section 281(4) of the 1952 Act). The Court held, first, that the offence arose by a combination of section 3(1) of the M.D.A. and what is now, section 170 of the C.E.M.A.: see *Menocal* [1980] A.C. 598 and *Williams* [1971] 1 W.L.R. 1029. Secondly, the underlying offence was an offence under the C.E.M.A. requiring an order of the commissioners to institute proceedings. Thirdly, that no such order was required if the appellants had been "detained" within the meaning of section 145(6) of the C.E.M.A. Finally, that the appellants had been so detained.

2–09   By section 145(6) of the C.E.M.A., an order is not required "... where any person has been detained for any offence for which *he is liable* to be detained under the customs and excise Acts." (Note the words in italics.) A contravention of section 170 of the C.E.M.A. is one such offence, but in *Whitehead*, neither appellant had been charged with that or any other substantive offence, under the Act. A conspiracy to evade section 3(1) of the M.D.A. is not, strictly speaking, an offence under the customs and excise Acts and therefore—if section 145(6) is strictly applied—such a conspirator is not a person "liable to be detained" under the Customs and Excise Acts.

However, the Court of Appeal held that the words in section 281(4)—now section 145(6)—should read "... where any person has been detained for conspiracy to commit any offence for which *he would be liable* to be detained under the customs and excise Acts."

On this basis, both appellants had been so detained and therefore section 145(6) of the C.E.M.A. should be construed as including cases of conspiracy to commit an offence for which an accused would be liable to be detained/arrested under the C.E.M.A.

2–10   Section 4(3) of the Criminal Law Act 1977 provides, in so far as it is material:

> "Any prohibition by or under any enactment on the institution of proceedings for any offence ... shall apply also in relation to proceedings under section 1 above for conspiracy to commit that offence ...."

Donaldson L.J. said, *obiter*, in *Whitehead* that section 4(3) confers authority on the Commissioners to make an order in relation to a statutory conspiracy to commit an offence under the Customs and Excise Acts.

II. LAWFUL SHIPMENTS

2–11   Section 3(2) and section 7 of the M.D.A. permit the Secretary of State to except any controlled drug from the relevant prohibitions. This he has done by virtue of reg. 4(1) of the Misuse of Drugs Regulations 1985, which provides that section 3(1) shall not have effect in relation to the drugs specified in Schedules 4 and 5 of the 1985 Regulations. The drugs listed in Schedule 4 will be exempt provided that they are in the form of medicinal products.

Other controlled drugs may only be imported or exported under and in accordance with the terms of a licence issued by the Secretary of State: see section 3(2)(b) of the M.D.A.

III. Defining the Moment of Importation or Exportation

This is dealt with in the C.E.M.A., by section 5, as follows: 2–12

"(1) The provisions of this section shall have effect for the purposes of the customs and excise Acts.

(2) Subject to subsections (3) and (6) below, the time of importation of any goods shall be deemed to be—

(a) where the goods are brought by sea, the time when the ship carrying them comes within the limits of a port;

(b) where the goods are brought by air, the time when the aircraft carrying them lands in the United Kingdom or the time when the goods are unloaded in the United Kingdom, whichever is the earlier.

(c) where the goods are brought by land, the time when the goods are brought across the boundary into Northern Ireland.

(3) In the case of goods brought by sea of which entry is not required under section 37 . . . [*particular documentation required on importation*], the time of importation shall be deemed to be the time when the ship carrying them came within the limits of the port at which the goods are discharged.

(4) Subject to subsections (5) and (7) below, the time of exportation of any goods from the United Kingdom shall be deemed to be—

(a) where the goods are exported by sea or air, the time when the goods are shipped for exportation;

(b) where the goods are exported by land, the time when they are cleared by the proper officer at the last customs and excise station on their way to the boundary.

(5) In the case of goods of a class or description with respect to the exportation of which any prohibition or restriction is for the time being in force under or by virtue of any enactment which are exported by sea or air, the time of exportation shall be deemed to be the time when the exporting ship or aircraft departs from the last port or customs and excise airport at which it is cleared before departing for a destination outside the United Kingdom.

(6) Goods imported by means of a pipe-line shall be treated as imported at the time when they are brought within the limits of a port or brought across the boundary into Northern Ireland.

(7) Goods exported by means of a pipe-line shall be treated as exported at the time when they are charged into that pipe-line for exportation.

(8) A ship shall be deemed to have arrived at or departed from a port at the time when the ship comes within, or, as the case may be, leaves the limits of that port."

A "port" means any port appointed by the Commissioners (under section 2–13

19). The Commissioners may also determine the "limits" of the port: see section 1(1). A large number of Statutory Instruments have ensured that the entire coastline has been embraced. It may happen, of course, that controlled drugs (destined for the United Kingdom) are, say, jettisoned at sea beyond the limits of a port. In these circumstances no offence would be committed contrary to the C.E.M.A. since there has been no importation within the meaning of section 5.

In *MacNeill* v. *H.M. Advocate* 1986 S.C.C.R. 288, the appellants carried cannabis on board a vessel which because of bad weather entered the limits of a port in Northern Ireland for a short time before entering the Port of Strathclyde in order to refuel for a voyage in international waters. The jury were directed that the importation had taken place in the Port of Strathclyde. The court rejected the argument that the prosecution had to prove that an importation occurred within the limits of the first appointed port within which the vessel passed. Importation occurs at any port where the goods are discovered and also at any port in the United Kingdom which has been entered en route to that port. In any event a temporary stop-over, at a point identified as coming within the limits of a port for the purposes of sections 5 and 19 of the C.E.M.A. 1979, will not preclude a charge under section 50 or section 170 of the 1979 Act if the evidence discloses an "importation" at the port where the drugs are discovered.

The term "ship" is broadly defined to include any boat or other vessel whatsoever: section 1(1).

It is not entirely clear why Parliament has provided that "prohibited goods" are deemed to be exported at the moment when the exporting ship or aircraft ". . . departs from the last port or customs and excise airport at which it is cleared before departing for a destination outside the United Kingdom . . ." (section 5(5)). If prohibited goods leave the United Kingdom from a place other than a recognised port or airport then, clearly, section 5(5) can have no application. In this event there is no reason why section 5(4)(*a*) should not prevail.

IV. Goods Sent by Post

2–14   The provisions of the C.E.M.A. apply to all goods imported or exported—however they may have been shipped. But, almost by way of a "belt and braces" provision, section 16 of the Post Office Act 1953 (as amended by section 87 of the Post Office Act 1969, article 9 of the Postal Services (Channel Islands Consequential Provisions) Order 1969 and article 11 of the Postal Services (Isle of Man Consequential Provisions) Order 1973), directs that the C.E.M.A. shall apply:

> ". . . in relation to goods contained in postal packets to which this section applies brought into or sent out of the United Kingdom by post from or to . . . any place outside the British postal area as they apply in relation to goods otherwise imported, exported or removed into or out of the United Kingdom from or to . . . any such place."

The postal packets, to which section 16 applies, are specified in the Postal Packets (Customs and Excise) Regulations 1975 (S.I. 1975 No. 1992), namely:

> "... all postal packets, other than postcards and telegrams, which are posted in the United Kingdom for transmission to any place outside it or which are brought by post into the United Kingdom": reg. 4.

Regulation 5 modifies section 5 of the C.E.M.A. by omitting the proviso to   2–15
subsection (2) while modifying subsection (3) so that:

> "... the time of exportation of goods shall be the time when they are posted (or re-directed) in the United Kingdom for transmission to a place outside it ...."

The Commissioners of Customs and Excise may require an officer of the Post Office to produce to an officer of Customs and Excise, postal packets either arriving in, or about to be despatched from, the United Kingdom for the examination of that packet: reg. 12. The customs officer may also open any packet for the purpose of that examination: reg. 12.

Furthermore, the Commissioners of Customs and Excise may, by reg. 17, require an officer of the Post Office to deliver a postal packet to a customs officer if the packet contains goods liable to forfeiture under (*inter alia*) the C.E.M.A. or the Postal Packet Regulations of 1975.

C. UNLAWFUL IMPORTATION: SECTION 50 C.E.M.A. 1979

Section 50 of the C.E.M.A. defines the offence arising out of an unlawful   2–16
importation as follows:

"(1) Subsection (2) applies to goods of the following descriptions, that is to say—
> (*a*) goods chargeable with a duty which has not been paid; and
> (*b*) goods the importation, landing or unloading of which is for the time being prohibited or restricted by or under any enactment.

(2) If any person with intent to defraud Her Majesty of any such duty or to evade any such prohibition or restriction as is mentioned in subsection (1) above—
> (*a*) unships or lands in any port or unloads from any aircraft in the United Kingdom or from any vehicle in Northern Ireland any goods to which this subsection applies, or assists or is otherwise concerned in such unshipping, landing or unloading; or
> (*b*) removes from their place of importation or from any approved wharf, examination station, transit shed or customs and excise station any goods at which this subsection applies or assists or is otherwise concerned in such removal,

he shall be guilty of an offence under this subsection and may be [arrested].

17

(3) If any person imports or is concerned in importing any goods contrary to any prohibition or restriction for the time being in force under or by virtue of any enactment with respect to those goods, whether or not the goods are unloaded, and does so with intent to evade the prohibition or restriction, he shall be guilty of an offence under this subsection and may be detained."

I. THE AMBIT OF SECTION 50(1)

2–17   Quite clearly the draftsman was careful to distinguish between "dutiable goods" (s.50(1)(a)) and "prohibited and restricted goods" (s.50(1)(b)): see *Superheater Co. Ltd.* v. *Commissioners of Customs & Excise* [1969] 1 W.L.R. 858. At first blush, a problem of construction arises when the wording of section 50(1)(b) is examined. If (b) was merely concerned with the unlawful *importation* of prohibited goods, and nothing else, what then does the draftsman gain by adding the words "landing" or "unloading"? Although it may be tempting to argue that Parliament was merely describing or demonstrating an act of importation, this contention is soon defeated once it is remembered that "importation" is sufficiently defined under the Act by reference to the moment when goods are deemed to be imported under section 5. Therefore, goods may be imported (and the prohibitions against importation evaded) before the goods are even unloaded. However, the solution to the problem lies in recognising that each of the three words ("importation," "landing," and "unloading") represents a wholly separate and distinct prohibition, or restriction, which must be expressly imposed by the relevant enactment. Thus, for the purposes of section 3(1)(a) of the M.D.A. the "importation" of controlled drugs is prohibited. Other statutes, for their respective purposes, prohibit or restrict the "landing" or "unloading" of certain goods but do not seek to prohibit their actual importation: see section 13(2) Criminal Justice (International Co-operation) Act 1990.

2–18   In *Smith (Donald)* [1973] Q.B. 924, cannabis was sent by air from Nairobi to Bermuda via London. The drug was unloaded at London Airport, transferred to another aircraft and flown to Bermuda. S was convicted of fraudulently evading the prohibition against its importation (contrary to section 304 of the Customs and Excise Act 1952) and its subsequent exportation (contrary to section 56(2) of that Act). The appellant argued that reference to "goods unloaded" in section 45 of the 1952 Act (now section 50) was excluded from the category of "goods imported" and therefore since S merely facilitated the unloading of goods he had therefore not imported them.

The Court of Appeal rejected that argument, concluding that section 45 of the old Act was concerned with the "improper importation" of goods. Willis J. said:

> "... it is to be observed that ss.44 and 45 are concerned with the improper importation of goods ... It seems quite clear that the Act contemplates that goods can be imported before they are either landed from a ship or unloaded from an aircraft ... it would be strange indeed for Parliament to have excluded from the various categories of 'goods

imported' a category of 'goods unloaded' without such an intention being precisely indicated. We cannot think … that there can be a category of goods which are simply 'unloaded' and not 'imported' when they are taken off an aircraft … until reloaded for onward transmission outside the country."

The result is patently right since to treat "imported goods" and "unloaded   **2–19** goods" as being mutually exclusive is to make a nonsense of the wording of the Act. It should be noted that the appellant was not charged with an offence under what is now section 50, but with the offence of being knowingly concerned in the fraudulent evasion of a prohibition against the importation of a controlled drug (*i.e.* what is now s.170(2)). When Willis J. described section 45 of the 1952 Act as being concerned with the "*improper* importation of goods" he was careful not to say that section 45 was concerned only with the *unlawful* importation of goods. He clearly recognised that goods might be lawfully imported but illegally unloaded or landed and he therefore described section 45 in neutral terms as being concerned with the "improper" importation of goods.

II. Section 50(2) Offences

It is clear that subsection (2) creates two sets of offences—one in relation to   **2–20** "dutiable goods" and another in respect of "prohibited or restrictive goods." Therefore, a person arriving in the United Kingdom knowing that the goods he is carrying are subject to a prohibition against importation, will commit an offence contrary to section 50(2)(*a*) if he removes them from a ship in a port, or unloads them from any aircraft.

Curiously, whereas section 50(2)(*a*) applies to goods removed from any aircraft in the United Kingdom (whether or not the aircraft has landed at a recognised "Customs and Excise airport"), it seems that no offence is committed contrary to section 50(2)(*a*) if goods are unshipped from a vessel outside the limits of "a port" as defined by section 19(1) of the C.E.M.A.

III. Section 50(3)

"**Concerned.**" The *actus reus* of the offence is very narrow, particularly   **2–21** when it is compared with the much broader offence of "being knowingly concerned in the fraudulent evasion of the prohibition," against importation, contrary to section 170(2). In essence, section 50(3) is concerned solely with the single word "importation." Consequently, if the prosecution is to succeed under section 50(3), it must prove that the accused participated in the actual importation, *e.g.* by carrying the drug, or that he was at least in such a position as to be able to lend his assistance if required, in the smuggling operation. Unlike section 170(2), the offence is not a continuing one and cannot therefore include persons who, subsequently, handle the drug—albeit aware of its origin—but who were not parties to the original importation.

The mens rea. Again, quite unlike section 170(2), the intent required is an   **2–22** intent to evade the relevant prohibition. Evidence of an intention to take the

the imported goods elsewhere without landing them or that he intended to keep the vessel, carrying the drug, in an anchorage only long enough to buy fuel for a voyage into international waters is irrelevant once it is proved that the accused knew that the goods were being imported contrary to a prohibition on importation: *MacNeill* v. *H.M. Advocate*, 1986 S.C.C.R. 288. The use of the words "the prohibition," implies that the accused must know the relevant prohibition which he is evading. Accordingly, an importer of drugs commits no offence, under this subsection, if he genuinely believes that the drugs are not subject to a prohibition. Similarly, if an importer makes a complete mistake as to the nature of the goods imported, believing for example, that he has smuggled weapons (which he knows to be "prohibited goods") whereas he has unwittingly imported heroin, then no offence under section 50(3) has been committed since he does not intend to evade the prohibition imposed by section 3(1) of the M.D.A. However, a mistaken belief that he is importing cannabis whereas he is importing heroin, is no defence since both commodities are subject to the same prohibition.

2–23   It is not necessary for the prosecution to prove dishonesty on the part of the importer. By "evade" Parliament meant no more than an intention on the part of the accused to "get around" the prohibition. "Evade," in this context, does not carry the connotation of fraud or dishonesty as it does in income tax law: see *Hurford-Jones* (1977) 65 Cr.App.R. 263. It follows that it would be no defence for a cannabis smuggler, knowing of the prohibition, to say that he considered he was doing nothing wrong, believing that the drug cured most ailments.

D. UNLAWFUL EXPORTATION: SECTION 68

2–24   Section 68(2) of the C.E.M.A. provides that:

> "Any person knowingly concerned in the exportation or shipment as stores, or in the attempted exportation or shipment as stores, of any goods with intent to evade any such prohibition or restriction as is mentioned in subsection (1) above shall be guilty of an offence under this subsection and may be detained."

Oddly, the draftsman has adopted a formula of words which is very different to section 50. It is difficult to see why there should be a difference. First, the use of the word "knowingly" appears to add nothing to the subsection since the prosecution is required in any event to prove that the accused intended to evade any prohibition or restriction in force with respect to those goods. Secondly, quite unlike section 50, the requirement that the prosecution must prove an intent "to evade any ... prohibition or restriction" is ambiguous; it may be sufficient for the prosecution merely to prove that the accused knew that the goods he was exporting were subject to some prohibition, albeit that he was unaware of the precise one. Thus, it would be no defence for an exporter to say that he believed he was exporting guns (knowing them to be subject to a prohibition on exportation) and not heroin. But, if he believed that he was exporting brandy then, there is no intention to evade a prohibition on exportation since brandy does not come within the category of "prohibited goods or restricted goods" (see section 1(1) of the C.E.M.A.) but "dutiable goods." Furthermore, whereas section 50 is principally directed against the persons who are physically involved in the actual importation, *e.g.* either by carrying, or unloading the drug or aiding and abetting its commission, section 68, by contrast, is not so restricted and may include persons who organise an exportation venture and who may never see or handle the goods in question.

E. FRAUDULENT EVASIONS: SECTION 170

Commercially motivated contraband smuggling almost always involves a   **2–25** high degree of planning and a team of participants to secure the distribution of smuggled goods and to prevent their confiscation by law enforcement officers. An evasion of a prohibition or restriction on the importation or exportation of goods is therefore a continuing process and not confined to the moment when the goods actually enter or leave the country. Accordingly, it is not surprising that statutory measures designed to combat smuggling cast a particularly wide net. The drawback is that these measures lack precision and create ambiguity and uncertainty—as section 170 demonstrates.

Thus section 170(1) reads as follows:

"Without prejudice to any other provision of the Customs and Excise Acts 1979, if any person—
(*a*) knowingly acquires possession of any of the following goods, that is to say—
   (i) goods which have been unlawfully removed from a warehouse or Queen's warehouse;
   (ii) goods which are chargeable with a duty which has not been paid;
   (iii) goods with respect to the importation or exportation of which any prohibition or restriction is for the time being in force under or by virtue of any enactment; or
(*b*) is in any way knowingly concerned in carrying, removing, depositing, harbouring, keeping or concealing or in any other manner dealing with any such goods,
and does so with intent to defraud Her Majesty of any duty payable on the goods or to evade any such prohibition or restriction with respect to the goods he shall be guilty of an offence under this section and may be [arrested]."

Note the words "acquires possession" in section 170(1)(*a*) and the activi-   **2–26** ties required to be proved in section 170(1)(*b*). Note also that the relevant *mens rea*, in cases of drug smuggling, is an intention to "evade any such prohibition or restriction with respect to the goods."

Now compare the above with the wording of subsection (2) set out below:

"Without prejudice to any other provision of the Customs and Excise Acts 1979, if any person is, in relation to any goods, in any way knowingly concerned in any fraudulent evasion or attempt at evasion—
  (a) of any duty chargeable on the goods;
  (b) of any prohibition or restriction for the time being in force with respect to the goods under or by virtue of any enactment; or
  (c) of any provision of the Customs and Excise Acts 1979 applicable to the goods,
he shall be guilty of an offence under this section and may be [arrested]."

I. General Statement of the Law

2–27   Interpreting section 170 has become something of a judicial nightmare—particularly in the last few years—and it would be idle to pretend that considerable difficulties of reconciliation do not exist between the many cases which have wrestled with drug-related importations. Nevertheless it is clear that a set of rules is not only crystallising but is also displaying signs of durability. Accordingly, before examining the wording of section 170 and the relevant decisions, it may be of assistance to summarise the basic legal position at this stage.

2–28   If a charge is brought under section 170(1) then the prosecution must prove that:

  (a) the accused *either*:
    (i) knowingly acquires possession of goods; *or*
    (ii) is "knowingly concerned" in carrying, removing, depositing, harbouring, keeping or concealing, "or in any other manner" dealing with goods; *and*
  (b) the goods in question are subject to a prohibition or restriction on importation in force under or by virtue of any enactment; *and*
  (c) the accused intended to evade a prohibition or restriction imposed with respect to the goods.

If, however, the charge is brought under section 170(2) then the prosecution must prove that:

  (a) the goods in question are subject to a prohibition or restriction on importation or exportation under or by virtue of any enactment; *and*
  (b) a *fraudulent evasion* or attempted evasion of a prohibition or restriction has taken place in relation to those goods; *and*
  (c) the accused is *concerned* in that fraudulent evasion; *and*
  (d) the accused was concerned in that fraudulent evasion "*knowingly.*"

2–29   In respect of each subsection the following propositions currently represent the law. Propositions referable to "importations" apply equally to "exportations" thus:

- There must be proof (at least for the full offence) that the goods were "imported": see *Watts* (1979) 70 Cr.App.R. 187.
- The prosecution must prove that the accused knew that the goods were, at least, prohibited or restricted from importation.
- However, the prosecution does not have to prove that the accused knew:
    - (*a*) the precise prohibition involved; or
    - (*b*) the class of drug actually imported; or
    - (*c*) the actual drug imported.

        See *Hussain* [1969] 2 Q.B. 567; *Hennessey* (1978) 68 Cr.App.R. 419, C.A.; *Shivpuri* [1987] A.C. 1; *Ellis* (1987) 84 Cr.App.R. 235.
- It is therefore a defence for the accused to say that he did not know that the goods imported were subject to any prohibition or restriction on importation.
- It is a defence for the accused to say that he believed he was importing goods not subject to a prohibition or restriction but that they came within some other category, for instance, "dutiable goods," *e.g.* brandy.
- It is a defence for the accused to say that he mistakenly believed that he was importing goods of a particular description (*e.g.* currency) which he believed to be prohibited from importation when, as a matter of law, they would not have been prohibited: see *Taaffe* [1984] A.C. 539.
- An offence may be committed by a person who is involved in the venture before or after the moment of importation of the goods into the country.
- Acts committed abroad are nevertheless punishable in England if the prohibited goods are consequentially imported into that country: see *Wall* [1974] 2 All E.R. 245.

II. Distinguishing Section 170(1) from Section 170(2)

In *Neal* (1983) 77 Cr.App.R. 283, Griffiths L.J. contrasted the language of   **2–30**
subsections (1) and (2) and commented that:

> "The language of [subsection (1)] is so embracing and casts the net so wide that one is left to wonder what purpose is served by subsection (2) ... We are satisfied that [subsection (2)] was inserted by the draftsman with the intention of casting his net as widely as words enabled him— note his language, 'if any person' and 'in any way.' "

Certainly both subsections are very widely drawn and catch individuals who were not party to the original smuggling operation. A person who conceals drugs at a safe house, long after the moment of importation, is therefore caught by either subsection, provided that he intended to evade a prohibition against the importation of the goods.

However, there is in fact a significant distinction to be made between the scope of subsections (1) and (2). It will be seen that section 170(1)(*a*) makes it plain that an acquisition or possession of the goods is a necessary prerequisite for an offence under section 170(1)(*a*). Similarly, proof of custody or control over prohibited goods is implicitly required in respect of any of the activities referred to in section 170(1)(*b*) of the Act. By contrast, subsection (2) imposes no such restrictions.

It may be said that there is another significant difference, namely that subsection (1) expressly requires proof of an intention to evade the prohibition or restriction, whereas subsection (2) does not. However, such an ingredient is imparted by the word "fraudulent" in subsection (2), that is to say "fraudulent" in this context means dishonest conduct, "deliberately intended to evade the prohibition or restriction with respect to, or the duty chargeable on, goods as the case may be": *per* Lord Lane C.J. in *Att.-Gen.'s Reference (No. 1 of 1981)* [1982] Q.B. 848.

III. EVADING THE PROHIBITION OR RESTRICTION

2–31   The popular image of smuggling is a venture involving the surreptitious landing of contraband at an unofficial point of entry into a country. However, the "evasion" of "any prohibition or restriction on importation" as required by subsection (1) or (2), is wider than simply the single word "importation," as Kenneth Jones J. vividly illustrated in *Neal* (1983) 77 Cr.App.R. 283:

> "A boat arrives in . . . this country . . . and it has on board cannabis resin. One of the sailors . . . actually carries the cannabis resin ashore. He hands it over to another man . . . who loads it into a van. The van is driven off to some place where the drug is . . . stored . . . and . . . at a later stage, it is transported to yet another building and is stored there and it may be . . . that behind all this operation . . . is some organising person. Now you see, of all those men . . . strictly speaking, only the sailor has imported the drugs into this country . . . and that is what importation means, but he and each of those other persons . . . have all taken a part . . . in setting at nought the ban which the law imposes on the importation of the drug."

2–32   The illustration effectively demonstrates that the evasion of a prohibition is a continuing process rather than an isolated act, and accordingly offences under section 170 are continuing offences. It follows that arguments which attempt to narrowly construe section 170 so as to include only those persons who were parties to the original smuggling operation must be fallacious. The organiser who never makes an appearance at the moment of importation is as guilty as the sailor who brings the goods ashore. Thus, in *Neal* (*supra*) Griffiths L.J. said:

> "Subsection (1) clearly includes those who are not a part of the original smuggling team. For example, it includes anyone who acquires possession of goods unlawfully removed from a warehouse, or anyone who hides goods on which duty has not been paid, or anyone who carries goods the importation of which is forbidden; and there can be no warrant for reading into the language of the subsection the qualification 'provided they are part of the original smuggling team' . . . ."

2–33   As MacKenna J. pointed out in *Ardalan* [1972] 1 W.L.R. 463, section

170(1)(a) (formerly section 304(a) of the 1952 Act) embraces an accused who "acquires possession" of prohibited goods. Obviously he can only "acquire" goods after (or before) the moment of importation or exportation. Equally, the person who (contrary to section 170(1)(b)) carries, removes or harbours prohibited goods, can only do so prior to, or subsequent to, the moment of importation. In other words, the very language of section 170(1), itself proves that offences under that subsection are continuing. Since subsection (2) merely widens the scope of subsection (1) it follows that offences under subsection (2) must also be continuing. Persons who are therefore not parties to the actual importation may nevertheless join or leave the venture at any time until the goods cease to be prohibited and are therefore criminally liable for their acts under section 170. Thus in *Green* [1976] Q.B. 985, a crate containing cannabis arrived at Southampton and was placed in a shed. Customs officers removed the cannabis and substituted a quantity of peat. A month after the importation G rented a garage in a false name. The crate was delivered to the garage where it was stored. The Court of Appeal dismissed G's appeal against his conviction under what is now section 170(2). The offence was a continuing one and the evasion did not cease when the drugs were seized. Renting the garage, knowing that it was to be used to store cannabis which had been unlawfully imported, completed the offence.

Again, in *Neal* (*supra*), the provision of a barn on a farm in which six hundredweight of cannabis was concealed behind a false wall was sufficient evidence of being concerned in the unlawful importation of drugs even though there was no evidence as to where, or how, the drugs had been imported.

It will be recalled that in *Green* (*supra*) customs officers removed the drug **2–34** shortly after it was imported and substituted a quantity of peat. Perhaps encouraged by this decision, it has long been the practice of customs officers to substitute an innocuous substance for the smuggled goods before allowing the container to be delivered to the consignee (see §2–81*infra*). Accordingly, where any person was "knowingly concerned" in the evasion of the prohibition on importation of a controlled drug (*i.e.* after the goods were imported and seized) he will still be guilty of an offence contrary to section 170(2) of the C.E.M.A.

This startling result has recently been confirmed by the Court of Appeal in **2–35** *Ciappara* [1988] Crim.L.R. 172.

> In Bolivia, C's sister addressed two packets containing cocaine to C. The packets were unsolicited by C. Customs officers intercepted the packets and substituted baking powder for the cocaine. Each packet consisted of a note (asking C for money) wrapped around a postcard to form a container for the drug. C threw away the note, and the postcard, but kept the powder which he believed to be cocaine. He was convicted of an offence under section 170(2) in respect of one packet (which was sent to his place of work) but he was acquitted of a similar charge in respect of the other packet which had been sent to his home address. C's appeal against his conviction was dismissed.

C contended, on appeal, that (a) the packets were unsolicited, (b) the importation was complete by the time the packages were intercepted, (c) the drug had been removed before C received the packages and therefore, (d) C could not be said to be "knowingly concerned" with the importation of cocaine. The Court of Appeal rejected C's contention. There was no dispute that the packets were unsolicited and that the importation was complete by the time the packages were intercepted. However, section 170(2) did not exclude those whose only involvement arose after the importation, provided they knowingly participated. The court's attention was drawn to *D.P.P. v. Doot* [1973] A.C. 807, *Neal* (1983) 77 Cr.App.R. 283 and *Ardalan* [1972] 1 W.L.R. 463, but not—it would seem—to *Green* (*supra*).

2–36   The commentary to *Ciappara*, provided by Professor J. C. Smith Q.C., is thought-provoking but, it is submitted, erroneous. Professor Smith remarked (at 173):

> "So he is convicted of being knowingly concerned in the fraudulent evasion of the prohibition on the importation of cocaine, although, in fact, the only substance he ever dealt with was baking powder! Surely that cannot be right.... How can a person properly be said to be concerned in evasion of a prohibition on importation when the importation is complete before he even knows anything about it.... The onus should surely be on the prosecution to show that there are words justifying the remarkable wider meaning given to the section. It is like saying I am knowingly concerned in killing X if, after finding that X has been killed, I help to dispose of the body."

But the definition of "murder," "manslaughter" (or even "killing") is very different to the wording of C.E.M.A., s.170(2). A "killing" denotes a very brief moment in time, as does the word "importation." However, it is not the fact of importation which is the continuing element of an offence under section 170(2). It is the *evasion* of a prohibition or restriction on importation which continues. Thus, the evasion continues until the goods cease to be prohibited or, possibly, until the goods are re-exported. The fact that they have been seized in the interim is irrelevant. *Cf. Mitchell* [1992] Crim.L.R. 594.

2–37   Applying the same reasoning, acts done *before* the moment of importation, with the requisite *mens rea*, are punishable under section 170 even if the acts are performed abroad. So where, in *Wall* [1974] 1 W.L.R. 930, W travelled to Afganistan with others and handled packages of cannabis which were later shipped to the United Kingdom, it was held that he had been knowingly concerned in the fraudulent evasion.

The appellant contended that if he had done nothing on the day of importation, and if what he did do earlier was not done in England, then he should not have been convicted. This contention implied that the offence is not a continuing one and therefore overlooked the fact that the court was not restricted to focussing its attention on acts done in England when the goods were imported. There was a clear causal link between the defendants' activities abroad and the eventual arrival of the drug into England. If *Wall* had been decided differently the ramifications would have been colossal. Organisers, operating abroad, who shipped vast quantities of drugs to England could therefore never be convicted of an offence under section 170.

2–38   The decision in *Wall* is, in fact, supported by a long line of authorities including *D.P.P.* v. *Doot* [1973] A.C. 807, *Treacy* v. *D.P.P.* [1971] A.C. 537, *Baxter* [1972] Q.B. 1 and *Millar* [1970] 2 Q.B. 54.

In *Smith (Donald)* [1973] Q.B. 924, Willis J. said:

> "It was quite unnecessary to prove that the applicant did anything to further the transaction in this country."

It follows that once steps are taken by an individual to bring about the fraudulent evasion of the prohibition, an act of remorse (even if coupled with a wish to abandon the enterprise) will not save that person from a conviction under section 170 if an importation in fact results.

> In *Jakeman* (1983) 76 Cr.App.R. 223, J was recruited to carry a case of cannabis from Ghana to Heathrow, via Paris. She withdrew from the enterprise in Paris by abandoning the suitcase at the airport. Baggage officials found the suitcase and, believing it to have been mis-routed, rushed it to London.
>
> *Held*: her appeal against conviction was dismissed. Her initial actions ultimately brought about the importation.

The result may seem harsh but it is consistent with the wording of section 170(2), under which Jakeman had been charged. As Wood J. observed in that case, the correct approach is to analyse the offence itself. At best her withdrawal from the enterprise was good mitigation; but it was not a defence. It was ingeniously contended on the appellant's behalf that she should not be convicted unless her guilty state of mind subsisted at the time of importation. Once again, the argument assumed that the offence is only committed at the moment of importation which, clearly, it is not. It will be remembered that in *Neal*, the accused prepared a hiding place in a barn to store cannabis; he was recruited after the moment of importation and therefore his mind could not possibly have been a "guilty" one when the drugs were imported into the United Kingdom from the Lebanon. Nevertheless, he was guilty of an offence under section 170(2). **2–39**

In *Jakeman*, Wood J. observed that:

> "What matters is the state of mind at the time the relevant acts are done, *i.e.* at the time the defendant is concerned in *bringing about the importation*. This accords with the general principles of common law. To stab a victim in a rage with the necessary intent for murder or manslaughter leads to criminal responsibility for the resulting death regardless of any repentance between the act of stabbing and the time of death, which may be hours or days later."

Although it is correct to say, as Wood J. effectively did on the facts of this particular case, that the applicant's initial actions ultimately brought about the importation, this is a feature which must not be taken too far. Wood J. went on to say: "For guilt to be established the importation must, of course, result as a consequence, if only in part, of the activity of the accused." **2–40**

Construed literally, those passages may be thought to suggest that in every case the prosecution must establish a chain of causation between the actions of the accused and the ultimate importation of the drug. This would obviously be impossible to prove in the case of a person who (not being a party to the original importation) committed acts in furtherance of the evasion *after* the drugs had been imported, yet such persons are caught by the section. Furthermore, construed literally, the words of Wood J. would mean that any act which breaks the chain of causation would provide a defence. If this is what was intended then it is hard to accept that the result in *Jakeman* would not have been decided differently since the intervention of the baggage officials, who redirected the suitcase from Paris to London, was itself a *novus actus interveniens*.

2–41   A person who is not a party to the original smuggling operation will still commit an offence if he acts in joint enterprise with one or more persons to contravene section 170. A classic example of this situation is *Williams* [1971] 1 W.L.R. 1029:

> H, an Indian, asked W if he had contacts for selling cannabis as H was returning to India and could send on "samples." W gave H a forwarding address, occupied by X. H said he would send a letter to W informing him of an impending delivery at that address. X opened one such letter in error but decided to tell W that no letter had arrived. Customs officers discovered a parcel containing cannabis at that address shortly thereafter. W was convicted of an offence contrary to section 304 of the 1952 Act [now s.170 of the C.E.M.A.]. W contended that the offence had not been made out since an agreement to sell cannabis after it had been imported into the United Kingdom was not a sufficiently proximate act to the original importation to be guilty of the offence charged.
>
> *Held*: the appeal was dismissed. There may well have been a joint enterprise to unlawfully import but, in any event, what W did was sufficiently proximate to make him guilty of the offence.

Of course W was sufficiently proximate to the actual importation to make him guilty of the offence. It was not necessary for W to be present at the moment of importation, or to know when the illicit parcel was being posted, or to know that the parcel had in fact arrived in the United Kingdom; indeed it is not apparent from the report that there was any evidence that W did know that the cannabis had arrived in the United Kingdom. Even so, the interval of time between the defendant agreeing to receive the drugs, and the moment of importation, was not so great as to make him insufficiently proximate to the importation. Like *Jakeman* (1983) 76 Cr.App.R. 223, W's initial actions brought about the eventual importation of the drug.

2–42   It follows from the above that the fact that the drugs were merely in transit to another country will not protect the shipper once the goods are technically imported.

> In *Smith (Donald)* [1973] Q.B. 924, packets of cannabis were sent by air from Nairobi to Bermuda, via London. S was a party to the shipment and there was evidence that he knew of the likely route. S was convicted, *inter alia*, of being knowingly concerned in the fraudulent evasion of the prohibition on the importation of cannabis. S argued, on appeal, that he did nothing in this country to further the transaction.

Held: the appeal would be dismissed. It was unnecessary for the prosecution to prove such an ingredient. The goods were deliberately "introduced" into this country and were therefore "imported."

A similar point was made in *Berner* (1953) 37 Cr.App.R. 113 where B took goods prohibited from *exportation* out of the United Kingdom with the intention that they be brought back in again. The fact that they were to be brought back did not mean that the exportation ceased to be prohibited.

In *MacNeill* v. *H.M. Advocate*, 1986 S.C.C.R. 288, it was held that to be concerned in the importation of goods, a person has to be involved in the enterprise in some way if only in the sense of having accepted a role to be performed if circumstances so required. It is not enough for the Crown to show merely that the accused was being kept informed of what others were doing. There must be evidence that the accused played or held himself available to play some role in furtherance of the smuggling venture.   **2–43**

The judgment in *MacNeill*, *supra*, is also of interest as to the extent to which dissociation from the enterprise is a relevant consideration when a person has played some part in it.

(a) Exportation: acts done before or after that moment

There is clear authority for the proposition that acts done before the moment of exportation are caught by the section. Thus, where in *Garrett* v. *Arthur Churchill (Glass) Ltd.* [1970] 1 Q.B. 92 the defendant handed goods over for export knowing that they were prohibited from exportation, he committed an offence contrary to section 170.   **2–44**

There is no logical reason why the principles applicable to importations should not equally apply to exportations.

(b) At what point in time does an offence under section 170 cease?

How far removed from the original smuggling operation does a person have to be, before he is no longer liable under section 170?   **2–45**

The answer is of some importance because, in theory at least, a person arrested in London in possession of one gramme of so-called "Lebanese Gold" (*i.e.* cannabis resin from the Lebanon) may be said to be evading the prohibition on importation of that drug by dealing with it unlawfully. Moreover, consider the case of a person in England, who plants cannabis seeds taken from a cannabis plant imported by another: is that person guilty of an offence under the same section?

In *Ardalan* [1972] 1 W.L.R. 463, A was recruited to collect packages, which contained drugs, long after they had arrived in the United Kingdom, Roskill L.J. observed that:

> "If once ... there can be an offence committed at some point of time and at some place after importation ... it is difficult to see why there should be any limit to that point of time or place provided always, of course, that the goods ... are the subject of a prohibition ... and with intent to evade that prohibition."

2–46   Logically, there can be no limit either as to time or place, before the offence is committed, providing—and this is the crucial point—that the acts are done with the intention of evading the relevant prohibition. It is when the prosecution ceases to be able to prove the requisite *mens rea* that the cut-off point is reached. In *Neal* (1983) 77 Cr.App.R. 283, Griffiths L.J. expressed the position thus:

> "If no more can be proved than that a piece of cannabis changed hands in Piccadilly Circus, no doubt it would be foolish of the prosecution to proceed under [s.170] of the Customs and Excise Management Act 1979 for it would be far-fetched to suggest that the real intent of such a transaction is to evade the prohibition on the import of cannabis."

The holder of a small piece of cannabis may know that the drug comes from the Lebanon but his intention is to use it either for his own or for another's benefit. He is unlikely to use the drug in a manner intended to avoid, or to get around, the ban on its importation.

2–47   In *Watts* (1979) 70 Cr.App.R. 187, S was arrested upon leaving a public house and found to be in possession of cocaine, scales and other drug-paraphernalia. A large sum of money was found at an address which S had earlier visited and where W was arrested. Bridge L.J. said, *obiter*:

> "Merely to establish that there has been a dealing with the prohibited goods, and that by virtue of the presumptions [see now s.154(2)] they are presumed at some time in the infinite past to have been unlawfully imported, would not, in our judgment, ever justify, without anything further, inviting a jury to conclude that the evidence established an intent to evade the prohibition on importation."

Accordingly, Bridge L.J. reached the conclusion that:

> "... on a true construction of section 170(1), in order to establish that any particular dealing with goods was done with intent to evade the relevant prohibition on importation, the onus on the Crown to prove that intent must involve *establishing a link or nexus between the actus reus of the offence and some prohibited importation*."

2–48   Just as one must be careful not to construe too literally the words of Wood J. in *Jakeman* (1983) 76 Cr.App.R. 223 when he said that the importation must result "... as a consequence, if only in part, of the activity of the accused ..." so one must be careful not to treat references made by Bridge L.J. to a "link" or "nexus" as establishing hard and fast ingredients of the offence. But, that said, there is a great deal of force in the dictum of Bridge L.J. in *Watts* which should not be overlooked. *Watts* was cited in *Neal* (1983) 77 Cr.App.R. 283 but, most unfortunately, the head-note to *Neal* [as it appears in the *Criminal Appeal Reports*], states that the dictum of Bridge L.J. was "not applied." In fact, this is not so. It is important to emphasise that their Lordships adopted the dictum for the purpose of stressing the importance of the prosecution leading evidence to prove the necessary intent to evade the prohibition. What the Court of Appeal in *Neal* could not accept was that the words of Bridge L.J. had the meaning attached to them by Counsel for the appellants who argued that a "nexus between the *actus reus* of the offence and some prohibited importation" meant that offences under section 170 could only be committed by persons involved in the initial smuggling operation. Such a contention was clearly going too far since Bridge L.J. was careful to use the words "link" or "nexus" to indicate a point of involvement beyond the initial smuggling operation but not so far removed as to be unrealistic and incapable of proving intent.

The appellant's argument in *Neal* ignored the fact that Bridge L.J. was merely describing a method of proving *mens rea*. He was not, it is submitted, setting out to redefine the *actus reus* of the offence.

If Bridge L.J. really did intend to express the construction, for which the appellants in *Neal* contended, then such a dictum would at least be in conflict with *Ardalan* [1972] 1 W.L.R. 463. But Bridge L.J. was careful to refer to *Ardalan*, and in any event, it was not the belief of their Lordships in *Neal* that Bridge L.J. intended any such conflict.

The decision in *Watts* (1979) 70 Cr.App.R. 187 is a revealing example of   2-49
how easy it is to be misled by the sweeping words of section 170 and to ignore the essential ingredient that there must be an intent to evade the prohibition and that there must be proof that the goods were imported. In *Watts* there was clear evidence that the accused dealt in cocaine but there was no evidence at all to show that they had imported the cocaine into the United Kingdom. The trial judge held that there was an evasion of a prohibition on importation of goods once goods of that description were shown to have been "dealt with" in the United Kingdom from which an intention to evade the prohibition could be inferred. Astonishing, perhaps, is the fact that the judge accepted the argument that the growing of cannabis plants in a back garden in England would be an evasion of the prohibition on the importation of cannabis, or that LSD manufactured in the United Kingdom, would similarly be an evasion of the prohibition on importation of LSD. In neither example could it be said that a prohibited importation had taken place. The absence of such a fact was fatal to the argument and accordingly, it was not advanced before the Court of Appeal.

The above examples pose very different situations to the facts in, say, *Neal*, where there was evidence that goods had been imported and the prohibition evaded—although there was no evidence as to when or how that importation had taken place. The only issue was whether the defendant was a party to that evasion of the prohibition on importation.

VI. PROVING THE IMPORTATION

Arising out of the above it follows that in every case of drug-smuggling the   2-50
prosecution is faced with the obvious practical problem of proving that the drug was in fact imported. This may not be very easy if there is no evidence as to the place or the time of importation of the goods. To circumvent this difficulty the Crown, in *Watts*, argued that section 154 of the Customs and Excise

Management Act 1979 (as it now is) enacts a series of presumptions in favour of the Crown so as to place the burden of proving that there had been no importation on the defendant. The Court of Appeal did not find that contention attractive. Bridge L.J. said:

> "The Court feels grave doubt as to whether the opening words of subsection (2) ... are apt to refer to an issue as to whether goods have been imported or not. We think it more probable that those words are directed to an issue, which may arise in determining at what rate import duty is to be levied, as to the country from which the imported goods have originated."

2–51   Nevertheless the court decided the appeal on the assumption that the contention was correct. The point is not straightforward. Section 154(2), insofar as it is material, provides that:

> "Where in any proceedings relating to customs and excise any question arises *as to the place from which any goods have been brought* or as to whether or not—
>
> (a) any duty has been paid or secured in respect of any goods; or
> (b) any goods or other things whatsoever are of the description or nature alleged in the information, writ or other process; or
> (c) any goods have been lawfully imported or lawfully unloaded from any ship or aircraft; or
> (d) any goods have been lawfully loaded into any ship or aircraft or lawfully exported or were lawfully water-borne; or
> (e) any goods were lawfully brought to any place for the purpose of being loaded into any ship or aircraft or exported; or
> (f) any goods are or were subject to any prohibition of or restriction on their importation or exportation
>
> then, where those proceedings are brought by ... the Commissioner ... the burden of proof shall lie upon the other party to the proceedings."

2–52   It is important to note that questions arising in connection with "... the place from which any goods have been brought ..." (see the opening words of section 154(2)) and questions arising as to any of the matters listed in section 154(2)(a) to (f), are separate and distinct.

To demonstrate how devastating these presumptions can be, consider *Mizel* v. *Warren* [1973] 1 W.L.R. 899. In 1962, M bought (in England) a second-hand bracelet from C. The bracelet was made of white gold and platinum. The bracelet was seized by Customs and Excise officers in 1970 on the basis that it was of Belgian manufacture and there was no evidence that duty had been paid on it when it had been imported. However, evidence adduced by M suggested that it could have been of English *or* foreign manufacture. The Crown Court preferred the evidence called by M. However, the prosecution relied on what is now section 154(2)(b), and argued that the place of manufacture formed part of the "description," and that the burden therefore fell on M to prove that the bracelet was manufactured in England. The Divisional Court agreed.

The repercussions of the decision in *Mizel* v. *Warren* are enormous. A person approached by a customs officer in connection with a camera in his possession may be faced with the task of proving that the camera was of British manufacture or, if he cannot do so, of proving that the duty was paid in respect of it—a task that is likely to be quite impossible to fulfil. Again, a person found in possession of cannabis may, likewise, be faced with the task of proving that the drug was grown in Britain.

It may be asked why the Court in *Mizel* v. *Warren* was so concerned with "description" and not with the opening words of section 154(2). Lord Widgery C.J. reflected on this aspect when he said: 2–53

> "Some time was spent in the Crown Court in considering the opening words of [section 154(2)] dealing with the place from which any goods have been brought; but it is obvious to me ... that that is not the point with which we are concerned ... The argument is concerned with their place of manufacture ... So we are not interested in the place from whence the goods have been brought; we are very much concerned in whether they have been imported in the sense they began life in a foreign country."

There is, of course, force in this line of reasoning on the particular facts of that case. M did not "bring" the bracelet from any "place." In any event, the opening words of section 154(2) apply, for example, to cases where different rates of duty are payable on goods brought into the United Kingdom from countries outside the EC, as opposed to payments on the same goods brought in from countries outside the EC. In such cases it is important to ascertain the place from which the goods were in fact brought. Identifying the exact country of origin was not relevant to the issue to be determined in *Mizel* v. *Warren*. It was not relevant to ascertain the actual place from which the bracelet was brought at all. It was only necessary to ascertain whether the bracelet was of "foreign manufacture" or not; if it was then it must have been imported. The court was therefore concerned with the description of the goods. "Havana cigars" or "Chinese silk" is clearly a description which includes the country of origin. But the fact that goods are said to be "foreign" is also part of the description.

Given the above, suppose D, an American tourist, is arrested in Piccadilly   2–54
and found to be in possession of LSD. The prosecution alleges that the drug was manufactured in the United States of America and imported into this country by D. D is adamant that he bought the LSD in Piccadilly. On such facts, the country of origin is likely to be regarded as part of the description of the drugs and accordingly, the burden will be on D to prove that the substance was manufactured in the United Kingdom and therefore could not have been imported by him.

It is important to note that, for the purposes of section 154(2)(b), the presumption arises once it is alleged in the information, writ, or other process, that the goods are of a particular description. In *Mizel* v. *Warren* it was alleged that the bracelet was of foreign manufacture. Evidence was called to support the allegation but the evidence does not appear to have been accepted by the court as being convincing. Nevertheless, it was enough to bring the presumption into play in favour of the Commissioner of Customs and Excise.

VII. PROVING MENS REA FOR AN OFFENCE UNDER SECTION 170(2)

2–55   In 1969, the Court of Appeal delivered judgment in *Hussain* (1969) 53 Cr.App.R. 448, a case which has been the subject of much scrutiny both in the Court of Appeal and in the House of Lords, but it continues to be the leading authority on the *mens rea* required for an offence under section 170 of the C.E.M.A. The facts are as follows:

> A motor vessel arrived at Liverpool from Las Palmas. The vessel was boarded by an officer who entered a cabin occupied by H and two other crew members. The officer removed the bulkhead panel in the cabin and discovered some 10 packets of cannabis resin concealed behind it. H told customs officers that the second engineer and a carpenter (who carried a bucket containing the 10 packets) came into his cabin and put the packets behind the bulkhead. H was told he would have his throat cut if he said anything about it. The chairman directed the jury in the following terms:
>
>> "The question is; has it been proved that the defendant was knowingly concerned in that operation? . . . 'Knowingly concerned in that operation' means co-operating with the smugglers . . . and it does not matter if he did not know precisely the nature of the goods the smugglers were dealing with. He would be just as guilty if he had thought they were dealing with brandy, for instance, but what has to be proved is that he was knowingly and . . . consciously and deliberately concerned in co-operating in what he must have known was an operation of smuggling or getting prohibited goods into this country."
>
> *Held*: *inter alia*, that "knowingly" in section 304 of the 1952 Act, is concerned with knowing that a fraudulent evasion in respect of goods is taking place. It is not necessary that the defendant should know the precise category of goods the importation of which has been prohibited.

2–56   In order to be able to follow the history of this case and to be able to understand the complaints that have been levelled against the decision, it is desirable that the reader should note the following features. First, on more than one occasion the chairman referred to "smugglers" and "smuggling" but on no occasion did he actually define those terms. This may seem a relatively unimportant omission until it is remembered that the C.E.M.A. applies not only to "prohibited goods" but also to other categories of goods—including "dutiable goods." Secondly, the chairman said (by way of example) that it did not matter if Hussain thought he was importing brandy. However, brandy is a *dutiable* commodity: it is not prohibited or restricted from importation. Thirdly, although the chairman directed the jury that it did not matter whether Hussain knew precisely the "nature of the goods" being dealt with, does this mean that an accused need not know the precise prohibition involved? It has to be noted that if Hussain did not know what was actually being imported, then he would not know which prohibition was being contravened.

As to the first point, the Court of Appeal rejected the complaint swiftly. The court took the view that there was no reason to suppose that the jury would associate the word "smugglers" solely with those who seek to evade Customs duty. The second and third complaints posed considerable problems, however.

In *Hussain* the Court of Appeal isolated the three essential elements of the   2–57 *mens rea*, which the prosecution is required to prove against an accused, namely:

(*a*) knowledge that the goods which are being imported are subject to a prohibition; and

(*b*) knowledge that he is concerned in an operation designed to evade that prohibition; and

(*c*) knowledge that the prohibition is to be evaded fraudulently.

The burden of proving the above rests on the prosecution because nothing in the C.E.M.A., or the M.D.A., suggests that section 170 or section 3(1) of the M.D.A. is subject to section 28 of the M.D.A. Furthermore, none of the statutory presumptions listed in section 154 of the C.E.M.A. shifts the evidential burden onto the accused to rebut a presumption of knowledge of any of the three elements.

There must be evidence from which a reasonable jury, properly directed,   2–58 may safely infer that a defendant knew that what was afoot was an unlawful evasion of the prohibition on the importation of prohibited goods. In practice this means there must be sufficient evidence that the accused knew of the existence of the prohibited goods which were being smuggled. In *Suurmeijer* [1991] Crim.L.R. 773, S was the passenger in a car driven by H which was stopped by customs officers in the "Nothing to Declare" channel at Sheerness. The petrol tank had been adapted to conceal 30.5 kilograms of cannabis. H hired the car and paid for the tickets on behalf of himself and S. The Court of Appeal quashed S's conviction in respect of the unlawful importation of drugs. The mere presence of S, in the company of H, in the car was insufficient: see also *Strong, The Times*, January 26, 1989, *Irala-Prevost* [1965] Crim.L.R. 606 and §3–51, *infra*.

VIII. MUST AN ACCUSED KNOW THE PRECISE PROHIBITION OR GOODS INVOLVED?

In *Hussain* (§2–55 *et seq*., supra), the appellant had submitted that the   2–59 prosecution was required to prove that the accused knew the precise nature of the goods that had actually been imported—in this case, cannabis resin. This was a very bold submission since one might have anticipated the appellant to have conceded that there was a sufficient *mens rea* if the accused knew that goods of a type subject to a particular prohibition (*e.g.* controlled drugs) had been imported. It will be necessary to return to this point when we examine *Hussain* in the light of the decision of the House of Lords in *Courtie* [1984] A.C. 463. In the event the Court of Appeal rejected the submission advanced on behalf of the appellant. Widgery L.J. said:

"It seems perfectly clear that the word 'knowingly' in the section in question is concerned with knowing that a fraudulent evasion of a prohibition in respect of goods is taking place. If, therefore, the accused knows that what is afoot is the evasion of a prohibition against importation and he knowingly takes part in that operation, it is sufficient to justify his conviction, even if he does not know precisely what kind of goods are being imported."

Widgery L.J. made it clear that it is essential that the accused should know that the imported goods are subject to a prohibition on importation, but he added that "... it is not necessary he should know the precise category of the goods the importation of which has been prohibited."

Accordingly, by the jury's verdict, Hussain knew that the packages were being smuggled contrary to a prohibition against their importation and that he was a party to that operation. The fact that he did not know precisely what those packages contained was held to be irrelevant.

2–60   *Hussain* has been held to have been correctly decided in a number of subsequent cases and notably, by the House of Lords in *Taaffe* [1984] A.C. 539 and *Shivpuri* [1987] A.C. 1. But, if all that has to be proved is that an accused knew that the goods imported were subject to "a prohibition," does that include a belief (mistakenly but genuinely held) that he was importing goods of a different description (*e.g.* firearms instead of heroin) but which would, if true, also have been subject to a prohibition against importation? On a strict reading of the judgment in *Hussain*, the answer must be in the affirmative since it was said, in terms, that it is not necessary for the prosecution to prove that an accused knew the precise "category of goods" prohibited from importation.

2–61   An attempt was made in *Hennessey* (1978) 68 Cr.App.R. 419 to challenge directly the correctness of the decision in *Hussain* and to renew the submission, (rejected in *Hussain*) that the prosecution had to prove that the accused knew what the imported goods actually were. Thus:

> In *Hennessey*, stolen cars were adapted so that cannabis could be hidden in them and then used to bring the cannabis over to the United Kingdom from the Continent. H drove one such car to the Continent and returned to Dover some six days later. Customs officers found 28.14 kilograms of cannabis resin in the vehicle. H said that he believed he was importing pornography into the United Kingdom of a type which would have been prohibited from importation.

Lawton L.J., giving judgment for the court, followed *Hussain*, "for the best of reasons—it was correctly decided," and added: "In plain English [Hennessey] was smuggling goods. It matters not for the purpose of conviction what the goods were as long as he knew that he was bringing into the United Kingdom goods which he should not have been bringing in."

2–62   The decisions of *Hussain* and *Hennessey* produce harsh results and pose special problems, not least on the issue of sentence. For example, many goods and products or animals (whether dead or alive) are prohibited from importation (see the Endangered Species (Import and Export) Act 1976). Smuggling such things attracts a maximum sentence of two years' imprisonment, whereas the penalty for smuggling a Class A drug is life imprisonment. Accordingly, if heroin is imported but the accused believed he was importing an article in contravention of the 1976 Act, he nevertheless faces life imprisonment; the accused's mistaken belief affords him no defence. The sentencer is thus confronted with a difficult sentencing problem. On which basis does he sentence the accused? In *Hennessey*, an application for leave to appeal against sentence was made on the basis that he should not have been sentenced as a drug smuggler but as a smuggler of pornography. The Court of Appeal side-stepped that issue, claiming that H's story "was not credible anyway" and secondly, that "he was lucky to be sentenced as leniently as he was."

A second, but far more subtle, attack has been made on the correctness of *Hussain* and *Hennessey*, on the grounds that both cases have wrongly attributed the *mens rea* of one prohibition to offences requiring proof of a very different prohibition and required proof of a corresponding *mens rea*; see *Shivpuri* [1987] A.C. 1, considered later in this chapter. If the complaint is valid then the prosecution is put in the very difficult position of having to prove that the accused knew that the goods imported were at least subject to a particular prohibition. Many guilty persons, it is said, would slip through the net as a result.

One solution is to impose a presumption of knowledge on the accused and   **2–63**
to shift the burden onto him to prove (on a balance of probabilities) that he neither knew, believed, suspected, nor had reason to suspect that the goods he was importing were the goods alleged, *i.e.* controlled drugs. In other words one solution is to direct that section 28 of the M.D.A. applies to drug-related importations.

In respect of offences created by sections 4, 5, 6 and 9 of the M.D.A., section 28(3) already applies to those offences. Obviously the reason why there is no corresponding provision for the purposes of section 3(1) of the M.D.A. is that Parliament considered that such a course was unnecessary: the difficulty lies in understanding why Parliament took that view. The basic explanation favoured by many lawyers is that Parliament was satisfied that *Hussain* already governed the position and therefore statutory intervention was not required. The problem with that explanation is that lawyers have not been agreed on the true *ratio* of *Hussain*. For this reason two opposing theories are worth mentioning.

The first theory is that Parliament was not fundamentally concerned with   **2–64**
whether or not an importer made a mistake about the goods actually imported. That was his concern. All that mattered was that he knew he was smuggling prohibited goods, whatever their description and whatever the prohibition involved. *Hussain*, it is argued, is authority for that proposition. Since *Hussain* already governed the position there was no need for Parliament to take any further action. The fact that an accused faces different penalties depending on the goods actually imported was not the legislature's concern but a matter for the sentencing court. Indeed, under the M.D.A. different penalties apply to Class A, B and C drugs (see Schedule 4 of the M.D.A., as amended by the Controlled Drugs (Penalties) Act 1985). Nevertheless, section 28 makes it plain that it is no defence for a person to say "but I thought

I was supplying methaqualone (Class C) and not heroin (Class A)."

2–65   The second theory, which advocates that *Hussain* should be narrowly construed, starts on the basis that Parliament accepted the principle that persons who believed they were dealing with substances other than controlled drugs should not be convicted of a drugs-related offence. Hence section 28, enacted in the light of *Warner* v. *M.P.C.* [1969] 2 A.C. 256. This was so whether a person produced, possessed, supplied, or *imported*, a drug. It was not intended that a supplier should be more favourably treated than an importer. Once it was established that an accused knew that he was dealing with a drug, it really did not matter thereafter what he believed that drug to be. However, there was no need to extend section 28(3) to importation cases, because the burden of proving knowledge (according to *Hussain*) rests entirely on the Crown and that burden never shifts. Parliament's understanding in 1971 (so the argument runs), was that *Hussain* did not establish the sweeping proposition that an accused need only be proved to have known that the goods were subject to any prohibition. That was not made clear until *Hennessey* was decided in 1978. The judgment in *Hussain* was understood to mean, in 1971, no more than that it did not matter whether an accused knew exactly what the imported goods were so long as he knew that they were of a type subject to the same prohibition. Thus, for example, an accused's belief that he was importing methaqualone (Class C) whereas he was importing heroin (Class A) was not fatal to a conviction under section 170(2) since he knew he was importing drugs. If Parliament knew in 1971, what it now knows, then section 28(3) would indeed have been expressed to apply to section 3(1).

2–66   It must be stressed that, for the moment at least, the position is that *Hussain* and *Hennessey* represent the law. All that the prosecution need prove is that an accused knew the goods were prohibited from importation. He does not need to know the precise prohibition involved and still less does he need to know the class of drugs actually imported. But, it is a defence for him to say that he mistakenly believed that the goods imported were not subject to any prohibition and, it is also a defence for him to say that he mistakenly believed he was importing goods subject to a prohibition when (as a matter of law) they would not have been; see *Taaffe* [1984] A.C. 539. However, because the matter is still regarded as being in a state of flux—and it will be surprising if the House of Lords is not required to look at this matter yet again—it is helpful to trace the history of drug importation offences in so far as it is relevant to do so.

VII. An Historical Perspective of Drug Importation Offences

2–67   Section 304(*b*) of the Customs and Excise Act 1952 was the fore-runner to section 170(2) of the C.E.M.A., and read:

> "... if any person; ... is, in relation to any goods, in any way knowingly concerned in any fraudulent evasion or attempt at evasion of any duty chargeable thereon or any such prohibition or restriction as aforesaid or of any provision of this Act applicable to those goods he may be detained

and ... shall be liable to a penalty. ...."

When *Hussain* was decided in 1969, the relevant prohibition on the importation of various drugs was imposed by section 2 of the Dangerous Drugs Act 1965. Under the Customs and Excise Act 1952 the maximum penalty for contravening section 304 was two years' imprisonment unless a different penalty was expressly imposed by a different enactment. But the Dangerous Drugs Act 1965 did not in fact provide a different penalty. Two years later, the Dangerous Drugs Act 1967 (section 7) increased the maximum sentence for drug-smuggling to 10 years' imprisonment. Thus, whether the drug imported was a Class A, B or C drug, the maximum penalty was the same. It was against this background that *Hussain* was decided.

Widgery L.J. said in *Hussain* (1969) 53 Cr.App.R. 448, 452, that it was essential that an accused should know that the goods which were being imported were subject to a prohibition but "it is not necessary he should know the precise category of the goods the importation of which has been prohibited."

These are crucial words but there was uncertainty as to whether or not   **2–68**
Widgery L.J. was saying that the *mens rea* for one prohibition would support an offence in connection with the importation of goods subject to another prohibition so that the accused only had to know that the goods were "prohibited goods." The fact that Widgery L.J. referred to "goods" and not to "drugs" is one indication that he was saying precisely that. His reference to knowledge of "a" prohibition (rather than "the" prohibition) is another indication. However, he went on to say that an accused must be proved to be engaged in an operation "designed to evade *that* prohibition" which might, on its own, suggest that proof of the specific prohibition was required.

The M.D.A. swept away the Dangerous Drugs Acts of 1965 and 1967, as well as the Drugs (Prevention of Misuse) Act 1964. New offences were created under the M.D.A., the most important of which are subject to the statutory defences created by section 28. Parts of that section are reminiscent of the judgment of Lord Pearce in *Warner*. A smuggler, charged with offences under the M.D.A. (*e.g.* possession with intent to supply) has a defence under section 28(3) of the M.D.A. which he does not have if he is charged under section 170 of the C.E.M.A.

(a) The *Courtie* argument

In *Courtie* [1984] A.C. 463, the House of Lords held that the Sexual   **2–69**
Offences Act 1967 created several different offences, given that proof of different factual ingredients attracted different penalties. Each offence would require the requisite *mens rea*.

In *Taaffe* [1984] 78 Cr.App.R. 301, a case involving a rather different point, Lord Scarman said (at 304), *obiter*, that:

> "While there can be no doubt that *Hussain* was correctly decided, it may be that *Hennessey* will have to be reconsidered in the light of the House's decision to-day in the case of *Courtie*. For the court in *Hennessey* appears to have paid no regard to the effect of section 26 of the Misuse of

Drugs Act 1971 upon section 304 of the Customs and Excise Act 1952 ... it would seem likely that these two sections (now consolidated into section 170 of the Act of 1979) have substituted several offences ... for one offence in relation to all prohibited imports which existed before the Misuse of Drugs Act 1971 was enacted. But the point does not arise and I therefore express no concluded opinion as to whether the decision in *Hennessey* can stand with ... *Courtie.*"

Those observations have resulted in two further cases reaching the appellate courts, namely, the House of Lords in *Shivpuri* [1987] A.C. 1 and, more recently, the Court of Appeal in *Ellis* (1987) 84 Cr.App.R. 235. The background to these two decisions should now be explained.

In 1971, offences contrary to sections 4, 5, 6 and 9 generally attracted identical maximum penalties depending on the class of drug involved. Thus, Class A and B drugs attracted 14 years' imprisonment while a Class C drug attracted five years' imprisonment (lesser penalties were imposed for offences of simple possession). Offences committed under the Customs and Excise Act 1952 in respect of drug-smuggling attracted like penalties: see section 26 of the M.D.A.

Section 26 was repealed with the passing of the Customs and Excise Management Act 1979 but the same penalties were then re-enacted in Schedule 1, 2, 3 of that Act. However, under the Controlled Drugs (Penalties) Act 1985, the maximum penalty for offences involving a Class A drug was increased to life imprisonment. Accordingly, each class of controlled drug now attracted a different maximum penalty. Moreover, unlawfully importing or exporting other prohibited goods attracted a maximum of two years' imprisonment (unless a different penalty was stipulated by the relevant enactment).

2–70   The impact of *Courtie* [1984] A.C. 463 is now evident. If separate offences are created, because separate penalties arise out of different factual ingredients which are required to be proved by the prosecution, then this means:

(*a*)   that separate offences exist where goods are subject to *different prohibitions* attracting different penalties; *and*

(*b*)   that, in the case of a drug-related importation, three separate offences exist in relation to Class A, B and C drugs because each class attracts a different penalty.

In other words, if different offences are created under section 170 of the C.E.M.A. then, in the case of drug smuggling, the prosecution is required to prove as part of the *actus reus* that an accused imported or exported the appropriate *class* of controlled drug. That being so, is it not also incumbent on the prosecution to prove a corresponding *mens rea*? If the answer is "yes" then *Hennessey*, and possibly *Hussain*, were wrongly decided.

2–71   In *Shivpuri* [1987] A.C. 1, S believed he was importing a suitcase of cannabis whereas he actually imported harmless vegetable matter and was accordingly, charged with attempting to contravene section 170. The House of Lords feared that if the answer to the question posed above was in the affirmative, then "the task of the prosecution in proving an offence in relation to the importation of prohibited drugs would in many cases be rendered virtually impossible" (*per* Lord Bridge).

Their Lordships in *Shivpuri* recognised the force of the arguments based on *Courtie*. Lord Bridge traced the history of the legislation, with particular reference to section 28, pointing out that Parliament overcame the "almost insurmountable difficulty ... of proving the appropriate guilty knowledge" for the purposes of offences under the M.D.A. by placing the burden of proving a lack of knowledge on the accused. Lord Bridge asked why section 28 did not apply to section 3(1) of the M.D.A., concluding that *Hussain* made such a provision unnecessary for the following reasons (at 996):

> "Irrespective of the different penalties attached to offences in connection with the importation of different categories of prohibited goods *Hussain* established that the only *mens rea* necessary for any such offence was knowledge that the goods were subject to a prohibition on importation."

It is to be noted that Lord Bridge referred to "goods," not "drugs," and also, that he, like Widgery L.J. in *Hussain*, referred to "a" prohibition, not "the" prohibition, Lord Bridge added (at 996): "Had [*Hussain*] been decided otherwise ... it is surely inconceivable that Parliament, in the 1971 Act, would not have made provision ... such as ... section 28(3) applicable to drug related offences connected with importation." **2–72**

However, this observation is not, with respect, a complete answer because by section 28(3) of the M.D.A. it is a defence for the accused to prove that he did not believe or suspect or had reason to suspect that the substance was a controlled drug at all. This is very different from the effect of *Hussain* and *Hennessey* which affords a defendant charged with an offence under section 170(2) no such defence.

Lord Bridge considered that the issue resolved itself once the history of the legislation was traced. Of course that is to assume that Parliament had the foresight to anticipate the decision in *Courtie*, which is highly unlikely. Lord Bridge has bravely attempted to rationalise the relevant history and, to the extent that it is capable of rationalisation, the broad construction of the *ratio* in *Hussain* is to be preferred. But ultimately, rationalising the authorities has proved to be somewhat artificial, and perhaps unnecessary, because in the final analysis it is the wording of the relevant enactment that counts. No matter how hard one tries to scrutinise the decisions of the courts, the colossal difficulties of reconciliation remain. For the moment *Hussain* and *Hennessey* remain the law. Suggestions that *Shivpuri* has not closed the doors to the argument that a mistaken belief that the goods were subject to a wholly different prohibition provided a defence, are unfounded. In *Shivpuri* (§2–71 *supra*) their Lordships did not expressly approve *Hennessey* and this may have generated confusion and the suspicion that the argument was still open so that a person who believes he is importing goods subject to one prohibition, when in fact he is importing goods subject to a different prohibition, does not have the requisite *mens rea*. It is submitted that this construction is a misreading of the opinions delivered in *Shivpuri*. Significantly, Lord Scarman who made the now famous remarks in *Taffe* (§2–69, *supra*) concerning the implications of *Courtie* also heard the appeal in *Shivpuri*, but said no more in *Shivpuri* than **2–73** that he agreed with the speech of Lord Bridge. It is not apparent why Lord Scarman in *Taffe* readily accepted that *Hussain* was rightly decided but queried the correctness only of *Hennessey*. This fuelled speculation in legal circles that the judgment in *Hussain* was to be narrowly construed—speculation which was not only proved to be unfounded but which also might have ended with the decision in *Shivpuri*. However, in *Ellis* (1987) 84 Cr.App.R. 235, the appellants imported cannabis believing that they were importing pornography. The facts were therefore identical to *Hennessey*. The Court of Appeal was invited to rule that *Hennessey* was wrongly decided and could not stand with subsequent decisions of the House of Lords. The Court of Appeal had no difficulty in holding that the true *ratio* of *Hussain* is that it does not matter what a person believes the nature of the prohibition to be. In *Ellis*, the appellants contended that in *Hussain* the defendant simply did not care what the material was, and accordingly, *Hussain* could be distinguished from *Hennessey*. But, by the jury's verdict, *Hussain* must have known as a fact that the goods were prohibited, even if he did not know of their actual description. O'Connor L.J. said: "... if a man does not know what prohibited material is being imported but only knows that it is prohibited, it follows that he cannot know which prohibition is being broken."

2-74 In *Shivpuri* [1987] A.C. 1, had Lord Bridge remarked that where the accused is charged with an attempt to contravene section 170 of the C.E.M.A. 1979 then to tell the jury that they may convict the accused if they are sure "that he knew or believed the substance was [a Class A drug] or ... [a Class B drug] or some other prohibited drug" included a misdirection, namely, the reference to "some other prohibited drug."

In *Ellis* (1986) 84 Cr.App.R. 234 O'Connor L.J. said *obiter*:

> "It is difficult to see why Lord Bridge thought it was a technical misdirection because Class C drugs are just as surely prohibited as A or B and on *Hussain* and certainly on *Hennessey*, a mistaken belief that it is a Class C drug would be no defence, and therefore no misdirection."

It should be borne in mind that at the time Shivpuri was tried, the maximum sentences imposed for the unlawful importation of Class A and B drugs were the same (14 years' imprisonment) and the observations of Lord Bridge were made with *Courtie* (*supra*) in mind. Furthermore, the remarks of Lord Bridge were directed to cases where the accused was charged with an attempt and not the full offence. The *mens rea* for an attempt is an intention to commit the *actus reus* of the offence. As Professor Smith has pointed out ([1987] Crim.L.R. 47), if an accused is charged with attempting to import a Class A drug, his intention to import a Class C drug (being a different offence) will not support the conviction but, in the light of *Shivpuri*, an accused may be convicted of attempting to import a Class C drug (intending to import a Class C drug) even if the drug actually imported is a Class A drug. The fact that the commission of the Class C offence is impossible is not defence under the Criminal Attempts Act 1981.

(b) Applying *Hussain* and *Hennessey*

Once it is proved first, that controlled drugs were imported contrary to section 3(1) of the M.D.A., secondly, that a prohibition was evaded fraudulently, thirdly, that the accused knew that the goods were subject to a prohibition, and finally that the accused was concerned in that fraudulent evasion, then an offence under section 170(2) is made out.   2-75

However, a person is to be judged "against the facts as he believed them to be" (*per* Lord Lane C.J. in *Taaffe* [1983] 1 W.L.R. 627)

> In *Taaffe*, T drove his car through the green channel of the ferry terminal at Sheerness. The vehicle was stopped. Packets of cannabis resin were found in a tyre and more packets of cannabis were found on T's person. T maintained that he thought the packets contained currency. He mistakenly believed that currency was prohibited from importation.
>
> *Held*: if T's story was true he was entitled to be acquitted. Had T indeed imported currency then no offence would have been committed and T's mistake of law could not convert his reprehensible belief into a criminal offence.

The House of Lords in *Taaffe* [1984] A.C. 539 adopted the reasoning of Lord Lane C.J. which they found compelling, Lord Lane C.J. said ([1983] 2 All E.R. 626, 628h):   2-76

> "He is to be judged against the facts as he believed them to be. Had this indeed been currency and not cannabis, no offence would have been committed. Does it make any difference that the appellant thought wrongly that by clandestinely importing currency he was committing an offence? Counsel for the Crown strongly submits that it does. He suggests that a man in his situation has to be judged according to the total mistake that he has made . . . . We think that that submission is wrong. It no doubt made his actions morally reprehensible. It did not . . . turn what he . . . believed to be the importation of currency into the commission of a criminal offence."

It may be said that the result in *Taaffe* is inconsistent with *Hussain* and *Hennessey* in that T was not judged on the facts as he believed them to be because T believed currency to be prohibited and that if his belief had been true then he would have had no defence. However, two points should be noted. First, that by the jury's verdict in *Hussain*, and by the defendant's admission in *Hennessey*, both defendants knew that the goods actually imported were subject to a prohibition. Secondly, when a person is judged against the facts, as he believes them to be, he is judged "according to law." Thus, in *Hennessey* (§2–61, *supra*) H believed that he was importing pornography. The law states pornography is prohibited from importation and so too were the drugs actually imported. Hennessey's belief that the goods were prohibited would, if true, have been correct in law. However, in *Taaffe*, T made a mistake of law which saved him. His views on the law were totally irrelevant.

It will be recalled that in *Hussain* the chairman directed the jury that it did not matter if the defendant did not know precisely what the imported goods   2-77 were; "He would be just as guilty if he thought [the smugglers] were dealing in brandy." This, of course, was a misdirection since brandy is not prohibited from importation. Accordingly, if *Hussain* believed he was importing brandy then he would have had a defence for the reasons given in *Taffe*. However, this was not a misdirection which the court regarded as being fatal to the conviction.

(c) Meaning of the words "knowingly" and "fraudulently"

2-78   This does not mean that a deception must be practised on officers of Customs and Excise in their presence. It simply connotes a deliberate intention to evade the relevant prohibition or restriction; see the *Att.-Gen.'s Reference (No. 1 of 1981)* [1982] Q.B. 848. The decision of *Borro* [1973] Crim.L.R. 513 to the contrary, was decided *ex tempore* and was therefore not followed by the court.

Lord Lane C.J. said (at 856): "the prosecution must prove fraudulent conduct in the sense of dishonest conduct deliberately intended to evade the prohibition or restriction with respect to, or the duty chargeable on, goods as the case may be."

The word "knowingly" in section 170 is explicit. It means that the prosecution must prove knowledge on the part of the accused of all the relevant elements of the offence. This would include knowledge that he is within the territorial jurisdiction of the United Kingdom; that the goods imported were of a type prohibited from importation; and that he knew that what was afoot was the evasion of that prohibition. In *Warner* v. *Metropolitan Police Commissioner* [1969] 2 A.C. 256, Lord Reid seemed to equate knowledge with "wilfully shutting one's eyes to the truth." However, that was a case dealing with the elusive concept of possession in respect of which their lordships attempted to define the mental element required (see §3–23, *infra* and *Lewis* (1988) 87 Cr.App.R. 270). There is now much authority to support the view that "wilful blindness" is a question of evidence—not law—and that what is required is proof of actual knowledge of the relevant elements of the offence: see *Panayi (No. 2)* [1989] 1 W.L.R. 187; *Grainge* [1974] 1 W.L.R. 619; *Griffiths* (1974) 60 Cr.App.R. 14; but see *Atwal* v. *Massey* (1971) 56 Cr.App.R. 6 D.C.

> In *Panayi (No. 2)* (*supra*), P and K were arrested on board their yacht which had been intercepted inside British territorial waters 1.1 nautical miles off the Isle of Wight (within Port Solent for the purposes of C.E.M.A. 1979, s.5), 690 kilogrammes of cannabis resin were found on board. The drug had been loaded on board in Spain. The appellants contended that the drugs were intended for Holland and that their presence in the United Kingdom was the result of navigational errors and contrary tides.
>
> *Held*: quashing the convictions, that the wording of s.170 precluded a construction which equated recklessness or negligence with knowledge.

2-79   The appellants' yacht was equipped with electronic navigational equipment but their intention was not to enter territorial waters of the United

Kingdom. Bush J. said:

> "... they cannot be knowingly concerned in the fraudulent evasion
> unless they intend dishonestly to evade the restriction. They cannot
> knowingly be involved in the evasion if one of the essential ingredients,
> namely the fact that they are within territorial waters, is unknown to
> them; provided of course that they never had any intention of entering
> the United Kingdom territorial waters. ... Though it is possible in some
> cases to equate recklessness with knowledge or general intent, this
> cannot be done in this kind of case where the specific intent is required of
> being knowingly concerned in any fraudulent evasion."

(d) When must the intent be formed?

In *Jakeman* (1983) 76 Cr.App.R. 223 it was held that what matters is the   2–80
state of the accused's mind at the time the relevant acts were done, *e.g.* at the
time when there was an intention to bring about an unlawful importation.
Accordingly, where a courier of drugs abandoned her intention to carry her
suitcase of cannabis into the United Kingdom in Paris, she could not escape
conviction under section 170 once the cannabis arrived in the United
Kingdom, albeit in an unexpected way.

(e) Innocuous substitutes

Article 11 of the 1988 Vienna Convention Against Illicit Traffic in Narcotic   2–81
Drugs and Psychotropic Substances provides "for the use of controlled deliveries at international level and paves the way for 'clean' deliveries."
   A "clean" delivery involves the substitution of an innocuous substance for
the controlled drug in question. This technique is frequently employed in
drug trafficking investigations and indeed this has been the case for many
years: see *Green* [1976] Q.B. 985.
   The "clean" delivery has the obvious advantage of removing the offending
substance from circulation and preserving vital evidence whilst permitting
the investigation to run its course without the risk of losing the drug if the
trafficker secures an advantage over his investigator. The substitution normally takes place in the country where the offender is likely to be apprehended and tried. Technical difficulties might arise if the substitution were to take
place abroad. It would mean, for example, that the substance actually imported into the United Kingdom was not a controlled drug at all whereas a
charge under section 170(2) of the C.E.M.A. 1979 requires proof that prohibited, restricted, or dutiable goods have actually been imported. Accordingly,
where the accused acts with others and the substitution takes place abroad,
then the appropriate charge would be one of conspiracy to contravene section
170(2): see *Sansom* [1991] 2 All E.R. 145 and *Somchai Liangsiriprasert* v.
U.S. Government [1990] 2 All E.R. 866.
   Note also the arguments in *Ciappara* (1988) 87 Cr.App.R. 316, *supra*, at
§§2–35—2–36.
   The "clean" delivery is to be contrasted with a "controlled" delivery in   2–82
which the law enforcement agency allows detected drugs to be moved down

the chain of supply. Drugs detected in one country may be allowed to travel across national frontiers in order to identify and to obtain evidence against the participants in international drug trafficking. In 1986, the Report of the Committee of Inquiry into the Drugs Problem in the Member States of the Community (European Parliament, September 1986, p. 56) suggested that controlled deliveries were rarely used by reason of legal restrictions in some countries or rivalry or mistrust between law enforcement agencies. No doubt it has been experienced that customs officials in one country will not permit a detected drug to be exported if a prosecution can be brought in that country. However, a substantial number of investigations depend on sound intelligence gathered at home and overseas and which also depend upon detected drugs being shipped across several national frontiers. In its Seventh Report, *Drug Trafficking and Related Serious Crime* (Session 1988–89, paras. 51 and 52), the Committee noted that since 1986 the "situation has improved."

Chapter 3
Possession of Drugs

A. AN INTRODUCTORY NOTE

Any person approaching the concept of possession for the first time could **3–01**
reasonably be forgiven if he expected the legal principles involved to be
straightforward. They are not. He might expect to find, for example, that the
ingredients of possession are encapsulated in a sentence or two, whereas the
ingredients differ from one branch of the law to another. As a general rule, a
person has in his possession anything which is in his physical custody, or
under his control. Although this bald statement represents the law (see *D.P.P.*
v. *Brooks* [1974] A.C. 862, P.C.) it is a statement heavily peppered with
qualifications and exceptions, notably in the field of criminal law, where a
strict adherence to the rule would produce intolerably harsh results. Is a
person to be held criminally liable when he does not know, for example, of
the existence of the article in his custody, or if he makes a mistake as to its
quality? Once such considerations are taken on board, then the simple rule
expressed above is liable to become radically redefined. Furthermore, it is
not initially obvious from the general rule that possession involves a mental
element. In law, however, proof of a mental ingredient of some sort is
required although it is not always clear just what the mental ingredient
entails. Such lack of clarity obviously generates confusion and uncertainty in
the law.

Not surprisingly, the Misuse of Drugs Act 1971 (the M.D.A.) does not
offer a simple definition of possession. Section 37(3) merely provides that:
"... the things which a person has in his possession shall be taken to include
anything subject to his control, which is in the custody of another."

Possession therefore includes constructive possession. A person who puts a **3–02**
suitcase (knowing that it contains cannabis) into the left luggage office at a
railway station while retaining the keys, no longer has custody of it but he
nevertheless falls within section 37(3) since he retains control of the case by
holding the keys. But the Act offers little more by way of assistance. It is important to remember that the Act is designed to *regulate the flow and use* of
controlled drugs: it is not designed to outlaw the majority of them. It follows
that the M.D.A. must distinguish between persons who are *lawfully* entitled
to possess controlled drugs but are merely restricted as to how they may use

them, and those persons who are *unlawfully* in possession of them. Only the latter, of course, will be guilty of the offence of unlawful possession.

For ease of understanding, it may be helpful to approach the law of possession in the following stages. First, look briefly at the sections of the Act which make possession of controlled drugs not only unlawful but also a criminal offence. Secondly, examine what may be lawfully possessed under the Act, and finally examine cases of unlawful possession.

B. MAKING POSSESSION UNLAWFUL

3–03   Section 5(1) is expressed as follows:

"Subject to any regulations under section 7 of this Act ... it shall not be lawful for a person to have a controlled drug in his possession."

Although section 5(1) establishes a general rule that it is unlawful to possess all controlled drugs, many exceptions are to be found in the Misuse of Drugs Regulations 1985. One must therefore look initially to the drugs listed in Schedule II to the M.D.A. to see if the drug is controlled. If it is, one then turns to the various Schedules set out in the Regulations (which do not correspond to the Schedules in the M.D.A.) to see if the drug in question comes within one of the exceptions.

Note that section 5(1) merely makes the possession of controlled drugs unlawful. The *offence*, of being in unlawful possession, is created by section 5(2) which provides:

"Subject to section 28 of this Act and to subsection (4) below, it is an offence for a person to have a controlled drug in his possession in contravention of subsection (1) above."

3–04   Three ingredients are required to be proved, by the prosecution, before an offence under section 5(2) is committed:

   (i)   the item must be in the physical custody or control of the accused,
   (ii)   the accused must know, or at least could reasonably have known, of the existence of the item in question,
   (iii) the item must be proved to be a controlled drug within the meaning of the Misuse of Drugs Act 1971.

For reference, both section 28 and section 5(4) provide an accused with a variety of defences in narrowly defined circumstances, being defences which, for the most part, did not previously exist. Both sections are examined in detail elsewhere but, significantly, the statutory defences so created are all concerned with the state of mind of the person said to be (*inter alia*) in unlawful possession of a controlled drug. Thus, by section 28 it is a defence for the accused to prove that he neither believed, suspected, nor had reason to suspect that what he had was a controlled drug, but it is no defence for him to say that he believed he had cocaine whereas the drug turned out to be heroin. Parliament was therefore making it plain that section 5(2) did not create an absolute offence: unlawful possession requires proof of the requisite *mens rea* before an offence is committed under that section.

Although many cases have considered the meaning of possession, it should **3–05** be borne in mind that some cases appear to be definitive of a proposition of law, whereas they merely demonstrate a general principle that is already well established. Secondly, there have been many changes to the law since a number of cases were decided. Thus, in *Warner* v. *Metropolitan Police Commissioner* [1969] 2 A.C. 256, the House of Lords considered the meaning of "possession" but that was, of course, prior to the passing of the M.D.A. Not all the opinions expressed in *Warner* have the significance that they had in 1969. It is, however, necessary to look at these authorities, since they affect the way in which a case of possession is to be approached, and they have a bearing on the terms in which a jury should be directed by the trial judge.

I. LAWFUL POSSESSION

If there were to be an absolute rule that nobody is entitled to possess any **3–06** controlled drug, ridiculous results would follow. A police officer seizing a controlled drug from an addict would himself be guilty of unlawful possession. Accordingly, the Secretary of State, after consultation with the Advisory Council, may, by regulations, permit certain persons to possess particular controlled drugs, or he may make it lawful for individuals to do a number of things in relation to controlled drugs that would otherwise be unlawful for them to do: see section 7. To this end, the Secretary of State may also make different provisions in relation to different controlled drugs; he may affect different categories of persons, he may impose conditions on the right to possess particular drugs, or he may grant an authority to possess them contingent upon the happening of certain events.

The relevant provisions are mainly to be found in the Misuse of Drugs Regulations 1985 (S.I. 1985 No. 2066) which came into operation on April 1, 1986 (as amended by S.I. 1986 No. 2330, S.I. 1988 No. 916, S.I. 1989 No. 1460, S.I. 1990 No. 2589 and S.I. 1990 No. 2630).

The Misuse of Drugs Regulations 1973 (S.I. 1973 No. 797) have been **3–07** revoked; similarly the following amending Regulations have also been revoked, namely: S.I. 1974 No. 402, S.I. 1975 No. 499, S.I. 1977 No. 1380, S.I. 1979 No. 326, S.I. 1983 No. 788 and S.I. 1984 No. 1143.

By section 10 of the M.D.A. 1971, the Secretary of State may also make regulations, as appears to him necessary or expedient, for preventing the misuse of controlled drugs. For example, the Secretary of State may require certain drugs to be kept in a locked safe or room, or in other secure conditions. The relevant regulations, made under section 10, are embodied in the Misuse of Drugs (Safe Custody) Regulations 1973 (S.I. 1973 No. 798) as amended by S.I. 1974 No. 1449, S.I. 1975 No. 294, S.I. 1983 No. 1909, S.I. 1984 No. 1146, S.I. 1985 No. 2067, and now S.I. 1986 No. 2332.

The Secretary of State is empowered (by virtue of section 10 of the M.D.A. **3–08** 1971), to regulate (*inter alia*) the issue of prescriptions or the supply of controlled drugs to drug addicts. This he has done by the Misuse of Drugs (Notification and Supply to Addicts) Regulations 1973 (S.I. 1973 No. 799) as amended by S.I. 1983 No. 1909.

It should be noted that, for the purposes of the Misuse of Drugs Regulations 1985 (S.I. 1985 No. 2066), controlled drugs are listed in five Schedules. It is these Schedules that must be referred to when considering the extent of the exemptions from section 5(1) and other provisions of the M.D.A. Schedules 1 to 4 have been amended by the Misuse of Drugs (Amendment) Regulations 1986 (S.I. 1986 No. 2330, S.I. 1988 No. 916, S.I. 1989 No. 1460, S.I. 1990 No. 2589 and S.I. 1990 No. 2630).

The major exemptions under the Misuse of Drugs Regulations 1985 are summarised and set out below.

(a) Persons who may possess any controlled drugs

3–09   There are two ways in which it is possible for a person to possess any controlled drug lawfully, no matter how dangerous it may be. The first protection is afforded by regulation 6(7), and the second is afforded by way of a licence issued by the Secretary of State.

(i) *Regulation 6(7)*

Regulation 6(7) provides six classes of persons with immunity from prosecution under section 5(1) when acting in the course of their respective duties, namely:

"(a) a constable when acting in the course of his duty as such;
(b) a person engaged in the business of a carrier when acting in the course of that business;
(c) a person engaged in the business of the Post Office when acting in the course of that business;
(d) an officer of customs and excise when acting in the course of his duty as such;
(e) a person engaged in the work of any laboratory to which the drug has been sent for forensic examination when acting in the course of his duty as a person so engaged;
(f) a person engaged in conveying the drug to a person who may lawfully have that drug in his possession."

The last category certainly protects those who convey drugs to one of the remaining five groups stated above but would seem, equally, to protect the person who, for example, collects controlled drugs from a pharmacist and delivers them to a person entitled to receive them under a prescription. Where a person acts outside the scope of his duties he will lose the protection of regulation 6(7) and so will be guilty of unlawful possession. Thus, a forensic laboratory technician would not be acting in the course of his duties if he took cannabis resin home to show his family what it looks like. Curiously, a disturbing omission from regulation 6(7) is any specific exemption for court staff, including counsel, jurors or members of the judiciary who frequently handle controlled drugs as court exhibits. Frankly, it is difficult to know by what authority court staff may lawfully handle such exhibits by virtue of any other provision of the M.D.A. or the Regulations.

(ii) *Regulation 5*

Another method of securing protection is afforded by regulation 5 which **3–10** enables the Secretary of State to issue a licence authorising any individual to possess any controlled drug. The licensee must abide by the terms and conditions attached to the licence. Failure to do so may amount to the commission of a separate offence (section 18) but such a breach is unlikely to vitiate the effect of the licence. However, the Secretary of State is empowered to revoke or modify the licence at any time.

Licence fees are controlled by the Misuse of Drugs (Licence Fees) Regulations 1986 (S.I. 1986 No. 416) and the Misuse of Drugs (Licence Fees) (Amendment) Regulations 1987 (S.I. 1987 No. 298).

(b) Persons who may possess Schedule 2 drugs

The following substances and products, their salts and stereoisomeric **3–11** forms, are included in Schedule 2 to the M.D. Regs. 1985:

"1. Namely:

Acetorphine
Alfentanil
Allylprodine
Alphacetylmethadol
Alphameprodine
Alphamethadol
Alphaprodine
Anileridine
Benzethidine
Benzylmorphine
   (3-benzylmorphine)
Betacetylmethadol
Betameprodine
Betamethadol
Betaprodine
Bezitramide

(Carfentanil)
Clonitazene
Cocaine

Desomorphine
Dextromoramide
Diamorphine
Diapromide
Diethylthiambutene
Difenoxin

Dihydrocodeinone
   O-carboxymethyloxime
Dihydromorphine
Domenoxadole
Dimepheptanol
Dimethylthiambutene
Dioxaphetyl butyrate
Diphenoxylate
Dipipanone
Drotebanol

Ecgonine, and any derivative of ecgonine which is convertible to ecgonine or to cocaine
Ethylmethylthiambutene
Etonitazene
Etorphine
Etoxeridine

Fentanyl
Furethidine

[Glutethimide]

Hydrocodone
Hydromorphinol
Hydromorphone
Hydroxypethidine

Isomethadone

Ketobemidone

[Lefctamine]
Levomethorphan
Levomoramide
Levophenacylmorphan
Levorphanol
(Lofentanil)

Medicinal opium
Metazocine
Methadone
Methadyl acetate
Methyldesorphine
Methyldihydromorphine
(6-methyldihydromorphine)
Metopon
Morpheridine
Morphine
Morphine methobromide, morphine N-oxide and other pentavalent nitrogen morphine derivatives
Myrophine

(N-hydroxy-tenamphetamine)
Nicomorphine
Noracymethadol
Norlevorphanol
Normethadone
Normorphine
Norpipanone

Oxycodone

Oxymorphone

Pethidine
Phenadoxone
Phenampromide
Phenazocine
Phencyclidine
Phenomorphan
Phenopcridine
Piminodine
Piritramide
Proheptazine
Properide

Racemethorphan
Racemoramide
Racemorphan

Sufentanil

Thebacon
Thebaine
Tilidate
Trimeperidine

4-Cyano-2-dimethylamino-4, 4-diphenylbutane
4-Cyano-1-methyl-4-phenylpiperidine
1-Methyl-4-phenylpiperdine-4-carboxylic acid
2-Methyl-3-morpholino-1, 1-diphenylpropanecarboxylic acid
4-Phenylpiperidine-4-carboxylic acid ethyl ester
(4-methyl-aminorex)

2. Any stereoisomeric form of substance specified in paragraph 1 not being dextromethorphan or dextrorphan.

3. Any ester or ether of a substance specified in paragraph 1 or 2, not being a substance specified in paragraph 6.

4. Any salt of a substance specified in any of paragraphs 1 to 3.

5. Any preparation or other product containing a substance or product specified in any of paragraphs 1 to 4, not being a preparation specified in Schedule 5.

6. The following substances and products are also included, namely:

Acetylihydrocodeine
Amphetamine

Codeine

Dextropropoxyphene
Dihydrocodeine

Ethylmorphine
  (3-ethylmorphine)

(Fenethylline)

(Glutethimide)

(Lefetamine)

Mecloqualone
Methaqualone
Methylamphetamine
Methylphenidate

Nicocodine
Nicodicodine
  (6-nicotinoyldihydrocodeine)
Norcodeine

Phenmetrazine
Pholcodine
Propiram

(Quinalbarbitone)

7. Any stereoisomeric form of a substance specified in paragraph 6.

8. Any salt of a substance specified in paragraph 6 or 7.

9. Any preparation or other product containing a substance or product specified in any of paragraphs 6 to 8, not being a preparation specified in Schedule 5."

[Glutethimide and lefetamine were deleted from paragraph 1 by the Misuse of Drugs (Amendment) Regulations 1986 (S.I. 1986 No. 2330). Carfentanil, lofentanil, fenethylline, glutethimide and lefetamine were inserted into paragraph 6 by the same Regulations. N-hydroxy-tenamphetamine was inserted by S.I. 1990 No. 2589. 4-Methyl-aminorex was inserted by S.I. 1989 No. 1460. Quinalbarbitone was inserted by S.I. 1986 No. 916.]

It will be seen that some of the drugs referred to in Schedule 2 to the 1985 **3–12** Regulations include some of the most dangerous drugs, *e.g.* heroin, cocaine, dipipanone, methadone, medical opium, morphine, DF 118 and methaqualone. However, because such substances are also recognised as being a valuable contribution to medicine when properly and professionally administered, regulation 10(1)(*a*) provides that the following classes of persons (set out in regulation 8(2)), are entitled to possess Schedule 2 drugs (and to supply them) namely:

"(*a*) a practitioner;

(*b*) a pharmacist;

(*c*) a person lawfully conducting a retail pharmacy;

(*d*) a person in charge or acting person in charge of a hospital or nursing home which is wholly or mainly maintained by a public authority out of public funds or by a charity or by voluntary subscriptions;

(*e*) in the case of such a drug supplied to her by a person responsible for the dispensing and supply of medicines at the hospital or nursing home, the sister or acting sister for the time being in charge of a ward, theatre, or other department in such a hospital or nursing home as aforesaid;

(*f*) a person who is in charge of a laboratory the recognised activities of which consist in, or include, the conduct of scientific education or research and which is attached to a university, university college or such a hospital as aforesaid or to any other institution approved for the purpose ... by the-Secretary of State;

(g) a public analyst appointed under section 76 of the Food Act 1984 or section 27 of the Food and Drugs (Scotland) Act 1956;

(h) a sampling officer within the meaning of the Food and Drugs (Scotland) Act 1956;

(i) a sampling officer within the meaning of Schedule 3 to the Medicines Act 1968;

(j) a person employed or engaged in connection with a scheme for testing the quality or amount of the drugs, preparations and appliances supplied under the National Health Service Act 1977 or the National Health Service (Scotland) Act 1978 and the Regulations made thereunder;

(k) a person authorised by the Pharmaceutical Society of Great Britain for the purposes of section 108 or 109 of the Medicines Act 1968."

A person who is an authorised member of a group may, in accordance with the terms of his group authority, have a Schedule 2 drug in his possession: see reg. 10(3).

(c) Persons who may possess Schedule 3 drugs

3–13   The following drugs are included:

"1.(a) Benzphetamine   Mephentermine
(Buprenorphine)   Meprobamate
(Cathine)   Methylphenobarbitone
Chlorophentermine   Methyprylone
Diethypropion   Pentazocine
Ethchlorovynol   Phendimetrazine
Ethinamate   Phentermine
Mazindol   Pipradol

(b) any 5,5 disubstituted barbituric acid (not being quinalbarbitone).

2. Any stereoisomeric form of a substance specified in paragraph 1 (not being phenylpropanolamine).

3. Any salt of a substance specified in paragraph 1 or 2.

4. Any preparation or other product containing a substance specified in any of paragraphs 1 to 3, not being a preparation specified in Schedule 5."

[Cathine and phenylpropanolamine were inserted by S.I. 1986 No. 2330, buprenorphine was inserted by S.I. 1989 No. 1460 and quinalbarbitone was inserted by S.I. 1988 No. 916.]

3–14   The drugs in Schedule 3 are less dangerous than those in Schedules 1 and 2. They include the barbiturates, e.g. methylphenobarbitone. The persons entitled to possess (and supply) these drugs include the following persons (see reg. 10(1)(b) in conjunction with reg. 9(2)):

"(a) a practitioner;
(b) a pharmacist;

(c) a person lawfully conducting a retail pharmacy;

(d) a person in charge of a laboratory the recognised activities of which consist in, or include, the conduct of scientific education or research;

(e) a public analyst appointed under section 76 of the Food Act 1984 or section 27 of the Food and Drugs (Scotland) Act 1956;

(f) a sampling officer within the meaning of the Food and Drugs (Scotland) Act 1956;

(g) a sampling officer within the meaning of Schedule 3 to the Medicines Act 1968;

(h) a person employed or engaged in connection with a scheme for testing the quality or amount of the drugs, preparations and appliances supplied under the National Health Service Act 1977 or the National Health Service (Scotland) Act 1978 and the Regulations made thereunder;

(i) a person authorised by the Pharmaceutical Society of Great Britain for the purposes of section 108 or 109 of the Medicines Act 1968."

By reg. 10(1)(c), (in conjunction with reg. 9(3)(b), (c) and 9(6)—as **3–15** amended by S.I. 1986 No. 2330), the following persons are also included and may therefore possess any Schedule 3 drug, namely:

(i) "... a person in charge or acting person in charge of a hospital or nursing home": *per* reg. 9(3)(b)—as amended by S.I. 1986 No. 2330;

(ii) "... in the case of such a drug supplied to her by a person responsible for the dispensing and supply of medicines at the hospital or nursing home, the sister or acting sister for the time being in charge of a ward, theatre, or other department in such a hospital or nursing home": *per* reg. 9(3)(c)—as amended by S.I. 1986 No. 2330;

(iii) a person in charge of a laboratory may possess (and supply or offer to supply) any drug specified in Schedule 3 which is required for use as a buffering agent in chemical analysis: see reg. 9(6)—inserted by S.I. 1986 No. 2330.

(d) Persons who may possess drugs under a practitioner's control

A person receiving, *e.g.* amphetamine (as a slimming tablet) or other con- **3–16** trolled drugs from a doctor, is entitled to possess them and to take them by reason of regulation 10(2) which provides:

"Notwithstanding the provisions of section 5(1) of the Act a person may have in his possession any drug specified in Schedule 2 or 3 for administration for medical, dental or veterinary purposes in accordance with the directions of a practitioner: ..."

Note that only Schedule 2 and 3 drugs are referred to. There was no point in the draftsman including Schedule 5 drugs since *anybody* may possess these (with or without the directions of a practitioner) by virtue of regulation 4(2)(b) which provides that:

"... Section 5(1) of the Act ... shall not have effect in relation to ... (b) the drugs specified in Schedule 5."

The same consideration applies to Schedule 4 drugs in medicinal form which are also excluded from section 5(1): see regulation 4(2)(a).

The reader may be wondering why no drugs listed under Schedule 1 are included under this heading. The reason is that Parliament has ensured that certain drugs are not supplied to any patient by any doctor, e.g. cannabis in all forms, coca leaf (but not cocaine), LSD, psilocin (extracted from the magic mushroom), or raw opium.

"Administration," within the meaning of regulation 10(2), clearly embraces persons who intend to administer drugs to themselves as well as to others; regulation 7(3) provides that:

"Any person other than a doctor or dentist may administer to a patient ... any drug specified in Schedule 2, 3 or 4."

3–17   As regulation 7(3) gives the general right to *administer* such drugs, in accordance with the directions of a doctor or dentist, it makes obvious sense to give a corresponding right to *possess* the drug(s) in question—hence regulation 10(2).

In cases of self-administration, it is equally important that the drug should be used for the purpose for which it was intended and in a manner that will not cause harm to the user. Accordingly, regulation 10 requires that drugs are administered for "medical, dental or veterinary purposes in accordance with the directions of a practitioner."

Thus, an individual originally in lawful possession of barbiturates will lose the protection of regulation 10 if he uses a drug for a non-medicinal purpose (e.g. to commit suicide) or if he displays mala fides by administering the drug in a way which does not accord with the directions of a practitioner.

> In *Dunbar* [1981] 1 W.L.R. 1536, D was a registered medical practitioner who had no patients. He obtained heroin and pethidine for "professional purposes" and administered them to himself. D told police that he intended committing suicide, but at his trial stated that he wished to alleviate his depression. The trial judge ruled that D had no defence to a charge of unlawful possession of the drugs, contrary to section 5(1) M.D.A. 1971, on the basis that regulation 10(2) had not been complied with since D had not acted "with the directions of a practitioner."

3–18   During the course of the appeal the Crown argued that a doctor who has no patients is not acting in his capacity as a doctor. The Court of Appeal did not find that argument attractive and held that a doctor who bona fide prescribed a controlled drug for himself was acting in his capacity as a doctor even though he was the person receiving the benefit.

The decision is patently right. The definition of a doctor is not dependent on whether he has patients or not. Moreover, regulation 10(2) is designed to ensure the prudent use of controlled drugs (e.g. for medical purposes), when those drugs are in the hands of persons who are not medically qualified. A doctor treating himself, in a bona fide fashion, clearly meets the object of this provision. Like anyone else, a doctor who administers a drug to himself for a non-medical purpose, *e.g.* for an attempt to commit suicide or simply to abuse the drug, cannot avail himself of the protection of regulation 10 and is accordingly guilty of an offence under section 5(2): see *Taylor* [1986] Crim.L.R. 680.

(e) Persons who may possess Schedule 4 drugs

Drugs falling within Schedule 4 include: 3–19

"Alprazolam	Ketazolam
Bromazepam	Loprazolam
Camazepam	Lorazepam
Chlordiazepoxide	Lormetazepam
Clobazam	Medazepam
Clonazepam	(Mefenorex)
Clorazepic acid	(Midazolam)
Clotiazepam	
Cloxazolam	Nimetazepam
	Nitrazepam
Delorazepam	Nordazepam
Diazepam	
	Oxazepam
Estazolam	Oxazolam
Ethyl loflazepate	
	(Pemoline)
(Fencamfamin)	Pinazepam
(Fenproporex)	Prazepam
Fludiazepam	(Propylhexedrine)
Flunitrazepam	(Pyrovalerone)
Flurazepam	
	Temazepam
Halazepam	Tetrazepam
Haloxazolam	Triazolam
	(*N*-Ethylamphetamine)

2. Any stereoisomeric form of a substance specified in paragraph 1.

3. Any salt of a substance specified in paragraph 1 or 2.

4. Any preparation or other product containing a substance or product specified in any of paragraphs 1 to 3, not being a preparation specified in Schedule 5."

[Fencamfamin, fenproporex, mefenorex, propylhexedrine, pyrovalerone and N-Ethylamphetamine were inserted by S.I. 1986 No. 2330. Midazolam was inserted by S.I. 1990 No. 2630. Pemoline was inserted by S.I. 1989 No. 1460.]

Any of the persons mentioned in regulation 9(2) (*supra*) may possess

Schedule 4 drugs. Moreover, *any person* may possess a Schedule 4 drug *provided* that the controlled drug so specified is in a "medicinal product": see reg. 4(2)(*a*).

(f) All persons may possess Schedule 5 drugs

3–20　　　By regulation 4(2)(*b*), all drugs specified in Schedule 5 to the 1985 Regulations are exempt from section 5(1) of the M.D.A. Accordingly, *any* person may possess such drugs.

Schedule 5, in so far as it is material, provides that:

"1.—(1) Any preparation of one or more of the substances to which this paragraph applies, not being a preparation designed for administration by injection, when compounded with one or more other active or inert ingredients and containing a total of not more than 100 milligrammes of the substance or substances (calculated as base) per dosage unit or with a total concentration of not more than 2.5 per cent. (calculated as base) in undivided preparations.

(2) The substances to which this paragraph applies are acetylihydrocodeine, codeine, dihydrocodeine, ethylmorphine, nicocodine, nicodicodine (6-nicotinoyldihydrocodeine), norcodeine, pholcodine and their respective salts.

2. Any preparation of cocaine containing not more than 0.1 per cent of cocaine calculated as cocaine base, being a preparation compounded with one or more other active or inert ingredients in such a way that the cocaine cannot be recovered by readily applicable means or in a yield which would constitute a risk to health.

3. Any preparation of medicinal opium or of morphine containing (in either case) not more than (0.2 per cent. of morphine calculated as anhydrous morphine base, being a preparation compounded with one or more other active or inert ingredients in such a way that the opium or, as the case may be, the morphine, cannot be recovered by readily applicable means or in a yield which would constitute a risk to health. [and see *Hunt* [1987] A.C. 325]

4. Any preparation of dextropropoxyphene, being a preparation designed for oral administration, containing not more than 135 milligrammes of dextropropoxyphene (calculated as base) per dosage unit or with a total concentration of not more than 2.5 per cent. (calculated as base) in undivided preparations.

5. Any preparation of difenoxin containing, per dosage unit, not more than 0.5 milligrammes of difenoxin and a quantity of atropine sulphate equivalent to at least 5 per cent. of the dose of difenoxin.

6. Any preparation of diphenoxylate containing, per dosage unit, not more than 2.5 milligrammes of diphenoxylate calculated as base, and a quantity of atropine sulphate equivalent to at least 1 per cent. of the dose of diphenoxylate.

7. Any preparation of propiram containing, per dosage unit, not more than 100 milligrammes of propiram calculated as base and compounded

with at least the same amount (by weight) of methylcellulose.

8. Any powder of ipecacuanha and opium comprising—

10 per cent. opium in powder

10 per cent. ipecacuanha root, in powder, well mixed with 80 per cent. of any other powdered ingredient containing no controlled drug.

9. Any mixture containing one or more of the preparations specified in paragraphs 1 to 8, being a mixture of which none of the other ingredients is a controlled drug."

II. UNLAWFUL POSSESSION

(a) Two special cases of unlawful possession

At this stage it is appropriate to look at two specific cases of unlawful pos- 3–21
session.

(i) *"Double-scripting" nullifies lawful possession*

The purpose of the Regulations is to ensure that controlled drugs remain in the hands of those persons entitled to possess them and who will deal with them in a way that produces no harmful effects resulting in a social problem. Since regulation 10(2) gives all individuals the right to administer drugs specified in Schedule 2 and 3 in accordance with the directions of a practitioner, including controlled drugs supplied to them on prescription from a doctor, the object of the regulations would be defeated if users could simply increase their supply by obtaining prescriptions from more than one doctor at a time.

Accordingly, regulation 10(2) shall not have effect in the case of a person to whom the drug has been supplied by or on the prescription of a doctor if:

> "(a) that person was then being supplied with any controlled drug by or on the prescription of another doctor and failed to disclose that fact to the first mentioned doctor before the supply by him or on his prescription; ..."

Thus, if A obtains drugs from Dr. 1 and Dr. 2, but fails to inform the latter of the prescription received from Dr. 1, then A will be guilty of unlawfully possessing the drugs received from Dr. 2. However, A will still be in lawful possession of the drugs received from Dr. 1.

(ii) *Persons dishonestly obtaining drugs*

Furthermore, regulation 10(2) shall not have effect in the case of a person 3–22
to whom the drug has been supplied by or on the prescription of a doctor if:

> "(b) that or any other person on his behalf made a declaration or statement which was false in any particular, for the purpose of obtaining the supply or prescription."

A person who falsely represents to a doctor that he is unable to sleep and needs a strong barbiturate, commits an offence contrary to section 5(1) if he obtains the drug to crush up and injects it for "kicks." The phrase "false in any particular" must refer to a material particular, the falsity of which was intended to induce the doctor to supply the controlled drug. Upon a literal construction of regulation 10(2)(*b*), the words "... for the purpose of obtaining ..." mean that it is the intention of the recipient that is all-important. It would not be necessary to show that the doctor was in fact induced to supply the drug by the false particulars.

III. THE GENERAL PRINCIPLES OF POSSESSION

(a) The mental element of possession

3–23   Given that, in general terms, a person has in his possession whatever is in his physical custody or under his control, it may be thought that possession is a purely physical concept involving no mental ingredient at all whereas, in fact, the law separates the physical element of possession (the *corpus*) from the mental element (the *animus possidendi*), *i.e.* the intention to possess. It is therefore implicit that in every case of possession, a person must at least know of the existence of the thing which he has or controls but it is not always apparent whether a person need know of the quality of the thing in question. For the purposes of the M.D.A. 1971, it must be stressed that the provisions of that Act make it plain that it is for the accused to discover for himself the nature of the substance which he has. He will not be liable if he neither believed, nor suspected, nor had any reason to suspect that the substance was a controlled drug (section 28(3)(*b*)(i)). By contrast, a mistake of fact as to the precise controlled drug possessed is no defence (see section 28(3)(*a*)). To prove the mental element of possession, the prosecution need only lead evidence to establish that the accused knew of the existence of the "thing" which it is said he has or controls. However, since the provisions of the Act are superimposed on to existing case law, it follows that the fine distinctions which remain relevant (and therefore affect the validity of a judge's summing-up at trial) require a close examination of the authorities concerned.

3–24   In *Warner* v. *Metropolitan Police Commissioner* [1969] 2 A.C. 256, W handled two boxes which he believed contained scent. In fact one box contained amphetamine sulphate. W was charged with an offence under section 1 of the Drugs (Prevention of Misuse) Act 1964 (now repealed), which provided that "(1) ... it shall not be lawful for a person to have in his possession a substance ... specified in the Schedule to this Act ... ." The House of Lords held that the offence was absolute and did not require proof of *mens rea*. However, the prosecution was required to prove that the accused knew of the existence of the thing alleged, although a mistake as to its quality was generally no defence. Moreover, special considerations apply in connection with "container cases" and it was a defence for the accused to show that he believed the contents to be of a wholly different character.

Lord Reid observed (at 391) that:

> "As a legal term 'possession' is ambiguous at least to this extent: there is no clear rule as to the nature of the mental element required. All are agreed that there must be some mental element in possession, but there is no agreement as to what precisely it must be. Indeed the view which

prevailed in *R.* v. *Ashwell* (1885) 16 Q.B.D. 190, and was approved in *R.* v. *Hudson* [1943] 1 K.B. 458, went so far that a person who received a sovereign thinking it to be a shilling was held not to possess the sovereign until he discovered the mistake."

The above passage demonstrates the reluctance of the courts to make per- **3–25** sons criminally liable for offences of possession without proof of some mental ingredient. As Lord Scarman remarked in *Boyesen* [1982] 2 All E.R. 161, 163g:

"Possession is a deceptively simple concept. It denotes a physical control or custody of a thing plus knowledge that you have it in your custody or control. You may possess a thing without knowing or comprehending its nature; but you do not possess it unless you know you have it."

Lord Scarman, with whom their Lordships in that case concurred, adopted the description of possession given by Lord Wilberforce in *Warner* v. *M.P.C.* (who also heard *Boyesen*) when he said (at 310):

"The question to which an answer is required … is whether in the circumstances the accused should be held to have possession of the substance rather than control. In order to decide between these two, the jury should, in my opinion, be invited to consider all the circumstances … the manner and circumstances in which the substance, or something which contains it, has been received … On such matters as these (not exhaustively stated) they must make the decision whether, in addition to physical control, he has, or ought to have imputed to him the intention to possess, or knowledge that he does possess, what is in fact a prohibited substance. If he has this intention or knowledge, it is not additionally necessary that he should know the nature of the substance."

When Lord Wilberforce in *Warner* referred to "… the intention to possess …" he was of course referring to the *animus possidendi* of possession. Again, Lord Pearce in *Warner*, observed (at 305) that:

"I think that the term 'possession' is satisfied by a knowledge only of the existence of the thing itself and not of its qualities, and that ignorance or mistake as to its qualities is not an excuse."

Accordingly, in *Warner*, the majority of their Lordships held that once pos- **3–26** session is proved then the offence is absolute and no proof of *mens rea* is required. As we have seen, section 28 of the M.D.A. now ameliorates some of the harshness of the decision in *Warner* by shifting the onus on to the accused to prove that he did not believe, suspect or had reason to suspect that the substance in question was a controlled drug.

It may be thought unrealistic to say that the offence was absolute in 1969 when their Lordships, in *Warner*, stated that the prosecution was required to prove an intention to possess. Perhaps it is a matter of academic debate whether such an intention can properly be termed "*mens rea*," but it is submitted that it cannot be so termed. The House of Lords did no more than exploit what had always been an ingredient of the concept of possession—

namely the *animus possidendi*. Had it been held necessary for the accused to know of the nature and quality of the substance then, clearly, this would involve more than proof of an *animus* and would therefore amount to the *mens rea* of the offence.

3–27   Bearing in mind that the prosecution is still required to prove the fact of possession (for the purposes of section 5(2)), it follows that the prosecution must still prove the *corpus* and the *animus* elements in possession. But, in *Wright* (1975) 62 Cr.App.R. 169, C.A. the prosecution argued that the M.D.A. effectively redefined the word "possession," by virtue of the wording of section 28, so as to place the burden of proving a lack of knowledge firmly on the accused. The Court of Appeal did not think that the Crown's contention was correct but the court was not prepared to make a decision on the point.

Section 28(2) reads as follows:

> "Subject to subsection (3) below, in any proceedings for an offence to which this section applies, it shall be a defence for the accused to prove that he neither knew of nor suspected nor had reason to suspect the existence of some fact alleged by the prosecution which it is necessary for the prosecution to prove if he is to be convicted of the offence charged."

3–28   The issue which was raised in *Wright* is whether the *animus possidendi* amounts to "... some fact alleged by the prosecution which it is necessary for the prosecution to prove." If it is, then the burden of proving a lack of knowledge shifts to the accused. The point was fully considered in *Ashton-Rickhardt* [1978] 1 All E.R. 173. The appellant was found asleep in his car. A cigarette, containing cannabis, was discovered in the vehicle. The trial judge directed the jury that "... the 'burden of proof' rests on the defendant ... that he did not know it [the cigarette] was there...." This was a clear misdirection in the light of *Warner* but the Crown contended that section 28(2) altered the position. Roskill L.J., who delivered the judgment of the court, had no difficulty in rejecting the Crown's argument. He said (at 178d):

> "When one construes [sections 28(2) and (3)] in the 1971 Act together with section 5(1) and (2) and one realises that s.5(2) and indeed (3) are each made subject to s.28 of the Act, it is apparent that whatever the precise scope of the various subsections of s.28 may be, their manifest purpose is to afford a defence to an accused person where no defence had previously existed. ... It would be very odd indeed if one effect of s.28 which ... is plainly designed to afford a defence where no defence had previously existed, was at the same time to remove from the shoulders of the Crown the burden of proof of one of the essential elements of the offence as stated by the House of Lords in *Warner*."

Accordingly, section 28 only adds defences. It was not intended to remove previous defences and, indeed, it does not do so.

(b) What the prosecution must prove

As we have noted, three ingredients are required to be proved, by the prosecution, before an offence under section 5(2) is made out:　**3–29**

   (i)　the item must be in the physical custody or control of the accused;

   (ii)　the accused must know, or at least could reasonably have known, of the existence of the item: see *Lewis* (1988) 87 Cr.App.R. 270; and

   (iii)　the item must be a controlled drug.

Ideally, one would prefer to examine the authorities in respect of each ingredient in isolation, but this approach is not appropriate since the first two ingredients heavily overlap. For this reason (although it is essential to keep the three ingredients very much in the forefront of one's mind) a better approach is to examine seven typical situations, namely, where:　**3–30**

   (1)　The defendant knows of the existence of the thing and he has the custody or control of it.

   (2)　The defendant has no knowledge of the thing, or article, and therefore he is not in a position to exercise control over it.

   (3)　The defendant has the custody of, or general control over, a number of articles but he does not know of the existence of the offending article.

   (4)　The defendant knows of the existence of the thing but he does not exert any control over it.

   (5)　The defendant knows of the existence of the thing and he has custody or control, but he makes a *mistake as to its quality*.

   (6)　The defendant has the custody, or control, of a *container* but he has no knowledge of its *contents*.

   (7)　The quantity is so minute that the presence of the drug indicates no more than previous possession.

(i) *Proof of knowledge and control*

Few problems are likely to be encountered where an accused is clearly proved to have the custody of a controlled drug or exercises control over it. However, prosecutors have a duty to ensure that the accused is charged appropriately. Thus, in *Muir* v. *Smith* [1978] Crim.L.R. 293, D.C., the defendant was charged with being in possession of "cannabis resin." Police had searched the defendant's flat and found 20 microgrammes of cannabis which could have been herbal cannabis or resin. There was no doubt that the defendant was in possession of some kind of cannabis. The Divisional Court held that the conviction had to be quashed since herbal cannabis and resin were two totally different substances.　**3–31**

However, if the prosecutor had amended the charge to read "a quantity of cannabis or cannabis resin" then it is difficult to see what answer the defendant would have had to the charge. Indeed in *Best* (1979) 70 Cr.App.R. 21, the Court of Appeal so held when dismissing appeals against conviction by five appellants who had been charged with possession of "cannabis or cannabis resin." The scientific evidence was that the drug found was *either* of those two substances. The charge was held not to be bad for duplicity and reliance on rule 7 of the Indictment Rules 1971 was not necessary.

(ii) *No knowledge of the thing*

3–32   Suppose D attends a party at which a number of guests are smoking cigarettes. The police raid the premises and a quantity of "joints" containing cannabis are found. If D does not know of the existence of the "joints" he cannot be said to be in possession of the drug contained in them. The position would be different if, upon the arrival of police, the accused unwittingly picked up the offending cigarettes in order to try to "tidy up." In the eyes of the law, D will now be in possession of the cigarettes—including the drug. Accordingly, D's possession will be unlawful unless he can prove, under section 28, that he neither believed, suspected, nor had reason to suspect that the cigarettes contained a controlled drug. In *Searle* v. *Randolph* [1972] Crim.L.R. 779, D.C., D picked up a number of cigarette ends in a tent used by a number of individuals. One cigarette contained cannabis. He was convicted on the basis that he had the drug in his custody and a mistake as to the quality of the substance was (at that time) no defence. Of course, now he would have a defence under section 28.

The crucial fact in *Searle* v. *Randolph* is that D knew of the existence of the articles, *i.e.* the cigarettes when he picked them up. Had he left them untouched, he would only have had a general interest in the contents of the tent, which would not have been sufficiently specific to amount to control.

3–33   Where unsolicited goods containing drugs are delivered to an individual's address in the absence of the addressee he is clearly not able to exercise control over them (by reason of his absence) and therefore he cannot be said to have custody or control over them until he returns and becomes aware of their existence. These principles are clearly demonstrated in *Cavendish* [1961] 1 W.L.R. 1083, a case involving the receipt of stolen property, in which it was held that in order to prove possession, something more must be proved in addition to the goods being found on the defendant's premises: namely, that upon his return he became aware of their presence and exercised some control over them, directly or indirectly. The point to note is that Cavendish was not responsible for the delivery of the goods. He was not exercising control. But if goods are solicited, having been ordered by D, then the converse is true and the fact that D is absent from the premises at the time of delivery can be no defence. D may not know of the time or the day of delivery, but it was he who ensured its delivery. He was in control. Accordingly, if the packet contains a controlled drug, D is guilty of unlawful possession, unless he can avail himself of a defence under section 28.

> In *Peaston* (1978) 69 Cr.App.R. 203, P occupied a bed-sit in a house made up of such accommodation. He received through the post a package containing amphetamine which he had ordered. P was unaware of its arrival. Police arrived shortly after it was delivered and handed the package to P who then opened it. He was charged and convicted of being in unlawful possession of the drugs.

Held: the conviction was right. P had ordered the drugs.

(iii) *General control but no knowledge*

There will often be cases where D exercises control over a considerable **3–34**
number of goods, not all of which he necessarily knows to exist. In *Lockyer* v.
Gibb [1967] 2 Q.B. 243, the defendant was stopped by police. She had in her
possession a holdall containing many items including a paper bag which contained a bottle in which white tablets were visible. The tablets were in fact
morphine sulphate. The defendant knew of the existence of the tablets but
there was a possibility that she did not know that the tablets contained a prohibited substance. Her conviction, for the unlawful possession of morphine,
was upheld. D was clearly aware of the existence of the tablets. She therefore
exercised clear control over them. Her mistake as to the nature of the tablets
was purely a mistake as to quality which, at that time, afforded D no defence.
Now she would have a defence under section 28. But Lord Parker C.J. took
the facts of that case several steps further and remarked: "If something were
slipped into your basket and you had not the vaguest notion it was there at all,
you could not possibly be said to be in possession of it."

It is not difficult to see how such a set of facts might arise in practice. For example, D arrives in the United Kingdom, having travelled from Morocco by
air. X, a passenger on the same flight, and fearing detection, slips two slabs of
cannabis resin into D's wicker basket before D enters the "nothing to
declare" channel. D certainly has control over the basket and has an interest
in the contents. In the ordinary way one would say that D "possesses" the
contents. So why should D escape conviction under section 5(2)? The answer
is that since possession requires an *animus* (see *Warner*), it follows that custody or control is subject to the knowledge that one has something that is *additional* to those articles which one already knows to exist. Thus, in *Searle* v.
Randolph the defendant knew of the existence of cigarette ends (the articles)
but only made a mistake as to the quality of the "tobacco." But, in our example, D knew she possessed the wicker basket and certain contents but not
the slabs of resin which another person had put there.

The same reasoning probably explains the decision in *Irving* [1970] **3–35**
Crim.L.R. 642, C.A. The defendant was in possession of a bottle of stomach
pills but one tablet was heroin. He said that his wife must have put it there.
His conviction was quashed since there was no evidence that he knew of its
existence. He knew of the existence of the bottle and the stomach pills but
that was all.

The same principles apply to all situations in which an individual has general custody of a number of items, some of which he knows to exist and others
which he does not. In *Warner*, the House of Lords approved that part of the
judgment of Lord Parker C.J., in *Lockyer* v. *Gibb*, when he said:

> "... it is quite clear that a person cannot be said to be in possession of
> some article which he or she does not realise is, or may be, in her hand-
> bag, in her room, or in some other place over which she had control."

The classic situation is a house used and occupied by a number of individ- **3–36**
uals.

In *Smith* [1966] Crim.L.R. 588, C.A., police found Indian hemp in a room at a house where S was arrested. The room was used in common by all the people living in the house but the judge directed the jury that they could convict if they concluded that "she did live in that room and had an interest in it so that she controlled all the things that were in it."

Held: the direction was defective since it did not go far enough to demonstrate control and the judge had not dealt with the issue of knowledge at all. S had a general interest in the room but that was all.

Smith is therefore distinguishable from *Searle* v. *Randolph* (cigarette ends in a tent) where the defendant, in *Searle* v. *Randolph*, knew of the existence of the articles, *i.e.* the cigarettes, when he picked them up. There is, of course, an apparent conflict between the results in *Irving*, *Smith*, the dictum of Lord Parker C.J. in *Lockyer* v. *Gibb* on the one hand, and the result of *Searle* v. *Randolph* on the other hand. Thus, if Irving was not in possession of a tablet which he did not know existed, then why should D, in *Searle* v. *Randolph*, be in possession of the cannabis which, again, he did not know existed in the cigarette? In both cases the offending material was held in a container over which the accused exercised custody and/or control. Why, then, was there a different result? The admittedly subtle distinction is that if the drug and the remaining articles are blended to form one substance then that is the commodity over which control is exercised. If the accused therefore knows of the existence of the blend (albeit that he may not appreciate its real quality), then he will have the necessary *animus* to put him in possession of it. In *Irving*, and *Smith*, the drug had a separate and distinct existence from its neighbouring articles. The issue was whether the defendant knew of the existence of the thing which was, in fact, a controlled drug and, if he did do so, whether he exercised control over it. By contrast, in *Searle* v. *Randolph* the tobacco and cannabis were mixed to form (in reality) one substance. The distinction is capable of producing curious results. If D is given a parcel which, upon examination, is found to contain two bags, one containing flour and the other containing heroin, D will not be guilty of possessing the heroin if he only knows of the existence of the bag of flour. It is for the prosecution to prove that the defendant had the necessary *animus* in respect of each commodity. However, if both drugs had been blended and put into the parcel, D would be in possession of the blend even though he believed the entire substance to be flour: he made a mere mistake as to quality. In these circumstances the burden would therefore be on the defendant to prove, under section 28, that he did not have reason to suspect that the substance included a controlled drug.

3-37   The point is again demonstrated in *Marriott* [1971] 1 W.L.R. 187:

Police searched M's flat. M was found to be in possession of a penknife. On the blade, forensic scientists detected the presence of cannabis resin. The judge directed the jury that if M was in possession of the knife then even if he did not know of the existence of the material on the blade, he was guilty of possessing what turned out to be cannabis resin. The Court of Appeal held that the judge misdirected the jury. M had to be aware of the existence of some foreign matter on the knife.

It was not enough for M to know of the existence of the knife, he also had to know of the existence of the extra substance as well. If he did know of its existence but simply thought that the substance was toffee, his mistake would merely be one of quality. Once again, by virtue of section 28, the burden would now be on the accused to prove a lack of knowledge: see also *Coffey* v. *Douglas*, May 20, 1976, unreported.

The problem of drug traces. Section 5(1) makes it unlawful to possess "*any* 3–38 controlled drug.*"* Strictly interpreted, that phrase means that the actual quantity involved is irrelevant. Unfortunately, the courts became confused as to whether a person can properly be said to be in possession of a drug (for the purposes of section 5) if the quantity involved is so small that it cannot be seen with the naked eye or that it can only be detected by the use of precise scientific equipment. Alternatively, it has been queried whether a person can properly be said to be in possession if the drug is capable of being weighed or otherwise measured but is merely too small to be of any practical value to a drug abuser. In a bid to mitigate the strictness of section 5, some courts effectively attempted to add words to section 5(1) in order to give effect to the spirit of the M.D.A. Thus, in *Worsell* [1970] 1 W.L.R. 111:

> W was found in possession of a tube which was apparently empty. However, a few droplets of heroin were detected under a microscope.
>
> *Held*: that the tube was in reality empty and therefore the prosecution could not prove that there was any drug for the defendant to possess at the time of his arrest. But there would have been no defence if the charge was amended to cover possession at an earlier stage.

The conclusion that the tube was in reality empty is, of course, a fiction 3–39 since the drug exists as a trifling amount. The courts refined this approach until they developed a so-called "usability" test. By virtue of this test, a person could only be in possession of the drug if it was either usable or sufficiently great to amount to "something." The House of Lords in *Boyesen* [1982] A.C. 768 later rejected the usability test. There really was no need to create the fiction in the first instance. In cases where presence of the drug is so minute as to be unusable or even (following *Worsell*) practically "non-existent," the prosecution is unlikely to be able to prove that an accused *knew of the existence of the drugs*. It is the issue of knowledge which would normally be at the heart of the case. In *Worsell*, W knew of the existence of the tube but that was all. He could only be guilty if he knew that he had, or controlled, something else, *i.e.* some substance or matter which in fact turned out to be a controlled drug. But he did not know any such thing. If a scientist would not have known of the presence of a drug without the use of special equipment, it is difficult to understand how can it be proved that the accused would have known of its existence.

Stinson J. upheld a submission of no case to answer in *Colyer* [1974] Crim.L.R. 243, where C possessed a pipe which was forensically examined. The scientist could not see anything in it but, by an elaborate process, approximately a millionth of an ounce of cannabis was found. There was no evidence that C knew of its existence albeit he exercised control of the pipe.

A similar submission was upheld in *Hieorowski* [1978] Crim.L.R. 563, where H admitted that three reefer ends were his. The presence of the drug was only detected by an elaborate chemical process. It could not be presumed that H would have been aware of such small amounts for had that been his state of mind, then he would probably have smoked the remainder.

3–40 One can only wonder whether the result in *Searle* v. *Randolph*, or *Muir* v. *Smith* [1978] Crim.L.R. 293, D.C. (20 microgrammes of cannabis), would have been the same if a similar point had been taken on behalf of the defence.

Whether an amount is so small that the prosecution cannot establish a prima facie case of knowledge is a matter of degree and is to be determined by the trial judge: see *Webb* [1979] Crim.L.R. 462 (0.4 milligrammes and 0.6 milligrammes of cannabis not enough).

It may be thought that, by virtue of section 28, the burden is on the defendant to show that he had no reason to suspect the presence of the trace, but this is not so. It is for the prosecution to establish a prima facie case in respect of all three ingredients to prove possession. Only when the prosecution succeeds in so doing, does section 28 come into play.

3–41 **Can possession be "lost" by forgetfulness?** The point arose in the interesting case of *Buswell* [1972] 1 W.L.R. 64:

> B, a drug addict, was prescribed 70 amphetamine tablets by his doctor. He put the tablets in his jeans. His mother washed the jeans. B, assuming the tablets to have been washed away, obtained a second prescription. He later found the original tablets in a drawer. The police made a search of B's home and found the drugs.
>
> *Held: inter alia*, that where a person in lawful possession of the drugs forgot their existence, he remained in possession of them. They were still in his custody. B's conviction was quashed.

The authorities of *Warner* v. *Metropolitan Police Commissioner* and *Lockyer* v. *Gibb* [1967] 2 Q.B. 243 were referred to in the judgment. Phillimore L.J. held that those two cases dealt with something "very different, *i.e.* the question whether an article ever came into the individual's possession at all." The example was given of the drug slipped into somebody's pocket without that person's knowledge. The court distinguished that situation from *Buswell's* case where the article was "undoubtedly in B's possession."

At this stage, it is worth bearing in mind that two separate considerations arose in *Buswell*. The first concerned the validity of the prescription, *i.e.* whether the legality of the original prescription was destroyed by the obtaining of a second prescription, and secondly, whether the accused continued to possess the drugs. If he did, and if the prescription was no longer valid, then his possession of the drugs would have been unlawful. In respect of the first point the court found nothing to show that the prescription was not, as it were, still "lawful."

Accordingly, since B had originally been in lawful possession of the drugs by reason of the earlier prescription, his right to possess those drugs under the prescription was not lost by his forgetfulness, or his mistaken belief that they had been destroyed.

3–42 That leaves the second point. The prosecution had contended that B had "lost" his original possession when he believed that the drugs were destroyed. Phillimore L.J. questioned whether possession could have been in a state of limbo and added:

" ... it is idle to say that if mistakenly you think your mother has dissolved the tablets which you put in the pocket of your jeans, whereas in fact they are still in the drawer, they have in some way passed out of your possession. They have never left your care and control accordingly, you are in possession."

The Court of Appeal in *Martindale* [1986] 1 W.L.R. 1042 followed the reasoning in *Buswell*, holding that possession did not depend on the alleged possessor's power of memory. In *Martindale*, M was given a piece of cannabis, in Canada, in 1983. Two years later he was arrested in the United Kingdom and searched by police. The officers discovered the cannabis in his wallet. M had forgotten all about it although he admitted that he had put it there some two years previously. Lord Lane C.J. delivered the judgment of the court and said:

"In our judgment ... he remained in possession, even though his memory of the presence of the drug had faded or disappeared altogether. Possession does not depend on the alleged possessor's powers of memory. Nor does possession come and go as memory revives or fails. If it were to do so, a man with a poor memory would be acquitted, he with the good memory would be convicted."

The Court of Appeal had been referred to *Russell* (1985) 81 Cr.App.R. 315, which the court declined to follow and implied that *Russell* was wrongly decided. But, in *Russell*, the Court of Appeal was concerned with a charge of possession of an offensive weapon, namely a cosh, which was under the driver's seat of a car driven by the defendant. Jupp J. delivered the judgment of the court, saying: "It would in our judgment be wrong to hold that a man knowingly has a weapon with him if his forgetfulness of its existence or presence in his car is so complete as to amount to ignorance that it is there at all."

In *Martindale* the Court of Appeal had little doubt that if the court in *Russell* had been referred to *Buswell* the decision " ... would almost certainly have gone the other way." However, it is submitted that it is difficult to see why that should be, since a charge under section 1(1) of the Prevention of Crimes Act 1953 (which, insofar as it is material, reads "any person ... who has with him ... any offensive weapon") is a very different type of allegation to a charge under s.5(2) of the M.D.A. The words "has with him," for the purposes of section 1(1) of the Prevention of Crimes Act 1953, clearly denote that the accused must know of the presence of the weapon at the moment of arrest: see *Cugullere* [1961] 1 W.L.R. 858. The case of *Martindale* serves to demonstrate the dangers of construing the ingredients of possession by reference to another branch of the law.

The reasoning of the Court of Appeal in *Martindale* was followed in *Gill* v. *Lockhart*, 1987 S.C.C.R. 599. In that case police found a piece of cannabis resin wrapped in clingfilm in a pocket of a golf bag in the appellant's room. He had placed it in there some two years earlier and had forgotten about it.

The court held that the appellant had the necessary *mens rea* which continued to be applied to the physical possession throughout the whole period.

3–44　　**Knowledge and imputed knowledge.** The question that arises here is whether the accused must have *actual* knowledge of the existence of the offending substance or whether there are circumstances in which the requisite knowledge may be imputed. There is some support for the proposition that knowledge includes deliberately "shutting one's eyes to the truth," but it is submitted that this is a concept which is currently ill-defined in English law, being perhaps no more than a forensic yardstick with which to test the quality of the evidence as to knowledge, and which (particularly in the light of the decision of the Court of Appeal in *Lewis* (1988) 87 Cr.App.R. 270) may not be apt to describe what is a sufficient *animus* for the purposes of possession under the M.D.A. 1971 (see *Atwal* v. *Massey* (1971) 56 Cr.App.R. 6, D.C., and *Grainge* [1974] 1 W.L.R. 69). In *Warner* v. *Metropolitan Police Commissioner* [1969] 2 A.C. 256, Lord Reid said (at 279): "The object of the legislation is to penalise possession of certain drugs ... And it is a commonplace that, if the accused had a suspicion but deliberately shut his eyes, the court or jury is well entitled to hold him guilty."

In *Murray* v. *MacPhail* [1991] S.C.C.R. 245, the appellant agreed with his co-accused that the latter could conceal cannabis in the appellant's room while the appellant was on holiday. The appellant expected the cannabis to have been removed by the time he returned. The appellant returned as police were searching his room during the course of which 21 grammes of cannabis were found under his bed. On appeal it was not disputed that the appellant had control of the cannabis because it was in his room. The court held that the element of knowledge was satisfied by the appellant's consent to the hiding of the drugs in his room. His consent imported the necessary knowledge.

3–45　　It is submitted that this case is not straightforward and should be read with the case of *Lewis* (1988) 87 Cr.App.R. 270 in mind. The appellant was absent when the drugs were placed under the bed. The appellant's room had no lock and access could easily be gained. The court concluded that the appellant had allowed the drugs to come into his possession, and control, by virtue of the standing arrangement he had with the co-accused. Although such a "standing arrangement" may be evidence of control, it does not necessarily prove knowledge of the existence of the offending substance. The co-accused may change his mind and not take advantage of the standing arrangement. The defendant may or may not be mistaken in his belief that the co-accused has concealed drugs in accordance with the open-ended arrangement. The court dismissed the appeal on the narrow basis that the cannabis had been put beneath his bed by the co-accused with the consent of the appellant. However, the appellant's state of mind was no more than merely anticipatory.

In *McNamara* (1988) 87 Cr.App.R. 246 it was said, correctly, that a person does not have possession of something which had been put into his pocket or house without his knowledge. That proposition is consistent with some of the speeches of their Lordships in *Warner* v. *Metropolitan Police Commissioner* [1969] 2 A.C. 256, *per* Lord Pearce at 302 and Lord Morris at 283. However, Lord Wilberforce said that the jury "must make the decision whether, in addition to physical control [the defendant] has, or ought to have imputed to him, the intention to possess, or knowledge that he does possess, what is in fact a prohibited substance." This description of "possession" was adopted by Lord Scarman in *Boyesen* [1982] A.C. 768 and by the Court of Appeal in *Lewis* (1988) 87 Cr.App.R. 270.

There is, of course, a world of difference between a mere intention to pos-   3–46
sess and proof that the defendant had actual knowledge of the offending substance under his control before the court can convict. If all that is required to be proved is an intention to possess then the result in *Murray* v. *MacPhail* (*supra*) was a foregone conclusion. The appellant's consent to the hiding of drugs in his room amounted (at the very least) to an intention to possess.

As Professor Smith has pointed out ([1988] Crim.L.R. 518) the starting point for Lord Morris, in *Warner*, is that the defendant is *knowingly* in control of the offending article (at 403–404):

> "In my view in order to establish possession the prosecution must prove that an accused was knowingly in control of something in circumstances which showed that he was assenting to being in control of it; they need not prove that in fact he had actual knowledge of the nature of that which he had."

The same point may be made in relation to the speech of Lord Pearce (at 427):

> "I think the term 'possession' is satisfied by a knowledge only of the existence of the thing itself and not its qualities and that ignorance of mistake as to its qualities will not excuse. This would comply with the general understanding of the word 'possess.' "

With respect, Lord Wilberforce's description of possession (although it   3–47
seems currently to represent the law) goes much further than the description of possession expressed by Lord Morris and Lord Pearce. The speeches on this aspect are difficult if not impossible to reconcile. On what basis should a defendant have imputed to him an intention which he does not in fact have? Is "imputed intention" not a contradiction in terms? Is there room for a concept of "reckless possession?" In *Lewis*, L was the sole tenant of a house which was searched by police in L's absence. The police found 42.5 grammes of amphetamine sulphate and one milligramme of cannabis resin. L claimed that he never intended to live there and that he only went to the premises occasionally. He never looked in the cupboards and he never suspected the presence of drugs. The Court of Appeal held that it was not necessary to direct the jury that they had to be satisfied that the defendant had actual knowledge that the drugs were under his control before they could convict. The question is whether the defendant is proved to have, or ought to have imputed to him, *either* the intention to possess *or* the knowledge that he possessed what was in fact a prohibited substance. It is not necessary for the jury to be directed that they had to be satisfied that the defendant had actual knowledge that he had the drugs in question under his control before they could convict. See also B. Boulter, "Possession of Drugs," L.S.Gaz., November 23, 1988, and *McKenzie* v. *Sheen*, 1983 S.L.T. 121, and *Bland* [1988] Crim.L.R. 41, §3–53, *infra*.

3-48 **Further examples of control.** In *Feeney* v. *Jessop* 1990 S.C.C.R. 565, F was convicted of possessing a small quantity of cannabis resin lying on his towel which was on a central heating pipe alongside the bed he was lying on. When charged, F said, "So it's my towel. I'm saying fuck all." The court held that the absence of any explanation from F was not evidence of knowledge, but that the place where the drugs were found coupled with the power F had to remove the drugs from the towel, and the relationship of the drug and towel to the place where the appellant was lying before the search began, was ample evidence of knowledge and control and therefore possession: see *Crowe* v. *MacPhail*, 1987 S.L.T. 316, *Mackay* v. *Hogg* 1973 S.C.C.R. Supp. 41.

Again, in *Davidson* v. *H.M. Advocate*, 1990 S.C.C.R. 699, police found cannabis under the bed of the co-defendant. Beside the bed police found a set of electric scales which D had bought. D did not live in the co-defendant's house but he was in the bedroom when the police arrived and he had visited the premises in order to get cannabis. When the police entered the bedroom D climbed out of the window. The court held that the facts amounted to sufficient evidence of possession to go before the jury. The evidence was the slightest but the High Court seem to have regarded the appellant's flight from the premises as being evidence from which the jury could infer control of the drug under the bed.

3-49 In *Hughes* v. *Guild*, 1990 S.L.T. 715, the two appellants were charged with the unlawful possession of cannabis resin contrary to section 5(2) of the M.D.A. 1971. The appellants lived together and were the only persons to occupy a house searched by police in which two small pieces of cannabis resin were found on the mantelpiece in the living room, and traces of cannabis were found on a knife lying in front of the fireplace. Two torn packets of cigarette papers were found in the living room. The High Court held that there was sufficient evidence of possession and control because (i) all the relevant articles were lying in the open in their own living room; (ii) the appellants were the only persons occupying the house; and (iii) if they knew that the drugs were in their own room they could have picked them up and done with them what they wished. The High Court correctly observed that each case must be decided on its own facts but that cases of joint occupancy are no different from any other case in which the elements of knowledge and control must be established by inference. In some cases it may be possible to distinguish the position of one occupier from another if drugs are concealed or if one occupier is absent at the crucial time, or where the fact that others have access to the premises makes it unreasonable to attribute knowledge or control to the occupiers: see *Lustmann* v. *Stewart*, 1971 S.L.T. 58 and see *Mingay* v. *Mackinnon*, 1980 J.C. 33.

(iv) *Knowledge of the substance but no control*

3-50 Mere knowledge of the presence of the offending substance is not enough because the person must be in a position to exercise practical control over it in some way: see *Black* v. *H.M. Advocate*, 1974 S.L.T. 247 and *Hughes* v. *Guild*, 1990 S.C.C.R. 527.

3-51 **Joint possession.** So far we have been looking at examples where only one person is said to be in physical custody or control of the drug. Not infrequently the suggestion is that a number of people are in joint possession. A typical case is where police raid a dwelling-house occupied by a number of residents and a quantity of a drug is found. The police may not be in a position to say to whom the drug belongs but they do find signs of communal living coupled with evidence of communal drug abuse. It may well be that all the residents know of the existence of the drug on the premises but only two or three of them are active users.

> In *Searle* [1971] Crim.L.R. 592, C.A., drugs were found in a vehicle which was used by the defendants on a touring holiday. The prosecution could not say which defendant intended to benefit from each type of drug found. The case was put on the basis of joint enterprise. The judge told the jury " ... if they all knew that those drugs were then in the possession of other people and they knew they were drugs then you probably will not have any difficulty in deciding that they are guilty ... ." It was held that the judge misdirected the jury by equating knowledge with possession. A direction that ought to have been given was to ask the jury to consider whether the drugs formed part of a common pool from which each defendant was entitled to draw.

It was unnecessary for the prosecution to assert joint enterprise. The crucial feature in this case was that each defendant intended to draw from the common pool, each defendant exercised control over the pool and accordingly, each defendant was in possession of the drugs in question. To equate mere knowledge of the existence of the pool of drugs, however, was a clear misdirection since such knowledge could not by itself amount to proof of control.

A similar problem occurred in *Tansley* v. *Painter* [1969] Crim.L.R. 139,   **3–52** D.C., where two persons were seen sitting in a car but of whom only X sold drugs from the vehicle. The Divisional Court allowed D's appeal on the basis that mere knowledge that X was selling drugs was not evidence that he was in joint possession since, again, mere knowledge of the existence of the drugs could not be equated with custody or control.

Again, in *Irala-Prevost* [1965] Crim.L.R. 606, D was a passenger in a motor vehicle driven by D2 on a journey from North Africa to England. A large quantity of a drug was concealed in the vehicle. The judge directed the jury that if both defendants knew of the existence of the drug, and both intended that it should be taken along in the car, then both were guilty of possessing the drug. The Court of Appeal held that the judge had not said enough to make the jury realise the *degree* of control required. Properly directed, a jury would have had abundant evidence upon which to convict each defendant of possession. The point here is that the mere presence of the passenger in the car is insufficient evidence of control even if he knows of the existence of goods in the vehicle: see *Bland* [1988] Crim.L.R. 41 (*infra*). In *Strong, The Times*, January 26, 1989, it was held that the evidence established only the presence of the passenger in the vehicle and failed to establish knowledge of the existence of the drug let alone control over it: see also *Suurmeijer* [1991] Crim.L.R. 773.

It should be noted that on the question of knowledge the prosecution is   **3–53** required to prove a narrower intent in the case of an aider or an abettor, namely that the accused knew that the principal was in possession of a controlled drug. It is not necessary that the prosecution prove the type of drug in question: see *Patel* [1970] Crim.L.R. 274 and *Fernandez* [1970] Crim.L.R. 277, C.A.

However, there must be evidence of assistance, active or passive. Passive assistance involves more than mere knowledge that the confederate possesses or supplies controlled drugs: it requires evidence of encouragement or some element of control. In *Bland* [1988] Crim.L.R. 41, C.A., the appellant had been living with her co-accused, R, in one room of a house which was occupied by others. The police had been observing the house and had seen a number of people calling. Some of the visitors were stopped and questioned and found to be in possession of drugs. A search warrant was executed and traces of drugs were found. The defendant denied knowledge of the presence of the drugs and said that she could not believe that R had either possessed or supplied drugs. She was charged with possession with intent to supply. The case against her rested solely on the fact that she was living with R at a time when he was undoubtedly dealing with drugs. Her conviction was quashed, the Court of Appeal ruling that the case should have been withdrawn from the jury at the close of the prosecution case. The fact that the appellant and R lived together in the same room was not sufficient evidence from which the jury could infer that she exercised custody or control. There was sufficient evidence to infer knowledge that R was dealing in drugs but no more: see also *Searle* [1971] Crim.L.R. 592, C.A. (§3–51, *supra*). On the facts in *Bland* there was no evidence from which a jury could impute even an intention to possession: see *Lewis* (1988) 87 Cr.App.R. 270, *Hughes* v. *Guild*, 1990 S.L.T. 715 (§3–49, *supra*) and *Allan* v. *Milne*, 1974 SLT (Notes) 76.

(v) *Knowledge is proved but there is a mistake as to quality*

3–54   It will be remembered that in *Warner* it was held that ignorance or mistake as to the quality of a substance will not prevent the accused being in possession of it if that substance turns out to be a controlled drug. In *Lockyer* v. *Gibb* [1967] 2 Q.B. 243, L was found in possession of a bottle of morphine sulphate. There was doubt as to whether she knew of the nature of the substance. Nevertheless, even if she did not, she merely made a mistake as to quality which afforded her no defence. For the same reason, it would have made no difference in *Marriott* [1971] 1 W.L.R. 187 if M believed that the substance on the blade of the knife was toffee. Both cases were, of course, decided before the passing of the M.D.A. Both cases remain relevant to demonstrate when a person will be held to be in possession of the offending article, but the significant difference now is that the accused's possession will not be unlawful if he can bring himself within section 28, section 5(4), or one of the categories exempt from section 5.

(vi) *The "container" cases*

3–55   Is a person who knowingly exercises custody or control of a parcel, box or other container thereby deemed to be in possession of its contents, if he (*a*) has no idea what they are; (*b*) cannot see inside the container; (*c*) has no opportunity to examine it, or (*d*) has no authority to do so? These were the issues that confronted the House of Lords in *Warner* [1969] 2 A.C. 256:

> W sold scent as a side line. The proprietor of a café told W that there were two boxes for him under the counter. One box contained scent but the other contained 20,000 tablets of amphetamine sulphate. W contended that he believed both boxes contained scent. He was convicted.
>
> *Held*: W had a defence since he claimed that he believed the contents to be of a wholly different character, but the evidence against him was so strong that the appeal would be dismissed.

Before going any further, it is as well to consider some of the situations that might reasonably arise in respect of "container cases." First, a person in possession of a container may believe that it is empty: in fact it contains drugs. Secondly, he may believe that it contains goods of a wholly different description, *e.g.* jewellery. Thirdly, he may believe that it contains one type of drug whereas, in fact, it contains another drug. Finally, he may believe that the container holds one commodity whereas he has been the victim of a trick, and drugs have been intermixed with innocent goods.

It has been asserted that section 28 (which permits a lack of knowledge to be a defence in certain cases) now governs each situation. This is not entirely correct. The first step is for the prosecution to prove that the accused was in possession of the drugs for the purposes of section 5. Only when it has done so does section 28 come into operation. Accordingly, the decision in *Warner* (and other container cases) is relevant in determining whether an accused ever came into possession of the container and its contents in the first place. Although in every case of possession there must be an *animus possidendi*, the question is whether that includes an intention to possess simply the container or the drugs as well. Only if the accused is in possession of the container and its contents is it possible to consider whether a mistake of fact is a defence and, again, section 28 comes into play.

The present position may be summarised as follows. In the ordinary way a **3–56** person who is in possession of a container will be presumed to possess the contents as well. However, that presumption may be displaced if he shows *either* that he had no right to open the container and had no reason to suspect that its contents were drugs or were in any way illicit, *or* alternatively, that he could have opened the container if he so wanted, but he received it innocently, and did not have a reasonable opportunity to acquaint himself with the actual contents or to discover their illicit nature. At this stage, the only issue is whether the fact of possession is established against an accused. If it is, then one considers whether that possession is lawful or unlawful.

When the above is compared with section 28 then an overlap does appear, but even so, section 28 does not replace the ingredients required to be proved for an offence under section 5.

It will be recalled that in *Warner* their Lordships were concerned with section 1(1) of the Drugs (Prevention of Misuse) Act 1964 which provided that "it shall not be lawful for a person to have in his possession [a prohibited substance]." Section 5(2) of the M.D.A. is worded in similar terms except that it is subject to section 28. The opinions expressed in *Warner* are therefore still relevant and it is on those opinions that the above summary is based: see also

McNamara (1988) 87 Cr.App.R. 246, *infra*, and *Lewis* (1988) 87 Cr.App. R. 270. However, the opinions in *Warner* vary enormously. They are also difficult to reconcile in places and rely on decisions which themselves conflict.

3–57   Lord Reid found great difficulty in accepting that Parliament intended to create an absolute offence. However, knowing where to draw the line between *mens rea* and absolute liability proved to be an equally difficult task:

> "... suppose that an innkeeper is handed ... a box or package by a guest for safe-keeping ... I cannot agree with the contention that if the possessor of a box genuinely believes that there is nothing in the box then he is not in possession of the contents but ... if he knows there is something in it he is in possession of the contents though they may turn out to be something quite unexpected."

In order to drive the point home Lord Reid added:

> "It would, I think, be absurd to say that the innkeeper is not guilty if he genuinely believes that the box is empty but that he is guilty of an offence ... if he truly believes that it contains jewellery, though it also contains some drugs secreted in it. If he is not guilty in the case where the box contains jewellery as well as drugs, on what rational ground can he become guilty if there is not jewellery in the box but only drugs."

By contrast Lord Guest felt that the words (in section 1 of the 1964 Act) created an absolute offence, while Lord Morris of Borth-y-Guest walked a middle course, holding that possession was established if (*a*) the accused knew he controlled a container; (*b*) he had the opportunity to know or to discover the contents; and (*c*) that the contents were in fact controlled drugs.

3–58   However, Lord Pearce (with whom Lord Wilberforce and, reluctantly, Lord Reid concurred) indicated that an appropriate direction to juries would be as follows:

> "The Act forbids possession of these drugs ... If a man has physical control or possession of a thing that is sufficient possession under the Act provided that he knows that he has the thing; but a man does not (within the meaning of the Act of 1964) possess things of whose existence he is unaware."

Accordingly, an accused is not in possession of the contents if he believes the container to be empty. Lord Pearce continued:

> "The prosecution has here proved that he possessed the parcel, but has it proved that he possessed its contents also? There is a very strong inference of fact in any normal case that a man who possesses a parcel also possesses its contents, an inference on which a jury would in a normal case be justified in finding possession."

Thus far the law establishes a presumption of possession of the contents, but it is capable of being rebutted by the accused in the following way:

> "... by evidence that, although a man was in possession of a parcel, he was completely mistaken as to its contents and would not have accepted

possession had he known what kind of thing the contents were. A mistake as to the qualities of the contents, however, does not negative possession … If the accused knew that the contents were drugs or were tablets, he was in possession of them, though he was mistaken as to their qualities."

In other words an accused must show that he believed the goods to be of a **3–59** totally different character. It is always a question of degree whether goods are of a similar character or not. In an earlier passage, Lord Pearce thought that sweets would be sufficiently similar, although it is difficult to see why. However, the matter is entirely one for the tribunal of fact to determine.

In *Lockyer* v. *Gibb* Lord Parker C.J. considered that:

"… while it is necessary to show that the appellant knew she had the articles which turned out to be a drug, it is not necessary that she should know that in fact it was a drug and a drug of a particular character."

This was not an approach that found favour with Lord Reid who thought that the distinction would not bear critical examination. Nevertheless, he recognised that the appeal in *Warner* would produce that result. It will be recalled that in *Lockyer* v. *Gibb*, L was found in possession of a bottle of morphine sulphate but she did not realise that the bottle contained that substance. She made a mere mistake as to its quality but it afforded her no defence. Today, she would still be held to be in possession of the contents, but her possession will not be unlawful if she can prove a defence under, say, section 28 of the M.D.A.

Opportunity to examine the contents. On this aspect the House of Lords in **3–60** *Warner* made three observations. First, where a person is entitled to open a container, but did not do so *at the first opportunity* to ascertain the nature of the contents, then the "proper inference is that he was accepting possession of them" (*per* Lord Pearce). Secondly, however, the converse is true if he had no authority to open the container. Finally, if any person had cause to suspect that there was something wrong with the contents, it was his business to verify them and if he failed to do so, an adverse inference may be drawn that he was accepting possession of them.

Thus, it should not be inferred, in the case of a secretary who receives a bulky letter (containing cocaine) which is addressed to her employer and marked "strictly private and confidential," that she was accepting possession of the contents, *providing* she did not suspect that there was anything wrong with the letter. If she did, then it would be her responsibility to open it to verify the contents. Consider, on the other hand, the position of a left-luggage attendant, who accepts baggage on the strict understanding that he has a general right to examine it at his discretion. In such a situation, if he is so busy that he chooses not to examine baggage, is it to be inferred that he is accepting possession of the contents of an item of baggage, even if he is unaware that it holds cannabis? Such a conclusion would be unfair on the custodian. But, once he is given that right, such an inference is difficult to resist. In *Warner*, Lord Pearce said:

"… a man takes over a package or suitcase at risk as to its contents being unlawful, if he does not immediately examine it (if he is entitled to do so). As soon as may be he should examine it and, if he finds the contents suspicious, reject possession by either throwing them away or by taking immediate sensible steps for their disposal."

Nevertheless, it is still open to him to rely on any defences available to him under section 28.

3–61　　　It is implicit in the decision in *Warner* that a person who fails to take the opportunity to ascertain the contents of a container, only accepts possession of those items that would be discovered by a reasonable examination of the container. Accordingly, if the drug was concealed, say in a false compartment of a suitcase, the attendant who failed to examine the case would not be accepting possession of the drug because (*a*) a reasonable examination would not have disclosed its existence in any event, and (*b*) even if he had done so there would be evidence that he knew of the existence of the case and of the visible contents but no evidence at all that he was aware of anything else (see *Irving* [1970] Crim.L.R. 642, C.A.).

The length of time a container remains in the hands of the recipient is also material. If the period of retention is so short that it prevented a reasonable examination of the contents then it could not be inferred that possession of the contents was accepted. In *Wright* (1975) 62 Cr.App.R. 169, C.A., W was a passenger in a motor vehicle. A fellow passenger gave W a tin which he almost immediately threw out of the window, before he had any idea what it contained. It actually contained cannabis. He therefore had an insufficient opportunity to examine the contents and accordingly he was not in possession of the drug.

3–62　　　More recently, in *McNamara*, the Court of Appeal has again wrestled with the concept of possession in so far as that concept has been affected by the interplay between section 28 of the M.D.A. and the seemingly conflicting opinions of their Lordships in *Warner*.

> M rode his motor cycle to an address occupied by a co-defendant. Police found a box containing cannabis resin on the back of the motor cycle. M denied that he knew the box contained drugs and insisted that he thought the box contained pornography or pirate videos. The trial judge directed the jury that if M was in possession of the box, and that he knew the box contained "something," then M had the burden of proving—on a balance of probabilities—that he did not know, or suspect, or had reason to suspect that the box contained a controlled drug.
>
> *Held*: the direction was correct.

3–63　　　Having regard to the aforementioned principles of law, it may be thought that the result in *McNamara* was inevitable. Nevertheless, the court took the opportunity to look again at the decision in *Warner* (in the light of section 28) and extracted the following propositions:

(1) A man did not have possession of something which had been put into his pocket or house without his knowledge.
(2) A mere mistake as to the quality of a thing under the defendant's control was not enough to prevent his being in possession, *e.g.* being

in possession of heroin, believing it to be cannabis or aspirin.

(3) If the defendant believed that the thing was of a wholly different nature from that which in fact it was, then to use the words of Lord Pearce, at 305 in *Warner*, "the result would be otherwise."

(4) In the case of a container or box the defendant's possession of it led to the strong inference that he was in possession of the contents. But, if the contents were quite different in kind from what he believed, he was not in possession of them.

(5) The draftsmen of the 1971 Act intended that the prosecution should have the initial burden of proving that the defendant had and knew that he had the box in his control and also that the box contained something.

(6) Thereafter, section 28(3) places the burden on the accused to prove that he neither believed, nor suspected, nor had reason to suspect that the thing in question was a controlled drug.

Mixed drugs and goods. A different problem arose in *Irving* [1970] Crim.L.R. 642, where I possessed a bottle containing stomach pills. Unbeknown to him one heroin tablet also found its way into the bottle. He contended that his wife must have put it there. His conviction was quashed. At first sight the decision seems to be at variance with the principle that a mistake as to quality does not negative possession (subject to section 28(3)), and seems not to accord with other "container cases," but the reasoning is sound. Irving admitted knowing of the existence of the bottle *and* the stomach pills. It was those pills over which he intended to exercise control. But he was not aware of the existence of a prohibited substance. The position is therefore identical to that of a lady carrying a wicker basket full of groceries, unaware of the fact that a slab of cannabis has been slipped into it. Only if the prosecution could prove that Irving knew of the existence of a thing *in addition* to the stomach pills would a mistake as to its quality not suffice: see *Searle* v. *Randolph* [1972] Crim.L.R. 779. The tenor of the opinions in *Warner* support the correctness of *Irving* although their Lordships were not then dealing specifically with a case involving a mixture of substances in one container of which only some were controlled drugs. Most interestingly, Lord Reid said: **3–64**

> "I do not know what the result would be ... if, in the present case, both the scent and the drugs had been in the same parcel. The appellant, if his story were accepted, would have rightly believed that the parcel contained scent, but would have been ignorant of the fact that drugs had been slipped in with the scent. Could it be right that if the appellant had taken possession of the parcel of scent and thereafter the drugs had been slipped in without his knowledge he would be innocent (which is Lord Parker's view), but that if the drugs had been slipped in without his knowledge before he took possession then he would be guilty? That seems to me to be quite unreasonable. ...."

It may be that in *Irving*, I's wife put the drug into the bottle *before* I took hold of it but, if she did then, as Lord Reid pointed out, it would be unreasonable to distinguish between drugs slipped into a container *prior* to possession, and afterwards, if the defendant's state of mind is identical in both instances.

Finally, it may be asked what constitutes a container? In *Searle* v. *Randolph* it was no defence for the accused to deny possession of cannabis in respect of cigarettes which he had picked up, merely because he did not know that they contained the drug. The cigarette paper certainly sealed in the tobacco and cannabis. To that extent the paper "tube" was a container. Nevertheless, the tobacco and cannabis were blended to form one substance. He knew of the existence of that substance (or thing) and therefore made a mere mistake as to quality.

(vii) *Quantity too minute to possess*

3–65   In *Worsell* [1970] 1 W.L.R. 111, referred to earlier, the Court of Appeal held that where the presence of a controlled drug is so minute that it cannot be seen with the naked eye, measured or poured, and amounted in reality to nothing, it could not be said that the accused was in possession of the drug. The evidence established no more than proof of an earlier possession.

The principle is, of course, a fiction because section 5(1) prohibits the possession of "*any*" controlled drug including, on a literal interpretation, a trace however slight. Undoubtedly, the principle is sensible, but the very words of section 5(1) indicate just how limited in scope the application of the principle must be. Over the years the courts have shifted their ground until eventually, in *Carver* [1978] Q.B. 472, they departed from the original point enunciated in *Worsell*. This shift can be clearly demonstrated by a brief chronological examination of the authorities. In *Hambleton* v. *Callinan* [1968] 2 Q.B. 427, C provided a urine sample in which was found a trace of "amphetamine powder." The justices held that C was not in possession because the powder, having been consumed, was now completely changed in its character. Lord Parker C.J. concluded that the justices were right and said:

> "It was contended by the prosecution . . . that a man can be in possession of a prohibited substance . . . if he has traces of it in his urine, in his intestines, or any other part of his body in which it can be found . . . once you had consumed something and its *whole character had altered* and no further use could be made of it . . . a man could not be said to be in possession of the prohibited substance."

3–66   It is significant that the emphasis was placed on the *changed character* of the substance. Clearly, in that event, it is impossible to hold that a person is in possession of the original controlled substance. The trace in the urine could only prove an earlier possession and the consumer should be charged accordingly. Lord Parker C.J. acknowledged that a person who swallows a diamond or a gold ring would still be in possession of it. That much is obvious because neither object would change character. Likewise, in *Worsell* (*supra*) the court was concerned with a minute quantity of a drug which, again, had not changed character. Even so, in *Worsell*, it was decided that the courts would equate minute quantities with "nothing." It was at this juncture that the fiction was created. How then was it to be determined whether a drug amounted to "something" or effectively "nothing"? One method is to adopt a principle akin to *de minimis non curat lex*, but to do so would be to add words to section 5 which prohibit possession of "any" amount of a controlled drug. Another approach is to discover whether the trace is capable of being weighed, measured, poured or seen with the naked eye. Such tests could not be performed in *Worsell*. However, in *Graham* [1970] 1 W.L.R. 113, G had scrapings of cannabis taken out of his pocket; they were very small but were capable of being weighed and measured. Accordingly, it could not be said that the amounts were so small that they amounted to nothing because they had at least been measured.

In *Frederick* [1969] 3 All E.R. 804, police searched F's flat. Traces of can-   3–67
nabis were found on two pipes and a tobacco pouch. But 307 grains of cannabis resin were found in a bag inside a television set. F denied knowledge of the cannabis. The judge directed the jury that if the jury were sure that F possessed the traces but not the 307 grains, then they should convict, and vice versa. The Court of Appeal held that there were logical difficulties in concluding that F was in possession of the traces alone, but the scientific evidence was not tested as to whether the traces were so small as to amount to nothing. Furthermore, the jury could infer from the existence of the traces that F was in possession of the 307 grains.

In *Bocking* v. *Roberts* [1974] Q.B. 307, Lord Widgery C.J. held that the *de minimis* rule did not apply to offences under section 5(1) but that slight traces merely indicated presence on an earlier occasion. Even 20 microgrammes of cannabis resin, found in a pipe, had been measured and therefore amounted to something. Interestingly, the point does not appear to have been taken that the quantity was so small that there was no evidence that the accused knew of its existence, *i.e.* no *animus possidendi*.

A different conclusion was reached by Stinson J. in *Colyer* [1974]   3–68
Crim.L.R. 243, who declined to follow *Bocking* v. *Roberts*, being, as it was, a decision of the Divisional Court. C was in possession of a pipe which had traces of cannabis weighing 20 microgrammes (one millionth of an ounce). Stinson J. held that to say this amount was "measurable," after a complicated process of extraction, was stretching the meaning of section 5(1). Alternatively, he held that there was no proof of knowledge. Likewise, in *Hierowski* [1978] Crim.L.R. 563, Edmonson J. upheld a submission of no case to answer when not less than 20 microgrammes of resin was found by chemical analysis. The judge regarded the amount as being effectively nothing.

By 1977 the principle in *Worsell* had been thoroughly glossed. However, in *Bayliss and Oliver* [1978] Crim.L.R. 361, D.C. the courts went even further. The defendants were tried for possession of 0.011 grammes and 0.083 grammes of cannabis. The Crown had adduced no evidence that the drug was "usable." It was held that there was no evidence that the defendants were in possession of a usable quantity. The learned judge cited Salmon L.J. in *Worsell*, concluding that the appropriate test was one of "usability."

The judgment has two curious features. First, the principle in *Worsell* was not one of usability but whether the drug was capable of amounting to "something." In *Worsell* the drug could not be weighed or measured. That certainly had been done in *Bayliss*. Secondly, the learned judge included an additional ingredient which the prosecution had to prove, namely that the drug was usable. Such an ingredient is not even implicit in the wording of section 5(1). It is true that one finds reference to the "use of the drug" in *Worsell* as one did in *Hambleton* v. *Callinan*, yet in neither case did the court intend to establish a usability test.

3–69   However, in *Carver* [1978] Q.B. 472, the Court of Appeal did exactly that. The reasoning in *Bocking* v. *Roberts* was accepted but Michael Davies J. at 477 added:

> "... if the quantity of the drug found is so minute as ... to amount to nothing *or ... if the evidence be that it is not usable in any manner which the Misuse of Drugs Act 1971 was intended to prohibit*, then a conviction for being in possession ... would not be justified." (Emphasis added.)

On this basis the "usability test" was no longer a mere guide to determine whether a drug amounted to something because, even if it did, it must be capable of being used "in any manner which the Misuse of Drugs Act 1971 was intended to prohibit." But what exactly did the M.D.A. intend to prohibit and, secondly, did the "use" of a drug imply obtaining the desired effect from it? These issues resulted in the appeal to the House of Lords in *Boyesen* [1982] A.C. 768.

> In *Boyesen*, B carried a metal tin which contained a polythene bag. Traces of cannabis resin were found in the bag. The traces were visible to the naked eye and weighed five milligrammes. An expert said that it could be picked up and put into a pipe or cigarette.

3–70   Lord Scarman, with whom all their Lordships agreed, held that section 5(1) did not depend upon the test of "usability" but simply whether the drug amounted to something. *Carver* was overruled. *Bocking* v. *Roberts* was approved. Lord Scarman found himself entirely persuaded by the reasoning of the Lord Justice-Clerk (Wheatley) in *Keane* v. *Gallacher* (1980) J.C. 77, 81–82:

> "The decision in *R.* v. *Carver* seems to entail the importation into section 5(1) of a qualification to the term 'controlled drug,' namely 'which is capable of being used.' If that be the case, it would add an additional onus on the prosecution to prove that fact. If Parliament had intended that such a qualification should be added it would have been simple to give express effect to it ... It is the possession of the controlled drug which is made punishable by section 5(1) and (2), not its use or potential use."

However, if the quantity of the drug involved is minute, *e.g.* it is invisible to the naked eye, it would be far-fetched to allege that the person in possession "knew" of the existence of the substance and was therefore in possession. To that extent the quantity of the drug involved is an important factor when considering the accused's knowledge.

3–71   **Using traces to prove past possession.** Even if the prosecution fails to prove possession of the trace, for the purposes of section 5, it is always open to the prosecution to rely on the existence of the trace to show that the accused was in possession of a much larger quantity of the drug on an earlier occasion; see *Worsell* and *Graham* (*supra*). This is so even if the prosecution cannot show how much of the drug was involved or when it was acquired. However, prosecutors must display wisdom and not act oppressively. The point is graphically demonstrated in *Pragliola* [1977] Crim.L.R. 612:

> A pipe belonging to P was taken by police in 1975 and found to contain traces of cannabis. He was not charged in relation to the traces and the pipe was returned to him. Much later P was charged with being in possession of the traces.
>
> *Held*: the charge was oppressive and could not be justified in the circumstances.

Each case must, of course, be decided on its own facts.

IV. STATUTORY DEFENCES UNDER SECTION 5(4)

In addition to any other defence open to an accused, the M.D.A. provides   **3–72**
two statutory defences to a charge of unlawful possession, notwithstanding that he knew or suspected the substance to be a controlled drug. In each case the burden of proving the defence is on the accused. Section 5(4) provides:

"In any proceedings for an offence under [section 5(2)] above in which it is proved that the accused had a controlled drug in his possession, it shall be a defence for him to prove—
  (*a*) that, knowing or suspecting it to be a controlled drug, he took possession of it for the purpose of preventing another from committing or continuing to commit an offence in connection with that drug and that as soon as possible after taking possession of it he took all such steps as were reasonably open to him to destroy the drug or to deliver it into the custody of a person lawfully entitled to take custody of it; or
  (*b*) that, knowing or suspecting it to be a controlled drug, he took possession of it for the purpose of delivering it into the custody of a person lawfully entitled to take custody of it and that as soon as possible after taking possession of it he took all such steps as were reasonably open to him to deliver it into the custody of such a person."

(a) Section 5(4)(*a*)

It follows that an accused must prove: **3–73**
  (i)   that he took possession of the drug; and
  (ii) that he did so for the purpose of preventing another committing or continuing to commit an offence in connection with that drug; and
  (iii) that, as soon as possible, he took all reasonable steps to:
    (*a*) destroy the drug; or
    (*b*) deliver it into the custody of a person lawfully entitled to take custody of it.

The clearest example is that of a parent finding his son or daughter unlawfully possessing a controlled drug. The parent is entitled to take the drug and to destroy it or to hand it over to a person entitled to receive it, *e.g.* a police officer (by virtue of regulations 6(6) and (7) of the M.D.Regs. 1985).

The words "preventing another from committing ... an offence ..." would include the parent who finds, in her child's absence, a cannabis plant growing in the bedroom and destroys the plant. However, no protection is afforded by section 5(4)(*a*) if no offence is being committed in relation to the drug in question. So, a parent who destroys heroin found in the son's bedroom, unaware of the fact that he is a registered heroin addict, and therefore entitled to possess it, will not be protected under subsection (4)(*a*). But protection would have been afforded under subsection (4)(*b*) had the drug not been destroyed but given to the police instead.

It is therefore unfortunate that section 5(4)(*a*) does not protect a person who has reasonable cause to suspect that an offence is or may be being committed in relation to that drug.

(b) Section 5(4)(*b*)

3–74 The accused must prove:

(i) that he took possession of the drug; and

(ii) that he did so for the purpose of delivering it into the custody of a person lawfully entitled to take custody of it; and

(iii) that, as soon as possible thereafter, he took all reasonable steps to deliver it into the custody of that person.

It will be noted that subsection (4)(*b*) is not dependent on preventing the commission of a crime and secondly, it is confined to delivery of the drug to a lawful custodian and it does not protect a person who destroys the drug.

In *Dempsey* (1986) 82 Cr.App.R. 291, MD was a registered drug addict and lawfully entitled to possess ampoules of physeptone. His wife D, held some of the ampoules for safe-keeping while MD went into a lavatory to inject himself with the remainder. It was held that D did not come within section 5(4)(*b*) since she took possession of the drugs for the purpose of removing them from MD albeit temporarily, and not for the purpose of delivering them within the meaning of the sub-paragraph.

3–75 It is not clear whether a person "lawfully entitled to take custody" of a drug includes all persons who would be lawfully entitled to possess a controlled drug of a particular description or whether the category of persons is limited to those listed in regulations 6(6) and (7) of the M.D. Regs. 1985. Parliament's use of the phrase "to take custody" implies a very restricted class and therefore that latter construction was probably intended by Parliament.

Chapter 4
Possession With Intent To Supply

A. SECTION 5(3)

Section 5(3) of the M.D.A. provides that: **4–01**

"Subject to section 28 of this Act, it is an offence for a person to have a controlled drug in his possession, whether lawfully or not, with intent to supply it to another in contravention of section 4(1) of this Act."

Section 4(1) makes it unlawful to supply or to offer to supply a controlled drug to another.

It has been said that there is a logical difficulty inherent in the wording of section 5(3) in that an intention to supply a controlled drug cannot make the possession of it lawful. (See Richard Lord, *Controlled Drugs, Law & Practice* (Butterworths, 1984).) If that is true then the words "whether lawfully or not" are redundant. However, there is no general proposition of law that possession is, or becomes, unlawful merely because the purpose for which the drug is intended to be used is unlawful. So where any person, by virtue of a prescription, lawfully and honestly obtains controlled drugs which he subsequently intends to supply, then his simple possession of those drugs remains lawful, even though his subsequent intention now makes him guilty of an offence contrary to section 5(3). In other words, what is being punished in section 5(3) is the guilty intent and it therefore does not matter whether his possession of the drugs was either lawful or unlawful. It is true that *Dunbar* [1981] 1 W.L.R. 1536 and regulation 10(2) of the Misuse of Drugs Regulations 1985 are concerned with rendering unlawful the possession of drugs (which had originally been lawful) in cases of dishonest "double-scripting," or where drugs have been dishonestly obtained from a doctor on prescription. However, these are isolated examples expressly catered for by the Regulations.

B. PROVING THE OFFENCE

The prosecution must prove (subject to section 28) first, that the accused **4–02**
was in possession of drugs; secondly, that those drugs were controlled by the

M.D.A.; and thirdly; that the accused intended to supply the drugs to another. Unfortunately, the Act does not define the word "supply" other than to say that "supplying includes distributing": see section 37(1).

No difficulty arises in the classic and most obvious example of supplying, namely, where a person transfers both custody and total control of a controlled drug to another so that he may do with it as he pleases: see *Mills* [1963] 1 Q.B. 522. Obviously, a person cannot be supplied with what he already has. In *Harris* [1968] 1 W.L.R. 769, H injected F with F's own heroin. The Court of Appeal held that H was not supplying F since the heroin was already in F's possession and undoubtedly belonged to him. H did no more than to help F administer his own drug. Of course, H did exercise some control over the substance in the sense that she controlled the top of the syringe and thus forced the drug into F's body, but physical control of the drug had not been transferred to H.

Where more than one person has an "interest" in the drug, for example, where one person buys cannabis on behalf of a number of others, then each party exercises some degree of control over the substance once it is acquired by the agent. To that extent each contributor may be said to be in possession of it. But, if the agent then allows each contributor to draw his share of the drugs from the pool or, if he distributes the drug to the contributors concerned, then he is supplying them because "supplying" is expressed by section 37(1) of the M.D.A. to include "distributing."

I. "Distributing"

4–03   In common usage, "distributing" means to "deal out in portions or to share among others." In *Holmes* v. *Chief Constable of Merseyside* [1976] Crim.L.R. 125, the Divisional Court held that the word "supply" had to be given its ordinary everyday meaning, so that a person who bought drugs on behalf of himself and others is to be regarded as supplying those drugs if he thereafter "distributes" them or shares them out. In delivering the judgment of the court, the Lord Chief Justice said (as cited in the judgement of Lane L.J. (as he then was) in *Buckley and Lane* [1979] 69 Cr.App.R. 371, 374):

> "... the question of joint possession can become highly relevant on a charge of possessing, but I do not believe that the question of possession or no, is a satisfactory route to an answer in the type of case we are dealing with at the present time where the charge is of supplying or possession with intent to supply. Section 37 of the Misuse of Drugs Act 1971 in terms says 'supplying' includes distributing, and in my judgment when a court has to consider an allegation of supply under this Act it must give the word 'supply' its perfectly ordinary natural everyday meaning. I have no doubt at all that a man who goes to market shopping for drugs on behalf of himself and others will often properly be regarded as supplying those drugs when he brings them home and distributes them because distribution is by statute a form of supply and that in itself is enough to cover such a case."

In *Buckley and Lane* [1979] 69 Cr.App.R. 371 B and G agreed to buy cannabis resin in bulk by pooling their money and thereafter, to take their respective shares. B, having been put in funds, visited Lane who supplied B with one pound of cannabis. B gave G three-quarters of a pound of the resin, and retained the remainder for himself. At his trial, B pleaded guilty to a charge that he "lawfully supplied to [G] three-quarters of a pound of cannabis resin." Despite his plea of guilty, B appealed on the grounds that since he was G's intermediary, G acquired ownership and legal possession of his share of the drug at the moment B handed the money over to L. On this basis it was argued that B could not be said to be supplying G with what was already his. The Court of Appeal described the argument as "recondite," but found a simple answer to the problem in section 37(1) of the M.D.A. in that "supplying" is expressed to include "distributing." Lane L.J. remarked:

> "Whatever else Buckley may or may not have been doing when he divided up the cannabis and gave three-quarters of a pound to Gilchrist and kept the other quarter pound for himself, he was without any shadow of a doubt—it seems to us—distributing the cannabis whoever may have been the owner or the custodian or in possession of the drug."

As the court in *Buckley and Lane* pointed out, had the appellant's contention been correct, any drug-pusher could effectively circumvent the provisions of section 4 by merely collecting monies in advance from all interested purchasers and then buying the controlled drugs so ordered. Such a conclusion would have made a mockery of section 4.

By contrast, in *Searle* [1971] Crim.L.R. 592, C.A., the defendants had been on a touring holiday. A motor vehicle used by them for that purpose was searched, as a result of which, controlled drugs were found. The drugs could not be attributed to any particular defendant. Accordingly, the Court of Appeal held that if the drugs represented a common pool from which the defendants were entitled to draw at will and, if there was a joint enterprise to do so, then each defendant who is proved to be a party to that joint enterprise is to be regarded as being in possession of the drugs. Obviously, on the special facts in *Searle,* an intention to distribute drugs to the others could not be established against any of the defendants.

Consider the example of D providing a platter of "reefer" cigarettes for the enjoyment of guests at a party. On these facts D is clearly in possession of the cigarettes with intent to distribute them and thus to supply the drug which they contain.

A more complex problem, which has never been satisfactorily resolved by the courts, arises in connection with the smoking of a "reefer" cigarette which is then passed round a circle of smokers. In *King* [1978] Crim.L.R. 288, K made reefer cigarettes in the presence of friends. The drug was taken from K's own supply. He passed the reefer round. Each person took it in turns to draw a puff from the reefer and then passed the reefer on. His Honour Judge Finlay Q.C. held that K was not guilty of possessing the reefer with intent to supply it, contrary to section 5(3), because the degree of control exercised by each person within the smoking circle was insufficient.

4–04

4–05

4–06

The reasoning of the court was as follows:

> "... only taking a puff and passing it on does not constitute supplying the material in the cigarette as it exists. It is only a supply if at the beginning the defendant has the material in his possession and at the end it has come into the possession of another in the sense that the other can do with it as he wishes."

This passage is not easy to understand. One supposes that the contention was that only the smoke (a puff) was being supplied and not the drug itself. Smoke was not the material in the cigarette "as it existed." Since only smoke was acquired at the beginning of the defendant's period of possession he did not, and could not, transfer it to another which that other could do with as he wished. Meanwhile the maker of the reefer retained control of the drug.

4–07   The strained reasoning adopted in *King* depends on drawing a distinction between the substance and the vapour (if any) which is produced. There is no sound reason for making such a distinction. What was being transferred was the control of the reefer. By drawing smoke the user was effectively diminishing the drug-stock in the cigarette. Since the words "supplying" and "distributing" must be given their everyday meaning it follows that the drug was being distributed for use within the circle of smokers.

> In *Moore* [1979] Crim.L.R. 789 M persuaded two girls to "go for a smoke." He rolled a reefer which he intended to share with them. It was submitted to the trial judge that the offer was an offer to supply "smoke" rather than the material in the cigarette.
>
> *Held*: there was a supply. The court declined to follow *King*.

The court accepted that what was being offered was not only smoke but the custody and temporary control of the reefer from which the two girls could draw smoke. To that extent there had been an offer to distribute the drug by sharing custody of the reefer. The fact that custody was retained for a very short period of time was irrelevant. It is also irrelevant that only a fraction of the drug would have been consumed. It is submitted that *Moore* is to be preferred and this would seem to be the current thinking of the Court of Appeal: *Chief Constable of Cheshire* v. *Hunt* (April 25, 1983; unreported).

II. THE PROBLEM OF "BAILMENT"

4–08   So far we have seen examples in which the intention has been to supply the drug for the use or for the benefit of another person. But suppose A intends to give B drugs purely for safe-keeping. Does A intend to supply B contrary to section 5(3)? Furthermore, if B actually receives the drug from A, intending to restore it to A at a later date, does B commit an offence contrary to section 5(3)?

On one interpretation of the term "supplying" it may be thought that all that is required to be proved is a transfer of physical custody of the drug to another. On this basis it hardly matters whether A gives drugs to B for safe-keeping or not, either way physical custody has been transferred.

But in order to avert conclusions which would either be regarded as an affront to common sense, or which would seriously weaken an ambition of the Act, the courts have attempted to define the concept of supplying in the context of the policy of the Act. As a result, various ingredients are said to exist which the prosecution may be required to prove in certain drug-related cases, *e.g.* by requiring proof of an intention on the part of the transferor, to enable the transferee to use the drugs for his own purposes. Unfortunately, the efforts of the courts to produce a logical and consistently applied set of qualifications or refinements to the concept of supplying have largely failed, so that the law produces some strange results. For the moment the law states that a person who deposits drugs with a custodian for safe-keeping will not ordinarily be guilty of supplying, contrary to section 4 of the M.D.A., whereas the custodian will be guilty of supplying the depositor if he returns the drug to him! This is the effect of the decision of the House of Lords in *Maginnis* [1987] 1 All E.R. 907, approving *Delgado* [1984] 1 W.L.R. 89, and *Donnelly* v. *H.M. Advocate*, 1985 S.L.T. 243. The conclusion that the custodian is put in a worse position than the depositor is both startling and, it is submitted, grossly illogical.

III. THE DIFFICULTY OF DEFINING "SUPPLY"

It is not always easy to state or to define the ordinary natural meaning of a   **4–09** word. "Supply" and "supplying" are two prime examples. Both expressions are not always used precisely and, in any event, not everyone perceives an act of supply in the same terms. The Shorter Oxford English Dictionary devotes almost an entire column to the word "supply" defining it as ". . . fulfilling a want or demand . . . to furnish with . . . to satisfy the wants of . . . provide for . . . to use," and so on. Accordingly, different instances of supplying may, in fact, possess different characteristics but, the existence (or absence) of a possible characteristic does not necessarily determine whether there has been a supply or not.

As the authorities are examined, it will be seen that different courts seem to focus on different characteristics and treat them as if they were conclusive of an act of supplying. Thus in *Dempsey* [1986] Crim.L.R. 171, the court looked to see if the transfer was an act designed to benefit the transferee: but not every supply necessarily benefits the recipient. Again, in *Delgado*, (*supra*), the court focussed its attention on the passing of physical control of the article to another. But in *Dempsey* (§4–10—4–11, *infra*) there was a transfer of physical control of a drug and yet the conviction for supplying the drug was quashed.

(a) A delivers the drug to B

Assume that A's intention is that B should act as custodian of the drug so   **4–10** that, upon demand, the drug is returned to A.

> In *Dempsey* [1986] Crim.L.R. 171, D was a registered drug addict. He
> lawfully obtained 25 ampoules of physeptone. Maureen held some of the

ampoules while D went into the lavatory to inject himself with the remainder. D pleaded guilty to supplying Maureen.

Held: the conviction must be quashed. The mere deposit of an article for safe-keeping and return could not amount to an act of supply.

Lord Lane C.J., giving the judgment of the court, referred to the word "supply" as it appears in the Shorter Oxford English Dictionary and noted that it seems to be an act designed to benefit the recipient, but he added that:

> "It does not seem to us that it is apt to describe the deposit of an article with another person for safe keeping, as was the case here. The example was canvassed in argument of a person who hands his coat to a cloak-room attendant for safe keeping during the show in a theatre or cinema. It could scarcely be said that the person handing the coat supplies it to the cloakroom attendant. Nor do we think it makes any difference that the cloakroom attendant wishes in one sense to get his coat, thinking that he may get a tip at the end of the evening. That is not the sort of wish or need which is envisaged by the definition of the offence."

4–11   Clearly, if the transfer of the drug to Maureen was so that she could use the drug for her own purposes, then there would have been a supply of the drug to her.

The Court of Appeal added that the jury had to decide whether the drug was being supplied to Maureen for her own purposes, *e.g.* to hand on to someone else, or to use upon her own body, in which case there would have been a supply, or whether it was simply for safe-keeping and return to D "who was lawfully entitled to the drug." The words quoted are perhaps unnecessary and even a little misleading since they may be thought to imply that a depositor who is not lawfully entitled to possess the drug commits an offence of supplying if he deposits the drug with another for safe-keeping. But this logically cannot be so. Custody and physical control of the drug was given to Maureen but ultimate control was nevertheless retained by D. In ordinary language the drug "belonged" to D and it was not intended that Maureen could deal with it as she pleased. Whether D was lawfully entitled to the drug or not was irrelevant.

4–12   In *Maginnis* [1987] 1 All E.R. 907, H.L. (which is now the leading case on this aspect of the law) Lord Keith said (at 909 f/g): "The word 'supply,' in its ordinary natural meaning, conveys the idea of furnishing or providing to another something which is wanted or required in order to meet the wants or requirements of that other."

The word "supply" does convey such ideas but it can also convey other ideas not dependent on what is either wanted or required by the recipient. Lord Keith, who delivered the majority opinion in the House of Lords, went on to say (at 909g): "It ['supply'] connotes more than the mere transfer of physical control of some chattel or object from one person to another. No one would ordinarily say that to hand over something to a mere custodian was to supply him with it."

In so holding, their Lordships were clearly approving at least part of the reasoning in *Dempsey*. However, Lord Keith then dealt with the "accidental concept" said to be involved in a supply, namely (at 909 g/h): ". . . that of enabling the recipient to apply the thing handed over to purposes for which he desires or has a duty to apply it."

This is not an easy concept to understand. Lord Keith may have meant no **4–13** more than a supply connotes the transfer of substantial or complete control in relation to the article handed over. But, construed literally, Lord Keith seems to be saying that the additional concept is satisfied once the recipient is given the opportunity of applying the thing to his own purposes if he so wishes or, if he is under a duty to apply it. But "enablement" is itself a broad concept. It is difficult to think of any physical transfer of goods to another which does not tend to "enable" the recipient to deal with the goods as he wishes, whether he is entitled to do so or not, and irrespective of the transferor's intentions. On this basis the cloakroom attendant is enabled, or given the opportunity, to apply the patron's coat to the purposes for which he desires (lawfully or otherwise) but that fact does not convert the transfer of the coat to the cloakroom attendant, into an act of supply.

Where a custodian is under a "duty to apply" the article in question then he may be said to have been supplied with it. For example, where B is given a power drill by A for safe-keeping (while A is on holiday) with a direction that B completes work on A's house in the meantime, then it is difficult to resist the view that B has been supplied with the drill. But this is, of course, a very different case to the custodian who is merely asked to look after the article in question.

(b) B holds the drugs intending to return them to A

In *Maginnis* [1987] 1 All E.R. 907 a package of cannabis resin was found **4–14** by police in M's motor car. He claimed that the package had been left there by a friend who was to collect it from him. He pleaded guilty to an offence under section 5(3) after the trial judge had ruled that the intention to return the package constituted the requisite intent. The Court of Appeal allowed the appeal against that conviction. The Crown appealed to the House of Lords.

Held: the Crown's appeal would be allowed. M intended to return the drug to his friend for that person's benefit.

The majority of their Lordships (Lord Goff dissented) analysed supply in the context of "enabling" the recipient to apply the thing for the recipient's own benefit. Thus, Lord Keith said (at 910i): "If on a later occasion the defendant had handed the drugs back to his friend, he would have done so in order to enable the friend to apply the drugs for the friend's own purposes."

Lord Keith examined earlier authorities and distinguished them by ascertaining whether the drugs were transferred "so as to enable those persons to apply the drugs to their own purposes." Of course, a person may, as a fact, enable another to apply the thing in question to his own purposes without actually intending to do so, but it is not clear whether the majority of their Lordships were in fact holding that such an intent is required. The tenor of the opinions delivered suggests that proof of such an intent is required although the certified question was amended by their Lordships to read only as follows:

> "Whether a person in unlawful possession of a controlled drug which has been deposited with him for safe-keeping has the intent to supply that drug to another if his intention is to return the drug to the person who deposited it with him."

The majority of their Lordships answered the amended question in the affirmative. Unfortunately, the certified question was not amended to include an intention, on the part of the transferor, to enable the transferee to apply the drugs for his own purposes. The amendment was considered necessary because the original question was said not to be "in all respects apt to raise the true issue in the case."

4–15   The legal position of a custodian, who merely intends to return the drugs to the person who deposited them, has posed a difficult analytical problem for the courts to resolve. The reason is that a custodian of controlled drugs must realise that, in almost every case, the depositor ultimately intends to either unlawfully use the drugs himself or to unlawfully pass them onto others. It is therefore tempting, for the purposes of section 5(3), to include an element that the person in possession must know that he is enabling the recipient to use the drugs for the latter's benefit. But the issue is whether the inclusion of such an ingredient gives "supply" an artificial meaning. Take, for example, the cloakroom analogy. The patron who hands a coat to the attendant relinquishes, temporarily, the custody and physical control of the coat but, it is not the attendant's coat to do with as he wishes since ultimate control remains with the depositor. The latter may call for its return. Accordingly, when the attendant returns the coat, he does not as a matter of common sense, "supply" the depositor with it. He knows perfectly well that the coat will be used by the depositor for his own use and has enabled him to use it. But that fact does not, it is submitted, ordinarily convert a return of an article in those circumstances into an act of supply. There is a mere resumption of total possession.

However, a very different view was taken in *Delgado* [1984] 1 W.L.R. 89. In that case the Court of Appeal analysed "supply" in the context of whether or not there had been a transfer of physical control.

> Police arrested D who was carrying 6.31 kilograms of cannabis in a holdall. He said that he was taking them to the persons who had given him the drugs for safe-keeping.
>
> *Held*: D intended to transfer the drug to another at an agreed time and place and had committed an offence contrary to section 5(3).

4–16   The court held that section 5(3) covered a wide range of transactions and that a feature common to all of them is a transfer of physical control of a drug from one person to another. Skinner J. observed (at 179) that: "In our judgment questions of the transfer of ownership or legal possession of those drugs are irrelevant to the issue whether or not there was an intention to supply."

Obviously, every case of supplying involves a transfer of *physical control* but the converse is not always true. The fact that physical control has been transferred cannot, without more, establish an act of supplying. *Maginnis* is itself authority for that proposition. Yet on the face of it *Delgado* appears to be establishing precisely that. By contrast, in *Dempsey* D gave ampoules (which belonged to him) to Maureen to hold temporarily. D therefore transferred physical control of the ampoules to Maureen, but the Court of Appeal held that D had not supplied her with the drug: something more was required, namely that there had to be a benefit transferred to the recipient as well.

Not surprisingly the Court of Appeal, in *Maginnis* [1986] 2 All E.R. 110, believed that a conflict existed between *Delgado* and *Dempsey*. Thus, Mann J., giving judgment for the court, said of those two decisions (at 113–114):

> "We find it impossible to reconcile the meaning put on the word 'supply' in R. v. *Delgado* with the meaning put on that word in R. v. *Dempsey*. The decision in *Delgado* is that the word is satisfied if there is a transfer of physical control of the drug in question. However, in *Dempsey* there was a transfer of physical control, yet the conviction was quashed ... In our judgement the meaning put on the word 'supply' in *Dempsey* is to be preferred."

The Court of Appeal could not accept that the word "supply," as a matter of ordinary language, is apt to mean merely the transfer of physical control. Mann J. said (at 113–114):

> "We agree with the view of the court in *Dempsey*, that for there to be a supply there must be a transfer of physical control which is for the benefit of the recipient of the article. Counsel for the Crown accepted that this was the correct formulation but agreed that the transferee obtains a benefit when he receives back an article which he has placed in the custody of another."

The only discernible benefit that the Court of Appeal in *Maginnis* could **4–17** find was the resumption of actual possession which the court could not accept was sufficient to amount to an act of supply.

But when *Maginnis* went to the House of Lords ([1987] 1 All E.R. 907), their Lordships held that both *Dempsey* and *Delgado* are distinguishable on the facts.

Lord Keith explained the distinction in the following terms (at 912d):

> "In R. v. *Delgado* a custodian was found to have the necessary intent to supply because his intention was to hand back controlled drugs to the persons who had deposited them with him so as to enable those persons to apply the drugs to their own purposes, and thus put them back into circulation. In R. v. *Dempsey* there was a mere placing in temporary custody, and no intention of enabling the custodian to use the drugs for her own purposes."

The House of Lords held *Delgado* to have been rightly decided and applied it.

Their Lordships approved, for the most part, the decision of the High Court of Justiciary in Scotland, in *Donnelly* v. *H.M. Advocate*, 1985 S.L.T. 243. In that case, the appellant claimed that a quantity of controlled drugs found in her possession had been put there by another. The court (approving

Delgado) said (at 244) "if the appellant intended to part with all or some of the drugs in her possession to Colin Stewart, even for his own use, she intended to supply Colin Stewart, and it matters not whether his intention was to use them himself or to supply others."

4–18   In *Maginnis* their Lordships remarked that if this passage was intended to mean that a mere transfer of physical control of a drug from one person to another may constitute supply then this was not "entirely correct."

The decision of the House of Lords in *Maginnis* is fraught with difficulty and throws up more issues than it settles. Whereas the Court of Appeal in that case looked to see what benefit was conferred on the recipient, the House of Lords by contrast, referred to the intention of the transferor to enable the transferee to use the drugs for his own purposes. The upshot is that the custodian will often be in a worse position than the depositor, as the custodian will know that he is enabling the depositor to use the drug, whereas the depositor, does not intend the custodian to do likewise. Lord Goff of Chieveley (who dissented in *Maginnis*), was clearly concerned that the word "supply" would not be given a common sense interpretation if the majority of their Lordships were right. He found himself in agreement with the Court of Appeal in *Dempsey* but he regarded *Delgado* and *Donnelly* v. *H.M. Advocate* to be wrongly decided.

Lord Goff considered that the primary rule of construction is that the courts should attribute to words their natural and ordinary meaning unless the context otherwise requires but he hesitated to attempt a definition " especially as the word is not always very precisely used"—and thus demonstrated how elusive the ordinary natural meaning of words, can be. However, Lord Goff observed (at 913f/g) that "the word [supply], as used in relation to goods, connotes the idea of making goods available to another from resources other than those of the recipient."

4–19   In other words, the act of making goods available to a recipient, when those goods already form part of the recipient's own resources, cannot amount to an act of supply. Put another way, a recipient cannot be given what he effectively already has. Thus, Lord Goff said (at 913j): "I would not describe the re-delivery by the depositee to the depositor as a supply of goods, because the goods are simply being returned to him, rather than being made available to him from resources other than his own."

Lord Goff agreed with that part of the judgment of Mann J. when he said ([1986] 2 All E.R. 110, 113–114; [1986] Q.B. 618, 624): "In ordinary language the cloakroom attendant, the left luggage officer, the warehouseman and the shoe mender do not 'supply' to their customers the articles which those customers have left with them."

However, Lord Keith pointed to the example of a storekeeper who provided equipment to employees out of the store (at 909h):

> "... if an employee draws from his employers store materials or equipment which he requires for purposes of his work, it involves no straining of language to say that the storekeeper supplies him with those materials or equipment, notwithstanding that they do not form part of the storekeeper's own resources and that he is merely the custodian of them ...."

In this example, however, it was not the employee who deposited the supplies or the equipment with the storekeeper in the first place. That is why the storekeeper could properly be described as a "distributor," and "supplying" of course includes "distributing." Lord Keith therefore gave the additional example of the owner of a business, who obtains tools and materials from his own storekeeper—being articles which formed part of the owner's assets—and concluded that the storekeeper "can be said to be supplying him what he needs" (at 909j). This was not an illustration which found favour with Lord Goff (see 914d/3) who did not think that it would be appropriate to use the word "supply" to describe this situation. He added:

> "Even if the word 'supply' were to be used in such a context, I would regard it as a loose or aberrant use of the word which should be regarded as providing any foundation for the proposition that the word can be appropriately used, or is normally used, in every case where a depositee returns the goods to a depositor."

Surprisingly, the majority of their Lordships, in *Maginnis* adopted a highly **4–20** legalistic approach to justify answering the amended certified question in the affirmative. Lord Keith observed that in *Dempsey* there was no intention of enabling Maureen (the custodian) to use the drugs for her own purposes and, accordingly, a transfer of the drugs to her in those circumstances could not amount to an act of supply. But Lord Keith added (at 912e):

> "One who deposits controlled drugs of which he is in unlawful possession with a temporary custodian has no legal right to require the drugs to be handed back to him. Indeed, it is the duty of the custodian not to hand them back but to destroy them or to deliver them to a police officer so that they may be destroyed. The custodian in choosing to return the drugs to the depositor does something which he is not only not obliged to do, but which he has a duty not to do."

There seems to be no good reason for introducing such legalistic considerations into the concept of "supplying" for the purposes of the M.D.A. If a custodian may be compelled, as a matter of law, to return goods to the depositor, does that mean that the depositor has therefore not been "supplied" with those goods, but that if a custodian cannot be compelled in law to return goods (*e.g.* controlled drugs) then he is guilty of supplying them if they are returned? Lord Goff tested the validity of that approach when he said (at 914):

> "Let us forget about controlled drugs for the moment; and let us suppose that, owing to some technical rule of law, a contract of deposit of goods is unenforceable . . . But the depositee is an honourable man, and returns the goods to the man who deposited them with him. Nobody would, I think, describe him in ordinary language as supplying the goods to the depositor, simply because he was not legally bound to return them. The fact is that the goods came from the depositor's own resources; and all the depositee was doing was returning them to him."

In *Carey* (1990) N.S.W.L.R. 292, the Court of Criminal Appeal (Australia) **4–21** declined to follow *Maginnis.* The court was concerned with the construction of section 3 of the Drug Misuse and Trafficking Act 1985 (Australia). "Supply" is defined in section 3 of that Act to include "having in possession for supply." However, the court decided the case on the basis of the ordinary meaning of the word "supply" in circumstances where a person has possession of the drug but intends merely to transfer the physical control of it to its owner or the person reasonably believed to be such (*i.e.* the "custodian to depositor" situation). In *Carey,* a folded handkerchief containing 15 small packages containing substances from cocaine to cannabis was found in a chest beside the appellant's bed. The appellant said the drugs belonged to her sister which the appellant agreed to "mind" overnight and that the sister would collect the drugs the next day. The appellant's only intention as to the destination of the drugs was to return them to her sister. In delivering the judgment of the court, Hunt J. said:

> "The word 'supply,' however, retains its ordinary meaning as well as the extended meaning for which that inclusive definition [s.3] provides. The various dictionary meanings of the word are generally agreed as being to furnish or to provide something which is needed or wanted or required by the person to whom it is given. They do not suggest that the use of the word is appropriate when that something is merely returned to its owner or the person reasonably believed to be its owner."

4–22   The court referred to *O'Brien* v. *Smith* (May 9, 1986; unreported, Australia) in which Yeldham J. ruled that the word "supply" did not apply to the mere return of the drugs to their owner or to the person reasonably believed to be such. In discussing *Maginnis* [1987] 1 A.C. 303, *Dempsey* (1985) 82 Cr.App.R. 291 and *Delgado* [1984] 1 W.L.R. 89, Hunt J. observed that the ordinary meaning of any word may change according to the context in which it is used and that (in relation to *Maginnis*):

> "... it must be that the special statutory context in which the word 'supply' was there used caused the House of Lords to give an extended meaning to the word which it does not bear in its ordinary use. The Misuse of Drugs Act 1971 which was there under consideration includes as a defence to one of the charges under section 5 ... that the accused, knowing the drug to be a controlled drug, took possession of it for the purpose of delivering it into the custody of a person lawfully entitled to take custody of it. It may be (I say no more) that in that context their Lordships were able to give an interpretation to the word 'supply' which appears on its face to go beyond the ordinary accepted meaning of the word."

Hunt J. agreed with the reasoning of Lord Goff in *Maginnis.* The court declined to follow *Maginnis* and *Excell* v. *Dellaca* (1987) F.L.R. 157 in which Kelly J. found the reasoning of Lord Goff more attractive but felt constrained to follow the opinion of the majority in *Maginnis.* In the opinion of Hunt J. the policy of the Drug Misuse and Trafficking Act 1985 (Australia) would not be thwarted by giving the word "supply" its ordinary accepted meaning:

> "Such a consequence will not open the floodgates. In many (if not in

most) cases, the circumstances of the delivery would be such as to establish that the accused was an accessory of the person to whom the delivery
was effected. The acts of the drugs storeman to which Lord Keith referred in *Maginnis* (at 309) would clearly fall within the ordinary meaning of the word 'supply.' "

There is much force in the reasoning of Hunt J. In *Carey* the case had to be   **4–23**
decided on the narrow basis that the appellant's only intention was to return
the drugs to her sister but, in many cases, the evidence may disclose a joint
venture (or a conspiracy) with the depositor to supply the drugs to a third
party. Where A and B possess drugs intending to supply C then both A and B
are guilty of an offence under section 5(3) of the M.D.A. 1971 (or alternatively of a conspiracy to supply a controlled drug contrary to the Criminal
Law Act 1977).

The court went on to consider the situation where one person obtains drugs
on behalf of a group of persons. The court concluded that this situation is in
no sense analogous to the "bailment" situation which would necessarily fall
within the ordinary meaning of the word "supply." The reasoning of the
court in *Carey* on this aspect is entirely consistent with the law in the United
Kingdom under the Misuse of Drugs Act 1971: see *Buckley and Lane* (1979)
69 Cr.App.R. 371, §4–04, *supra*.

(c) The special case of *Harris*

> In *Harris* [1968] 1 W.L.R. 769, H and F were heroin addicts. H was   **4–24**
> registered as an addict whereas F was not. At Kingston railway station H
> and F were seen sitting close together in the waiting room. Sticking in F's
> arm was a syringe, containing F's heroin. H was seen injecting F's arm by
> pushing the top of the syringe. At the police station H told police, "I
> didn't give him the jack, it was one of his own. I was only helping him."
> *Held*: the conviction would be quashed. The jury should have been
> directed to be sure that the drug belonged to the appellant and that the
> drug administered to the co-defendant was not already his.

This case has sometimes been cited to support the contention that a transfer
of custody or physical control of a drug cannot amount to a supply even if the
transfer was for the benefit of the recipient. In fact one should approach this
case with caution since the Court of Appeal had to decide the appeal on the
basis that the drug belonged to F and indeed he pleaded guilty to possessing
the drug. In allowing the appeal Lord Parker C.J. said: "If B has obtained in
some way the possession of the heroin, and all that A is doing is to assist in
injecting that heroin into B, then A is not supplying heroin contrary to the
Regulation."

In ordinary language, the heroin "belonged" to F and as a matter of com-   **4–25**
mon sense, F could not be supplied with what he already had. It would not
appear from the facts, as reported in *Harris*, that the defendant had been in
possession of the drug (whether jointly or otherwise) moments before she
injected F with "his" drug and, again, there appears to have been no evidence
that H inserted the needle into F's arm—which would otherwise have meant

that she had been in possession of the drug prior to administering it. If H was not in possession of the drug before, or at the moment of injection, then clearly there was nothing for H to supply. On one view of the facts F was administering his own drug—H merely helped him. Accordingly, one may be compelled to treat *Harris* as having been decided on its own very special facts. In *Delgado* (1984) 78 Cr.App.R. 175 Skinner J. seems to have interpreted the facts in *Harris* in this way for he said (at 178): "The drugs which were injected never left the presence of the owner nor, as it was strongly argued, his physical control."

(d) B possesses drugs intending to act jointly with A

4–26   Again, in *Maginnis* [1987] 1 All E.R. 907, 909j Lord Keith said:

> "If a trafficker in controlled drugs sets up a store of these in the custody of a friend whom he thinks unlikely to attract the suspicions of the police and later draws on the store for the purposes of his trade, or for his own use, the custodier is in my opinion rightly to be regarded as supplying him with drugs."

In practice the prosecution may have no difficulties in proving that a custodian (in the circumstances described by Lord Keith) was acting in concert with the depositor and therefore both may be convicted of supplying a third party in accordance with the usual rules of joint enterprise. Thus, the facts of *Delgado* were capable of showing more than just an intention to return the drugs to his friends. There was at least a prima facie case that D was engaged in a joint venture (or a conspiracy) to supply persons unknown; a matter which clearly loomed large during the course of the hearing of the appeal in that case.

4–27   But even if the custodian intended to supply the depositor, knowing that the latter would supply the drug to others, that does not mean that the custodian possesses the drug intending to supply those third parties. Thus in *Greenfield* (1984) 78 Cr.App.R. 179, G was stopped by police in his car. Between the front seats was a plastic bag containing cannabis. G told police that a friend left the bag with him but he knew that his friend was a supplier of cannabis. The judge directed the jury principally on the basis that G held the drug for X knowing that X would supply it. Less emphasis was placed, by the judge in his summing-up, on the alternative case, namely, that G himself was engaged on a joint venture with X to supply. G's appeal against conviction for an offence under section 5(3) was allowed on the basis that the intent of somebody else to supply the drugs was not enough. "The words . . . 'with intent to supply . . .' predicate that it should be the intent on the part of the person who possesses to supply and not the intent of someone other than that who is in possession of drugs to supply."

A similar point arose in *Downes* [1984] Crim.L.R. 552, where the trial judge directed the jury that a defendant was guilty under section 5(3) if he knew full well that the depositor was ultimately going to supply the drugs to others even if he, personally, was not going to be involved in the supply. The Court of Appeal quashed the conviction. The prosecution must establish a joint venture with the requisite joint intention. *Greenfield* does not appear to have been cited in *Downes* but both decisions are clearly consistent: see also *Tansley* v. *Painter* [1969] Crim.L.R. 139, D.C.

Chapter 5
Supplying Controlled Drugs

5–01   Section 4 of the Misuse of Drugs Act 1971 reads as follows:

"(1) Subject to any regulations under section 7 of this Act for the time being in force, it shall not be lawful for a person—
  (*a*) to produce a controlled drug; or
  (*b*) to supply or offer to supply a controlled drug to another.
(2) Subject to section 28 of this Act, it is an offence for a person—
  (*a*) to produce a controlled drug in contravention of subsection (1) above; or
  (*b*) to be concerned in the production of such a drug in contravention of that subsection by another.
(3) Subject to section 28 of this Act, it is an offence for a person—
  (*a*) to supply or offer to supply a controlled drug to another in contravention of subsection (1) above; or
  (*b*) to be concerned in the supplying of such a drug to another in contravention of that subsection; or
  (*c*) to be concerned in the making to another in contravention of that subsection of an offer to supply such a drug."

It will be seen that section 4(1) merely imposes prohibitions on the production or supplying of controlled drugs, (or against the making of an offer to supply such drugs) but offences, arising out of a contravention of any of the prohibitions, are created by subsections (2) and (3).

5–02   Unfortunately, the concept of supplying is not straightforward and the M.D.A. offers little assistance. By section 37(1), "supplying" includes "distributing."

In *Mills* [1963] 1 Q.B. 522, it was suggested by the Court of Appeal that "supply" involves the passing of possession from one person to another. This statement is plainly an over-simplification and not apt to cover every situation. In the wake of the decision of the House of Lords in *Maginnis* [1987] 1 All E.R. 907, it is now more appropriate to view a supply in the context of a transfer of physical control of a controlled drug, to another, with the intention of enabling the recipient to use that drug for his own purposes. Although many cases of supply will involve the passing of a benefit, or reward, to the transferee, it is going too far to "gloss" the meaning of "supply" in those terms. So, where a chain of persons is involved in the distribution of controlled drugs, it follows that each member who transfers the drug to the next person in the chain will commit a separate act of supply, even if each distributor receives no discernible benefit or reward himself.

Many of the authorities which have considered the meaning of "supplying" and "distributing" are examined in Chapter 4 ("Possession With Intent To Supply") which the reader is strongly invited to read.

A. DRUGS WHICH MAY LAWFULLY BE SUPPLIED

Bearing in mind that the object of the M.D.A. is to regulate the flow of controlled drugs and their use, and that not all controlled drugs are equally dangerous to use, Parliament has endeavoured to introduce as flexible a system of distribution as it can under a statute. For this reason some drugs may be more freely supplied than others. Indeed, one substance, "Poppy-straw," is not subject to section 4(1) of the M.D.A. at all (see regulation 4(3) of the Misuse of Drugs Regulations 1985). "Poppy-straw" is defined in Part IV of Schedule 2 to the M.D.A. to mean "all parts, except the seeds, of the opium poppy, after mowing." The extent to which various classes of persons are permitted to supply specified controlled drugs are set out in the Misuse of Drugs Regulations 1985 (S.I. 1985 No. 2066) as amended by S.I. 1986 No. 2330.

5–03

B. PERSONS WHO MAY LAWFULLY SUPPLY ANY CONTROLLED DRUG

I. LICENSEES

Any person may supply any controlled drug if authorised by licence so to do: see regulation 5. The licence is issued by the Secretary of State. Obviously, any supply (or offer to supply), not in accordance with the terms and conditions attached to the licence will render such a supply (or offer to supply) unlawful, although it is unlikely to render the licence invalid.

5–04

II. GENERAL AUTHORITY TO SUPPLY

Regulation 6(1) provides that:

5–05

"Notwithstanding the provisions of section 4(1)(*b*) of the Act, any person who is lawfully in possession of a controlled drug may supply that drug to the person from whom he obtained it."

Regulation 6(1) protects the person who, for example, is prescribed a course of controlled drugs—and is therefore lawfully entitled to possess them—but who then wishes to return all unused drugs to the prescribing doctor. Regulation 6(1) cannot be used to protect a "bailee" who is given controlled drugs for safe-keeping, which are then returned to the "bailor," if the bailee is not a person lawfully entitled to take possession of them in the first instance.

By virtue of regulation 6(5), and notwithstanding the provisions of section 4(1)(*b*) of the Act, "any of the persons specified in regulation 6(7) may supply any controlled drug to any person who may lawfully have that drug in his possession." The six classes of persons listed in regulation 6(7) are:

"(*a*) a constable when acting in the course of his duty as such;
(*b*) a person engaged in the business of a carrier when acting in the course of that business;
(*c*) a person engaged in the business of the Post Office when acting in the course of that business;
(*d*) an officer of customs and excise when acting in the course of his duty as such;
(*e*) a person engaged in the work of any laboratory to which the drug has been sent for forensic examination when acting in the course of his duty as a person so engaged;
(*f*) a person engaged in conveying the drug to a person who may lawfully have that drug in his possession."

III. GENERAL AUTHORITY TO SUPPLY SCHEDULE 2, 3, 4, & 5 DRUGS

(a) Drugs returned by patient to practitioner

5–06 Regulation 6(2) provides that:

"Notwithstanding the provisions of section 4(1)(*b*) of the Act, any person who has in his possession a drug specified in Schedule 2, 3, 4 or 5 which has been supplied by or on the prescription of a practitioner for the treatment of that person, or of a person whom he represents, may supply that drug to any doctor, dentist or pharmacist for the purpose of destruction."

Accordingly, a patient who has been supplied controlled drugs by a "practitioner," and who now wishes to see some or all of those drugs destroyed, may deliver (*i.e.* supply) those drugs to any doctor, dentist or pharmacist for that purpose. It is therefore not necessary to return the drugs only to the person who supplied them. Nor is it necessary for the patient, who was the original recipient, to deliver them up for destruction: he may appoint another person to perform that task. The latter will also be protected by regulation 6(7). The term "practitioner" is not defined by the Regulations, but is stated in section 37(1) of the 1971 Act to mean "a doctor, dentist, veterinary practitioner or veterinary surgeon."

(b) Drugs returned to veterinary practitioners

5–07 It is often forgotten that controlled drugs are also supplied, prescribed and administered in the treatment of animals as well as human beings.

Accordingly, persons who have such drugs in their possession will be protected if they are supplied to them in a form authorised by the Regulations. Any person who intends to deliver them up for destruction will be protected by regulation 6(3) if certain conditions are fulfilled. Regulation 6(3) provides that:

"Notwithstanding the provisions of section 4(1)(*b*) of the Act, any person who is lawfully in possession of a drug specified in Schedule 2, 3, 4 or 5 which has been supplied by or on the prescription of a veterinary practitioner or veterinary surgeon for the treatment of animals may supply that drug to any veterinary practitioner, veterinary surgeon or pharmacist for the purposes of destruction."

(c) Administration of drugs

Every act involving the administration of a controlled drug to another is an   5–08
act of supply. In respect of drugs specified in Schedule 5 to the 1985 Regulations, any person may administer such drugs to any one else (regulation 7(1)).

Doctors and dentists may lawfully administer drugs listed in Schedules 2, 3 and 4 to a patient under regulation 7(2). Indeed, any person may administer such drugs to another *providing* that the drugs are administered in accordance with the directions of a doctor or a dentist: see regulation 7(3).

C. PERSONS WHO MAY SUPPLY SCHEDULE 3 DRUGS ONLY

The drugs which come within Schedule 3 include the following: 5–09

"1(*a*). Benzphetamine   Meprobamate
        (Cathine)   Methylphenobarbitone
        Chlorphentermine   Methyprylone
        Diethypropion   Pentazocine
        Ethchlorvynol   Phendimetrazine
        Ethinamate   Phentermine
        Mazindol   Pipradrol
        Mephentermine

(*b*) any 5,5 disubstituted barbituric acid.

2. Any stereoisomeric form of a substance specified in paragraph 1 "not being phenylpropanolamine"—[words added by the Misuse of Drugs (Amendment) Regulations 1986 (S.I. 1986 No. 2330)].

3. Any salt of a substance specified in paragraph 1 or 2.

4. Any preparation or other product containing a substance specified in any of paragraphs 1 to 3, not being a preparation specified in Schedule 5."

(a) Wildlife licensees

5–10   Subject to an appropriate licence being granted under section 16 of the Wildlife and Countryside Act 1981, it is not unlawful to supply or to offer to supply a controlled drug falling within Schedule 3: see regulation 6(4).

(b) Buffering agents in chemical analysis

5–11   It is often necessary for laboratory personnel to use a variety of chemicals (some of which may be controlled) in order to carry out chemical analysis. Limited protection is afforded by regulation 9(6) (as amended by the Misuse of Drugs (Amendment) Regulations 1986 (S.I. 1986 No. 2330) which provides:

> "Notwithstanding the provisions of section 4(1)(b) of the Act, a person in charge of a laboratory may, when acting in his capacity as such, supply or offer to supply any drug specified in Schedule 3 which is required for use as a buffering agent in chemical analysis to any person who may lawfully have that drug in his possession."

D. PERSONS WHO MAY SUPPLY SCHEDULE 2 OR 5 DRUGS

(a) Classes of persons lawfully entitled to supply others

5–12   Eleven categories of persons may, by regulation 8(2), lawfully supply or offer to supply Schedule 2 or 5 drugs to any person who may lawfully have that drug in his possession, namely:

"(a) a practitioner;

(b) a pharmacist;

(c) a person lawfully conducting a retail pharmacy;

(d) a person in charge or acting person in charge of a hospital or nursing home which is wholly or mainly maintained by a public authority out of public funds or by a charity or by voluntary subscriptions;

(e) in the case of such a drug supplied to her by a person responsible for the dispensing and supply of medicines at the hospital or nursing home, the sister or acting sister for the time being in charge of a ward, theatre, or other department in such a hospital or nursing home as aforesaid;

(f) a person who is in charge of a laboratory the recognised activities of which consist in, or include, the conduct of scientific education or research and which is attached to a university, university college or such a hospital as aforesaid or to any other institution approved for the purpose ... by the Secretary of State;

(g) a public analyst appointed under section 76 of the Food Act 1984 or section 27 of the Food and Drugs (Scotland) Act 1956;

(h) a sampling officer within the meaning of the Food and Drugs (Scotland) Act 1956;

(*i*) a sampling officer within the meaning of Schedule 3 to the Medicines Act 1968;

(*j*) a person employed or engaged in connection with a scheme for testing the quality or amount of the drugs, preparations and appliances supplied under the National Health Service Act 1977 or the National Health Service (Scotland) Act 1978 and the Regulations made thereunder;

(*k*) a person authorised by the Pharmaceutical Society of Great Britain for the purposes of section 108 or 109 of the Medicines Act 1968.

Provided that nothing in this paragraph authorises—

(i) the person in charge or acting person in charge of a hospital or nursing home, having a pharmacist responsible for the dispensing and supply of medicines, to supply or offer to supply any drug;

(ii) a sister or acting sister for the time being in charge of a ward, theatre or other department to supply any drug otherwise than for administration to a patient in that ward, theatre or department in accordance with the directions of a doctor or dentist."

(b) Group authority

Protection is given to any person who is "authorised as a member of a   5–13
group" to supply, or offer to supply, drugs specified in Schedule 2 or 5, to any person who may lawfully have that drug in his possession: regulation 8(3). However, such a member must comply (*a*) with the terms of his group authority, and (*b*) with any conditions attached to that authority.

By regulation 2(1), a person is "authorised as a member of a group" if he is:

"... authorised by virtue of being a member of a class as respects which the Secretary of State has granted an authority under and for the purposes of Regulations 8(3), 9(3) or 10(3) which is in force, and 'his group authority,' in relation to a person who is a member of such a class, means the authority so granted to that class;"

(c) Provisions applicable to non-doctors at sea

By regulation 8(5):   5–14

"... (a) the owner of a ship, or the master of a ship which does not carry a doctor among the seamen employed in it;
(b) the installation manager of an offshore installation,
may supply or offer to supply any drug specified in Schedule 2 or 5—

(i) for the purpose of compliance with any of the provisions specified in paragraph (6), to any person on that ship or installation;

(ii) to any person who may lawfully supply that drug to him;

(iii) to any constable for the purpose of the destruction of that drug."

By regulation 8(6):   5–15

"The provisions referred to in paragraph (5) are any provision of, or of any instrument which is in force under—

(a) the Merchant Shipping Acts;
(b) the Mineral Workings (Offshore Installations) Act 1971; or
(c) the Health and Safety at Work Act 1974."

E. PERSONS WHO MAY SUPPLY SCHEDULE 3 OR 4 DRUGS

(a) Classes of persons lawfully entitled to supply others

5–16　　The following nine classes of persons may, by regulation 9(2), lawfully supply or offer to supply controlled drugs to any person lawfully entitled to have such drugs in his possession, namely:

"(a) a practitioner;
(b) a pharmacist;
(c) a person lawfully conducting a retail pharmacy;
(d) a person in charge of a laboratory the recognised activities of which consist in, or include, the conduct of scientific education or research;
(e) a public analyst appointed under section 76 of the Food Act 1984 or section 27 of the Food and Drugs (Scotland) Act 1956;
(f) a sampling officer within the meaning of the Food and Drugs (Scotland) Act 1956;
(g) a sampling officer within the meaning of Schedule 3 to the Medicines Act 1968;
(h) a person employed or engaged in connection with a scheme for testing the quality or amount of the drugs, preparations and appliances supplied under the National Health Service Act 1977 or the National Health Service (Scotland) Act 1978 and the Regulations made thereunder;
(i) a person authorised by the Pharmaceutical Society of Great Britain for the purposes of section 108 or 109 of the Medicines Act 1968."

[Not surprisingly, the regulations also permit a retail pharmacist to supply what he is authorised to produce. Thus, by regulation 9(4)(b) "a person who is authorised under paragraph 9(1)(c) may supply or offer to supply any drug which he may, by virtue of being so authorised, lawfully produce to any person who may lawfully have that drug in his possession."]

5–17　　As from April 1, 1987 the Misuse of Drugs (Amendment) Regulations 1986 (S.I. 1986 No. 2330) substituted the following paragraph for regulation 9(3), thus:

"(3) Notwithstanding the provisions of section 4(1)(b) of the Act—
(a) a person who is authorised as a member of a group, under and in accordance with the terms of his group authority and in compliance with any conditions attached thereto;
(b) the person in charge or acting person in charge of a hospital or nursing home;
(c) in the case of such a drug supplied to her by a person responsible

for the dispensing and supply of medicines at that hospital or nursing home, the sister or acting sister for the time being in charge of a ward, theatre or other department in a hospital or nursing home, may, when acting in his capacity as such, supply or offer to supply any drug specified in Schedule 3, or any drug specified in Schedule 4 which is contained in a medicinal product, to any person who may lawfully have that drug in his possession:

Provided that nothing in this paragraph authorises—
  (i) the person in charge or acting person in charge of a hospital or nursing home, having a pharmacist responsible for the dispensing and supply of medicines, to supply or offer to supply any drug;
  (ii) a sister or acting sister for the time being in charge of a ward, theatre or other department to supply any drug otherwise than for administration to a patient in that ward, theatre or department in accordance with the directions of a doctor or dentist."

(b) Provisions applicable to non-doctors at sea

By regulation 9(5):   **5–18**

"... (a) the owner of a ship, or the master of a ship which does not carry a doctor among the seamen employed in it;
(b) the installation manager of an offshore installation,
may supply or offer to supply any drug specified in Schedule 3, or any drug specified in Schedule 4 which is contained in a medicinal product—
  (i)   for the purpose of compliance with any of the provisions specified in Regulation 8(6), to any person on that ship or installation; or
  (ii) to any person who may lawfully supply that drug to him."

F. PERSONS WHO MAY SUPPLY SCHEDULE 5 DRUGS

We have already seen that any person may administer to another a controlled drug providing that it is a drug specified in Schedule 5. The drugs coming within this category are as follows: **5–19**

"1.—(1) Any preparation of one or more of the substances to which this paragraph applies, not being a preparation designed for administration by injection, when compounded with one or more other active or inert ingredients and containing a total of not more than 100 milligrammes of the substance or substances (calculated as base) per dosage unit or with a total concentration of not more than 2.5 per cent. (calculated as base) in undivided preparations.

(2) The substances to which this paragraph applies are acetylihydrocodeine, codeine, dihydrocodeine, ethylmorphine, nicocodine, nicodicodine (6-nicotinoyldihydrocodeine), norcodeine, pholcodine and their respective salts.

2. Any preparation of cocaine containing not more than 0.1 per cent. of

cocaine calculated as cocaine base, being a preparation compounded with one or more other active or inert ingredients in such a way that the cocaine cannot be recovered by readily applicable means or in a yield which would constitute a risk to health.

3. Any preparation of medicinal opium or of morphine containing (in either case) not more than 0.2 per cent. of morphine calculated as anhydrous morphine base, being a preparation compounded with one or more other active or inert ingredients in such a way that the opium or, as the case may be, the morphine, cannot be recovered by readily applicable means or in a yield which would constitute a risk to health [and see *Hunt* [1986] 3 W.L.R. 1115, H.L.]

4. Any preparation of dextropropoxyphene, being a preparation designed for oral administration, containing not more than 135 milligrammes of dextropropoxyphene (calculated as base) per dosage unit or with a total concentration of not more than 2.5 per cent. (calculated as base) in undivided preparations.

5. Any preparation of difenoxin containing, per dosage unit, not more than 0.5 milligrammes of difenoxin and a quantity of atropine sulphate equivalent to at least 5 per cent. of the dose of difenoxin.

6. Any preparation of diphenoxylate containing, per dosage unit, not more than 2.5 milligrammes of diphenoxylate calculated as base, and a quantity of atropine sulphate equivalent to at least 1 per cent. of the dose of diphenoxylate.

7. Any preparation of propiram containing, per dosage unit, not more than 100 milligrammes of propiram calculated as base and compounded with at least the same amount (by weight) of methylcellulose.

8. Any powder of ipecacuanha and opium comprising—
    10 per cent. opium in powder
    10 per cent. ipecacuanha root, in powder, well mixed with 80 per cent. of any other powdered ingredient containing no controlled drug.

9. Any mixture containing one or more of the preparations specified in paragraphs 1 to 8, being a mixture of which none of the other ingredients is a controlled drug."

G. WRITTEN AUTHORITY TO SUPPLY

5–20   "A person who is authorised by a written authority issued by the Secretary of State under . . . [paragraph 8(4)] may, at the premises specified in that authority and in compliance with any conditions . . . supply or offer to supply any drug specified in Schedule 5 to any person who may lawfully have that drug in his possession": see regulation 8(4).

H. ISSUING A PRESCRIPTION NOT A "SUPPLY"

In *Taylor* [1986] Crim.L.R. 680 a general practitioner prescribed 70   **5-21**
people quantities of methadone, a Class A controlled drug. At the close of the
prosecution case, it was successfully submitted on behalf of the defence that
even assuming T acted unlawfully and in bad faith, the mere issuing of a prescription authorising a pharmacist to dispense a drug did not amount to "supplying" for the purposes of section 4 of the Misuse of Drugs Act 1971. In the
judgment of His Honour Judge Hickman, "supplying" involves the physical
transfer of the substance involved from the supplier to the supplied. The case
of *Taylor* raises a number of interesting points. The doctor was not in possession of methadone and therefore, even if his intention had been to supply
the drug to patients, he could not be convicted of an offence under section
5(3) of the 1971 Act. However, the pharmacist supplies patients with drugs
once they are handed over to the patient. As Professor Smith has pointed out
([1986] Crim.L.R. 681) if the doctor was acting unlawfully and in bad faith,
the "patient" was not entitled to have the drug and therefore the supply by the
pharmacist was an *actus reus* and the defendant, with *mens rea*, had caused
that *actus reus* to occur. Although the pharmacist is an innocent agent he
nevertheless acts on the directions and with the authority of the doctor: see
Cogan [1976] Q.B. 217, C.A.

I. THE UNLAWFUL SUPPLY OF CONTROLLED DRUGS

Offences arising out of a contravention of section 4(1)(*b*) appear in section   **5-22**
4(3) which reads:

"Subject to section 28 of this Act, it is an offence for a person—
  (*a*) to supply or offer to supply a controlled drug to another in contra-
       vention of subsection (1) . . . ; or
  (*b*) to be concerned in the supplying of such a drug to another in con-
       travention of that subsection; or
  (*c*) to be concerned in the making to another in contravention of that
       subsection of an offer to supply such a drug."

Although the offences of supplying and offering to supply appear together
in section 4(3)(*a*), they must be regarded as distinct offences so that charges or
counts in the indictment must clearly specify which offence is being alleged.

It will be seen that section 4(3) creates a total of four offences. The difference between (*b*) and (*c*) is that in (*b*) there must be an actual supply made by
an accused, whereas in (*c*) the accused need only be concerned in making an
offer to supply: see also *Clements* v. *H.M.Advocate* 1991 S.L.T. 388 and
§5-28, *infra*. Again, in respect of both (*b*) and (*c*), the word "knowingly"
does not appear since both offences are subject to section 28.

In *Hughes* (1985) 81 Cr.App.R. 344, the Court of Appeal listed the three
elements which the prosecution must prove for any offence under s.4(3),

namely:

(1) the supply of a drug to another or, as the case may be, the making of an offer to supply the drug to another; and

(2) participation by the accused in an enterprise involving such a supply or, as the case may be, such an offer to supply; and

(3) knowledge by the accused of the nature of the enterprise; either knowledge that it is a venture to supply or to make an offer to supply the drug in question.

It is not apparent from the report whether the court heard argument as to the effect of section 28 on section 4.

5–23　　"Supplying" includes "distributing": see section 37(1). In *Holmes* v. *Chief Constable Merseyside Police* [1976] Crim.L.R. 125, counsel for the defence submitted that a person who held drugs on behalf of himself and others was in joint possession and that a subsequent division of the drugs could not amount to a supply. The Divisional Court rejected that submission, holding that the word "supply" had to be given its ordinary natural meaning (see also *Searle* [1971] Crim.L.R. 592).

> In *Buckley* (1979) 69 Cr.App.R. 371, B and G pooled their money intending to buy cannabis in bulk. B took the money to L, the supplier, and bought 1lb. of cannabis resin. Thereafter, B gave 3/4 lb. of the drug to G representing the latter's contribution to the purchase price. B argued that he could not "supply" to G what he already possessed.
>
> *Held*: B was guilty of supplying the drug because he distributed it. *Holmes* v. *Chief Constable Merseyside Police* applied.

As the law presently stands, there is a supply upon the transfer of custody and physical control of a controlled drug to another, so as to enable that other to benefit from its use: see *Maginnis* [1987] 1 All E.R. 907. Many of the authorities relevant to this topic have been considered in Chapter 4, entitled "Possession with Intent to Supply."

I. MAKING AN OFFER TO SUPPLY

5–24　　Where an offer is made to supply a drug in the belief that it is one which is controlled under the Misuse of Drugs Act 1971, an offence is committed even though the substance sold is not the drug it was thought to be and was not even a controlled drug: see *Goddard* [1992] Crim.L.R. 588 and *Mitchell* (June 3, 1992; unreported).

> In *Haggard* v. *Mason* [1976] 1 W.L.R. 187, D.C., M bought 1,000 tablets of what he believed to be lysergide (LSD), a Class A controlled drug, and sold some of the tablets to Heward. Heward similarly believed the substance to be LSD whereas, in fact, the substance was Bromo STP (another hallucinogenic drug, similar in effect and appearance to LSD but not then controlled under the 1971 Act). M was convicted of offering to supply a controlled drug to H contrary to s.4(3)(*a*) of the 1971 Act.
>
> *Held*: appeal dismissed *per* Lawson J. at 190:

"In my judgment the offence was completed at the time when ... the appellant met Heward and offered to sell him a quantity of lysergide. ... It matters not in relation to the offence of offering to supply that what is in fact supplied pursuant to that offer, the offer having been accepted, is not in fact a controlled drug."

Section 4(3)(c) has been particularly widely drawn so as to involve people who may be at some distance from the actual making of the offer: see *Blake* (1979) 68 Cr.App.R. 1, C.A. and *Hughes* (1985) 81 Cr.App.R. 344, C.A.   **5–25**

The decision of *Haggard* v. *Mason* (*supra*) is of some importance. Three situations often fall to be considered in respect of charges under section 4(3)(a) and (c). The first is where the accused makes an offer to supply a controlled drug of one description (*e.g.* cocaine) which in fact turns out to be a controlled drug of a wholly different description. On these facts there exists no difficulty and section 28(3) affords no defence. The offence would seem to be in the making of the offer to supply a controlled drug. The fact that a different controlled drug is involved, is irrelevant.

The second situation is where an accused offers to supply what he believes to be a controlled drug, whereas the substance is in fact not controlled. It was this situation which arose in *Haggard* v. *Mason*. That case makes it plain that the accused has no defence. The third situation is where an accused offers to supply a controlled drug which in fact, and to the knowledge or belief of the accused, is not controlled at all. The Divisional Court in *Haggard* v. *Mason* did not need to consider the state of mind of an accused falling into this latter category. If the offence is solely in the making of the offer then it is submitted that the defendant's state of mind is totally irrelevant. However, section 28 of the Act applies to offences under section 4(3). Construed literally it follows that section 28 applies to offences under section 43(3)(a) and (c). The question arises whether an accused falling within the third category has a defence under section 28(3)(b)(i), *i.e.* that he neither believed nor suspected nor had reason to suspect that the substance was a controlled drug. Obviously no such defence is afforded to him by virtue of this provision if section 28(3)(b)(i) is construed as coming into operation only in circumstances where the substance in question is proved to be controlled.

Although, in the ordinary way, a person is entitled to be judged on the facts as he believed them to be (see *R.* v. *Taaffe* [1984] A.C. 539 and *D.P.P.* v. *Nock* [1978] A.C. 979) it is submitted that the mischief which the legislature has sought to punish is the act of making an offer to supply a controlled drug, irrespective as to whether the offer was bogus in nature or not.   **5–26**

(a) "Being concerned"

Where a prosecution is brought under section 4(3) (b) or (c), it is the duty of the trial judge to assist the jury as to the meaning of the word "concerned": see *Hughes* (*supra*). A failure to do so may result in the conviction being quashed. Given that "concerned" involves some identifiable act of participation, it follows that the assistance given to the jury, by the judge, will vary   **5–27** from case to case. However, any direction must have regard to the relevant evidence of the accused's conduct in the transaction.

For the purposes of section 4(3)(*b*) a person may be guilty of being concerned in the supplying of a controlled drug to another even if no supply actually took place: in *Kerr* v. *H.M. Advocate*, 1986 S.C.C.R. 81, Lord Hunter said:

> "Section 4(3)(*b*) ... covers ... the whole process of supplying to others, a process which may not be completed ... The provision is designed to catch any person who is concerned at any stage in the process of supplying to others from the beginning of that process to the end."

The Lord Justice-Clerk said, by way of example, that if a man were to assist a drug user by introducing him to a supply of controlled drugs, that could involve the former being concerned in the supplying of a controlled drug to another even though no actual supply took place on the occasion in question (see p. 89).

There exists, at present, a rather speculative interpretation as to whether the use of the word "concerned" was intended by the legislature to replace the principles of aiding and abetting. If not then why did Parliament enact (*b*) and (*c*) at all? As Eveleigh L.J. said in *Blake* (1979) 68 Cr.App.R. 1, section 4(3)(*c*) is very widely drawn so as to include people "who may be at some distance from the actual making of the offer."

> In *Blake*, O made an offer to supply drugs to X in Piccadilly. B was not present but X and O went to B's flat to obtain the drugs. B's conviction for being concerned in the making of an offer to supply was upheld.

5–28   In *Clements* v. *H.M. Advocate*, 1991 S.L.T. 388, the High Court of Justiciary had to consider whether acts done in England were triable in Scotland. In that case the only evidence led by the Crown was to the effect that "X" and "Y" collected 7 kilogrammes of cannabis resin in London and gave it to a co-accused who had travelled from Scotland and then returned to Scotland by train. Both "X" and "Y" were convicted of an offence under section 4(3)(*b*). It was submitted on their behalf that nothing in the 1971 Act overcame the presumption that a criminal statute was not intended to have extra-territorial effect. In refusing the appeals, the Court held that the problem posed was as to territorial limitations between different jurisdictions within the United Kingdom. The answer depended on constitutional practice and not international comity. The 1971 Act created a statutory offence which operates within the United Kingdom and accordingly there was nothing in precedent, comity or good sense to inhibit the Scottish courts from treating as justiciable acts committed in another part of the United Kingdom which formed part of the chain in supplying controlled drugs to persons in Scotland. The court distinguished *Somchai Liangsiriprasert* v. *Government of the United States of America* [1990] 3 W.L.R. 606.

(b) Supplying to "another"

In cases where defendants were charged with an offence of supplying a con- 5–29
trolled drug to another, it was common to find that the "another" was himself
a person named in the indictment.

Thus, suppose A supplied heroin to B. Some prosecutors charged both A
and B with being concerned in the unlawful supply of heroin to another. Such
a charge is misconceived since B cannot be charged with unlawfully supplying
drugs to himself: see *Smith* (February 14, 1983; C.A., unreported), and *Paolo
Ferrara* (July 17, 1984, C.A.; unreported). Accordingly, it was common practice for prosecutors to draft separate counts against each defendant so that A
was charged with unlawfully supplying heroin to B, whereas the latter was
charged merely with unlawfully possessing the drug. It is submitted that such
a course is perfectly sensible notwithstanding the fact that both defendants
appear on the same indictment. However, the Court of Appeal in *Adepoju*
[1988] Crim.L.R. 378, C.A. appeared to hold that the "another," for the purposes of section 4, cannot be a person "in the indictment." If that was truly
the *ratio decidendi* of *Adepoju* then the decision is surprising to say the least.
However, upon a closer examination of *Adepoju* it is clear that the case discloses no new law but merely confirms the decisions of the Court of Appeal in
Smith (*supra*) and *Paolo Ferrara* (*supra*). In *Adepoju*, A, L and a Carol Curmi
were all charged with being concerned in the unlawful supply of heroin to
another (*i.e.* to Curmi) contrary to section 4(3) of the M.D.A. 1971. At the
end of the prosecution case Curmi successfully submitted that there was no
case for her to answer. She could not supply herself. But the prosecutor
successfully applied to the court for leave to amend the indictment so as to
delete Curmi as a defendant from that charge but to name her as the
"another" to whom the supply was made.

That amendment prevented the appellants from successfully submitting 5–30
that there was no case for them to answer on the basis that the prosecution
had failed to prove that the appellants had supplied another. Even if supply to
Carol Curmi could be established she was not "another" so long as she was
included in the count on the indictment. The Court of Appeal held that the
appellants had been entitled to a ruling in respect of their submission of no
case to answer as the indictment stood "at the time." The judge had accordingly been wrong to allow the amendment. As the court remarked, ". . . the
trouble had arisen because of careless drafting of the indictment." The Court
concluded that "it was a matter of common sense that 'another' could not be
a person in the *indictment*." It was most unfortunate that the Court, throughout its judgement used the word "indictment," as opposed to "count,"
because if the word "count" had been employed then the decision would have
made perfect sense. Happily, the ambiguity has been resolved by the Court of
Appeal in *Connelly* [1992] Crim.L.R. 296. That case makes it plain that
where A, B and C were charged on a particular count with supplying a drug to
another, that other could not be A, B or C. The cases of *Smith* (*supra*), *Ferrara*
(*supra*) and *Adepoju* (*supra*) did not hold that the other person could not be
somebody who was a defendant on the same indictment. In *Connelly*, the
court sought to explain *Adepoju* on the basis that, in strict law, each count

was a separate indictment.

(c) Can one supply to another outside the United Kingdom?

5–31 It has not been resolved by an appellate court whether an intention to supply a person abroad with a controlled drug is an offence under section 5(3) of the Act. It is submitted that it is not. This is because offences under the Act are local. Offences under section 20 fall into a very different category. It would not be an offence under section 4 for a person having travelled from England, on holiday in India, to supply a controlled drug to another person there. Again, a person who posts drugs to another abroad commits no offence under section 4 although he commits at least an exportation offence. Accordingly, a person who possesses a drug intending to "supply" a person abroad, commits no offence under section 5(3) because the supply must be contrary to section 4.

II. INTOXICATING SUBSTANCES

5–32 So far we have only been concerned with offences in connection with controlled drugs. However, by the Intoxicating Substances (Supply) Act 1985, Parliament made it an offence to supply or to offer to supply, to a person under 18 years of age, a substance other than a controlled drug, if he knows or has reasonable cause to believe that the substance is, or its fumes are, likely to be inhaled by the recipient for the purpose of intoxication: see section 1(1) of the Intoxicating Substances Act (Supply) 1985.

However, the substance must be supplied to a person who is under 18 years of age *and* whom the accused knows, or has reasonable cause to believe, to be under that age: see section 1(1)(*a*). Alternatively, the substance must be supplied or offered to a person who is acting on behalf of a person under 18 years of age, *and* whom he knows, or has reasonable cause to believe, to be so acting: see section 1(1)(*b*) of the Intoxicating Substances (Supply) Act 1985.

If the accused can prove (because the burden is on him) that he was under 18 years of age at the time when it is alleged that he contravened subsection (1), *and* that he was acting otherwise than in the course or furtherance of a business, he is entitled to be acquitted: see subsection (2).

It follows that an accused aged 18 years or over commits an offence under the Act whether he supplies an intoxicating substance in the course of a business or not. The Act does not make it an offence for, say, a 17-year-old solvent abuser to supply the substance he is abusing to another 17-year-old. However, if a minor regularly sells part of his stock, he may (for the purposes of the Act) be engaged in a "business."

Chapter 6
The Manufacture and Production of Controlled Drugs

A. SUBSTANCES USEFUL FOR MANUFACTURE OF CONTROLLED DRUGS

The Criminal Justice (International Co-operation) Act 1990 received its **6–01** Royal Assent on April 5, 1990, just a few days prior to the World Ministerial Summit to Reduce the Demand for Drugs and to Combat the Cocaine Trade was held in London, on 9–11 April, 1990.

Part II of the Act was aimed at regulating the manufacture and supply of a variety of substances which may have a legitimate use in industry but which are also used in the unlawful production of controlled drugs. Enactment of Part II of the Act enables the Government to ratify the 1988 Vienna Convention against Illicit Traffic in Narcotic Drugs and Psychotropic Substances.

Section 12 and section 13 regulate and control the manufacture, transportation or distribution of substances listed in Schedule 2 of the Act to prevent their use for the unlawful production of a controlled drug (see Art. 3, Art. 12 and Art. 13 of the 1988 Vienna Convention).

The substances (particularised in Schedule 2 to the 1990 Act) are set out in two distinct groups.

Table I lists "precursors," that is to say, chemicals which may have a legitimate use clinically or in the pharmaceutical industry but which are also used in the unlawful production of a controlled drug. Notification of the proposed exportation of the substances listed in Table I may be required by regulations made under section 13(1)(*b*) and section 13(2) of the Act. Thus:

EPHEDRINE	(methamphetamine production)
ERGOMETRINE	(LSD production)
ERGOTAMINE	(LSD production)
LYSERGIC ACID	(LSD production)
1-PHENYL-2-PROPANONE	(amphetamine production)
PSEUDOEPHEDRINE	(amphetamine production)

The salts (if any) of the above are also included.

Table II lists those chemicals which also have a legitimate purpose in indus- **6–02** try and commerce (or generally) but which may also be used as reagents or solvents in the production of a controlled drug. Thus:

ACETIC ANHYDRIDE	(heroin production)
ACETONE	(cocaine and heroin production)
ANTHRANILIC ACID	(methaqualone production)
ETHYL ETHER	(cocaine and heroin production)
PHENYLACETIC ACID	(amphetamine production)
PIPERIDINE	(phencyclidine production) ("Angel Dust")

Again, the salts (if any) of the above are included.

Section 13(1) of the C.J. (I.C.) A 1990 empowers the Secretary of State to make Regulations for the keeping of records and the furnishing of information in respect of those substances while regulations made under section 13(2) may require manufacturers and suppliers to give notification of any proposed exportation to any country specified in the regulations in respect of a scheduled substance. Where the requisite notice has not been given the substance shall be deemed to be exported for the purposes of section 68 of the C.E.M.A. 1979 (offences relating to the exportation of prohibited or restricted goods): see section 13(2).

Parliament was concerned to ensure that nothing in sections 12 or 13 undermined the voluntary system (which has been in operation for a number of years) of passing information to law enforcement agencies by manufacturers and distributors of scheduled substances.

I. OFFENCES IN RESPECT OF SECTION 13

6–03   Two offences (non-compliance with the regulations and furnishing false information) are created by C.J. (I.C.) A 1990, s.13(s) which provides:

> "Any person who fails to comply with any requirement imposed by the regulations or, in purported compliance with any such requirement, furnishes information which he knew to be false in a material particular is guilty of an offence . . . ."

It would seem that neither offence is extraditable since they are not specified as "drug trafficking offences" for the purposes of the D.T.O.A. 1986 (and see section 22 and Schedule 4 of the 1990 Act).

By section 13(2) a failure to give notification of the proposed exportation of a substance specified in Table I of Schedule 2 (required by regulations made under section 13(1)(b)) shall be deemed to be exported contrary to a restriction in force for the purposes of section 68 of the C.E.M.A. 1979. A conviction under section 68 of the C.E.M.A. 1979 is a "drug trafficking offence" for the purposes of the D.T.O.A. 1986 (section 38(1) of the 1986 Act) and is therefore extraditable: see section 22 of the C.J. (I. C.) A 1990 and *Governor of Pentonville, ex p. Chinoy* [1992] 1 All E.R. 317.

B. THE PRODUCTION OF CONTROLLED DRUGS

Subject to any regulations which the Secretary of State may make pursuant to section 7 of the M.D.A., it is not lawful for any person to produce a controlled drug: see section 4(1)(*a*). Contravention of this subsection is made a criminal offence by section 4(2) of the M.D.A.   **6–04**

I. What is Meant by "Production of a Controlled Drug"

According to M.D.A., s.37(1), the legislature has defined the word "produce" to mean "producing [a controlled drug] by manufacture, cultivation or any other method, and 'production' has a corresponding meaning."   **6–05**

It is worth pointing out at this stage that although "production" includes "cultivating," Parliament (by section 6(2) of the Act) makes it a distinct offence to cultivate plants of the genus *Cannabis*, unless the grower is authorised to do so by a licence issued by the Secretary of State: see regulation 12 of the Misuse of Drugs Regulations 1985, which provides that:

> "Where any person is authorised by a licence of the Secretary of State issued under this Regulation and for the time being in force to cultivate plants of the genus *Cannabis*, it shall not by virtue of section 6 of the Act be unlawful for that person to cultivate any such plant in accordance with the terms of the licence and in compliance with any conditions attached to the licence."

It is not immediately apparent why Parliament specifically created this separate offence until one gives "producing" and "production" a narrow meaning. It is clear from section 37(1) that what has to be produced is the controlled drug itself, *i.e.* as specified in Schedule II to the Misuse of Drugs Act 1971. Some drugs are produced by a process of synthesis, *e.g.* LSD, some by cultivation, in the sense that penicillin, for example, is produced from the mould *Penicillium notatum*. Other drugs are produced after a process of extraction; thus cannabis resin is the resin separated from the cannabis plant.

The word "cultivation" certainly includes the act of nursing plants to fruition, but not every cultivated plant, in which a drug naturally subsists, is an act of "production," within the meaning of section 37(1), since what is physically produced is not the drug itself—that still subsists in the plant. In 1971, when the Misuse of Drugs Act was passed, "cannabis" was a controlled drug, but the definition of "cannabis" was restricted to the flowering and fruiting tops of the plant: see *Goodchild (No. 2)* [1977] 1 W.L.R. 1213. Accordingly, in 1971, a cannabis plant which had not flowered, or produced fruiting tops, was not a controlled drug, even though the active ingredient subsisted in the plant. If the infant plant had been cultivated, it follows that a controlled drug had not, at that stage, been "produced" either. Accordingly, in order to prohibit persons growing the plant of the genus *Cannabis* at all, Parliament enacted section 6.   **6–06**

By contrast, cocaine is a controlled drug, extracted from the coca-leaf. Obviously, the process of extraction is an act of production. But the coca-leaf itself, is a controlled drug, and is "produced" by growing it.

6–07   In 1977, the definition of "cannabis"—as a controlled drug—was extended to include virtually the entire plant (see Criminal Law Act 1977, s.52). As a result, there is now no reason at all why the act of growing the cannabis plant should not be regarded as an act of "production" for the purposes of section 4 of the M.D.A.

In *Taylor v. Chief Constable of Kent* [1981] 1 W.L.R. 606:

> Police found cannabis plants in T's premises but not in a room occupied by him. Nevertheless T knew that the plants were there and that they had been cultivated by X who was convicted under section 6 for so doing. T was charged with permitting or suffering the "production" of the plants in the premises under section 8. The defence argued that the plants had not been produced but only cultivated which was not an activity included in section 8.
>
> *Held*: the appeal would be dismissed. The 1977 amendment of the term "cannabis," included virtually the whole plant, and now equated production with its cultivation.

However, the so-called "magic mushroom" gives rise to special problems. The mushroom is not a controlled drug although the substance which subsists within it, psilocin, is a Class A drug. Therefore, merely to cultivate the mushroom cannot amount to cultivating the drug: see *Stevens* [1981] Crim.L.R. 568, *Cuncliffe* [1986] Crim.L.R. 547 and *Walker* [1987] Crim.L.R. 565, C.A.

6–08   The Misuse of Drugs Act 1971 also controls "preparations" containing a substance or product that is controlled by the Act. The meaning of "preparation" is discussed in Chapter 10, §10–04 and the reader is invited to read that section. Put shortly, it is submitted that "preparation" may amount to an act of production. At least four cases have decided that "preparation" involves a process or "the hand of man" for bringing a substance into a suitable state for consumption: see *Stevens, Cuncliffe, Walker* and now *Hodder v. D.P.P.* [1990] Crim.L.R. 261. In each case the appellant had been charged with simple possession which was no doubt sensible and appropriate in each case save, perhaps, in *Walker* where the appellant was found in possession of between 1,000 to 2,000 magic mushrooms.

> In *Hodder*, police searched premises occupied by H and another where they found bags of frozen magic mushrooms (containing psilocybin) in the freezer compartment of the refrigerator belonging to the defendants. The mushrooms had therefore been picked, packaged and frozen by the appellants.
>
> *Held*: (i) There was no evidence that freezing the mushrooms brought them into a suitable state to be consumed. They could not be used until defrosted. The act of freezing the mushrooms was not an act of "preparation," but:
>
> *Held*: (ii) the act of picking, packaging and freezing the mushrooms

was enough to bring them within the definition of "product" or "other product" in paragraph 5 of Schedule 2 to the Act and therefore the appeal would be dismissed.

The Court of Appeal, in *Hodder*, sought to place an ordinary and natural meaning to the word "product" as it appears in the Act but, with respect, it is submitted that "product," "produce" and "production" have a corresponding meaning which involve putting the substance into a form ready and intended to be used as a drug controlled by Schedule 2 to the Act. It is a startling result that a person who picks and immediately consumes 10 magic mushrooms would not be in possession of a controlled drug, but if—due to lack of appetite—he packs and/or freezes them for later consumption, he is then said to be in possession of a controlled "product." If the Court of Appeal is right, then is he also said to have committed an offence of unlawfully producing a Class A drug (or, more accurately, producing a product containing psilocybin) contrary to section 4(2) of the Act? 6–09

In *Russell* (1992) 94 Cr.App.R. 351 the appellant's car was stopped and searched. He was found in possession of equipment used by the appellant for converting cocaine hydrochloride (a salt) into free base cocaine. Coca leaf, cocaine and its salt are controlled as Class A drugs. It was conceded that the base and hydrochloride forms of cocaine are chemically different and have different properties. Paragraph 5 of Schedule 2 of the 1971 Act includes and "preparation or other product containing a substance or product" specified in that schedule. 6–10

Held: the conversion of one form of a Class A drug into another form of the same genus may be production. The conversion of the salt was production of a substance described in paragraph 5.

The Court of Appeal pointed out, correctly, that coca-leaf is also controlled as a Class A drug. It may be converted into a salt (hydrochloride). Such a conversion would amount to production: and see §15–13, *infra*.

The conversion of cocaine, from its salt form to base, involves adding an alkali (*e.g.* bicarbonate of soda) to a solution of the cocaine hydrochloride and water, which is then boiled. (Alternatively the salt may be moistened, the soda added and heated in a microwave oven.) Either method involves a process. It is not artificial to describe that process as an act of "production."

But for the decision in *Greensmith* [1983] 3 All E.R. 444 it might not have been necessary to have relied on paragraph 5, because some analysts would say that the reference to "cocaine" in paragraph 1 of Schedule 2 to the Act, is in fact a reference to base cocaine ("crack" when dried). Paragraph 4 includes cocaine as a salt. However, in *Greensmith* it was held that whether the drug is the coca-leaf, in its base form or a salt, it is still "cocaine" generically speaking for the purposes of paragraph 1 of Schedule 2. See §10–11 and Chapter 15.

II. LAWFUL PRODUCTION

Since many controlled drugs have a medicinal value, the policy of the M.D.A. and the Regulations is to restrict the category of persons who may 6–11 lawfully produce controlled drugs so that their activities may be closely monitored and regulated.

Accordingly, if the Secretary of State is of the opinion that it is in the public interest (*inter alia*) for the production, supply and possession of specified controlled drugs to be either totally unlawful, or unlawful except for research purposes, or except under licence, then he may, by Regulation, "designate" the drugs as being so affected: see section 7(4) of the M.D.A. 1971; and the Misuse of Drugs (Designation) Order 1986 (S.I. 1986 No. 2331) which, as from April 1, 1987, revoked earlier orders, namely S.I. 1977 No. 1379 and S.I. 1984 No. 1144.

The most important drugs which are thus subject to section 7(4) of the M.D.A. appear in Part I of the Schedule to the 1986 Order, and include:

Cannabinol	Coca-leaf
Cannabinol derivatives	LSD
Cannabis	Psilocin
Cannabis resin	Raw Opium

Thus, regulation 8(1)(*a*) of the M.D.Regs. permits a practitioner or pharmacist to manufacture or compound any drug specified in Schedule 2 or Schedule 5 of the M.D.Regs. providing that they act in their respective capacities. Thus, a pharmacist cannot "produce" a controlled drug merely to demonstrate to family and friends how drugs are made.

6–12   Again, by regulation 8(1)(*b*) a person who lawfully conducts a retail pharmacy business may manufacture or compound controlled drugs provided (i) that he acts in his capacity as such and (ii) that the production is carried on at the business premises of the registered pharmacy. A person "lawfully conducting a retail pharmacy business" means, by section 37(1) of the M.D.A., (and subject to subsection (5)) "a person lawfully conducting such a business in accordance with section 69 of the Medicines Act 1968";

Section 37(5) qualifies the above in the following terms:

"So long as sections 8 to 10 of the Pharmacy and Poisons Act 1933 remain in force, this Act in its application to Great Britain shall have effect as if for the definition of 'person lawfully conducting a retail pharmacy business' in subsection (1) above there were substituted—

'a person lawfully conducting a retail pharmacy business' means an authorised seller of poisons within the meaning of the Pharmacy and Poisons Act 1933; ..."

A similar concession is given to the aforementioned persons in respect of drugs listed in Schedule 3 and Schedule 4 of the M.D.Regs. see regulation 9(1)(*a*) and regulation 9(1)(*b*). Because the controlled drugs in Schedules 3 and 4 are considered by the Legislature to be less dangerous to use, a further exemption is given to persons who hold a written authority to produce controlled drugs. Such written authority is granted by the Secretary of State, subject to any conditions which he may provide: see regulation 9(1)(*c*).

6–13   A written authority is to be distinguished from a Licence to Produce which may be issued by the Secretary of State in respect of any controlled drug and subject to the terms and conditions attached to the licence: see regulation 5. However, where a person is authorised to produce drugs either by written authority or under licence, he will be obliged to keep a record of each quantity of drug produced by him: see regulation 22(1). Such a record must be preserved for a period of two years (regulation 23(2)).

In any event any producer of a Schedule 3 or 5 drug must keep every invoice (or similar record) in respect of any such drug which is either obtained by him for the purposes of that production or supplied by him: see regulation 24(1).

Clearly, it is important that the Secretary of State (or an authorised agent) is able to demand the production and inspection of records kept by a drug manufacturer. Such a power is afforded to him by regulation 25(1)(*a*).

For a multitude of reasons a person entitled to produce drugs under section 4(1)(*a*) may wish to destroy the end product, *e.g.* because they are not of the required standard or the stock is getting old. Nevertheless, to ensure that such controlled drugs do not fall into the wrong hands, Parliament has provided that drugs listed in Schedules 1 to 4 are destroyed only in the presence of an authorised person and in accordance with his directions: see regulation 26(1). The producer is obliged to keep a record of the date of destruction and the quantity of the drug destroyed: see regulation 26(3).

III. THE UNLAWFUL PRODUCTION OF CONTROLLED DRUGS

Although section 4(1)(*a*) of the Act imposes a general prohibition on the   **6–14** production of controlled drugs, it is section 4(2) which creates offences arising out of a contravention of subsection (1).

Thus section 4(2) provides:

"Subject to section 28 of this Act, it is an offence for a person—
> (*a*) to produce a controlled drug in contravention of subsection (1) above; or
> (*b*) to be concerned in the production of such a drug in contravention of that subsection by another."

In respect of both sections 4(2)(*a*) and (*b*) the prosecution must prove that the accused played some identifiable part in the production process.

> In *Farr* [1982] Crim.L.R. 745 F admitted to police that on one occasion A and C arrived at his house, asking to use his kitchen, which he allowed. He knew that A and C produced "pink heroin" there. F was charged with an offence under section 4(2). He had not been charged with an offence of allowing his premises to be used for the production of a drug under section 8.
> *Held*: F's conviction would be quashed. He took no identifiable role in the production although he would have had no answer to a charge under section 8.

It will be noted that section 8 of the M.D.A. prohibits an occupier to suffer   **6–15** or permit premises to be used for the purpose of producing a controlled drug.

Sections 4 and 8 are not mutually exclusive since the premises could be made available as part of the act of production, *e.g.* by a pre-arrangement that the premises would be so used. This had not occurred in *Farr*. Passive conduct would not in itself be enough. It may be said that giving encouragement is a sufficient participation in accordance with the usual principles of aiding and abetting the commission of an offence. The difficulty is that section 4(*b*) also makes it an offence to be "concerned" in the production of a controlled drug. This implies that, once again, some identifiable part in the production of the drug, is required and that accordingly, there is no room for the application of the principles of aiding and abetting: see *Carmichael & Sons (Worcester) Ltd.* v. *Cottle* [1971] R.T.R. 11 and *cf. Blake* (1979) 68 Cr.App.R. 1.

The word "concerned" in section 4(2)(*b*) is not qualified by the word "knowingly" for the simple reason that section 4(2)(*b*) is subject to section 28. The burden will therefore be on an accused to show that he did not believe, or suspect or have any reason to suspect that what was actually being produced was a controlled drug (section 28(3)(*b*)(i)); or that he did not know, or suspect or have reason to suspect that what he was in fact concerned in was a production venture (section 28(2)).

C. THE CULTIVATION OF CANNABIS

6–16   Although the word "produce" for the purposes of section 4(1)(*a*) includes "cultivation" (see: section 37(1)), it is the drug which is to be cultivated and not simply the plant in which the drug naturally subsists unless that plant is it-self listed as a controlled drug in the Schedules to the M.D.A. Thus, growing the magic mushroom is not an offence merely because a controlled drug (psi-locin) naturally subsists within that plant. On the other hand, the entire cannabis plant is a controlled drug. Originally, only the flowering and fruiting tops of the plant were controlled by the M.D.A. in 1971, and hence the prob-able reason why section 6 was enacted. But today there is no good reason why the cultivation of a cannabis plant should not be an offence under section 4(1)(*a*) (production) and section 6. It follows that an occupier, or manager of premises, who permits or suffers the "production" of cannabis will be guilty of an offence under section 8: see *Taylor* v. *Chief Constable of Kent* [1981] 1 W.L.R. 606, the facts of which are given at §6–07, *supra*. Both offences are subject to section 28.

Section 6 provides:

"(1) Subject to any regulation under section 7 of this Act for the time being in force, it shall not be lawful for a person to cultivate any plant of the genus *Cannabis*.

(2) Subject to section 28 of this Act, it is an offence to cultivate any such plant in contravention of subsection (1) above."

The exception to section 6(1) is, in the case of plants cultivated under a li-cence issued by the Secretary of State, and subject to his terms and conditions endorsed on the licence: see regulation 12 of the M.D.Regs. The principal reason for this exemption is to facilitate research into the drug.

An offence under section 6(2) is made out once the prosecution has proved,   **6–17**
first, that the accused was cultivating a plant, and, secondly, that the plant
was in fact a cannabis plant. It is not necessary for the prosecution to prove
that the accused knew that what was being cultivated was in fact a cannabis
plant. Thus, in *Champ* (1981) 73 Cr.App.R. 367:

> C was a herbalist who cultivated a plant in a window box. She believed
> the plant to be hemp which, according to an elderly gypsy, was good for
> various ailments. The plant was actually cannabis.
>
> *Held*: the burden was on C to prove, under section 28, that she did not
> know the plant to be cannabis.

[See Chapter 7.]

Champ has the curious feature that the defendant believed the plant to be
hemp: but hemp is another term for cannabis. However, the point does not
seem to have been taken either by counsel or by the court.

An offence under section 6 is not absolute since it is expressed to be subject
to section 28.

D. DRUG ACTIVITIES ON PREMISES

Policing and enforcing the prohibitions imposed by the M.D.A. on the pro-   **6–18**
duction, supply and use of controlled drugs is an expensive and difficult task,
particularly since many offences are likely to be committed on premises
which are owned, occupied or managed by persons who may not themselves
be concerned in the commission of the offences. They may be absent at the
material time. Nevertheless, it was clearly Parliament's hope that obligations
imposed on occupiers and managers not to permit, or suffer, a limited range
of activities to take place on their premises, would encourage them to "police" the Act. Thus, by section 8:

> "A person commits an offence if, being the occupier or concerned in the
> management of any premises, he knowingly permits or suffers any of the
> following activities to take place on those premises, that is to say—
>> (*a*) producing or attempting to produce a controlled drug in contra-
>>   vention of section 4(1) of this Act;
>> (*b*) supplying or attempting to supply a controlled drug to another in
>>   contravention of section 4(1) of this Act, or offering to supply a
>>   controlled drug to another in contravention of section 4(1);
>> (*c*) preparing opium for smoking;
>> (*d*) smoking cannabis, cannabis resin or prepared opium."

As a piece of Parliamentary drafting, section 8 represents a quite extraordi-   **6–19**
nary example, peppered, as it is, with a host of obvious anomalies. Thus, an
occupier is forbidden to permit the smoking of cannabis or prepared opium to
take place on his premises, but not the smoking or injecting of heroin, the
snorting of cocaine, the cooking of a "cannabis cake," or the preparation of

LSD tablets to take place. Given that such drug practices must have been well known to the Legislature in 1971, the wording of section 8 is all the more astonishing. Moreover, Parliament made no attempt to define several key words and phrases which would obviously require guidance. Thus, the terms "occupier" and persons "concerned in the management of premises" are not defined by the Act. A Report by Justice, *Drugs and the Law* (June 1991), recommended that the law be changed to embrace premises that are used for the "ingesting of any controlled drug" (para. 7.8) and that the definition of "premises" be clarified (para. 7.9).

I. PREMISES

6–20   Defining "premises" for the purpose of the M.D.A. is not straightforward. Unfortunately, the draftsmen failed on this occasion to provide a "clarifying definition"—a device to state expressly that certain matters are to be treated as coming within a definition.

In tort, we find that the word "premises" has been broadly construed to include real property; appliances and objects upon it, *e.g.* ships in dry dock (*London Graving Dock* v. *Horton* [1951] A.C. 737); and also includes movables not in transit such as ships (see *Duncan* v. *Cammell Laird & Co* [1946] A.C. 401); aircraft (see *Fosbroke-Hobbes* v. *Airwork Ltd.* [1937] 1 All E.R. 108); or permanently moored house-boats (see *West Mersea Urban District Council* v. *Fraser* [1950] 2 K.B. 119). If these authorities can be relied upon as being definitive of the word "premises" for the purposes of section 8 then some curious results follow. Thus, on one view of the authorities it might be argued that the owner of a river cruiser, knowing that cannabis is being smoked on board while the vessel is in motion, will not be guilty of an offence contrary to section 8(*d*). However, in *Darby* (unreported, 1989; Southwark Crown Court) His Honour Judge Rivlin Q.C., ruled that a pleasure vessel cruising on the river Thames was "premises" within the meaning of section 8. The learned judge derived some support for his conclusions from the decisions of *Andrews* v. *Andrews and Mears* [1908] 2 K.B. 567 and *Gardiner* v. *Sevenoaks Rural District Council* [1950] 2 All E.R.84. There is no logical reason for excluding movables from the scope of this section providing, of course, that the offence is committed within the jurisdiction of the courts.

6–21   There is abundant authority for the proposition that buildings (whether subject to a lease or not) are "premises," but mere land without structures upon it probably falls outside the definition of "premises": see *Bracey* v. *Read* [1963] Ch. 88. In *Brown* (unreported, 1991; Snaresbrook Crown Court) an "acid house" party was organised at which it was alleged controlled drugs were consumed. The party was held within a marquee. Unhappily, the trial judge was not required to decide whether the marquee temporarily erected on land was "premises," but it is submitted that it is: see *Norton* v. *Knowles* (1969) 1 Q.B. 572; *Metropolitan Water Board* v. *Paine* (1907) 1 K.B. 285; *Field Place Caravan Park* v. *Harding* [1966] 2 Q.B. 484.

II. WHO IS RESPONSIBLE?

Responsibility is clearly based on occupancy or control and not merely on **6–22**
ownership. Section 8 is expressly aimed at the occupiers or the managers of
premises since it is they who may exercise immediate supervision over the activities carried on within them. As the Court of Appeal pointed out in *Tao*
[1977] Q.B. 141 the fact that the term "occupier" was not defined in the Act
suggests that the intention of the Legislature was to leave it to the tribunal of
fact to decide whether an accused exercised "sufficient exclusivity of possession so that he can fairly be said to be 'the occupier' "; (*per* Roskill L.J.).

The court held that a common sense rather than a legalistic meaning should
be given to the term "occupier" so that a person who was in a position to
exercise a sufficient degree of control to exclude, say, a cannabis smoker was
an occupier for the purposes of section 8.

> In *Tao*, the accused, an undergraduate, occupied a room allocated to him
> by his college. He lived there and held the key to the room. Police found
> traces of cannabis resin and they smelt burning cannabis.
> *Held*: T had sufficient exclusivity of possession to be an occupier for
> the purposes of section 8 of the M.D.A.

The argument advanced by the appellant was that a distinction had to be
drawn between "an occupier" and "being in occupation."

There is force in this argument. A number of persons may decide to occupy **6–23**
premises as "squatters." They are certainly in occupation but scarcely enjoy a
legal exclusivity of possession. Can they therefore properly be said to be
"occupiers"? Support for the argument was found in *Mogford* (1970) 63
Cr.App.R. 168, which was then concerned with the word "occupier" as it
appeared in section 5 of the Dangerous Drugs Act 1965. On that occasion,
Neild J. held that it must be shown that an accused was in "legal possession"
of the premises. He said (at 169):

> "... the word 'occupier' is not defined in this enactment ... it is a penal
> statute ... the provisions must be construed strictly and favourably to
> accused persons ... it seems quite impossible to say here that the word
> 'occupier' must mean 'owner' ... the word 'occupier' is used in this Act
> in its advisory sense ... in a context which shows clearly that the person
> ... is in legal occupation and in control of premises."

Accordingly, where two sisters, aged 20 and 15 years, allowed cannabis to
be smoked in their parents house (while their parents were away on holiday),
they were not to be regarded as occupiers since they were not in legal possession of the house and therefore, they committed no offence under section 5
of the 1965 Act.

In *Tao*, however, the Court of Appeal approved the result in *Mogford*, the **6–24**
court did not approve of the reasoning. It was not entirely clear what Neild J.,
in *Mogford*, meant by "legal possession," given that an individual can be in
legal possession of premises without being a tenant or having any estate in
land; (see: *Errington* v. *Errington* [1952] 1 K.B. 290 and *cf. Heslop* v. *Burns*
[1974] 1 W.L.R. 1241). Furthermore, it is not entirely clear from the report

what the facts in *Mogford* really were. It may be that a jury would not have been able to say exactly what the nature of the possession was, so as to amount to occupation of those premises—a matter which evidently troubled the court in *Campbell* [1982] Crim.L.R. 595. But, it is submitted that it is not necessary to embark on an enquiry to determine the exact nature of the proprietary rights (if any) of an accused. For the purposes of section 8, it is sufficient if the prosecution can show that the accused demonstrably exercised control, or had the authority of another, to exclude persons from premises or to prohibit any of the activities referred to in section 8. On the facts of *Tao* it was held to be enough that the accused had a contractual licence to use the room. He may not have been able to exclude college staff from entering his room but he could exclude cannabis smokers or, for that matter, any smoker. In other words he was in a position to exercise control over the activities that took place there.

6–25   Both *Tao* and *Mogford* were considered by His Honour Judge Oddie in *Campbell* [1981] Crim.L.R. 595:

> S lived at his mother's address. With her approval, but in her absence, S held a party at the address. G, who lived elsewhere, attended. Following a police raid at the party, G and S were arrested and both accepted responsibility for the cannabis smoking by other guests at the party.
>
> *Held*: the facts were undistinguishable from *Mogford* and accordingly, G and S were not "occupiers" for the purposes of section 8.

The decision is of interest for several reasons but only a brief report of the case is available. As reported, the court explained *Mogford* in the following terms:

> "Not every transient use of premises or physical ability to remove another from the premises would enable the court or jury to find the nature, extent and degree of possession sufficient for finding that the person was the occupier of premises . . . ."

6–26   The court went on to point out that, in *Campbell*, the parents remained occupiers but had delegated to G and S the task of permitting the guests a licence to enter the premises for the purposes of the party while their parents were away overnight. For those reasons G and S were not occupiers. However, on its facts, *Campbell* poses a problem. S arranged the party, he organised it, he decided who should be invited and, no doubt, decided who should remain. In short, he was in control. In *Mogford*, Neild J. observed that:

> "Upon the second aspect of the test, namely, control, it was no doubt open to these daughters to invite guests and indeed to exclude persons from their parents house in the absence of those parents but . . . that does [not] amount to the nature and measure of control which is envisaged in the present statute."

Although the court in *Campbell* felt that the facts were indistinguishable from *Mogford*, in fact, the position in *Mogford* was very different—an aspect which it is now necessary to examine.

The section then being considered was section 5 of the Dangerous Drugs   6–27
Act 1965 which made it an offence to permit premises "to be used for the purpose of smoking cannabis." [Note the words "for the purpose of."] By contrast, section 8 refers to permitting the activity to take place "on those
premises." Neild J. explained section 5 of the 1965 Act when he said that the
words of that section "denote a purpose which is or has become a significant
one or a recognised one though certainly not necessarily the only one."

Examples were given in *Mogford* of the bowling alley or a hairdressing
salon or a cafe. Thus, for the purposes of the 1965 Act, "control" meant control over premises used for a primary purpose. But in the 1971 Act, section 8
is drafted so as to include a temporary use of the premises for any of the activities referred to in that section.

Accordingly, the decision of *Campbell* should be viewed with caution. It is
submitted that *Tao* establishes the correct test for the purposes of section 8 of
the 1971 Act.

(a) Liability of one occupier for the acts of a co-occupier

A co-occupier who permits or suffers another co-occupier to do any of the   6–28
activities referred to in section 8 commits an offence under that section as if
the co-occupier had invited a friend to the premises and permitted him to perform the prohibited activity: *Ashdown* (1974) 59 Cr.App.R. 193.

In that case, four defendants were charged with an offence under section 5
of the Dangerous Drugs Act 1965 in the following terms, that "being the
occupiers of premises," they "permitted those premises to be used for the purpose of smoking cannabis resin." All four defendants were co-tenants having
jointly entered into a tenancy agreement. It was argued that it was not possible in law for one co-tenant knowingly to permit another co-tenant to smoke
cannabis on the premises. The Court of Appeal held the argument to be fallacious. Roskill L.J. said (at 194):

> "The important point is that the essence of the offence is knowingly per-
> mitting that activity to be carried on . . . why is there any privilege or im-
> munity attaching to his position of co-tenant which would prevent him
> being guilty of an offence against what was section 5 of the 1965 Act
> merely because he happens to be one co-tenant and the offender who is in
> possession of the cannabis which he is unlawfully smoking is another co-
> tenant?"

III. PERSONS IN UNLAWFUL POSSESSION OF PREMISES

In *Tao* [1977] Q.B. 141 the court held that the person charged must be   6–29
proved to have had, "whether lawfully or otherwise," sufficient exclusivity of
possession of the premises to be an "occupier." There is no authority, specifically on the point, as to whether or not trespassers may nevertheless be "occupiers" for the purposes of section 8. In *Mogford*, and *Tao*, the court was
concerned with lawful possession or occupation. Indeed, in *Tao*, the court
went so far as to classify T's right to possession on the basis that he was a

"contractual licensee," although Roskill L.J. commented that it would be "somewhat astonishing" if a squatter could not be an "occupier" under the Act. The matter is not free from difficulty but there exists no logical reason why "occupier" should be glossed to mean only a person in lawful possession of premises. One must also have regard to the mischief which the Act seeks to prevent and, as the court in *Tao* remarked, the concept of occupation and possession should not be construed too legalistically.

IV. PERSONS CONCERNED IN THE MANAGEMENT OF PREMISES

6–30   "Management" imports the notion of control over the running of the affairs of an enterprise, venture or business. If a person therefore controls premises by running, organising or planning them then he will be "managing" them: see *Josephs* (1977) 65 Cr.App.R. 253. In order to be concerned in the management, it is enough to share, or assist in, the running of the premises. But there must be something more than the performance of purely menial or routine duties, see *Abbott* v. *Smith* [1965] 2 Q.B. 622. Thus, the cleaner of a nightclub would not be assisting in the management of that club even if he knew that the reason for its existence was primarily the smoking of cannabis.

Although many occupiers may also be concerned in the management of premises the converse need not necessarily follow. Indeed, there is no reason why a manager should have any proprietary interest in the premises at all. Thus, in *Josephs* (*supra*) the appellants were squatters on premises but nevertheless ran a "card school" in the basement. They were convicted of being concerned in the management of premises upon which they knowingly permitted the supplying of cannabis, contrary to section 8. Their appeal against conviction was dismissed. They were managing premises and the fact that they were trespassers was irrelevant.

(a) Knowingly

6–31   In *Thomas* (1976) 63 Cr.App.R. 65 the court was asked to consider whether the word "knowingly" in section 8 added anything to the section. The court held that it did not: the words "permitting" and "suffering" clearly implied knowledge of the relevant activity.

The point referred to in *Thomas* is hardly novel given the abundance of authority that exists in respect of similar phrases as they appear in other statutes [see: *Gray's Haulage Co. Ltd.* v. *Arnold* [1966] 1 W.L.R. 534; *Taylor's Central Garages (Exeter) Ltd.* v. *Roper* (1951) 2 W.N. 383; *Lucas* v. *Peek* [1947] 2 All E.R. 574].

In *Gray's Haulage* Lord Parker C.J. said:

"... knowledge is really of two kinds; actual knowledge and knowledge which arises either from shutting one's eyes to the obvious, or what is much the same thing put in another way, failing to do something or doing something not caring whether contravention takes place or not."

The next question is whether proof of knowledge necessarily implies permission or sufferance in respect of that activity.

In *Gray's Haulage*, Lord Parker C.J. said:

> "Knowledge is not imputed by mere negligence but by something more than negligence, something which one can describe as reckless ... not caring what happens."

The Court of Appeal in *Thomas* (*supra*) went a little further, observing that knowledge was not to be implied "from neglect to make such inquiries as a reasonable and prudent person would make, which, generally speaking, has no place in the criminal law."

It is therefore important to note that section 8 does not impose on occupiers 6–32 and persons concerned in the management of premises any duty to exercise vigilance to prevent the activities listed in section 8. This is particularly important in respect of persons who do not, for example, live on the premises. They are not required to investigate the affairs of persons using their premises. However, shutting one's eyes to the truth is a very different matter.

> In *Thomas* (*supra*), police found cannabis and cannabis smoking equipment at T's home. T said that it belonged to a friend saying, "I have asked him not to smoke in my house but what can you do?"
> *Held*: that the jury were properly directed. Knowledge may include shutting one's eyes to the obvious. The appellant did little to prevent cannabis being smoked on his premises.

A very different conclusion was reached in *Souter* [1971] 1 W.L.R. 1187:

> S let rooms in his house to drug addicts, retaining the living room for his own occupation. He put a notice on the door of that room to the effect that the police would be called immediately if illegal drugs were found on the premises. On several occasions S had turned away illegal drug users from his premises. There was evidence that cannabis had been unlawfully smoked on the premises.
> *Held*: S could do no more to stop the unlawful smoking (Court of Appeal).

Every case must, of course, be decided on its own facts.

(b) "Permits or suffers"

In *Thomas* it was said that the trial judge was right to direct the jury to dis- 6–33 regard the alternative phrase, namely, "or suffers" because " 'permits' and 'suffers' mean the same thing." In most cases there is no need to draw a distinction, but there is in fact a difference which is highlighted by the words of Lord Parker C.J. in *Gray's Haulage*. Thus, "to suffer" an activity involves a failure to act but knowing what is taking place. To "permit" an activity is to do something but not caring whether contravention takes place or not. The distinction is admittedly a fine one but it is safer not to regard these phrases as being synonymous.

It may be asked why the word "knowingly" should be added by the Legislature in the light of the decision of *Sweet* v. *Parsley* (1969) 53 Cr.App.R. 221. The answer can only be that the draftsman considered the addition necessary to make it plain that (*a*) *mens rea* is required to be proved by the Crown, and (*b*) constructive knowledge is not enough. In *Sweet* v. *Parsley* the House of Lords considered whether section 5 of the Dangerous Drugs Act 1965 created an absolute offence given that the word "knowingly" did not appear in the section which made it an offence for a person to permit premises to be used for the smoking of cannabis. Their Lordships held that *mens rea* was implied by the use of the word "permits" (and see *Yeandel* v. *Fisher* [1966] 1 Q.B. 440).

Section 8 of the M.D.A. is worded differently to section 5 of the Dangerous Drugs Act 1965 and it is not made subject to section 28. Accordingly, the draftsman was making it plain that nevertheless *mens rea* is required.

E. PROHIBITING OPIUM SMOKING

6–34   Section 9(1), provides, *inter alia*:

"Subject to section 28 of this Act, it is an offence for a person—
  (*a*) to smoke or otherwise use prepared opium; or
  (*b*) to frequent a place used for the purpose of opium smoking; or
  (*c*) to have in his possession [certain equipment for use in connection with opium smoking]."

[Prepared opium is defined by section 37(1) to mean prepared for smoking and includes the dross and other residues after opium has been smoked.]

Section 9(2) is considered separately in the next chapter concerning the provision of drug kits as a result of the addition of section 9A of the M.D.A. as enacted by the D.T.O.A. 1986.

The section is largely self-explanatory. The words "otherwise use" in subsection (*a*) must, it is submitted, refer to other methods of consumption. If the allegation is that opium was being sold by an accused then the proper charge is one alleging the supplying of the drug, *e.g.* under section 4(1)(*b*) or a kindred offence.

Opium "dens" have a notorious history. Subsection (*b*) is intended to attack their survival by prohibiting opium smokers frequenting such premises. The prosecution must prove that the main use or recognised purpose of the premises is for smoking opium although, of course, that need not be its only one (see *Mogford* [1970] 1 W.L.R. 988).

The courts have not been asked to define the word "frequent" for the purpose of section 9.

6–35   As a matter of natural construction, the word "frequent," in this context, implies a regular course of conduct or, at least, conduct that is repeated more than once. In *Airton* v. *Scott* (1909) 25 T.L.R. 250, the appellant had attended an athletics ground for the purpose of betting. Lord Alverstone C.J.

observed at p.250 that: "As to the word 'frequent,' it was plain that being long enough on the premises to effect the particular object aimed at was 'frequenting'."

However, in *Clark* v. *The Queen* (1884) 14 Q.B.D. 92 it was held that merely being in a public place does not amount to "frequenting" and in *Rawlings* v. *Smith* [1938] 1 K.B. 675, it was held that frequenting involved "the notion of something which to some degree . . . is continuous or repeated" (*per* Lord Hewart C.J.). Both *Clark* and *Rawlings* were applied in *Nakhla* v. *The Queen* [1976] A.C. 1, a decision of the Privy Council. Lord Morris of Borthy-Gest considered that "frequents" must be considered in its context which may require an enquiry as to the reason why a person is at the premises, the nature of the place, the time spent on the premises, his movements and continuing or recurrent activities.

It is submitted that a similar approach is likely to be adopted if the issue ever arose in section 9.

F. DRUG KITS AND ARTICLES FOR USE IN DRUG MISUSE

I. Articles for Opium Smoking

Section 9 of the M.D.A. is directed entirely to prohibiting the possession of   6–36
opium smoking equipment. Section 9 reads:

"Subject to section 28 of this Act, it is an offence for a person—
(*a*) to smoke or otherwise use prepared opium; or
(*b*) to frequent a place used for the purpose of opium smoking; or
(*c*) to have in his possession—
    (i) any pipes or other utensils made or adapted for use in connection with the smoking of opium, being pipes or utensils which have been used by him or with his knowledge and permission in that connection or which he intends to use or permit others to use in that connection; or
    (ii) any utensils which have been used by him or with his knowledge and permission in connection with the preparation of opium smoking."

Opium addiction, notably in the Far East, spans a period of history that is   6–37
both well-known and well recorded. It is therefore not at all surprising to discover that Parliament, for decades, has forbidden opium smoking in the United Kingdom and has sought to punish those who are in possession of opium smoking equipment. Section 9 of the M.D.A. reflects that established policy. Broadly speaking, section 9(*c*)(i) makes it an offence to possess equipment used in connection with the *smoking* of opium, while section 9(*c*)(ii) is targeted against those persons who possess articles used in connection with the *preparation* of opium for smoking. It will therefore now be obvious that the ambit of section 9 is incredibly narrow and presents more interest in terms of what is glaringly omitted than what is actually included. Thus, Parliament

has made no provision for the possession of equipment used in connection with opium taken other than by smoking. Furthermore, it is not an offence to possess articles used in the preparation or administration of other controlled drugs, *e.g.* hubble-bubble pipes used for smoking cannabis. Such omissions are all the more remarkable when it is remembered that the M.D.A. was passed to combat a rising tide of drug abuse which then, and now, involves the misuse of many dangerous substances. Indeed, opium smoking now represents a very small part of the overall drug problem. Moreover, Parliament has not sought to broaden section 9. In the wake of public concern at the number of so-called "drug kits" hitting the market, Parliament inserted section 9A into the M.D.A. in order to prohibit their sale: see section 34A of the Drug Trafficking Offences Act 1986. But, section 9A is only concerned with the supply of articles used to unlawfully *administer* controlled drugs and makes no corresponding provision for being *in possession* of articles supplied in contravention of that section.

(a) Section 9(*c*)(i)

6–38   Section 9(*c*)(i) applies to "pipes or other utensils." It is not clear whether "pipes" includes any conduit used in connection with opium smoking or whether it is restricted to the complete smoking apparatus including the bowl. If the latter interpretation is to be preferred, then although various parts of the smoking apparatus such as the mouthpiece or the connecting tube would fall outside the definition of a "pipe," they may come within the word "utensils."

It is clear from section 9 that the words "pipes or other utensils" are qualified by the words "made or adapted for use in connection with the smoking of opium." A typical tobacco pipe could not be said to be "*made*" for opium smoking but can it be said to be "adapted for use," if it is in fact used for that purpose? Certainly, one would normally say that the word "adapt" imparts the requirement of change, adjustment or alteration, *e.g.* to the original article. Merely to adapt an article for a different purpose would not be sufficient. But section 9(*c*)(i) refers to "pipes or utensils which have been used by him or which he intends to use in that connection."

There is therefore force in the view that those words embrace the adoption of a normally innocent piece of equipment, *e.g.* a tobacco pipe which has been used for the purposes of opium smoking.

Once it has been proved that the article is a "pipe" or "utensil" made or adapted for opium smoking, the prosecution must then prove that the article:

(1) was so used by the accused; *or*
(2) was so used with his knowledge *and* with his permission; *or*
(3) was *intended* to be so used by the accused, or (with his permission) by others.

Accordingly, it is not enough that an accused knew that a pipe had been used by another. It must be proved that the accused went further and gave his permission for the article to be used in connection with opium smoking.

(b) Section 9(*c*)(ii)

It is not necessary for the prosecution to prove that the utensils have been **6–39** made or adapted for use in connection with the preparation of opium for smoking. Any article which has been used in that regard will come within section 9(*c*)(ii). However, articles merely intended by the accused to be so used fall outside the section.

Again, if the utensils have been used by a person other than the accused, the prosecution must prove that the accused knew of that other person's use of those items and that he permitted him to use them. Permission may be granted expressly or by implication, *e.g.* conduct.

II. Drug Administration Kits Generally

Not very long ago the appearance of so-called "drug-kits" on the legitimate **6–40** consumer market became prevalent. Some kits were elaborate and did little to hide the fact that they would be of particular interest to drug users but of limited interest to anyone else. Thus, pouches containing a small mirror, a knife, a fairly broad tube, matches, etc., were handy "kits" for the purpose of snorting cocaine or heroin. Other kits were far less elaborate and, indeed, many of the items sold could not even be described as "kits," *e.g.* the sale of a mirror and a packet of wide straws. To the ordinary bystander the sale looked innocent enough but, to the retailer, it may have been apparent that he was selling articles to a drug user whom he believed would use them for that purpose.

To meet this situation, Parliament, by section 34A of the D.T.O.A., **6–41** inserted section 9A into the M.D.A. which provides:

"(1) A person who supplies or offers to supply any article which may be used or adapted to be used (whether by itself or in combination with another article or other articles) in the administration by any person of a controlled drug to himself or another, believing that the article (or the article as adapted) is to be so used in circumstances where the administration is unlawful, is guilty of an offence.

(2) It is not an offence under subsection (1) above to supply or offer to supply a hypodermic syringe, or any part of one.

(3) A person who supplies or offers to supply any article which may be used to prepare a controlled drug for administration by any person to himself or another believing that the article is to be so used in circumstances where the administration is unlawful is guilty of an offence.

(4) For the purposes of this section, any administration of a controlled drug is unlawful except—

　(*a*) the administration by any person of a controlled drug to another in circumstances where the administration of the drug is not unlawful under section 4(1) of this Act, or

　(*b*) the administration by any person of a controlled drug to himself in circumstances where having the controlled drug in his possession is not unlawful under section 5(1) of this Act.

(5) In this section, references to administration by any person of a

controlled drug to himself include a reference to his administering it to himself with the assistance of another."

(a) Section 9A(1)

6-42   It should be made clear at this stage that section 9A is not concerned with kits sold to abusers of solvents. That matter is dealt with by the Intoxicating Substances (Supply) Act 1985. Section 9A of the M.D.A. is solely concerned with kits supplied in connection with the administration of controlled drugs: solvents are not controlled under the M.D.A.

Section 9A(1) is very widely drawn. Unlike section 9 which refers to "utensils," section 9A(1) applies to any article which "may be used" or which may be "adapted to be used" in the administration of a controlled drug. In other words *any* article that has the capability of being used by another to abuse any controlled drug falls within this subsection. Parliament has been careful not to prohibit merely the supply of a *collection* of articles which may be termed a "kit." Thus, even if only one article is supplied, which by itself could not be used to facilitate drug abuse but which, if combined with other articles, could be so used, then it falls within section 9A(1).

It is not necessary for the prosecution to prove that the article has been sold or supplied for any consideration or to prove that the article was supplied to a person who himself intended to use that article for drug abuse. It is enough that the supplier (or the offeror) *believes* that the article is to be used (not "*may* be used") "in circumstances where the administration is unlawful. ...."

(i) *Mens rea under section 9A(1)*

6-43   Merely to *suspect* that the supplier would use the article for the unlawful administration of a controlled drug is not enough. However, the prosecution need prove no more than that the accused *believed* that the article would be so used "in circumstances where the administration is unlawful."

But what is the position if the supplier's belief is, in fact, erroneous? It is submitted that his mistake affords him no defence. His belief is all-important particularly since section 9A(1) prohibits the supplying of (or an offer to supply) of any article which *may* be used or adapted to be used in the administration of a controlled drug. Presumably an accused's belief must be reasonably held having regard to all the circumstances of the case, but it is not clear whether his belief is to be judged subjectively or objectively. Presumably the test is subjective. Section 28 is not expressed to have any application. Therefore, a perfectly innocent mirror which is sold in the belief that it will be used in connection with the unlawful snorting of heroin or cocaine is an offence contrary to section 9A(1). Of course, some harsh results will flow if a mistaken belief affords the supplier of an article with no defence in circumstances where the recipient never actually intended to use the mirror for anything other than a perfectly lawful purpose. Suppose X supplies a box of wide straws, to Y knowing that Y regularly snorts cocaine using straws and believes that all or some of the straws will be so used. In fact Y never intended any such thing but planned to use them for milk-shake consumption at a children's party. On a strict interpretation of section 9A(1), X is damned by his own mistaken belief.

Again, suppose Y (weeks later) does in fact use one of the remaining straws   6–44
to snort cocaine. Is X's fate sealed? It is important that X has more than just a
suspicion that the straws will be used for the administration of controlled
drugs. However, nothing in section 9A prevents the supply or the offer to supply any article for use in connection with the administration of a controlled
drug if the drug may be lawfully administered to another by the recipient or
may be possessed by him for self-administration: see section 9A(4).

The maximum sentence is six months' imprisonment and/or a financial
penalty on level five.

(b) Section 9A(2)

It may seem surprising that hypodermic syringes are excluded from sub-   6–45
section (1). As a matter of logic, no doubt they ought to have been included,
but as a matter of policy one can see reasons why they are not. First, there is
the quite considerable problem of regulating the distribution of such syringes
if they were to be included. Secondly, it is now well known that serious disease can be readily spread by the use of contaminated needles. The distribution of clean needles and syringes—even from dubious sources—may have
been considered by the Legislature as being the lesser of two evils.

(c) Section 9A(3)

Not unlike section 9(*c*)(ii) of the M.D.A., section 9A(3) is concerned to pro-   6–46
hibit the supply, or an offer to supply, any article which may be used to *pre-*
pare any controlled drug for administration. Again, like section 9, it is not
necessary for the prosecution to prove that the article had been "adapted" for
use in the preparation of a controlled drug.

Chapter 7
Section 28 of the Misuse of Drugs Act 1971

A. SECTION 28

7–01   This section provides a number of statutory defences as follows:

"(1) This section applies to offences under any of the following provisions of this Act, that is to say section 4(2) and (3), section 5(2) and (3), section 6(2) and section 9.

(2) Subject to subsection (3) below, in any proceedings for an offence to which this section applies it shall be a defence for the accused to prove that he neither knew of nor suspected nor had reason to suspect the existence of some fact alleged by the prosecution which it is necessary for the prosecution to prove if he is to be convicted of the offence charged.

(3) Where in any proceedings for an offence to which this section applies it is necessary, if the accused is to be convicted of the offence charged, for the prosecution to prove that some substance or product involved in the alleged offence was the controlled drug which the prosecution alleges it to have been, and it is proved that the substance or product in question was that controlled drug, the accused—

(a) shall not be acquitted of the offence charged by reason only of proving that he neither knew nor suspected nor had reason to suspect that the substance or product in question was the particular controlled drug alleged; but

(b) shall be acquitted thereof—

(i)   if he proves that he neither believed nor suspected nor had reason to suspect that the substance or product in question was a controlled drug; or

(ii) if he proves that he believed the substance or product in question to be a controlled drug, or a controlled drug of a description, such that, if it had in fact been that controlled drug or a controlled drug of that description, he would not at the material time have been committing any offence to which this section applies.

(4) Nothing in this section shall prejudice any defence which it is open to a person charged with an offence to which this section applies to raise apart

from this section."

Without section 28, the offences to which this section relate, would lead to   **7–02**
some very harsh results. Thus section 6(2) (cultivation of cannabis) would
arguably be an absolute offence. The decision in *Warner* v. *Metropolitan
Police Commissioner* [1969] 2 A.C. 256 produced an unhappy compromise
between absolute liability and *mens rea* in cases of the alleged possession of
prohibited drugs. Indeed, section 28 reflects many of the sentiments
expressed by Lord Pearce in *Warner* and the reader is invited to read the
speech of Lord Pearce in its entirety. However, section 28(4) makes it plain
that nothing in this provision was intended to alter the earlier law but merely
runs parallel to established principles. Furthermore, drug importations or
exportations contrary to section 3(1) are not subject to this provision, perhaps for the reasons expressed by Lord Bridge in *Shivpuri* [1987] A.C. 1.
Similarly, section 28 has no application in respect of a charge of conspiracy:
McGowan, The Times, January 27, 1990.

B. SECTION 28(2)

In respect of each charge to which section 28 applies, the prosecution is   **7–03**
required to prove the existence of certain factual ingredients. Thus, for an
offence under section 6(2), the prosecution is required to prove that the
accused (i) cultivated a plant and (ii) that the plant cultivated was of the genus
Cannabis. However, by section 28(2), it is a defence for the accused to prove
that he did not know that a plant was being cultivated or, even if he did, that
he did not know that the plant was a cannabis plant.

It is sometimes said that there exists a difficulty in understanding the re-   **7–04**
lationship between subsections (2) and (3). The wording is certainly confus-
ing and an overlap undoubtedly exists. Thus if X did not know that the plant
was of the genus *Cannabis*, then he has a defence under section 28(3)(*b*)(i) as
well as section 28(2).

> In *Champ* (1981) 73 Cr.App.R. 367, C had a window box which con-
> tained a cannabis plant. Her defence to a charge under section 6(2) was
> that she thought the plant was "hemp" which she believed was good for
> alleviating ailments. The trial judge ruled that the burden was on C to
> prove that she did not know the plant was cannabis.
>   *Held*: the judge's ruling was correct. Section 28(2) was subject to sub-
> section (3) " which is not relevant in this case" but subsection (2) placed
> the burden of proof on C.

The decision, when examined, highlights the confusion that can arise. It is
not clear why the court thought that subsection (3) was not relevant, since
one complaint made by the appellant was that the judge ruled that the burden
of proof was on her that she did not know that the plant was cannabis by virtue of that very subsection. Another complaint was that the trial judge was
wrong to rule that section 28(2) had no application to a charge under section
6(2): yet the court held that the judge directed the jury correctly. Clearly, the

burden of proof was on the appellant by reason of subsection (2) and/or (3)(*b*)(i). In any event her defence was extraordinarily thin since "hemp" is regarded as another term for cannabis.

7–05   The point to note is that subsection (2) is subject to subsection (3) but only in so far as subsection (3) is concerned with knowledge of the "substance or product." To that limited extent there is an overlap between them. Suppose an accused (X) is charged with frequenting premises used for the purposes of smoking opium (section 9(*b*)). The prosecution must prove (*a*) that the premises were being used for smoking; (*b*) that opium was being smoked on those premises; and (*c*) that the accused frequented those premises. If X does not know of the existence of (*a*) then section 28(2) gives X a defence which he must prove. If X does know of fact (*a*) but not fact (*b*) then he has a defence under section 28(2) and section 28(3)(*b*)(i).

C. DOES SECTION 28(2) ALTER THE DEFINITION OF POSSESSION?

7–06   Whereas in *Warner* the prosecution was held to be required to prove that an accused had the intention to possess the substance which was prohibited, the question arises whether this amounts to "some fact alleged by the prosecution which it is necessary for the prosecution to prove . . ." and therefore, by section 28(2), the onus is now on the accused to prove that he neither knew of, nor suspected, nor had reason to suspect, the existence of this fact.

In *Wright* (1975) 62 Cr.App.R. 169, the argument was raised but the Court of Appeal did not need to consider it. However, in *Ashton-Rickhardt* [1978] 1 W.L.R. 37:

> Police officers found the appellant asleep in his car. A cigarette, containing cannabis, was found in the pocket of the driver's door. The appellant denied knowledge of the reefer or that it contained cannabis. The judge directed the jury that the burden of proving a lack of knowledge fell on the appellant.
>
> *Held*: section 28(2) had not altered the burden of proof. The burden of proving knowledge of the article rested on the prosecution.

Accordingly, where drugs are planted on an accused, or added to the goods which he knows he controls (see *Irving* [1970] Crim.L.R. 642, C.A.) the onus of proving knowledge remains on the prosecution. Again, where the accused is in possession of a "trace" the burden of proving knowledge of the trace falls on the prosecution (*per* Stinson J. in *Colyer* [1974] Crim.L.R. 243) and see the interesting and very helpful article by Ribeiro and Perry, "Possession and section 28 of the Misuse of Drugs Act 1971" [1979] Crim.L.R. 90.

D. WHAT IS TO BE PROVED BY THE ACCUSED?

When the burden of proof does shift to the accused under section 28, the   7–07
standard of proof is on a balance of probabilities: see *Carr-Briant* [1943] K.B.
607.

However, the accused is also required to meet a subjective and an objective
test if his defence is under s.28(2) or s.28(3)(*b*)(i). Thus, he must prove:

- (i)   that he did not know the existence of the relevant fact (subjective);
  and
- (ii) that he did not suspect the existence of the same (again subjective);
  and
- (iii) that he had no reason to suspect the existence of that fact.

The last requirement is objective.

> In *Young* [1984] 1 W.L.R. 654, Y, who was seriously affected by drink
> and was almost incapable, sold LSD to W. As Y was about to negotiate a
> further sale of the drug he was arrested. Y was charged with possessing
> LSD intending to supply it contrary to section 5(3). Y relied on section
> 28(3)(*b*)(i). At a District Courts-Martial, the assistant Judge Advocate
> General directed that the test to be applied under s.28(3)(*b*)(i) was that of
> an "ordinary, reasonable and sober man."
> *Held*: the appeal against conviction would be dismissed. Although it
> was unnecessary to gloss the direction by referring to the "reasonable,
> sober man," it was a correct direction since self-induced intoxication did
> not avail Y. The third limb of s.28(3)(*b*)(i) is objective.

The assistant Judge Advocate General was clearly influenced by *D.P.P.* v.   7–08
Majewski [1977] A.C. 443,H.L., but the Courts-Martial Appeals Court had
doubts as to whether the same criterion applies when knowledge (as distinct
from intent) is under consideration.

Because the third limb to section 28(3)(*b*)(i) is objective, it follows that only
to a limited extent can an accused be judged on the basis of what he believed
the facts to be; see Lord Diplock in *Sweet* v. *Parsley* [1970] A.C. 132, H.L.
Suppose X possesses "snow" believing this term to be a popular name for
"snuff." Snuff is not a controlled substance. "Snow" is in fact a popular name
for cocaine which is actually what X possessed. X may say that he did not
believe or suspect that the substance was a controlled drug, but the third limb
of s.28(3)(*b*)(i) presents X with colossal difficulties having regard to its
"wider concept of objective rationality" (*per* Kilner Brown J. in *Young*
(*supra*). Accordingly, a phrase popularly used to denote a controlled drug is
likely to be a sufficient reason to cause a person to suspect that the substance
which he possesses, bearing that description, is in fact a controlled drug. (A
contrary view is expressed by Richard Lord in *Controlled Drugs, Law &
Practice*, Butterworths (1984).)

E. SECTION 28(3)(*b*)(ii)

7–09   As the M.D.A. permits the Secretary of State, by regulations, to exempt certain controlled drugs from the activities prohibited by that Act, *e.g.* sections 4 and 5, it is conceivable that a person may deal with drug X (which is not exempt) while believing that he is dealing with drug Y (which is exempt). Thus regulation 4(2) of the 1985 Regulations permits any person to possess drugs listed in Schedule 4 of those regulations (*e.g.* Lorazepam) notwithstanding section 5(1).

Accordingly, section 28(3)(*b*)(ii) affords a defence to an accused who in fact possesses heroin believing that the drug is Lorazepam. The test is entirely subjective.

Chapter 8
Offences Contrary to a Corresponding Law

A. GENERAL NOTE

Section 20 Misuse of Drugs Act 1971 provides that: 8–01

"A person commits an offence if in the United Kingdom he assists in or induces *the commission* in any place outside the United Kingdom of an offence punishable under the provisions of a corresponding law in force in that place."

It is submitted that the following propositions represent the law: 8–02

(1) Section 20 creates a statutory offence punishable under the Act: the section does not merely give the courts of the United Kingdom jurisdiction to try offences that would otherwise be "local" to courts of foreign jurisdiction.
(2) To prove the full offence under section 20:
   (a) the "foreign offence" must actually have been committed: *Panayi (No. 1)* (1988) 86 Cr.App.R. 261;
   (b) the "foreign offence" must be punishable under the provisions of a "corresponding law"; see section 20 and section 36.
(3) Where the foreign offence has *not* been committed then:
   (a) a conspiracy to commit an offence under section 20 may lie if two or more persons agree to commit a foreign offence: *Vickers* (1975) 61 Cr.App.R, 48;
   (b) an attempt to commit a section 20 offence may lie if the accused performs acts in the United Kingdom (being more than merely preparatory) in an attempt to induce the commission of the "foreign offence."

B. WHAT IS CAPABLE OF AMOUNTING TO "ASSISTANCE"

In *Vickers* [1975] 1 W.L.R. 811, the Court of Appeal held that the words 8–03 "assisting in or inducing the commission of" in section 20 were chosen by

Parliament: "so as to leave to a jury the opportunity of exercising a common sense judgment on the facts of a particular case" (*per* Scarman L.J.).

> In *Vickers, ibid.*; V and J agreed in England and elsewhere that V would obtain a truck in London to collect and load, a number of speaker cabinets which he would then deliver to Italy knowing (as was the case) that cannabis would be fitted into the cabinets and shipped to the United States of America. V performed his part of the agreement. He was convicted of conspiracy to contravene section 20 of the Misuse of Drugs Act 1971 by agreeing to assist in, or induce the commission in the United States of America of offences punishable under the United States Comprehensive Drug Abuse Prevention and Control Act 1970, "corresponding" to the United Kingdom law (namely section 3(1) of the M.D.A. 1971 and what is now section 180 of the C.E.M.A. 1979).
>
> *Held*: V's acts in obtaining the truck and collecting the speakers was sufficient "assistance" within the United Kingdom for the purposes of section 20.

8–04   V contended that the words "assists in or induces the commission," as they appear in section 20 M.D.A. must be narrowly construed as covering only acts directly concerned with the actual importation. Two arguments were advanced in support of this proposition. The first was that the offence was one of strict liability and therefore the words must be narrowly construed. This argument was swiftly rejected on the basis that "one who assists knows what he is doing and the purpose with which it is done" (*per* Scarman L.J. at p.818): and see §8–08, *infra*. The second argument was founded on the wording of the previous legislation which, by section 13(*d*) of the Dangerous Drugs Act 1965, provided that:

> "A person ...
>
>   (*d*) who in the United Kingdom ... does an act preparatory to, or in furtherance of, an act which if committed in the United Kingdom would constitute an offence against this Act; shall be guilty of an offence."

The wording of section 13(*d*) therefore embraced merely preparatory acts falling short of an attempt to commit the full offence. By contrast, section 20 omits those words: see *Johnston*, March 22, 1974 (unreported, but summarised in *Evans* (1976) 64 Cr.App.R. 237).

8–05   In *Vickers*, the appellant argued that if preparatory acts now fall outside the scope of section 20 then Parliament must have intended to restrict the meaning of the phrase "assist in or induces the commission of ... an offence" to acts directly concerned with the actual importation of the drug into the United States of America. Presumably, as part of that submission, the appellant also contended that if preparatory acts are excluded from section 20 then the answer should not be different merely because the accused is charged with conspiracy. The Court of Appeal rejected that argument on the straightforward basis that the offence under section 13(*d*) is abolished and what matters now is the construction of section 20 as a matter of plain English.

In order to understand the submissions made by the appellant in *Vickers*, it is helpful to look at the historical development of section 20.

Under the Single Convention on Narcotic Drugs 1961, to which the United   8–06
Kingdom is a party, each member state agreed to "assist each other in the
campaign against the illicit traffic in narcotic drugs": Article 35(*b*). To that
end Article 36 provides that:

> "1. *(a)* Subject to its constitutional limitations each party shall adopt such
> measures as will ensure that cultivation, production, manufacture,
> extraction, preparation, possession, offering, offering for sale, dis-
> tribution, purchase, sale, delivery on any terms whatsoever, brok-
> erage, dispatch, dispatch in transit, transport, importation and
> exportation of drugs contrary to the provisions of the Convention
> ... shall be punishable offences when committed intentionally
> ...."
>
> 2. (*a*) (i) Each of the offences enumerated in paragraph 1, if committed
> in different countries, shall be considered as a distinct offence;
>
> (ii) Intentional participation in, conspiracy to commit and
> attempts to commit, any of such offences, and preparatory acts
> and financial operations in connection with the offences re-
> ferred to in this article, shall be punishable offences as provided
> in paragraph 1;"

It will be seen that Article 36(2)(*a*)(ii) embraces "preparatory acts." Al-   8–07
though at common law, the test of an attempt has been expressed differently
over the years, the law recognised in essence that acts which are merely preparatory to the commission of an offence do not amount to an attempt to commit the full offence if the accused is not yet "on the job": *per* Rowlatt J. in
Osborn (1919) 84 J.P. 63. See also *Gullefer* [1987] Crim.L.R. 195, C.A.

Accordingly, ratification of Article 36(2)(*a*)(ii) necessitated a radical depar-
ture from the position at common law: hence section 13(*d*) of the Dangerous
Drugs Act 1965, cited at §8–04, *supra*.

Section 13(*d*) was concerned with two sets of offences. First, "aiding, abetting, counselling or procuring" the commission of a foreign offence. The
foreign offence had actually to have been committed because one cannot
otherwise aid or abet its commission: see *Panayi (No. 1)* (1988) 86 Cr.App.R.
261, 266, and see §8–08, *infra*. The second set of offences concerned conspiracies, or preparatory acts falling short of an attempt, to commit an offence
contrary to the 1965 Act. This included an offence punishable under a corresponding law in a foreign country, providing that the acts complained of
would, if committed in the United Kingdom, constitute an offence under the
1965 Act: see *Johnston*, (March 22, 1974; unreported).

The Misuse of Drugs Act 1971 simplified this framework. It deleted any   8–08
reference to preparatory acts but (for the purpose of section 20 of the M.D.A
1971) it replaced the words "aids, abets, counsels or procures" as they
appeared in section 13(*d*) with the broad words "assist in or induces the commission of."

The submission of the appellant in *Vickers* appears to have been that if section 20 now excludes acts which are merely preparatory, Parliament must

have intended that the words "assists" in section 20, should be narrowly construed so as to relate to acts proximate to the moment of importation. The Court of Appeal rejected the argument founded on section 13(*d*) of the 1965 Act as being "beside the point" and that the meaning of the plain English words in a statute is a question of fact (see *Cozens* v. *Brutus* [1973] A.C. 854, 861).

In the view of the Court of Appeal in *Vickers*, Parliament chose the plain English phrase "assist in the commission of" so as to leave to a jury the opportunity of exercising a common-sense judgment on the facts of a particular case: *per* Scarman L.J. In this regard the Court of Appeal was plainly right because there exists no logical reason why those words should be subject to an artificially restricted meaning.

8–09 All that need be proved, for the full offence, under section 20, is that a foreign offence was actually committed (whether that offence be substantive or inchoate: and see *Panayi (No. 1)* (1986) 86 Cr.App.R. 261) and that the defendant did acts within the United Kingdom which assisted or induced the commission of that offence.

> In *Panayi (No. 1)* (1988) 86 Cr.App.R. 261, a yacht carrying 690 kilogrammes of cannabis worth £1.3 million from Spain to Holland sailed into British territorial waters within the limits of Port Solent (see section 5 of the C.E.M.A. 1979) whereupon the appellants, who crewed the yacht, were arrested and charged on count 2 with an offence under section 20, that they assisted in the United Kingdom in the commission in the Netherlands of an offence punishable under the provisions of a corresponding law in force in the Netherlands.
>
> *Held*: the conviction would be quashed. The offence, said to be punishable under a corresponding law in the Netherlands, was not committed.

In *Panayi* the "foreign offence" relied upon, appears to have been a substantive offence contrary to the laws of the Netherlands.

"Preparatory acts" are relevant if they provide evidence that the defendant assisted in, or induced, the commission of the foreign offence.

8–10 In cases where a foreign offence has not been committed, the prosecutor may wish to consider whether he can properly charge an attempt to induce the commission of the foreign offence contrary to section 20 of the M.D.A. 1971 under section 1(1) and (4) of the Criminal Attempts Act 1981 or, to charge a conspiracy to contravene section 20. Indeed, where two or more persons are involved, the prosecution may find it easier to allege a conspiracy even if a foreign offence has been committed and this seems to have been the situation in *Vickers* itself.

Acts which are merely preparatory (although not sufficient to prove an attempt) may provide some evidence of an agreement to contravene section 20: see *Cooper and Compton* [1947] 2 All E.R. 701, *D.P.P.* v. *Bhagwan* [1972] A.C. 60; *Knuller (Publishing, Printing and Promotions) Ltd.* v. *D.P.P.* [1973] A.C. 435 and *Vickers* itself.

8–11 Suppose A and B agree in England to import cannabis into country X. The drug is concealed in furniture and stored in London. Both A and B visit X in order to familiarise themselves with the airport: they return to England the following day. Assume that it is an offence in country X to import cannabis, and that the government of X certifies that the offence is punishable under a corresponding law for the purposes of section 36. On those facts A and B are guilty of the full offence under section 20. They are also guilty of conspiring to commit an "exportation offence" contrary to section 68 or section 170(2) of the C.E.M.A. 1979 and section 3 of the M.D.A. 1971.

Furthermore, it would be open to the prosecution to charge A and B with   8–12
a conspiracy to commit the section 20 offence on the basis that if the agreement had been carried out "in accordance with their intentions," the substantive offence (by the law of X) would have been committed: see section 1(1) of the Criminal Law Act 1977; and see *Vickers* (1975) 61 Cr.App.R. 48 where a conspiracy was charged. If the appellants in *Panayi* had been charged with a conspiracy to contravene section 20 itself (as opposed to a conspiracy to commit the foreign offence), by agreeing in the United Kingdom to assist in the commission of a substantive offence punishable under a corresponding law in the Netherlands, the result might have been different providing there was evidence that the appellants, whilst they were within British territorial waters, agreed to assist or to induce the commission of the "foreign offence." *Panayi*'s defence appears to have been that he was asleep on board at the time the vessel entered British territorial waters. If true, it is difficult to see how he could be said to have formed an agreement with Karte to contravene section 20.

The cases of *Vickers* and *Panayi* (*supra*) demonstrate the importance of identifying carefully the "foreign offence" alleged to have been committed and drafting an appropriate count to meet the facts of any given case: see *Mushtaq Ahmed* [1990] Crim.L.R. 648.

C. ASSISTING "IN THE UNITED KINGDOM"

The acts relied upon by the prosecution to prove that the defendant assisted   8–13
in, or induced, the commission of an offence punishable under a corresponding law abroad must have been performed in the United Kingdom.

> In *Evans* (1977) 64 Cr.App.R. 237, E agreed with J to go to Brussels and to pick up a parcel of cannabis and to take it to Canada. E was provided with his airline ticket and met J at an hotel in Brussels where he was given a holdall containing the drug which E then took with him to Montreal and delivered the holdall to X, contrary to the Narcotic Control Act 1960–61 of Canada. On appeal, against his conviction under section 20 of the M.D.A. 1971, E contended that he had done nothing in the United Kingdom which was capable to amounting to "assisting" in the commission of the offence charged.
>
> *Held*: dismissing the appeal, E's conduct in going to London airport and collecting his ticket, knowing the illicit purpose of his journey, was sufficient evidence of "assistance" to go to the jury.

D. "OFFENCE PUNISHABLE UNDER A CORRESPONDING LAW"

8–14   By section 36:

"(1) In this Act the expression 'corresponding law' means a law stated in a certificate purporting to be issued by or on behalf of the government of a country outside the United Kingdom to be a law providing for the control and regulation in that country of the production, supply, use, export and import of drugs and other substances in accordance with the provisions of the Single Convention on Narcotic Drugs signed at New York on March 30th, 1961 or a law providing for the control and regulation in that country of the production, supply, use, export and import of dangerous or otherwise harmful drugs in pursuance of any treaty, convention or other agreement or arrangement to which the government of that country and Her Majesty's Government in the United Kingdom are for the time being parties.

(2) A statement in any such certificate as aforesaid to the effect that any facts constitute an offence against the law mentioned in the certificate shall be evidence, and in Scotland sufficient evidence, of the matters stated."

On a proper construction of section 20 a person cannot be guilty of committing an offence in a place outside the United Kingdom unless the offence outside the United Kingdom was in fact committed: see *Panayi (No. 1)* (1986) 86 Cr.App.R. 261. The Court of Appeal reviewed the authorities of *Vickers* [1975] 1 W.L.R. 811 and *Evans* (1977) 64 Cr.App.R. 237 and said: "A whole series of acts might be done preparatory to the commission of an offence, but if no offence is in fact committed, it is difficult to see how you can assist in its commission": *per* O'Connor L.J.

E. IMPORTATION EFFECTED BY AN INNOCENT THIRD PARTY

8–15   In *Ahmed* [1990] Crim.L.R. 648 cannabis concealed in a quantity of raisins was sent to Rotterdam but the goods were not collected there as intended. An innocent third party, employed by a firm of shipping agents, sent the goods to Belgium in the name of the consignee. Documents relating to the consignment were found at the appellant's address in the United Kingdom hidden behind a lavatory cistern. He had earlier visited Amsterdam to collect the shipping documents. He was also observed by officers meeting an accomplice named Bashir whom the appellant knew to be a drug smuggler.

Held: on appeal, that "it was not necessary to prove that the appellant intended that the goods should be import into Belgium. It was enough to prove that [the appellant] assisted in a course of business which had that result being well aware, as he was, that Bashir was involved in drug smuggling."

It is submitted that the position on this point is analagous to the reasoning in *Jakeman* (1983) 76 Cr.App.R. 223: §§2–38 and 2–80, *supra*. In each case the accused brought about the *actus reus* of the offence in question. The accused must know, of course, what is afoot and what he is doing and the purpose with which he acts. However, whereas in *Jakeman* the defendant did intend to import the drugs into the United Kingdom before she abandoned the enterprise, in *Ahmed* the appellant did not intend to import the drug into Belgium: and see *Panayi (No. 2)* [1989] 1 W.L.R. 187 in this regard. See, also, §8–08, *infra* (mental element).

It is not necessary for the prosecution to identify the "principal offender": **8–16** see *Ahmed, ibid*. In that case the submission appears to have been that acts of assistance must relate to the activities of an identifiable principal offender (and not an innocent third party) who affected the actual importation. That submission, rejected by the Court of Appeal, overlooked the unique nature of the offence under section 20. The section is aimed at those who give assistance. For the purposes of that section, the persons who "assist" are the principal offenders. The person who effects the importation into a foreign country may not, in fact, be guilty of any offence contrary to English law at all. To seek to distinguish between so-called "principal offenders" and "assistances" as if they were mere accessories or secondary parties in these circumstances is, with respect, fallacious. It must, of course, be proved that somebody committed the offence: see *Panayi (No. 1)* (1988) 86 Cr.App.R. 261, *supra*.

F. MENS REA FOR AN OFFENCE UNDER SECTION 20

In *Vickers, supra* V, knew the object of the venture but he did not know whether it would be carried out, or how, or by whom. To say (as was said in **8–17** *Cozens* v. *Brutus*, §8–08 *supra.*, and by Scarman L.J. in *Vickers*), that the meaning of a plain English word is a question of fact, may be an oversimplification in the context of a statutory provision creating a criminal offence. In plain English, "assisting in" may or may not involve knowledge of the object or venture. This is not always an issue to be left to a jury to determine in a criminal case and indeed, in *Vickers*, Scarman L.J. answered that aspect when he said that "in ordinary English one who assists knows what he is doing and the purpose with which it is done; and . . . this appellant was well aware of the purpose for which the containers he conveyed to Italy were wanted." To that extent the *mens rea* imported into the word "assists" as it appears in section 20, has been determined as a matter of law.

Chapter 9
Conspiracy and Attempt to Commit a Drug Offence

A. INTRODUCTION

9–01   In the last 10 years the law of conspiracy and attempt has undergone much change; indeed the common law offences of conspiracy and attempt have been largely abolished by statute. Furthermore, the old offences of inciting the commission of, or attempting to commit, a conspiracy are also abolished (section 5(7) of the Criminal Law Act 1977).

Instead the Criminal Law Act 1977 now creates a statutory offence of conspiracy which, by section 1(1) [as amended by section 5 of the Criminal Attempts Act 1981] provides:

> "Subject to the following provisions of this Part of the Act, if a person agrees with any other person or persons that a course of conduct shall be pursued which, if the agreement is carried out in accordance with their intentions, either—
>> (a) will necessarily amount to or involve the commission of any offence or offences by one or more of the parties to the agreement, or
>> (b) would do so but for the existence of facts which render the commission of the offence or any of the offences impossible,
> he is guilty of conspiracy to commit the offence or offences in question."

It follows that an agreement to do any of the acts prohibited by the Misuse of Drugs Act 1971 or the Customs and Excise Act 1952 may be charged as a statutory conspiracy.

9–02   To be guilty of a conspiracy, it is not necessary that the accused was a party to the original scheme. Conspirators may enter and leave a conspiracy at any time during its operation: see *Simmonds* [1969] 1 Q.B. 685. The role of each conspirator must be seen in the context of the concerted course of conduct: see *Ardalan* [1972] 1 W.L.R. 463 and *Bailey* (1913) 9 Cr.App.R. 94.

It used to be said that the essence of a conspiracy is the plotting by two or more persons to do an unlawful act, or to do a lawful act but by unlawful means, with the intention of carrying out the unlawful purpose: see *Thompson* [1966] 1 W.L.R. 405. However, this formulation is no longer apt in the light of the terms of section 1 of the 1977 Act as interpreted by the House of

148

Lords in *Anderson* (1985) 81 Cr.App.R. 253. Indeed, in relation to conspiracies arising out of offences under the Misuse of Drugs Act 1971, the reader should have in mind the combined effect of *Anderson (supra)*; *Courtie* [1984] A.C. 463; *Siracusa* (1990) 90 Cr.App.R. 340; and now *Patel* (August 7, 1991; unreported). The facts of *Siracusa* and *Patel* are summarised at §9–09 and §9–10 respectively.

It is submitted that the following propositions emerge from those authorities: **9–03**

(1) The accused must agree to commit an unlawful object: *Walker* [1962] Crim.L.R. 458; *Anderson (supra)*;

(2) the accused must know, in general terms, that an offence will be committed if the agreed course of conduct is carried out: see *Siracusa, ibid.*, at 349 *per* O'Connor L.J.; and *Anderson* (1985) 81 Cr.App.R. 253, 258, *per* Lord Bridge;

(3) however, the accused need not know the name of the offence or the relevant provision which will be contravened: *per* O'Connor L.J. *Siracusa, ibid.*, at 349; and see Woolf L.J. in *Patel, ibid.*;

(4) the accused must intend to play some part in the agreed course of conduct in furtherance of the criminal purpose which the agreement was intended to achieve: *per* Lord Bridge in *Anderson, ibid.*, at 258;

(5) the prosecution must prove the terms of the agreement. "You do not prove an agreement to import heroin by proving an agreement to import cannabis": *per* O'Connor L.J. in *Siracusa, ibid.*, at 350; but:

(a) a different penalty attaches to each Class of drug under Sched. 2 of the M.D.A. 1971 and therefore each Class of drug creates a separate offence: *Courtie (supra)* and *Shivpuri* [1987] A.C. 1. Therefore:

(b) different answers may result depending on the accused's belief as to the nature of the drug he thought he was dealing with; and depending on whether the charge of conspiracy identifies the drug in question as part of the Particulars of Offence: see (6) and (7) below:

(6) the accused must know that the drugs to which the conspiracy relates were controlled drugs: see *Patel, per* Woolf L.J., at 17 D/E of the transcript;

(7) if the drug is identified in the Particulars of Offence then the accused is to be:

(a) *acquitted*, if he may have mistakenly believed that the conspiracy related to a different drug (*e.g.* cannabis, Class B) from that identified in the Particulars of Offence (*e.g.* heroin, Class A), provided that:

(i) the "different drug" is in another Class and,

(ii) that "other Class" attracts a *lesser* penalty than the Class of drug identified in the Particulars of Offence; see *Patel, ibid.*,

(b) *convicted*, if the accused believes he was dealing with a drug attracting a "higher" penalty (*i.e.* this is the converse of 7(a) above: see *Patel, per* Woolf L.J. at 18 A/C;

(c) *convicted*, if the accused believes the drug belonged to the same

Class as the drug identified in the Particulars of Offence: *Patel, per* Woolf L.J. at 18 C/D;

(d) *convicted*, if the accused knows that controlled drugs are involved but he does not know what they are: *Patel, per* Woolf L.J. at 18E.

One implication of the decision in *Patel* is that the difficulties in *Siracusa* could be avoided if the Particulars of Offence did not specify any particular controlled drug.

9–04   In *Patel*, Woolf L.J. (at 16 B/F) regarded the name of the drug as a "material allegation," relevant to sentence, but he did not regard the name as a "material averment" so long as the defendant did not believe he was dealing with a drug in a different Class (*i.e. the Courtie* principle). Nevertheless, Woolf L.J. emphasised the desirability that the Particulars of Offence should identify the drug if the Crown is clear as to which drug was involved: see p. 18F.

Although Woolf L.J. thought that the name of the drug was relevant to sentence, this should not normally be the case since all drugs coming within a particular Class are subject to the same maximum penalty and therefore, in the ordinary way, they should all be treated similarly.

B. PROVING THE CONSPIRACY

9–05   The *actus reus* is the agreement to commit an unlawful object but the whole concept is heavily dependent on the mental element, namely, on the terms of the agreement and the beliefs held by each party to the agreement.

Considerations applicable in the civil law have little place in the construction of section 1 of the Criminal Law Act 1977.

In *Anderson* [1986] A.C. 27, the House of Lords explored the scope of section 1 of that Act.

> In *Anderson*, X and A shared a cell. A agreed to help X escape. A was bailed and received £2000 in order to buy equipment in order to facilitate X's escape. At his trial A claimed that he never actually intended to take part in X's escape although he had planned to smuggle equipment into the prison. A's object was primarily to make money out of X.
>
> The House of Lords held that the fact that A did not intend to participate any further in the escape bid, or that A believed the escape to be impossible, afforded A no defence (and see *Gortat and Pirog* [1973] Crim.L.R. 648).

There is little difficulty where the evidence shows that the parties to the conspiracy all intended to commit an unlawful object and acted in furtherance of that unlawful object "in accordance with their intentions": such an intent is joint. However, in *Anderson*, their Lordships were concerned to look at the position of those who are subordinates in a conspiracy (say C and D) who may or may not know the true objects of the conspiracy but which is well known to the prime movers (A and B). The point is graphically demonstrated in the case of an undercover officer who infiltrates a drug-trafficking ring. Such an officer may be a party to discussions (or even to an agreement) concerning the shipment of narcotics but he does not intend that the criminal enterprise should be successful nor does he necessarily intend to participate in the agreed course of conduct. Is he to be convicted in such circumstances merely by joining an agreement—to be carried out in accordance with the intentions *of the instigators?* In other words, when section 1 refers to an agreement being carried out "in accordance with *their* intentions," must each party to the agreement have precisely the same intention?

In dealing with this issue, Lord Bridge in *Anderson* said (i) that the accused   9–06
must enter into an agreement that a course of conduct be pursued; (ii) the accused must know that the conduct, if pursued, would involve the commission of an offence; but (iii) the prosecution does not need to prove that each conspirator intended that the offence should in fact be committed. This last point has been forcefully criticised on the basis that if no intention need be proved in the case of one conspirator, then why should it be proved on the part of any other, and yet, if it is not proved in respect of at least two persons there is no conspiracy which anyone intends to carry out: see Smith and Hogan, *Criminal Law* (6th ed., Butterworths). However, in practice, the position seems to be that once the conspiracy is proved to be "up and running," the prosecution does not need to prove that any subsequent party joining that conspiracy intended that the offence should be committed. An undercover police officer, engaged in a covert operation, would therefore not be protected on this basis. Their Lordships in *Anderson* had such officers well in mind when analysing the effect of section 1 of the 1977 Act which caused Lord Bridge to remark that "the *mens rea* implicit in the offence of statutory conspiracy must clearly be such as to recognise the innocence of such a person" who did not desire the performance of the object. The solution given by their Lordships was that:

> "... the necessary *mens rea* of the crime is ... established if, and only if, it is shown that the accused, when he entered into the agreement, intended to play some part in the agreed course of conduct in furtherance of the criminal purpose which the agreed course of conduct was intended to achieve": *per* Lord Bridge (at 39).

This *obiter* has been described as a "novel proposition" (Smith and Hogan,   9–07
Criminal Law, 6th ed.) and arguably contrary to *El Ghazal* [1986] Crim.L.R. 52, decided before *Anderson* was heard. However, it is submitted that *El Ghazal* is reconcilable.

> In *El Ghazal* [1985] Crim.L.R. 52, E, T and C were charged with a conspiracy to obtain cocaine. T asked E if he could arrange a meeting between T and C so that both T and C could "make a deal about cocaine." E arranged the meeting and attended it for a short period of time. E complained that the judge misdirected the jury by implying that an agreement to do acts that were merely preparatory to commit a crime amounted to a conspiracy under section 1(1).
>
> *Held*: the appeal would be dismissed. If E introduced T to C, knowing of T's intention and knowing that one of them would seek to obtain

cocaine, then that was the agreement for the purpose of section 1(1).

At first sight the decision is a little difficult to understand since E, on one interpretation of the facts, seems to have done no more than to arrange a meeting between T and C so that a conspiracy to possess cocaine could take place. For this reason the decision, or at least the basis for attaching liability, has been criticised, notably by the learned commentator in the *Criminal Law Review* (see [1986] Crim.L.R. 52) and the reader is encouraged to consult this. However, it was the prosecution's case that E knew from the start that either T or C would obtain the cocaine and therefore E had conspired with T to obtain the drug. C only joined the conspiracy at a later stage. It is submitted that, if the jury reached the conclusion that E did know of the object of the meeting right from the start, then it is not illogical to hold that E conspired with T to obtain drugs. That was the conspiracy. The fact that C might have been a necessary link to complete performance (C not yet having been recruited) is not a relevant consideration.

9–08   In *Siracusa* (1990) 90 Cr.App.R. 340, O'Connor L.J. observed that Lord Bridge did not intend to say that the organiser of a crime who recruited others to carry it out would not be guilty of conspiracy unless it could be proved that he intended to play some active part himself thereafter. In the judgment of the Court of Appeal in *Siracusa*, an intention to participate in the furtherance of the enterprise can be established by the accused's failure to stop the unlawful activity (*per* O'Connor L.J. at 349). This, of course, raises an interesting question as to when he should do so. To infer intention from such failure is a speculative concept. An undercover officer, for example, may wait until the very last moment before arrests are made and the venture is halted.

I. Proving the Terms of the Agreement

9–09   The House of Lords in *Anderson* [1986] A.C. 27 did not resolve the question whether all the conspirators must be of one mind in respect of the course of conduct to be pursued.

> In *Siracusa* (*supra*) the appellants were convicted on two counts of conspiracy—one to import cannabis (count 1) and the other to import heroin (count 2). The cannabis was imported from India and the heroin from Thailand. Each drug arrived on different dates but each drug was concealed in furniture. Each count specified the drug imported and that, in essence, the appellants conspired to import that drug. The appellants contended that, as charged, the prosecution had to prove that each defendant knew the precise drug being imported.
>
> *Held*: the submissions were correct but the appeals against conviction would be dismissed on other grounds.

It is important to bear in mind that on each count the name of the drug had been particularised and the case was therefore decided on that basis. The Court referred to *Anderson* [1986] A.C. 27 but, in the final analysis, the point made was a short one: "you do not prove an agreement to import heroin by proving an agreement to import cannabis": *per* O'Connor L.J. at 350.

The result and the reasoning is plainly right. The prosecution had alleged an agreement on a narrow basis and they had to prove it. O'Connor L.J., as if to reinforce the point, said (at 350):

"If the facts suggest that the agreement was to import prohibited drugs of more than one class, that can be appropriately laid because section 1(1) of the Criminal Law Act 1977 expressly provides for the agreed course of conduct to involve the commission of more than one offence."

On the facts in *Siracusa* the two drugs (heroin and cannabis) fell into Class 9–10 A and B respectively. Different penalties attach to each of the three Classes of controlled drugs under Schedule 2 to the M.D.A. 1971, and therefore create three separate offences: see *Courtie* [1984] A.C. 463 and *Shivpuri* [1987] A.C. 1.

In *Siracusa* the Court did not need to consider whether the result would have been different if drugs *of the same Class* had been imported.

In *Patel* (August 7, 1991; unreported), three men named Patel and two others operated a pharmacy which supplied chemicals used to manufacture amphetamine sulphate (Class B). They were convicted on two counts of conspiracy—one to produce amphetamine and the other to supply that drug. Each count named the drug in the Particulars of Offence. The Patels denied any knowledge that any drugs were being manufactured or supplied as alleged. The trial judge directed the jury that they had to decide in the case of each defendant whether "his knowledge of the scheme and the actual scheme was sufficiently close that it can properly be said that he attached himself to that scheme and not to something different."

Held: the Patels were not prejudiced by the directions of the judge given their complete denial of the knowledge of the scheme. The naming of the drug was not a material averment but it was a material allegation relevant to sentence.

The narrow ground on which *Patel* was decided turned on the effect of the 9–11 Patels' denials. In the opinion of the Court: "If they were not believed then they either did not know precisely what drugs were involved or they knew it was amphetamine sulphate." If they did not know which drugs were involved then this would span drugs falling into three Classes of drugs and therefore (following *Courtie*) three categories of offences. The question was whether this made any difference.

In a lengthy judgment Woolf L.J. held that *Siracusa* was only authority for the proposition that:

"... if a defendant joined a conspiracy believing it involved one Class of drug, he is not guilty of that conspiracy if he believes the drug involved is a drug which belongs to a lesser Class to that named."

The Court gave as its reason that "the conspiracy in which the defendant intended to become involved would then relate to a *different* and *less serious offence*."

By a "different" offence, the court meant that if a defendant believes he is dealing with cannabis (Class B) whereas it is alleged that he conspired to supply heroin (Class A), then the two drugs relate to two different offences (see *Courtie*). By "a less serious" offence, the Court was referring to what it understood to be the effect of the decision in *Courtie*.

9–12   If the Court in *Patel* is right, then where an accused believes he was dealing with heroin when in fact he was dealing with cannabis, he has no defence to a charge of conspiracy to supply cannabis because his mistaken belief went to a "graver offence": indeed this is precisely what Woolf L.J. suggests (at 18 B/C). It is respectfully submitted that this is not what *Courtie* decided when read in conjunction with *Shivpuri* (*supra*): see also *Ellis* (1986) 84 Cr.App.R. 235. Each Class creates a separate offence. It is a startling conclusion (if correct) that a mistake as to the quality of the substance may be sufficient *mens rea* depending on the seriousness of his mistake.

There exists, however, a fundamental challenge to the correctness of *Patel*, based on a natural construction of the word "agree," as it appears in section 1(1) of the Criminal Law Act 1977. Put shortly, if the prosecution alleges by its Particulars of Offence an agreement based on one set of terms then either the defendant entered into that agreement or he did not. As Professor Smith remarked in his commentary to *Siracusa* [1989] Crim.L.R. 712, 713: "It is the defendant's belief as to the nature of the drug, not how it is classified by the law, that is relevant."

9–13   In *Patel*, the Court drew on the law which is undoubtedly relevant in respect of the *mens rea* of a substantive offence but, as O'Connor L.J. pointed out in *Siracusa* (1990) 90 Cr.App.R. 340, 350, the *mens rea* sufficient to support the commission of a substantive offence will not necessarily be sufficient to support an inchoate offence: and see section 19(2) of the 1977 Act.

The Court of Appeal in *Patel* advanced a number of other propositions which should be carefully noted: see §§9–01 *et seq.*, *supra*.

C. CONSPIRACIES FORMED ABROAD

9–14   Historically the jurisdiction to try criminal cases was summarised by the phrase "all crime is local" and by Lord Halsbury L.C. in *MacLeod* v. *Attorney-General for New South Wales* [1891] A.C. 455, 458 when he said: "The jurisdiction over the crime belongs to the country where the crime is committed." Accordingly, an agreement made in England to commit an unlawful act constitutes the crime of conspiracy only if the act is unlawful by the law of England and Wales. It is not enough that it is unlawful only by the law of the country in which the act is to be committed: *Board of Trade* v. *Owen* [1957] A.C. 602.

Where the agreement to commit an offence contrary to the law of the United Kingdom is made entirely abroad, one might have thought that such an agreement falls outside the jurisdiction of the courts of England and Wales and indeed this was the view of the Court of Appeal in *Doot* [1973] Q.B. 73. However, two cases of the Court of Appeal, following the decision of the Privy Council in *Somchai Liangsiriprasert* v. *Government of the United*

States of America (1991) 92 Cr.App.R. 77, made it plain that an agreement made abroad to commit a crime in England is triable in the English courts even if nothing was done in England by the conspirators to further that agreement: see *Sansom* [1991] 2 Q.B. 130 and *Murchia* (December 20, 1991; unreported; 89/344/Y3). The principle enunciated in those cases goes further than the *ratio* of the House of Lords in *D.P.P.* v. *Doot* [1973] A.C. 807 which confined itself to circumstances where acts in furtherance of the conspiracy (whether legal or illegal in themselves) were done in England. No distinction is to be made for these purposes between the position at common law and under the Criminal Law Act 1977: see *Sansom*, §9–20, *infra*.

Although the House of Lords has yet to confirm that the decisions in *Som-* **9–15** *chai Liangsiriprasert* and *Sansom* are correct, it is submitted that they are sound and consistent with the *dicta* of a majority in the House of Lords in *Doot*. A brief historical sketch perhaps makes this clear.

In *Doot*, the appellants conspired in Belgium or Morocco to obtain cannabis resin in Morocco and to import it into the United States of America, having shipped it from England. In pursuance of the conspiracy the appellants drove three specially adapted cars concealing the cannabis into Southampton whereupon the appellants were arrested. In holding that the conspiracy was not triable in England, it was central to the reasoning of the Court of Appeal that *the offence* of conspiracy was completed when the agreement was made.

In other words, the offence itself was said not to be continuous, having been completed when the agreement was made, although the effect of the agreement would endure until it was performed or terminated. There seemed to be some support for this proposition on one interpretation (not adopted in the House of Lords) of a passage in the judgment of Brett J.A. in *Aspinall* (1876) 2 Q.B.D. 48 when he said that the crime of conspiracy "was completed when they agreed."

In *Doot* the Court of Appeal held that acts in performance of the agreement **9–16** were evidence to prove the existence of the conspiracy which, on the facts in *Doot*, was made by the appellants in Morocco and therefore the offence was committed in Morocco. The conviction was quashed. The Court of Appeal took on board the fact that the charge was framed as a conspiracy to contravene section 304(*b*) of the Customs and Excise Act 1952 (now section 170(2) of C.E.M.A. 1979) although, even on this point, the judgment suggests that there had been argument as to whether the substantive offence under that section was a continuing one, and if it was, whether that fact had any bearing on the ingredients of the charge.

On appeal the House of Lords restored the conviction. Their Lordships held that the offence of conspiracy was continuing and, to that extent, the Court of Appeal had been in error. Viscount Dilhorne said that "a conspiracy does not end with the making of the agreement. It will continue so long as there are two or more parties to it intending to carry out the design."

He was driven to conclude that:

"If [conspiracy] is a continuing offence then the courts of England, in my view, have jurisdiction to try the offence if and only if, the evidence suffices to show that the conspiracy whenever or wherever it was formed was in existence when the accused were in England."

9–17   It is important to bear this passage in mind when considering the decisions of *Somchai Liangsiriprasert* and *Sansom*. In that particular passage, jurisdiction is not expressed as being dependant upon proof of overt acts in furtherance of the agreement being performed in England and it therefore seems that Viscount Dilhorne considered such an ingredient not to be essential to the question of jurisdiction. Not all of their Lordships were united on this aspect. By contrast, Lord Pearson (with whom Lord Wilberforce concurred) opined that "a conspiracy to commit in England an offence against English law ought to be triable in England if it has been wholly or partly performed in England." Lord Kilbrandon said no more, other than he would answer the certified question in the affirmative (a question certified on the basis that the agreement was carried out by importing the drug into England), while Lord Salmon considered that a conspiracy entered into abroad was "certainly" triable in England if acts in furtherance of the conspiracy are done in this country but he left open "what the position might be if the conspirators came to England for an entirely innocent purpose."

The diversity of opinion, as to whether anything had to be done in England in pursuance of the agreement, reflects understandable anxiety as to the extent to which English courts may claim jurisdiction to try persons (who may not be British nationals) in respect of unperformed agreements made entirely abroad. If X and Y conspire in France to smuggle drugs into England, should that conspiracy be triable in England if X and/or Y arrive in England on holiday and not with an intention to do anything in pursuance of that conspiracy? Is the position any different if either X or Y abandons performance of their agreement prior to their arrival or may they be tried on the basis of their agreement at the time it was alive? (See the opinion and example given by Lord Salmon in *Doot* [1973] A.C. 807, 833F.)

9–18   If an agreement to commit a crime had been made in England then an English court would only be concerned with the nature of the agreement. It is not an essential element for a conspiracy made in England that anything overt should be done, beyond the agreement, in pursuance of the conspiracy (see *Aspinall* (1876) 2 Q.B.D. 48, 58–59) and it is no defence for a conspirator to say that he subsequently had second thoughts and withdrew from the criminal enterprise: see *Gortat* [1973] Crim.L.R. 648 and *Anderson* [1986] A.C. 27. Why, then, should different considerations apply merely because the agreement was made abroad? Both the Court of Appeal and the House of Lords in *Doot* attached much significance to the existence of overt acts performed in England and, in the opinions of Lord Wilberforce and Lord Pearson, regarded their existence as being necessary to found jurisdiction. But why should this be so? The real significance of the existence of overt acts is evidential, namely, to prove (1) that an agreement had been made to commit a crime in England; (2) the terms of that agreement; and (3) that the agreement was alive at the time the acts were done. This accords with opinions expressed by their Lordships in *D.P.P. v. Doot* [1973] A.C. 807. Lord Salmon observed (at 956h):

"It was unusual until recently to have any direct evidence of conspiracy.

Conspiracy was usually proved by what are called overt acts . . . . Today, however, it is possible to have direct evidence such as tape recordings or oral agreements."

It was against this background that *Somchai Liangsiriprasert* [1990] 3   **9–19**
W.L.R. 606 and *Sansom* (1991) 92 Cr.App.R. 115 were decided.

In *Somchai Liangsiriprasert*, the Privy Council was concerned with a conspiracy to import heroin into the United States of America from Thailand, the proceeds to be collected in Hong Kong. Lord Griffiths stated that in general terms the English criminal law does not concern itself with crimes abroad but added that (at 620):

"Their lordships can find nothing in precedent, comity or good sense that should inhibit the common law from regarding as justiciable in England inchoate crimes committed abroad which are intended to result in the commission of criminal offences in England."

In *Sansom*, the appellants agreed abroad to import half a ton of cannabis   **9–20**
resin from Morocco into Belgium (according to the appellants) or England (according to the Crown). A vessel, commissioned by one conspirator (acting in England) to carry the drug was arrested in the English Channel. The appellants submitted that if the vessel had been arrested outside British territorial waters then no unlawful act had been performed in England in furtherance of the conspiracy. The Court of Appeal rejected the submission. First, an overt act had been performed in England when commissioning the vessel at a time when the agreement was still subsisting. Secondly, that the principle propounded in *Somchai* by Lord Griffiths "should now be regarded as the law of England on this point" and that the principle applies equally to common law conspiracies and extra-territorial conspiracies charged under the Criminal Law Act 1977: *per* Taylor L.J. (1991) 92 Cr.App.R. 115 (at 120).

The decisions of *Somchai Liangsiriprasert* and *Sansom* reflect the reality that crime is international and that much has been done between nations to improve mutual assistance and co-operation to combat it: see the Criminal Justice (International Co-operation) Act 1990; the Single Convention on Narcotic Drugs, 1961, Cmnd. 2631; the European Convention on Mutual Assistance 1959; the Vienna Convention Against Illicit Traffic in Narcotic Drugs & Psychotropic Substances, 1988, Cmnd. 804; and the Extradition Acts 1870 and 1989.

In *Borro and Abdullah* [1973] Crim.L.R. 513, the appellants agreed   **9–21**
abroad to send cannabis from Beirut to Antigua via London. The appellants did no more than to stay overnight in a hotel in London while control over the baggage was retained by the airline. The Court of Appeal dismissed their appeals against their conviction and found no basis upon which *Doot* could be distinguished.

Where goods have been imported and thereafter two or more persons join the conspiracy to deal with the goods, knowing that the goods were prohibited from importation, a conspiracy to fraudulently evade the prohibition contrary to section 170(2) of the C.E.M.A. will lie against them because the section 170 offence is also a continuing one. In *Ardalan* [1972] 1 W.L.R. 463

drugs were posted from Beirut to London and, long after the moment of importation, A arranged to collect them. A's appeal against his conviction for a conspiracy to contravene what is now section 170, was dismissed.

9–22   The court in *Ardalan* indicated that terms such as "wheels," "chains," "sub-conspiracies," etc., should be used with care and only to illustrate and to clarify the definition of conspiracy and for no other reason.

In every case the facts must not disclose more than one conspiracy (see *Griffiths* (1965) 49 Cr.App.R. 279) for if they do the count is bad and may be quashed. Alternatively, a submission of no case can only be upheld: by then it may well be too late for the prosecution to amend the indictment.

D. CONSPIRACY TO DO THE PHYSICALLY IMPOSSIBLE

9–23   Section 1(1) of the Criminal Law Act 1977 (as amended) now overrules the decision in *D.P.P.* v. *Nock* [1978] A.C. 979 in so far as section 1 applies to offences committed after August 1981. If two or more persons agree to pursue a course of conduct but, for reasons unknown to them, the object is incapable of performance, a statutory conspiracy will still be committed. In *Nock* the defendants attempted to extract cocaine from powder which was not capable of releasing cocaine and so the object was incapable of performance. The House of Lords held that no offence had been committed. But today section 1(1) covers the position. *Nock* was distinguished in *Harris (K.A.)* (1979) 69 Cr.App.R. 122:

> H and other persons attempted to make amphetamine. They had the correct formula but incompetently obtained the wrong ingredients and did not fully understand the process of production. They were convicted of conspiring to produce a controlled drug contrary to section 4(1) of the M.D.A.
>
> *Held*: the offence was capable of performance but merely ineptly carried out.

E. ATTEMPTING TO COMMIT A DRUG OFFENCE

9–24   Criminal attempts are now given a statutory footing by the Criminal Attempts Act 1981. Section 1 of that Act provides:

> "(1) If, with intent to commit an offence to which this section applies, a person does an act which is more than merely preparatory to the commission of the offence, he is guilty of attempting to commit the offence.
>
> (2) A person may be guilty of attempting to commit an offence to which this section applies even though the facts are such that the commission of the offence is impossible.
>
> (3) In any case where—
>
> (*a*) apart from this subsection a person's intention would not be

regarded as having amounted to an intent to commit an offence; but

(*b*) if the facts of the case had been as he believed them to be, his intention would be so regarded,

then, for the purposes of subsection (1) above, he shall be regarded as having had an intent to commit that offence."

The 1981 Act repealed that part of section 19 of the M.D.A. which was concerned with attempts to commit offences contrary to that Act. Section 19 is now only concerned with "inciting" the commission of any offence under the M.D.A. More radical still is the effect of section 6 of the 1981 Act, which abolished the offence of attempt at common law.

However, some of the earlier authorities help to define the limits of the   9–25
offence under the 1981 Act. Thus, an accused commits an offence contrary to section 1(1) if he does an act that is "more than merely preparatory" to the commission of the offence. The practical significance of these words is not dissimilar to the proximity test laid down in *Osborn* (1919) 84 J.P. 63, namely that the actor is effectively "on the job": *per* Rowlatt J. In *D.P.P.* v. *Stonehouse* [1978] A.C. 55, Lord Diplock provided a neat test to be applied when determining whether or not the facts of a given case amount to an attempt or not, namely that "the offender must have crossed the Rubicon and burnt his boats." This test has since been criticised: see *Gullefer* [1987] Crim.L.R. 195, C.A, but see *Widdowson* (1985) 82 Cr.App.R. 314 and commentary at [1986] Crim.L.R. 233.

Turner J. adopted a six-fold classification of attempts in *Donnelly* [1970] N.Z.L.R. 980, thus an accused:

(1) may change his mind before committing any act sufficiently overt to amount to an attempt;

(2) may change his mind, but too late to deny that he had got so far as an attempt;

(3) may be prevented from completing the offence by an outside agency, *e.g.* the arrival of police;

(4) may fail to complete the offence by ineptitude;

(5) may find that commission of the offence is impossible by virtue of some physical fact;

(6) may find that his course of conduct does not amount to an offence.

An offence is clearly established in cases (2) and (3); and most probably es-   9–26
tablished in cases (4) and (5). No offence is committed in case (1). The House of Lords in *Haughton* v. *Smith* (*R.D.*) [1975] A.C. 476 held that no offence was committed in respect of case (6).

With the passing of sections 1 and 6 of the 1981 Act, it was thought that case (6) no longer afforded an accused with a defence. But in *Anderton* v. *Ryan* [1985] A.C. 567, the House of Lords held that an accused who purchased a video recorder believing it to be stolen (when in fact it was not) was not guilty of an offence of attempting to handle stolen goods. The decision is now overruled by *Shivpuri* [1987] A.C. 1:

While in India, S was persuaded by D to receive a suitcase containing drugs which a courier would give to him in Cambridge. S was to deliver the drugs in accordance with D's instructions to third parties. S believed the drugs to be cannabis or heroin but, upon analysis the substance was found to be either snuff or some such vegetable matter.

Held: a person was guilty of an offence under section 1(1) of the 1981 Act if the performed steps (that) were more than merely preparatory. The fact that such an offence was impossible to commit affords S with no defence.

9–27   In *Anderton* v. *Ryan* the House of Lords had tried to distinguish between "guilty acts" and those acts which were "objectively innocent"; in the latter case the mind was said to be guilty but the act was actually innocent (*per* Lord Bridge).

In *Shivpuri*, however, Lord Bridge reflected on the distinction he drew in *Anderson* v. *Ryan* saying (at 21B): "If we fell into error, it is clear that our concern was to avoid convictions in situations which most people, as a matter of common sense, would not regard as involving criminality."

Later Lord Bridge added (at 21G):

> "I am satisfied on further consideration that the concept of 'objective innocence' is incapable of sensible application in relation to the law of criminal attempts. The reason for this is that any attempt to commit an offence which involves an 'act which is more than merely preparatory to the commission of the offence' but which for any reason fails, so that in the event no offence is committed, must *ex hypothesi*, . . . be 'objectively innocent.' What turns what would otherwise . . . be an innocent act into a crime is the intent of the actor to commit an offence."

Arguably, every case where the offence is impossible to commit involves the taking of steps which are only merely preparatory to the commission of the offence. Accordingly, Lord Bridge considered that the distinction sought to be drawn in *Anderton* v. *Ryan* could not be maintained and that "there is no valid ground on which *Anderton* v. *Ryan* can be distinguished."

> "If I could extract from the speech of Lord Roskill or from my own speech a clear and coherent principle distinguishing those cases of attempting the impossible which amount to offences under the statute from those which do not, I should have to consider carefully on which side of the line the instant case fell. But I have to confess that I can find no such principle."

Their Lordships therefore overruled *Anderton* v. *Ryan* in accordance with the 1966 *Practice Statement* [1966] 3 All E.R. 77.

Chapter 10
Evidence

A. PROOF THAT THE DRUG IS CONTROLLED AND PROHIBITED

All drugs controlled by the M.D.A. are listed in Schedule 2 of the Act and   **10–01**
fall into one of three Classes (*i.e.* Classes A to C in Parts I to III respectively of
Schedule 2). Classification depends on the potential of the drugs for causing
"harm." The list is not closed. The Secretary of State may, by Regulation, add
other drugs to the list, re-classify existing controlled drugs or he may remove
some or all of them from Schedule 2 completely.

Since the M.D.A. was passed, Schedule 2 has been extensively modified by
a number of Misuse of Drugs Act 1971 (Modification) Orders: S.I. 1973 No.
771; S.I. 1975 No. 421; S.I. 1977 No. 1243; S.I. 1979 No. 299; S.I. 1983 No.
765; S.I. 1984 No. 859; S.I. 1985 No. 1995; S.I. 1986 No. 2230; S.I. 1989
No. 1340; S.I. 1990 No. 2589.

It is important to note that the Act also controls (where appropriate) any
stereoisomeric form of a controlled drug, any of their *esters, ethers or salts* or
certain "*preparations*" which contain a controlled substance or product.

I. Determining Whether a Given Substance or Product is a Controlled Drug

In the ordinary way determining whether a substance or product is con-   **10–02**
trolled or not, is a straightforward matter: one simply looks to see if the substance is listed in Schedule 2. But the matter is only made straightforward
because Parliament has been careful to ensure that the term "a controlled
drug" is narrowly defined so that (except where expressly provided) it is the
chemical which is the controlled "substance" or "product" and nothing else.

Accordingly, a drug that naturally subsists in a plant or material and which
has not been extracted is not a controlled drug unless that plant or substance
has itself been expressly controlled by the Act. Thus, in *Goodchild (No. 2)*
[1977] 1 W.L.R. 1213:

> G was charged with being in possession of cannabis resin after the police

found four ounces of stalks and leaves of cannabis plants at G's address. At that time the stalks and leaves were not expressly controlled by the Act—just the flowering and fruiting tops of the plant. However, the scientific evidence was that the stalks and leaves would naturally contain cannabis resin. Hence the charge. However, section 37(1) defines "cannabis resin" as "separated resin ... obtained from [a cannabis plant]." This implied some form of extraction which, on the facts, had not occurred. Accordingly, G's conviction had to be quashed.

The definition of cannabis has now been extended to include all of the plant except the mature stalk, fibre and the seeds.

Similarly, cocaine is extracted from the coca-leaf but without further provision the coca-leaf itself would not be a controlled drug. Accordingly, Parliament specifically included the leaf as a Class A substance. "Poppy-straw" (Class A) is yet another example.

Surprisingly, perhaps, the so-called "magic mushroom" (*psilocybe mexicana*) is not controlled even though it contains psilocin which is a controlled drug (Class A). Accordingly, it is therefore not unlawful to pick the mushroom or to possess it or to supply it.

(a) Esters, salts and ethers are also controlled

10–03   As we have noted, any esters, ethers, salts or any stereoisomeric forms of drugs specified in Classes A, B and C are "controlled" substances. These are terms of science. Thus a salt of diamorphine is still heroin (*cf. Greensmith* [1983] 1 W.L.R. 1124; and see (1992) 94 Cr.App.R. 351).

(b) Meaning of "preparation"

10–04   "Preparation" is broadly defined by the *Shorter Oxford English Dictionary* to mean, *inter alia*, the "composition, manufacture of a chemical, medicinal, or other substance."

The appearance of the word "manufacture" in this definition is of particular interest since it is undoubtedly the case that "preparing" a drug may amount to an act of "production" for the purposes of section 4 of the M.D.A. However, much will depend on the facts of a given case. It would be unsafe to assume that every act of production amounts to an act of preparation or indeed, conversely, that every act of preparation amounts to an act of production. It is submitted that the M.D.A. contemplates a subtle distinction, namely, that an act of "preparation" is calculated to convert a controlled drug into a form suitable for consumption, whereas "producing" a controlled drug is generally confined to the act of creating the drug. It must be remembered that many drugs are synthetically created in a laboratory, *e.g.* LSD. Steps taken to create such drugs are obviously steps taken to "produce" them. However, applying drops of LSD to sugar cubes for human consumption is an act of "preparation," not an act of production.

The distinction has practical significance in cases involving the mushroom *psilocybe mexicana*. The potency of *psilocin* (the drug that subsists in that particular mushroom) is considerably increased if the mushroom is dried. In

Stevens [1981] Crim.L.R. 568, C.A. it was held that the term "preparation" had to be given its natural and ordinary meaning. It is not a term of art. So, where S had dried magic mushrooms at a low heat, thereby converting them into a powder, he had accordingly made a "preparation" containing a controlled drug (psilocin). The mushrooms ceased to be in their natural growing state and were now "altered by the hand of man." The intervention of the "hand of man" is the crucial test.

Stevens was applied in *Cuncliffe* [1986] Crim.L.R. 547. In that case C, by the jury's verdict, had subjected a quantity of magic mushrooms to sunlight so that they dried out. He had therefore "prepared" them and he was held to be rightly convicted of possessing a controlled drug.

There is clearly a mental element in the act of preparation, namely, an **10–05** intention to alter the condition of the thing coupled with an intention that the substance should serve as a drug in the future. Accordingly, no offence is committed if the mushrooms in D's possession had dried out of their own accord. The prosecution must show that someone deliberately brought about the change.

> In *Walker* [1987] Crim.L.R. 565, C.A. police found between 1000 to 2000 dried magic mushrooms in a cupboard at W's premises. W said that they must have dried out of their own accord. Two-thirds of them had been seized by police in 1982 and then returned. The remainder he had since picked. The jury asked why the mushrooms were returned to W and were they then unlawful for him to possess. The judge directed the jury that they were unlawful to possess in 1982. During the appeal the prosecution argued that *picking* the mushrooms amounted to an act of "preparation."
>
> *Held*: that the court was not inclined to accept that merely picking the mushroom amounted to preparation. However, the jury's question, although difficult to understand, was answered incorrectly since it had to be proved that someone deliberately brought about a change in the condition of the mushrooms.

The court was right not to hold that merely to pick the mushroom was an **10–06** act of preparation since it does not follow that the mushroom will dehydrate as a result. It could not have been the intention of the legislature to include, for example, persons who innocently pick the mushrooms which then dry out of their own accord. Obviously, if the mushrooms are picked and are then deliberately kept in a dry environment so that they dry out, then a process is being adopted to alter the condition "by the hand of man." But deliberate conduct implies the existence of a mental ingredient. However, as yet, the courts have not been asked to examine the nature or the limits of that mental ingredient.

Suppose, now, that a person picks a *psilocybe mexicana* mushroom which is then deliberately allowed to dry out so that it may be preserved for botanical study. Is such a person now guilty of being in unlawful possession of psilocin? Such a harsh result could be avoided if "preparation" is construed to include a gloss to the mental element, namely, that the accused intended to put the thing into a form so as to achieve the desired chemical effect. It is submitted that such a construction is consistent with the ordinary natural meaning of the word "preparation" in the context of drug use and abuse; see *Hodder* v. *D.P.P.* [1990] Crim.L.R. 261 (discussed *supra* at §6–08), in relation to the production of controlled drugs and the reader is invited to refer to that section.

10–07 If a substance or product is not expressed in Schedule 2 of the M.D.A. to be a controlled drug, and if the prosecution fails to prove that it amounts to a "preparation," then that substance or product cannot be regarded as a controlled drug. This may seem obvious but consider the case of a person who innocently picks magic mushrooms which dry out naturally. He will not be guilty of unlawful possession if he subsequently learns that the powder is a narcotic and uses it as such. Moreover, if he then shares the substance with others, he cannot be guilty of unlawfully supplying it.

(c) Meaning of "product"

10–08 In *Hodder* v. *D.P.P.* [1990] Crim.L.R. 261, it was held that the picking, packaging and freezing of several bags of magic mushrooms was a process which brought the mushrooms within the definition of a "product" for the purposes of the Act. This case, and its facts, are considered in relation to the production of controlled drugs (see Chapter 6).

In *Russell* (December 11, 1991, unreported) the Court of Appeal held that the conversion of cocaine hydrochloride (the salt) into cocaine base, was an act of production: see §§6–08—6–10, *supra*.

(d) Definition of cannabis

10–09 Section 37(1) of the M.D.A. as amended by section 52 of the Criminal Law Act 1977, defines cannabis as:

"... any plant of the genus *Cannabis* or any part of such a plant (by whatever name designated) except that it does not include cannabis resin or any of the following products after separation from the rest of the plant, namely—
(*a*) mature stalk of any such plant,
(*b*) fibre produced from mature stalk of any such plant, and
(*c*) seed of any such plant."

Cannabis resin means:

"... the separated resin, whether crude or purified, obtained from any plant of the genus *Cannabis*."

Both cannabis (herbal) and cannabis resin are Class B drugs. However, cannabinol and cannabinol derivatives are Class A drugs since they are far more potent. Cannabinol is not further defined but cannabinol derivatives are defined in Part IV of Schedule 2 to mean:

"... the following substances, except where contained in cannabis or cannabis resin, namely tetrahydro derivatives of cannabinol and 3-alkyl homologues of cannabinol or of its tetrahydro derivatives."

10–10 Although all of the above are types of cannabis, it would not be right to regard them as generic for the purpose of drafting charges of indictments. Each drug is separately controlled and should be separately particularised in any charge: see *Muir* v. *Smith* [1978] Crim.L.R. 293 and *cf. Best* (1979) 70 Cr.App.R.21, and §3–31, *supra*.

Since the seeds of the cannabis plant are not controlled it follows that these may be lawfully possessed. But it is an offence to sow them and to cultivate the plant: see section 6 of the M.D.A. 1971.

Although "cannabis resin" means resin that is separated from the plant, it does not mean that the prosecution has to show that the resin was separated to the extent that all the cannabis had been removed from the oil-bearing glandular trichomes, since resin includes "crude resin": see *Thomas* [1981] Crim.L.R. 496.

(e) **Meaning of "cocaine"**

> In *Greensmith* [1983] 1 W.L.R. 1124, G was convicted of possession of 9.04 grammes of powder containing 40 per cent. cocaine with intent to supply it. The prosecution called no evidence as to whether the drug was in fact cocaine, or a stereoisomeric form or a salt of cocaine. The expert said whatever it was "it was still cocaine."
>
> *Held*: G's appeal would be dismissed. "Cocaine" was generic in paragraph 1 of Part I of Schedule 2 and included a natural substance, *e.g.* coca-leaf or a substance resulting from a chemical transformation. Both are cocaine. There was no need for the prosecution to prove the exact form.

10–11

The court attached importance to the words "any substance or product." The word "substance" has a wider meaning than "product." Lawton L.J. noted that "any kind of matter comes within 'substance,' whereas 'product' envisages the result of some kind of process."

Two Crown Court cases, *Leaman* (May 17, 1978; unreported; Maidstone Crown Court) and *Steeper* (September 27, 1979; unreported: Inner London Sessions), were referred to in the judgment of the Court of Appeal. Both cases held that the prosecution was bound to specify in the indictment whether the drug was of a form expressed in paragraph 1 of Schedule 2, Part I or whether it was an "ester, ether, salt etc." The Court of Appeal in *Greensmith* advised that neither decision should be followed and indeed this must be correct upon a literal reading of the M.D.A. Paragraph 1 of Part I indicates those substances and products which are controlled. It does not matter for present purposes that neither the word "substance" nor "product" is defined. What does matter, as a matter of science, is that a given substance or product referred to in Schedule 2 may have related to it certain stereoisomeric forms, esters, ethers, or salts. In other words they are generic. Accordingly, the prosecution is not obliged to particularise which form the drug takes. It is still the same substance or product. See also *Watts* [1984] 1 W.L.R. 757.

In *Russell*, the Court of Appeal held that the conversion of cocaine hydrochloride to base cocaine was an act of production: see §6–10, *supra*.

(f) Opiate related definitions

10–12　　**"Raw opium"** includes:

> "... powdered or granulated opium but does not include medicinal opium": see Part IV of Schedule 2.

"Medicinal opium" is defined in Part IV of Schedule 2 to mean:

> "... raw opium which has undergone the process necessary to adapt it for medicinal use in accordance with the requirements of the British Pharmacopoeia, whether it is in the form of powder or is granulated or is in any other form, and whether it is or is not mixed with neutral substances."

"Prepared opium," by section 37(1) of the M.D.A., means:

> "... opium prepared for smoking and includes dross and other residues remaining after opium has been smoked."

"Opium poppy" means the plant *Papaver somniferum* L."

"Poppy straw" means, by Part IV:

> "... all parts, except the seeds of the opium poppy, after mowing."

"Concentrate of poppy straw" means, by Part IV:

> "... the material produced when poppy-straw has entered into a process for the concentration of its alkaloids."

II. Using an Admission to Prove the Substance is a Drug

10–13　　Usually, it is the result of scientific analysis which will prove or disprove that the substance is a drug of a particular description. But, occasionally, an accused may equally be in a sound position to express an expert opinion as to the nature of the substance he possess. In *Bird* v. *Adams* [1972] Crim.L.R. 179, D.C. the defendant was found in possession of 15 tablets. He maintained that they contained LSD, and that he had been selling them. The prosecution called no scientific evidence. The Divisional Court held that (1) where an accused was not an expert then an "admission" was in reality no admission at all; and (2) an admission may be valueless where an accused could not have the necessary knowledge; but (3), on the facts, the defendant had sufficient knowledge, having peddled the drug, to make his admission a prima facie case against him.

Each case must of course be decided on its own facts, but a mere belief that a substance is a controlled drug is certainly not sufficient: *Mieras* v. *Rees* [1975] Crim.L.R. 224, C.A.

By contrast, in *Wells* [1976] Crim.L.R. 518, C.A., W admitted taking cannabis and amphetamine sulphate. She pleaded guilty to possessing those drugs. The Court of Appeal held that her pleas were good since "in the last analysis all evidence as to the nature of the substance was an expression of opinion, though scientists might be able to express more reliable opinions than others." The court distinguished *Mieras* v. *Rees* on the basis that there was a plea of not guilty in which the circumstances required proof of the nature of the substances.

To describe the results of chemical analysis as an expression of "opinion" is **10–14** an understatement to say the least. However, most users will have their own method of ascertaining the nature of the substance they have acquired in order to avoid being deceived into receiving a substance of a totally different description. Consuming the drug and noting its effects is one method. Once *Wells* had consumed the substance and thereafter pleaded guilty to possessing drugs of a type specified by the prosecution, the court was entitled to act on the basis that she knew perfectly well what the drugs were. Her pleas were the best evidence: *cf. Porter* [1976] Crim.L.R. 58.

Again, a person who admits injecting himself with heroin but later retracts that admission by asserting that he in fact used flour has at least a case to answer: see *Chatwood* [1980] 1 All E.R. 467. The original admission is a declaration against interest in circumstances in which, as a user of the drug, he is likely to know the effects of heroin consumption. But his subsequent assertion is self-serving; it does not neutralise the admission, still less does it prove innocence: see *Storey* (1968) 52 Cr.App.R. 334.

III. ANALYST'S REPORTS AND THE DECISION IN *HUNT*

(a) Proof that the drug is in prohibited form

It is for the Crown to prove that the substance in question is the controlled **10–15** drug alleged but, in certain cases, it is also incumbent on the prosecution to prove that the drug had been in prohibited form at the material time. Thus, where (by virtue of the M.D.A. and the regulations) it is an offence to have a controlled substance in one form but it is not an offence to have that substance in another form, then it is for the prosecution to prove that the substance is in the prohibited form for otherwise no offence is established: *Hunt* [1987] A.C. 352.

Hunt—the facts. One hundred and fifty-four milligrammes of white pow- **10–16** der was found in a packet at the appellant's home. H told the police that the powder was amphetamine sulphate. The analyst's statement, which was read to the jury, stated that, "This powder was found to contain morphine mixed with caffeine and atropine. Morphine is a controlled drug within the Misuse of Drugs Act 1971, Part I of Schedule 2 (Class A drugs). Caffeine and atropine are not controlled under the Misuse of Drugs Act 1971."

Counsel for the appellant unsuccessfully submitted that there was no case to answer whereupon the appellant pleaded guilty.

By regulation 4 of and Schedule 1 to the Misuse of Drugs Regulations 1973 (S.I. 1973 No. 797) (now regulation 4(1) and 4(2) and Schedule 5 of the Misuse of Drugs Regulations 1985) the Secretary of State directed, pursuant to section 7 of the Misuse of Drugs Act 1971, that section 5(1) (dealing with possession) "shall not have effect in relation to" any preparation of morphine containing "not more than 0.2 per cent. of morphine calculated as anhydrous morphine base . . . being a preparation compounded with one or more other active or inert ingredients in such a way that ... the morphine cannot be re-covered by readily applicable means ...." The Court of Appeal dismissed the appeal on the basis that although the regulation and the Schedule created an exception, the burden of proving the exception rested on the accused and, in this instance, the appellant had pleaded guilty.

On appeal to the House of Lords, their Lordships, in allowing the appeal held that (what is now regulation 4(1) and 4(2) and Schedule 5 of the M.D. Regs. 1985) "deals not with exceptions to what would otherwise be unlawful but with the definition of the essential ingredients of an offence" (*per* Lord Griffiths at 1130B) and that the burden was on the prosecution to prove that the morphine in the possession of the appellant had been in the prohibited form. The prosecution only tendered facts which might or might not amount to an offence (under section 5(2)) (*per* Lord Templeman at 1118G).

10–17　　**An explanation of *Hunt*.** It is important to bear in mind that in *Hunt* the relevant regulation and Schedule were made pursuant to section 7(1)(*a*) of the Misuse of Drugs Act 1971. Whereas section 7(1)(*a*) empowers the Secretary of State to "except" a controlled drug from any of the prohibitions set out in the section, by contrast, section 7(1)(*b*) merely enables the Secretary of State to make lawful various activities which would "otherwise be unlawful" under sections 4, 5 and 6. In other words, regulations made under section 7(1)(*a*) go directly to the elements of the offence which must be proved, whereas regulations made under section 7(1)(*b*) give an immunity—or pro-vide a defence—in cases where the offence is otherwise made out.

10–18　　In *Hunt*, the effect of the analyst's ambiguous report meant that the accused may or may not have come within the exception. The question then arose as to whether the burden was on the prosecution to negate the possi-bility that he did, or whether it rested on the accused to prove that he came within the exception on a balance of probabilities. Both the Court of Appeal and the House of Lords accepted the fundamental rule that the prosecution must prove every element of the offence charged. But, in *Edwards* [1975] Q.B. 27 the Court of Appeal stated that there was an exception to this "fun-damental rule" so as to shift the burden on the defendant to prove that he was entitled to do the "prohibited act"—but this exception was "limited to offences arising under enactments which prohibit the doing of an act save in specified circumstances": *per* Lawton L.J. (at 39–40). This, of course, begs the question. In *Hunt*, the "prohibited act" had yet to be established. Accord-ingly, the Court of Appeal held (in effect) that the principle in *Edwards* could have no application to "exceptions" made under section 7(1)(*a*). As if to underline the point, the Court of Appeal observed that by contrast, most, if not all of the remaining regulations (not made under section 7(1)(*a*)) "must fall within the principle in *Edwards* [1975] Q.B. 27" (*per* Robert Goff L.J. at 233G/H) because the effect of them is simply to make lawful (in specified circumstances) that which would otherwise be unlawful.

10–19　　However, this did not dispose of the matter, because both the Court of Appeal and the House of Lords held that practical considerations may be taken into account when construing a particular piece of legislation, in order to determine upon whom the burden of proof rests. In this instance the Court of Appeal considered that only rarely would an accused wish to bring himself within one of the exceptions whereas, if the burden rests on the prosecution, then in many cases it would be necessary "to produce evidence from an analyst" ([1986] 2 W.L.R. 225, 234). Furthermore, the Court of Appeal felt that the burden of proof in the regulations should be applied consistently (at 234 A/B).

The House of Lords, however, noted that in cases where the burden lies on the defendant, the burden can be easily discharged: *per* Lord Griffiths ([1987] A.C. 352, 365). Their Lordships did not share the "anxieties of the Court of Appeal" (at 1130 F-H) and accordingly held that the burden was on the prosecution to negate the possible application of the statutory exceptions. See also Patrick Healy, "Proof and Policy: No Golden Threads" [1987] Crim.L.R. 355.

The importance of a precise analyst's report. In *Hunt* Lord MacKay of   **10–20**
Clashfern remarked (at 1131G/H):

> "I consider that this case emphasises the need for absolute clarity in the terms of the analyst's certificate founded on by the prosecution in cases of this sort and, in my opinion, it would be wise where there is any possibility of one of the descriptions in the relevant Schedule applying . . . that the analyst should state expressly whether or not the substance falls within that description as well as stating whether or not it is a controlled drug within the meaning of the Act of 1971."

In the ordinary way a report from an authorised analyst to the effect that the substance in question is the controlled drug alleged is sufficient evidence of the matters set out therein for the purposes of the M.D.A. 1971 and there exists no burden on the Crown to exclude the possibility that the substance in question had been manufactured synthetically: *Guild* v. *Ogilvie* 1986 S.C.C.R. 67.

B. LETTERS: DOCUMENTS: BOOKS

I. DUTY OF THE PROSECUTION

In the ordinary way the prosecution is under a duty to disclose to the   **10–21**
defence all probative evidence on which the prosecution intends to rely in support of the prosecution case. Frequently, documents are seized by police or customs officers during the course of a search which are retained by them but not formally exhibited or identified. When the defendant comes to be cross-examined, prosecuting counsel may then seek to put to him material not previously disclosed in order to undermine or to rebut the defendant's evidence. Obviously the prosecution is not obliged to overload their case by including every single article or document seized merely because it has some probative value. However, where the prosecution foresees an issue which is likely to form a rational basis for a plea of not guilty, then the prosecution should not wait until the defendant gives evidence before disclosing the relevant material to the defence. In *Phillipson* (1990) 91 Cr.App.R. 226 the Court of Appeal quashed the appellant's conviction for an offence of being

knowingly concerned in the prohibited importation of 350 grammes of heroin concealed inside her body on the basis that the prosecution had been wrong not to disclose various letters in their possession which, prima facie, undermined the appellant's claim that she acted under duress.

> In *Phillipson*, P admitted that the heroin had been imported at the instigation of Icheke with whom P lived and was the father of her baby. During her trial she testified that Icheke frequently assaulted her. In cross-examination the prosecution put to her letters written by Icheke to P as well as one letter written by P to Icheke and a photograph. The purpose of putting the letters to her was to demonstrate a loving relationship and to undermine her evidence that she acted under duress. There was no evidence as to where the letters had been found and the defence was not told of their existence.
>
> *Held*: on appeal, that the evidence of the letters and photograph should have been included as part of the prosecution case. The letters, written by a person not called as a witness (Icheke) were not evidence of the truth of the various statements contained in them. They could not therefore be evidence of the true reason why P had gone to Pakistan or of the true relationship between P and Icheke.

10–22   The court recognised that by disclosing probative material in advance of trial, a defendant may be afforded the opportunity of trimming his evidence, but the rationale in favour of disclosure rested not on the view that the law wished to help liars to tell more convincing lies but because an accused needed to know in advance the case which would be made against him if he was to have a proper opportunity of giving his answers to the best of his ability. "It was better in the interests of justice that an accused was not induced, by thinking that he was safe is he did so, to exaggerate, or to embroider, or to lie": *per* Gibson L.J.

10–23   The importance of the principles referred to in *Phillipson* (1990) 91 Cr.App.R. 226 were repeated in *Sansom* (1991) 92 Cr.App.R. 115. In that case the Court of Appeal quashed the conviction of S in circumstances where documents were put to S in cross-examination which had not previously been disclosed to the defence. The duty of the Crown is to disclose all the evidence upon which it proposes to rely by the end of the prosecution case: see also *Rice* [1963] 1 Q.B. 857; *Kane* (1977) 65 Cr.App.R. 270. If the prosecution decides not to rely on certain documents as part of their case, then they fall into the category of unused material within paragraph 2 of the *Attorney-General's Guidelines* (1982) 74 Cr.App.R. 302 and should be disclosed. In *Sansom* (1991) 92 Cr.App.R. 115, the Court of Appeal emphasised that it is the duty of the prosecuting authority to sift and evaluate the material in its possession in good time. Unused material required to be disclosed under the *Attorney-General's Guidelines* should be disclosed at the proper time and in proper manner: *per* Taylor L.J. (at 123).

II. Evidence as to "Propensity" May Become Relevant

Evidence tending to show a propensity to commit the offence charged is not **10–24** admissible: but see *P.* [1991] 2 A.C. 447, H.L. There does exist, however, a line of cases on which the prosecution has been held entitled to rely concerning the finding of drug-related material in the possession of the defendant in order to prove *mens rea* of the offence charged or to rebut a defence of innocent association or "plant." Astonishingly, only *Madden* has been reported: see *Willis* (January 29, 1979; 2934/B/78); *Thrussell* (November 30, 1981; 1608/A1/81); *Alexiou* (November 14, 1983; 3399/A/82); *Madden* [1986] Crim.L.R. 804 and *Bagga* (May 21, 1986; 1878/C385).

As will be seen, these cases do not establish new law but they are increasingly relied upon by advocates appearing on behalf of the prosecution.

The general principle of law was stated by Lord Herschell in *Makin* v. *Attorney-General for New South Wales* [1894] A.C. 57, when he said (at 65):

"... the mere fact that the evidence adduced tends to shew the commission of other crimes does not render it inadmissible if it be relevant to an issue before the jury, and it may be so relevant if it bears upon the question whether the acts alleged to constitute the crime charged in the indictment were designed or accidental, or to rebut a defence which would otherwise be open to the accused. The statement of these general principles is easy, but it is obvious that it may often be very difficult to draw the line and decide whether a particular piece of evidence is on the one side or the other."

The principle in that case was fully discussed in *D.P.P.* v. *Boardman* [1975] A.C. 421, and again in *P.* (*supra*).

The overriding consideration is whether the evidence is relevant and proba- **10–25** tive—subject to the general discretion to exclude in cases where the prejudicial effect of the evidence outweighs its probative value (see sections 78 and 82(3) of P.A.C.E. 1984). In some of the cases, referred to *infra*, the basis upon which the evidence was admitted seems strained (*e.g.* *Willis*) and in others briefly examined (*e.g.* *Madden*). In *Madden*, the court appears to have had evidence before it which, if it had been discussed in the judgment, would have done much to explain the decision.

In *Willis*, W arrived at Heathrow carrying her handbag and a suitcase. A **10–26** photograph album found in her handbag contained 134.5 grammes of opium. Another album in her suitcase contained 75 grammes of heroin. From her home address was seized a spoon bearing traces of heroin and a box containing a folded piece of paper inside which was 80 milligrammes of heroin. W was charged with the unlawful importation of the drugs found in her luggage under the fore-runner to section 170 C.E.M.A. 1979 (Customs and Excise Act 1952, s.304). In interview W had denied knowledge of the drugs in her luggage.

Held: the finding of the items at her flat showed that W was connected with heroin inside the United Kingdom. That fact, in the ordinary way, would not have been relevant but it became relevant in the light of her defence disclosed in the interviews.

The Court of Appeal stated as its reason that:

> "... what the prosecution were doing was to show that her seeming possession in the United Kingdom of a small quantity of heroin was the odd coincidence in the case of a woman who was saying that she had no knowledge whatsoever that she was bringing dangerous drugs into the country. The jury was entitled to consider ... that coincidence."

During the course of argument the appellant contended that the finding of the items at the flat were not relevant to the offence charged. The Court of Appeal replied:

> "Prima facie that is so. The Court, however, has to look to see what was the defence which the appellant disclosed in the course of her interviews ... what she was saying was that she had no knowledge whatsoever of the fact that inside the ... albums ... there was opium in one and heroin in the other."

10–27   The approach, if not the result, is undoubtedly correct. The finding of articles, prima facie unconnected with the offence charged, may become relevant and admissible if they are probative of an issue in the case. The facts in *Thrussell, infra,* provide a good example of this. However, the validity of the result in *Willis* is less certain. A person who imports prohibited goods may or may not be a victim of a trick; a "plant" or misinformation. Why a user of a particular drug should be less likely to be a "victim" is difficult to follow. The court replied on what it described as the "odd coincidence" of the presence of heroin found at the premises and drugs found in the albums. But was the coincidence really "odd," or so odd as to be probative? A vast number of people abuse drugs in this country. Not every abuser is an importer nor is he to be assumed to be in a better position to know what he is carrying than anyone else. There was the "coincidence" that heroin was carried in one album but the coincidence would have been much more cogent if opium had been found at the premises as well. Suppose the whole consignment had been opium or cannabis. Would the result have been different?

10–28   In *Thrussell*, H and T travelled together on May 20, 1980 from London to Peru via Miami. On May 25, H returned to London. In a suitcase, which H carried, 2.93 kilogrammes of cocaine was discovered by customs officers. On May 26, T returned to London. T's home address was searched and the sum of $45,400 and a book entitled the *Cocaine Consumer's Handbook* were seized. The book described the methods of using cocaine; how to import it; the countries most suitable for export as well as data and advice on how the trade should be carried out. When asked about the cocaine in H's suitcase T replied, "Where would I get that sort of stuff?"

Held: the book was relevant and admissible to prove knowledge by T of the importation of the drug in respect of a charge under C.E.M.A. 1979, s.170.

The court said that the book showed knowledge by the appellant of the drug trade. It may be questioned how the book (which was found in the possession of the courier) could be probative evidence against T that he knew importation of the drug by the courier. The answer to this question has to be seen in the light of the other evidence but, it is submitted, that the decisive factor was the appellant's claim that he would not know where to get cocaine. The book was undoubtedly capable of rebutting that assertion. When coupled with the journey made by both defendants, and the circumstances in which the two men returned separately over two days, that was sufficient to render the book relevant, probative and admissible. As the court remarked, the book was "the one piece of evidence which showed knowledge by the Appellant of the drug trade": *per* Waller L.J.

> In *Alexiou*, 24 boxes arrived at Heathrow airport. The boxes contained   **10–29**
> chandeliers but their false bottoms concealed a total of 107.45 kilogrammes of cannabis resin. The boxes were loaded onto a van and taken to an address where the appellant was waiting and he helped to carry the boxes into the house. The appellant's own home was searched. A suitcase and scales were found. Both items had traces of cannabis on them. Officers also seized £600 in cash in a bread bin, and a diary containing calculations said to relate to drug dealings.
>
> *Held*: that the evidence was admissible to rebut the defence that his presence at the premises to which the drugs were delivered was innocent.

The court in *Alexiou* placed much reliance on the decision in *Willis*. Although the articles found at the Alexiou's home may have shown that he was connected with cannabis inside the United Kingdom, it is submitted that those items could not by themselves prove that the appellant knew the boxes contained cannabis. It may be that the court was influenced by the fact that there was an abundance of other evidence, including articles found at the premises to which the boxes were delivered, that was admissible to prove *mens rea*. One such article was a jig-saw with traces of cannabis resin upon it: the invoice for the jig-saw being at the appellant's home address.

> In *Madden*, a trunk was sent from Jamaica to England and the addressee   **10–30**
> was a child of M's. M arranged for the collection of the trunk. She paid some of the freight charges. Officers found the trunk at M's home address. Cannabis was found in the trunk. The officers also found two letters in a chest of drawers; written by the father of some of the children. The letters were at least one year old. They referred to smuggling small amounts of cannabis into the United Kingdom in batteries and tapes and "the reasons why you didn't get any herbs is because the man didn't have much."
>
> *Held*: the letters were addressed to M which she clearly read. They were admissible to rebut the defence that the trunk was unsolicited and that she did not know of its contents.

In dismissing the appeal, the court referred to *Alexiou* and *Thrussell*. However, the decision in *Madden* is, with respect, not without difficulty. The letters were adduced to show that the appellant knew the trunk contained cannabis and that she solicited the trunk, but neither letter suggested any such delivery and the court did not in its judgment point to any evidence that the author was instrumental in shipping the trunk to her in pursuance of anything said in the letters. The suggested probative value of those letters therefore seems speculative. However, there was evidence before the court that the appellant said to the disguised officer who delivered the trunk, "Now we can see what is in it. We know what is in it. We have been told." The true basis for the decision may be that her response showed a connection between the letters and the delivery of the trunk.

10–31   In *Bagga*, Mrs. R arrived at Heathrow airport with a suitcase found to contain 12.3 kilogrammes of heroin. She was met by her husband and B. Officers searched B's house. They found a briefcase and electronic scales capable of weighing in grammes to an accuracy of two decimal points. Traces of heroin were found in the briefcase and on the scales. In interview, B asserted that his presence at the airport was innocent and that he had no knowledge of the presence of heroin carried by Mrs. R.

Held: the evidence of the traces found in the briefcase and on the scales was relevant and admissible.

10–32   The court concluded that it was open to the prosecution to invite the jury to consider whether the evidence of prior unexplained handling of heroin by the appellant destroyed his defence of innocent and ignorant presence. Again, it was not explained by the court how this evidence would logically achieve that result. At first sight, the facts in *Bagga* were more strongly weighted in favour of admissibility than those in *Willis*. Bagga only came to be tried after the courier had been convicted and after her husband had been given immunity from prosecution: both then gave evidence against Bagga. If their evidence was true the jury had to consider whether Bagga's visit to the airport was innocent or part of a concerted plan to import heroin. The presence of the traces of heroin *inside* the briefcase and on the scales (consistent arguably with the acts of a dealer) went, it was said, to that issue. Curiously, the trial judge in *Bagga* withdrew from the jury a charge of conspiracy to supply heroin on the basis *inter alia* that the "possible findings in relation to importation might, despite the most careful direction as to propensity, be very damaging to the appellant." On appeal it was contended that this reasoning justified the exclusion of the evidence in respect of the charge under section 170, C.E.M.A. 1979 as well. The Court of Appeal queried whether the conspiracy should have been withdrawn and cited, in support of its own reasoning, the judgment in *Willis*.

In the final analysis each case must, of course, be decided on its own facts. It is respectfully submitted that the Court of Appeal in *Alexiou* erred in describing *Willis* as a decision "of this Court, which is of course binding upon us." In fact neither *Willis* nor any of the authorities cited above, establishes new law. These cases are illustrative of existing principles and nothing more.

III. EVIDENCE OF INFORMERS AND OBSERVATION POSTS

There has been much discussion as to the extent to which officers may be   **10–33**
permitted *not* to give evidence that would or might disclose the identity of
informers or the whereabouts of observation posts or matters relating to surveillance. The general rule, in relation to informers, is clear: a witness may not
be asked, and he will not be allowed to disclose, the channels through which
information has been obtained by the law enforcement agencies: *Marks* v.
Beyfus (1890) 25 Q.B.D. 494. This rule was extended in *Rankine* [1986] Q.B.
861 to observation posts in circumstances where disclosure will "embarrass
[the officers'] sources of co-operation [and] imperil person or persons from
whom they had co-operation into the affording of the vantage point."

It will be noted that the rule in *Rankine* is founded not upon the disclosure
of the observation post or vehicle itself, but upon the need to protect the
owner or occupier of the premises or the vehicle in question. The rule is therefore designed to protect individuals and not operational efficacy: see *Brown*
(1982) 87 Cr.App.R. 52.

In each case ("informers" and "observation posts") there is an exception to
the general rule, namely, where disclosure is necessary to avoid a miscarriage
of justice (see *Rankine*, also *Slowcombe* [1991] Crim.L.R. 198); or where the
evidence is necessary to show the innocence of the accused: *Marks* v. *Beyfus*
(1890) (above); *D.* v. *N.S.P.C.C.* [1978] A.C. 171; *Rogers* v. *Home Secretary*
[1973] A.C. 388, H.L.

In *Johnson* [1988] 1 W.L.R. 1377 the Court of Appeal gave guidance on   **10–34**
the evidence to be given during a *voir dire* to determine whether the information (albeit relevant) should be withheld or disclosed. The judge must then
balance the interests of the defence and the interests of the prosecution as well
as the interests of informers, owners or occupiers who may be affected by disclosure. In *Hewitt, The Times*, January 1, 1992; (decided December 20,
1991; 89/5135/X3) submissions that the cases of *Johnson, Brown* and *Rankine* were wrongly decided, were rejected: and see *Brown* (November 25,
1991; unreported).

C. PROVING PREMISES ARE USED FOR SUPPLYING

The presence of drugs on premises, particularly if separately wrapped; the   **10–35**
existence of drug paraphernalia consistent with the commercial supply of
drugs; large sums of money; cutting agents; books and records may all be
relied upon in appropriate cases to prove that premises are being used for the
purposes of supplying drugs. The evidence, if relevant, may or may not go one
step further and prove that the defendant himself was engaged in supplying:
see *Morrison* v. *Smith* 1983 S.C.C.R. 171.

The distinction between adducing evidence to prove (i) that the *premises*
were used to supply drugs, and (ii) proving that the *defendant* himself was a
supplier, may or may not be significant depending on one's interpretation of
an unsatisfactory line of authority culminating in the decision of the House of

Lords in *Kearley* (1992) 95 Cr.App.R. 88, discussed at §10–39, *infra*.

In a considerable number of drug trafficking prosecutions, the "high point" has been evidence of surveillance, carried out by police officers in respect of the number of visitors calling at the premises; the movement of such visitors; their conversations, and even details of telephone calls made to the occupiers enquiring about drugs.

In cases where it is not possible for the prosecution to call the visitors or telephone callers as witnesses the question arises whether the observing police officers may give evidence of (i) the number of visitors arriving and leaving the premises, and (ii) statements made by callers enquiring about the purchase of drugs. The objection to the admissibility of such evidence is that it infringes the hearsay rule.

I. PROVING VISITS

10–36   Evidence of observation describing the movement of persons visiting or leaving the premises is admissible if relevant and probative of any fact in issue in the proceedings. The hearsay rule has no application since the evidence is adduced to prove no more than the fact that the visits have taken place and not to impliedly assert that the visits were drug related. Usually there will be other surrounding circumstances that may give such visits probative significance, *e.g.* the presence of drugs, drug paraphernalia and cash on the premises.

II. REQUESTS MADE FOR DRUGS

10–37   This has proved to be a far more difficult problem. Police may have overheard visitors or telephone callers enquiring whether drugs are available for sale and negotiating a price. The callers themselves may not be willing to give evidence of their association with the premises or with the accused.

The general rule is well established and clearly stated by the Privy Council in *Subramaniam* v. *Public Prosecutor* [1956] 1 W.L.R. 965, 969:

> "Evidence of a statement made to a witness by a person who is not himself called as a witness may or may not be hearsay. It is hearsay and inadmissible when the object of the evidence is to establish the truth of what is contained in the statement. It is not hearsay and is admissible when it is proposed to establish by evidence, not the truth of the statement, but the fact that it was made."

10–38   The distinction between a statement being admissible because it was *made*, but inadmissible as to its *truth*, is sometimes so fine as to be illogical. The significance of the statement being made often depends on the truth of its content. There will be cases where what matters is not what was said but how it was said. Thus, the fact that words were spoken in a distressed fashion may make conversation recorded by a third party admissible: *Ratten* v. *R.* [1972] A.C. 378. In that case it was said: "A question of hearsay only arises when the words spoken are relied on 'testimonially' *i.e.* as establishing some fact narrated by the words": *per* Lord Wilberforce at 387.

Similar reasoning is said to explain the decision in *Woodhouse* v. *Hall* (1980) 72 Cr.App.R. 39. In that case the question was whether a massage parlour was in fact a brothel. Police officers were offered "hand relief" by the ladies at the premises. The Divisional Court held that the evidence of the officers as to what they had heard was admissible and did not infringe the hearsay rule. Donaldson L.J. (as he then was) said that the offers were not a matter of truth or falsity but a matter of what was really said. The evidence was held to be admissible to prove that the premises were in fact being used for immoral purposes.

With respect, it is difficult to see how the offers made by the ladies could have the significance attached to them by the Divisional Court without reference to their truth or falsity. If they were a joke they could hardly prove that the premises were being used as a brothel.

In *Kearley* (1991) 93 Cr.App.R. 222, the Court of Appeal applied *Wood-* **10–39** *house* v. *Hall*. In *Kearley*, the appellant was convicted of possessing amphetamine with intent to supply it. Police raided the appellant's home. However, at the time of the raid the appellant was absent. A number of telephone calls had been made to his home which had been answered by the police in which the caller had enquired whether he could speak to "Chippie" (the appellant's nickname) and asked to be supplied with controlled drugs. The requests were therefore not spoken in the presence or hearing of the appellant and were not made by persons called witnesses.

The Court of Appeal held that the requests were admissible (and were not hearsay) to prove that the premises were used to supply controlled drugs. The reasoning of *Woodhouse* v. *Hall* was applied in this regard. However, the Court of Appeal went further and held that the evidence was admissible to prove that the appellant himself was the supplier. The Court of Appeal held that if the evidence was admissible to prove the fact that the premises were used to supply drugs then it was admissible to prove that the appellant was the supplier.

Again, it is difficult to see how this latter step can be arrived at without reference to the truth or falsity of the statements themselves. The makers of those utterances were not available for cross-examination.

The House of Lords (1992) 95 Cr.App.R. 88, reversed the decision of the Court of Appeal but the certified question was confined to whether the evidence may be added "for the purpose ... of inviting the jury to draw an inference from the fact that the words were spoken (*namely that the defendant was a supplier of drugs*)," (emphasis supplied).

It follows that the House of Lords was not invited to consider whether the **10–40** fact that such requests were made was evidence that the *premises* were used for the purpose of supplying drugs.

A majority of their Lordships (Lord Griffiths and Lord Browne-Wilkinson dissented) held that the requests were inadmissible for the purposes set out in the certified question for two separate reasons. First, they were irrelevant. The requests went to the makers state of mind but that was not an issue in the case. The content of the statements relied upon did not assert that the appellant had previously engaged in drug supplying to any of the callers in question. Secondly, the hearsay rule was infringed. The request was made in a form which contained an assertion that the premises were being used as a course of supply of drugs and that the supplier was the appellant. What the prosecution therefore sought to do was to rely on the requests as evidence of the truth of the proposition asserted.

It is submitted that the decision of the majority of their Lordships in the House of Lords in *Kearley* is correct. Their Lordships regarded the facts in *Woodhouse v. Hall* as amounting to "original" and not hearsay evidence.

10–41   Ironically, perhaps, the decision of the Court of Appeal in *Kearley* sought to address some of the criticism levelled at another decision of that court in *Harry (D.)* (1988) 86 Cr.App.R. 105 in which it was held that evidence as to the content of telephone calls enquiring whether drugs were for sale, and asking for P by his nickname, was inadmissible on the grounds that the evidence was sought to be relied upon to establish some facts narrated by the words used. The sole question in *Harry* was whether the appellant could rely on the telephone calls to prove that the supplier of the drugs was his co-defendant and not himself. Lawton L.J. said (at 11):

> "He was seeking to rely upon the contents of the telephone calls not to prove their purpose but to establish his case that it was the co-accused and not he who was doing the drug dealing on the premises."

10–42   In other words, if the appellant had sought to rely on the content of the calls to "prove their purpose," namely that the premises were being used to supply drugs, then the content would have been admissible: see *Subramaniam* v. *Public Prosecutor* [1956] 1 W.L.R. 965, 970; *Ratten* [1972] A.C. 378; *Woodhouse* v. *Hall (supra)*; *Davidson* v. *Quirke* (1923) N.Z.L.R. 552 and *McGregor* v. *Stokes* [1952] V.L.R. 347. In *Harry* it was common ground that the premises were being so used and so that particular issue did not arise. In the opinion of the court, the appellant sought to cross the line between what is admissible or inadmissible, by relying on the content of the conversations to show that the co-defendant was the supplier. The main criticism of this part of the decision in *Harry* is that the distinction drawn by the Court of Appeal in that case simply does not exist because the identity of the recipient of the calls is all part and parcel of the same purpose: see D.J. Birch in her commentary on *Harry* [1987] Crim.L.R. 325; also *Archbold: Criminal Pleading, Evidence and Practice* (1992 edition) para. 11–7.

D. EXPERT EVIDENCE

I. GENERAL NOTE

10–43   In the ordinary way parol evidence is not admissible in respect of matters which are not within the personal knowledge of the witness hearsay evidence is inadmissible. Usually a witness may not express an opinion or belief but there exists a necessary exception in respect of witnesses who are able to express a credible opinion, empirically based, on specialised topics of learning or knowledge.

It is important to bear in mind that evidence of an expert may fall into two categories. The first relates to findings of fact made or discovered by him, *e.g.* that a substance is a controlled drug of a particular description: see *Hunt* [1987] A.C. 352. The second relates to an expression of opinion as to the probable results or consequences flowing from facts found or proved. Thus an expert may give evidence as to the amount of heroin found in the body of the deceased at the time of the autopsy and that the drug found was the sole or substantial cause of death: *Clarke* (January 21, 1992; unreported; 4101/W3/91).

Objection is sometimes taken to the admissibility of a conclusion which is **10-44** said to be less than probable. The basis of the objection is that any such conclusion is inherently unreliable, speculative and therefore worthless or, put another way, that its prejudicial effect outweighs its probative value. In the author's experience some judges conduct a *voir dire* to determine admissibility and to seek clarification from the expert as to his findings and conclusions: and see *Ward, The Times,* June 8, 1992, C.A.

The duty of experts has been said to be the duty:

> "... to furnish the judge or jury with the necessary scientific criteria for testing the accuracy of their conclusions, so as to enable the judge or jury to form their own independent judgment by the application of these criteria to the facts proved in evidence": *Davie* v. *Edinburgh Magistrates* 1953 S.C. 35, 40.

Laudible though these sentiments are, the performance of this duty is easier said than done. Some conclusions will depend on complicated tests, or a series of tests, the results of which are then subject to interpretation not easily understood by lay persons and which are difficult to explain to a court. In practice, and where the conclusion or method of analysis is in dispute, the expert will tend to summarise techniques employed and to rely on models, photographs and diagrammatic representations to explain the basis for his findings and conclusions.

II. QUALIFICATIONS OF AN EXPERT

As Bingham L.J. remarked in *Robb* (1991) 93 Cr.App.R. 161 a defendant **10-45** could not fairly be asked to meet evidence of opinion given by "a quack, a charlatan, or even an enthusiastic amateur."

It is a matter for the court to decide on the facts of a particular case whether a witness has sufficient "expertise" to give the evidence sought to be adduced. There is no logical reason why an "enthusiastic amateur" should not be an expert, providing that he or she has the necessary expertise. Experienced members of the "drug squad" may give expert evidence as to the street value of a drug. In *Bryan*; (November 8, 1984; unreported; 3923B84) the Court of Appeal held that the evidence of a Drug Squad officer with experience of street dealing is admissible as to the fact of what happens on the street. He was therefore entitled to give evidence of the street value of drugs. However, this was not a matter for a pharmacist who would probably have less information concerning black market prices than a Drug Squad officer. Wood J. said:

> "The view of this court is that police officers with their expertise of dealing with these problems, being on the streets and with their knowledge and meeting those having a drug problem and those pushing drugs, have a very wide experience and can give evidence of fact of what takes place on many occasions on the streets."

> In *White* v. *H.M. Advocate*, 1986 S.C.C.R. 224, a Drug Squad officer was permitted to give evidence that (i) LSD was a social drug and not an addictive drug; (ii) that "trips" may be pleasant or awful; and (iii) that 25 squares of LSD would not be taken by a user within a fortnight.
> *Held*: the evidence was rightly admitted "provided such a witness' qualification as a police officer and his experience in the Drug Squad are first established, such evidence ... is clearly competent. Evidence of this nature is not exompetent only to medically qualified witnesses": *per* Lord Justice-Clerk.

III. Sources of Information Used by Experts

10–46   Experts often give evidence of findings and conclusions even if the various tests employed (and results obtained) were carried out by laboratory technicians who are not called as supporting witnesses. Usually an expert will say that he supervised delegated tasks and so pre-empt objection that the evidence of an expert is founded on hearsay. However, most learning and the acquisition of expert knowledge is empirical and dependent upon the researches and findings of others. Accordingly, there is ample authority for the proposition that experts are entitled to rely on textbooks, materials and the experiments of others: see *Somers* [1963] 1 W.L.R. 1306.

10–47   Drug Squad officers are permitted (and have been for many years) to give evidence as to the street value and the rate and method of consumption of a particular drug: see *Bryan* (*supra*). The source of the information may derive from data collated by the National Drugs Intelligence Unit which, in turn, may have been derived from answers given by arrested persons to the police; see also *Patel* [1987] Crim.L.R. 839 and *Afzal, The Times,* June 25, 1991. The officer may well be able to add his own experiences to support the opinion he expresses. The complaint that such evidence infringes the hearsay rule has been advanced on a number of occasions at first instance but there is not one reported authority in which that complaint has been upheld.

> In *Wilson* v. *H.M. Advocate*, 1988 S.C.C.R. 384, Drug Squad officers and forensic scientists gave evidence that cannabis resin in the form of cannabis oil was commonly illegally imported into the United Kingdom from Morrocco via Spain by putting it inside a condom or a balloon and secreting this capsule internally. The basis of this knowledge was acquired, in the course of their respective duties by attending seminars and by discussing drug enforcement questions with officers of the customs

and excise.

Held: the submission that this evidence was hearsay and should not have been admitted was rejected. The Lord Justice-General said:

"... it appears to us that the evidence given by the drug squad officers and the forensic scientists could be described as simply disclosure of the received wisdom of persons concerned in drug enforcement, wisdom which they were bound to have picked up in various ways in order that they might perform their duties,": and see *Bryan*, *(supra)*.

It will be noted that the court did not deal head-on with the issue as to why **10–48** the evidence was not inadmissible as being contrary to the hearsay rule. However, the answer to this question is already covered by authority.

In *Abadom* [1983] 1 W.L.R. 126 fragments of glass were found embedded in the shoes of the appellant. One forensic expert ("X") gave evidence that the glass found on the shoes, and glass taken from a window at the scene of a robbery, were subjected to chemical analysis and were "similar on analysis." A second expert ("Y") measured the refractive index of both samples which was found to be identical. "Y" concluded that the glass from the shoes originated from the window. He based his conclusion on the findings of himself, and "X," but also on statistics compiled by the Home Office Control Research Establishment which showed that the refractive index in question occurred in only four per cent. of all analyses which had been made. On appeal it was argued that the evidence, founded on the Home Office data, was hearsay and therefore inadmissible.

Held: the evidence was not hearsay. In dismissing the appeal the Court of Appeal explained the basis of admissibility in terms of cogency and the role of the expert. Thus, it was said that the expert:

"... must be entitled to draw upon material produced by others in the field in which their expertise lies. Indeed, it is part of their duty to consider (such material) ... and not to draw conclusions merely on the basis of their own experience, which is inevitably likely to be more limited that the general body of information which may be available to them ... the statistical results of the work of others in the same field must inevitably form an important ingredient in the cogency or probative value of his own conclusion in the particular case."

The Court of Appeal made it plain that where an expert relies on the exist- **10–49** ence or non-existence of primary facts which are basic to the conclusion reached by the expert, then those facts must be proved by admissible evidence. If "Y" had not himself determined the refractive index it would have been necessary to call the person who had done so before "Y" could have expressed any opinion based on their determination (see the judgment of Kerr L.J. at 52): and see *English Exporters* v. *Eldonwall* [1973] Ch. 415: *Turner* [1975] 1 Q.B. 834; *Somers* [1963] 1 W.L.R. 1306; *Crayden* (1978) 67 Cr.App.R. 1.

IV. Weight and Reliability

10–50   As has been mentioned above, whether a particular witness has the necessary "expertise" before he may be permitted to give evidence of an opinion is a matter for the court to determine on the facts of each case. Once that criterion is met then evidence of opinion may be admissible even if the expert relied on a technique which was accepted by the majority of professional opinion to be unreliable unless supplemented or vertified by other methods: see *Robb* (1991) 93 Cr.App.R. 161. In that case evidence was admitted of voice identification notwithstanding the questioned technique employed by the expert. Presumably the court had in mind the general rule that relevant evidence which is more probative than prejudicial is admissible and that, thereafter, the weight to be attached to the evidence is a matter for the tribunal of fact and that it is open to the other party to the proceedings to adduce their own expert evidence in rebuttal.

To what extent inherently unreliable evidence can properly be said to be probative evidence at all has not been definitively decided by any appellate court. Plainly, evidence which is inherently unreliable may be inadmissible because its prejudicial effect outweighs its probative value or because it ought to be excluded under section 78 of P.A.C.E. 1984: see *Deenik* [1992] Crim.L.R. 578 89/6444/W3 where the evidence of a customs officer who recognised the voice of the appellant during his detention as being the person to whom the officer had spoken on the telephone during a covert operation, was admissible and would not be excluded under section 78 of P.A.C.E. 1984.

Schedule 2 to the Misuse of Drugs Act 1971 deals with matters of a technical nature and the words employed in that Schedule must be given the meaning attributed to them by a person qualified to understand such words: see *Couzens*, April 10, 1992, C.A.

V. Evidence of Voice Recognition

10–51   In *Deenik, supra* the appellant was convicted of the unlawful importation of 500 kilogrammes of cannabis resin packed in boxes and concealed in a lorry. An undercover customs officer spoke on the telephone to a man she had never met called "Lloyd." The appellant was arrested in a telephone kiosk and taken to an office of Customs and Excise. The officer who made the call was also at that office and recognised the voice of the appellant as being the person she spoke to on the telephone. Objection was taken to the admissibility of the evidence of voice recognition at the premises of Customs and Excise. In dismissing the appeal, the Court of Appeal held that here was no justification for the exclusion of the evidence under section 78 of P.A.C.E. 1984 on the facts of that case. What was done was not unfair and that nothing else could be done to reduce the chance of error; and also *Robb (supra)* in which it was held that evidence of voice recognition was admissible notwithstanding that the test carried out by the analyst was called into question as being unreliable.

VI. Effect of a Drug

As to the admissibility of expert evidence as to the effect of certain drugs on an individual see *Skirving; Grossman* [1985] Q.B. 819.   **10–52**

E. INTERVIEWS

I. Interviews Conducted by Customs Officers

Doubt has sometimes been expressed as to whether the Codes of Practice made under section 66 of P.A.C.E. 1984 apply to customs officers. It would be a startling result if they did not. In *Sanusi* [1992] Crim.L.R. 43 it was pointed out that section 67(9) of P.A.C.E. 1984 had the effect of placing a duty upon customs officers to observe the provisions of the Codes of Practice although P.A.C.E. (Application to Customs & Excise) Order 1985. (S.I. 1985 No. 1800) did not specifically apply section 66 of P.A.C.E. 1984 to the activities of customs officers: see Schedule 1 to S.I. 1985 No. 1800. On the facts in *Sanusi* there was a breach of Code C:3.1 and C:3.2 in not informing S of his rights and the interview in question ought to have been excluded: see also *Twaites* (1991) 92 Cr.App.R. 106. Similarly, in *Bailey* (March 17, 1992; unreported; Croydon Crown Court) the court excluded answers given by a suspect to customs officers in circumstances where a caution should have been administered under Code C:10.1 but which was not.   **10–53**

II. Failure to Make Contemporaneous Note

In *White* [1991] Crim.L.R. 779, W was charged with possessing a Class B drug with intent to supply. A short conversation took place at W's house when the premises were searched. A note of the conversation was not made until the officer arrived at the police station. It was submitted that there were three breaches of the Code to P.A.C.E. namely (1) no time was entered recording the end of the interview: Code C:11.3(b)(i); (2) there was no contemporaneous note of the interview: Code C:11.3(b)(ii); (3) no reason for non-completion of the interview was recorded: Code C:11.6.   **10–54**

Held: that in all the circumstances, and despite the three breaches, it was not unfair to admit the interview and accordingly the arguments for its exclusion under section 78 of P.A.C.E. 1984 were rejected.

III. Unfairness/Oppression/*Agent Provocateur*

(a) Drug addict withdrawing in interview

The relationship between sections 76(2)(*b*), 78 and 82(3) has been the subject of much attention by the courts and commentators alike: see *McGovern*   **10–55**

(1991) 92 Cr.App.R. 228; *Everett* [1988] Crim.L.R. 826; *D.P.P.* v. *Blake* [1989] 1 W.L.R. 432; *Goldenberg* (1989) 88 Cr.App.R. 285; *Rennie* (1982) 74 Cr.App.R. 207; and *Crampton* (1991) 92 Cr.App.R. 369.

For the purposes of section 76(2)(*b*), the cases seem to suggest a distinction, which the courts have not in fact expressly propounded, namely between words said and things done which are intrinsically likely to produce an untrue confession (*e.g.* threats), and mere circumstances "existing at the time" which fall outside the scope of section 76(2)(*b*) because the circumstances do not amount to "anything … done" by the police within the meaning of that section.

> *Crampton* (1991) 92 Cr.App.R. 369. The appellant, a heroin addict, made admissions during an interview in the police station 19 hours after his arrest in respect of an allegation that he conspired to supply heroin. The appellant complained at his trial that the admissions were made whilst experiencing withdrawal symptoms. The police relied on their own judgment to decide whether he was fit to be interviewed. They would not have interviewed the appellant if they had known he was withdrawing. After the interview, a doctor examined the appellant and concluded that he had been fit to be interviewed.
>
> *Held*: the argument that the confession should have been excluded under section 76(2)(*b*) or section 78 was rejected. Although the police had instigated the interview, the court doubted whether the mere holding of an interview when the appellant was withdrawing from heroin, came within section 76(2)(*b*). The subsection seemed to postulate something said or done *by the police* which was likely to induce an unreliable confession.

10–56 The court observed that whether or not a drug addict was fit to be interviewed (in the sense that his answers could be relied upon as being true) was a matter for those present at the time subject to Code C: 9B. The judge on the *voir dire* had to decide whether the assessment of those present was correct. On the evidence the appellant was fit to be interviewed at the relevant time.

It will be noted that in *Crampton* the Court of Appeal doubted whether the mere holding of an interview when C was withdrawing came within section 76(2)(*b*) but nevertheless the court assumed, for the purposes of the appeal, that it did.

It is submitted that on a natural reading of section 76(2)(*b*) the interviewer must say or do something which, "in the circumstances existing at the time," was likely to render unreliable a confession made in consequence. In the ordinary way, merely putting elementary questions to a suspect, who in fact is withdrawing during interviews, falls outside the scope of section 76(2)(*b*). In *Goldenberg* (1989) 88 Cr.App.R. 285, G requested an interview during which he made a number of admissions although the evidence showed that he was withdrawing at the time. On those facts nothing had been said or done by the interviewers within the terms of section 76(2)(*b*) to render a confession unreliable and the Court of Appeal so held. However, drawing the line between things "said" or "done," and mere circumstances prevailing at the time which fall outside section 76(2)(*b*) may be difficult to draw (see the commentary to *Crampton* [1991] Crim.L.R. 277, 279). If officers instigate an interview knowing that the suspect is withdrawing then, it is submitted, the fact that questions are asked in such circumstances in consequence of which a confession follows, is enough to bring section 76(2)(*b*) into play: see *Everett* [1988] Crim.L.R. 826; *D.P.P.* v. *Blake* [1989] 1 W.L.R. 432.

Even if "mere circumstances" fall outside the scope of section 76(2)(*b*), it is **10–57** of course open to the court to exclude a confession made in those circumstances under section 78. The courts have yet to decide whether it must be shown, for the purposes of section 78, that the circumstances of the case are likely to render unreliable any confession or whether the court is entitled to examine the truth of the confession in question. Ultimately, the test is "will the admission of the relevant evidence have such an effect on the fairness of the proceedings that the court ought not admit it?": *O'Leary* (1988) 87 Cr.App.R. 387, C.A.

F. VIEW OF THE SCENE OF THE CRIME

In *Hunter* [1985] 1 W.L.R. 613 a ship's officer was tried for the unlawful **10–58** importation of cannabis carried on his ship. At the judge's instigation a view of the *locus in quo* took place in the presence of the jury, the clerk of the court, counsel and solicitors and the witness under examination. The judge himself did not take part. The Court of Appeal quashed the conviction. The judge and jury had to be present throughout the giving of evidence: see *Tameshwar* v. *The Queen* [1957] A.C. 476.

Chapter 11
Powers of Police and Customs Officers

11–01   Recognising that much has been written by others concerning the powers of the police (but comparatively little concerning the powers of customs officers) what follows is intended only to be a summary of the most important powers, rights and duties conferred on officers insofar as they affect the investigation and prosecution of drug offences. The Police and Criminal Evidence Act 1984 (P.A.C.E.) and the Drug Trafficking Offences Act 1986 (D.T.O.A.) have radically altered much of the earlier law, and therefore earlier authorities, to the extent that they may appear to be relevant, must be considered and applied with care. However both P.A.C.E. and the D.T.O.A. do little to affect the powers exercisable under the Customs and Excise Management Act 1979 (C.E.M.A.).

Section 24 of the M.D.A., previously concerned with the powers of arrest under that enactment, has been totally repealed.

Accordingly, the duties, rights, powers and privileges conferred on police and customs officers are chiefly to be found in five statutes, namely:

(i)   The Police and Criminal Evidence Act 1984.
(ii)   The Misuse of Drugs Act 1971.
(iii) The Customs and Excise Management Act 1979.
(iv)   The Drug Trafficking Offences Act 1986.
(v)   The Criminal Justice (International Co-operation) Act 1990.

Citizens may also take certain steps in the prevention of crime—but very much at their peril. The overriding principle of our constitutional law is that no one in the United Kingdom may lay hands on another, or on his property, without his permission and without lawful justification. For this reason greater powers are given to police and to customs officers than to anyone else.

A. POWERS OF THE CITIZEN

I. SEIZING A CONTROLLED DRUG

11–02   A citizen possesses no inherent right at common law to seize property under the control of another, but section 5(4) of the M.D.A. provides a defence to a person charged with the unlawful possession of a controlled drug

186

if he proves that he took possession of it for the purpose of preventing another from committing an offence in connection with the drug (section 5(4)(*a*)), or that he took it for the purpose of giving it to a person lawfully entitled to take custody of it, for example a police officer or customs officer (see section 5(4)(*b*) of the M.D.A.).

II. A CITIZEN'S ARREST

Under section 24(4) of P.A.C.E. any person may arrest, without a warrant, **11–03** anyone who is in the act of committing an arrestable offence, or anyone whom he has reasonable grounds for suspecting to be committing such an offence. Again, he may arrest, without a warrant, anyone who is guilty of the offence, or whom he has reasonable grounds for suspecting to be guilty of it: see section 24(5) of P.A.C.E.

Both subsections 24(4) and (5) follow the earlier law, so where no arrestable offence has in fact been committed, a private person who performs an arrest faces an action for false imprisonment: see *Walters* v. *W.H. Smith & Son Ltd.* [1914] 1 K.B. 595 and *Beckwith* v. *Philby* (1872) 6 B. & C. 635.

An individual once arrested by another must be taken to a police station, by a constable, as soon as practicable: P.A.C.E., s.30(1).

There is no general power conferred by the law on a private person to effect a search of another.

B. POWERS OF THE POLICE

I. ARRESTS

Powers of arrest are conferred on constables by section 24 of P.A.C.E. and **11–04** include offences arising under the Customs and Excise Acts: see section 24(2) of P.A.C.E and section 1(1) of the C.E.M.A.

No warrant is needed where a constable has reasonable grounds for suspecting that an arrestable offence has been committed (section 24(6) of P.A.C.E.). He may also arrest anyone who is, or is reasonably suspected to be, about to commit an arrestable offence (section 24(7)). An arrest involves an act of compulsion so that a mere invitation to a person to accompany an officer to a police station is not an arrest: see *Alderson* v. *Booth* [1969] 2 Q.B. 216, *Wheatley* v. *Lodge* [1971] 1 W.L.R. 29 and *Inwood* [1973] 1 W.L.R. 647.

Reasonable suspicion is not the same as prima facie proof and may be based on the receipt of information which, at the trial, would in fact be inadmissible: see *Hussain* v. *Chong Fook Kam* [1970] A.C. 492 and *Dumbell* v. *Roberts* [1944] 1 All E.R. 326.

A person is to be told of the reason for the arrest at the time, or as soon as is practicable after the arrest: see P.A.C.E. 1984, s.28(3) and *Christie* v. *Leachinsky* [1947] A.C. 573.

II. Searches Without a Warrant

11–05   A constable who has reasonable grounds to suspect that any person is in possession of controlled drugs may stop and search that person and detain him for that purpose (section 23(2)(*a*) of the M.D.A.), or to search a vehicle or vessel in which the drug may be found (section 23(2)(*b*) of the M.D.A.). Section 23(2)(*a*) expressly authorises detention for the purpose of searching a suspect; it does not give the officer a general right to question him. But in *Green* [1982] Crim.L.R. 604, the Court of Appeal considered that a right to detain involved the right to ask questions which were at least incidental to the exercise of that statutory power.

Furthermore, an officer has no right to stop a vehicle, or to search it simply because he suspects that the vehicle (and not the occupants) has been used in connection with a drugs offence.

> In *Littleford* [1978] Crim.L.R. 48 an officer stopped a vehicle and searched it and the occupants. The officer had been informed by radio that the car was suspected of being involved in drug trafficking.
>
> *Held*: the searches were illegal. The officer's suspicion was in connection with the vehicle and not the occupant.

11–06   By section 2(2) of P.A.C.E. if a constable contemplates a search he must take reasonable steps to bring to the attention of the appropriate person the fact that he is a constable (if not in uniform) and, in any event, he must give his name, the name of the police station to which he is attached, the object of the search and his grounds for making the search (see section 2(3) of P.A.C.E.): *cf. Brazil* v. *Chief Constable of Surrey* [1983] 3 All E.R. 537 and *Lindley* v. *Rutter* [1981] Q.B. 128.

An officer may also search an unattended vehicle but he must leave a notice inside the vehicle (if possible) of the fact that he has searched it and stating that an application for compensation may be made at the constable's police station: section 2(6) and (7) of P.A.C.E. The officer shall record details of a search: section 3(1) of P.A.C.E.

Where a person has been arrested, a constable may then search that person for anything which might be evidence relating to an offence (section 32(2)(*a*)(ii) of P.A.C.E.) providing that the constable has reasonable grounds to believe that the person may have concealed something on him relevant to an offence (section 32(5)).

III. Search of Premises Without a Warrant

11–07   At common law there was no right vested in the police or anyone else to enter a private house without a warrant, no matter how serious the crime being investigated. The one exception was following a culprit in "hot pursuit": see *McLorie* v. *Oxford* [1982] Q.B. 1290.

If a person is arrested by police in any premises, and that person is a danger to himself or to others, the police are perfectly within their rights to search those premises but only for evidence relating to the offence for which he has been arrested (section 32(2)(*b*) of P.A.C.E.) and only to the extent that the search is reasonably required (section 32(3)) but there must be reasonable grounds to believe that there is relevant evidence on the premises (section 32(6)).

Irrespective of whether or not a person arrested is a danger to himself or to others, a constable, under section 18 of P.A.C.E., may enter and search any premises occupied or controlled by the person arrested if he has reasonable grounds for suspecting that on the premises there is evidence relating to that offence or indeed another similar offence. However, before invoking section 18, the constable needs the written authorisation of an officer of at least the rank of inspector unless (and this seems a curious addition to the section) the presence of the arrested party at the premises is "necessary for the effective investigation of the offence" (section 18(5)). This would presumably include a person who had stashed drugs, and items relevant to the offence, and who would therefore be able to assist the police (if he wishes to do so) to find them.

IV. Searching for an Individual

In addition to these powers, a constable in uniform (section 17(3) of P.A.C.E.) may enter and search any premises—without a warrant—if the object of gaining entry is (*inter alia*) to execute a warrant of arrest, or to arrest a person for an arrestable offence (section 17), providing there are reasonable grounds to believe that the person is on the premises (section 17(2)(*a*)) and only if it is reasonably required for the purpose of finding the person concerned. **11–08**

All former rules of common law which emerged to give a constable power to enter premises without a warrant are now abolished: section 17(5). It follows that section 17 is a codifying provision (*cf. Thomas* v. *Sawkins* [1935] 2 K.B. 249; *Davis* v. *Lisle* [1936] 2 K.B. 434; *Robson* v. *Hallett* [1967] 2 Q.B. 939). Parliament has now empowered officers not merely to enter premises in order to prevent the commission of an offence therein, but also to investigate crime generally.

V. Intimate Searches and Searches at Police Stations

Previous statutes and rules at common law affecting the ability of the police to search suspects at police stations and to carry out intimate searches have been abolished (section 53 of P.A.C.E.). **11–09**

Instead, a new set of principles has been enacted by section 55 of P.A.C.E. Thus, an intimate search is restricted to certain purposes only; *e.g.* where a Class A drug is concealed on the suspect and that he "was in possession of it with the appropriate criminal intent before his arrest"—a passage which may present some difficulties of application and construction (see section 55(1)(*b*)). In any event an intimate search must be authorised in writing by an officer of at least the rank of superintendent (section 55(1) and (3)) providing that he has reasonable grounds to believe that the Class A drug cannot be found without such a search (section 55(2)) and that it is carried out by a registered medical practitioner or registered nurse (unless the superintendent thinks this impracticable): see subsections 55(4), (5) and (17) of P.A.C.E. An intimate search for a Class A drug must not be carried out at a police station but at a hospital; or at the surgery of a general practitioner, or some other place used for medical purposes (see sections 55(9) and (8)).

Again, intimate samples (*e.g.* blood, saliva, urine) may not be taken unless a person is reasonably suspected of having committed a "serious arrestable offence"—a term which is narrowly defined by the Act (see section 116 of and Schedule 5 to P.A.C.E.) but which includes an arrestable offence, aggravated by the happening of certain events listed in section 116(6), *e.g.* substantial financial gain to any person. Therefore, a person reasonably suspected of being a major drugs supplier who has substantially benefited financially as a result is liable to be a person from whom intimate samples may be taken subject to the requirements of section 62. Other samples may be taken with the accused's consent.

VI. SEARCHES WITH A WARRANT

11–10   Warrants may be obtained under a number of different enactments but three principal statutes are dealt with here. The first is section 23 of the M.D.A.; the second is section 8 of P.A.C.E. and the third is section 28 of the D.T.O.A.

(a) Warrants granted under section 23 of the M.D.A.

11–11   A justice of the peace is authorised by this section to grant a warrant authorising a constable to search premises at "any time or times" within one month from the date of the warrant. But there must be reasonable cause to suspect that controlled drugs are in the possession of a person on any premises, or that documents exist in relation to a drugs transaction.

In *Adams* [1980] Q.B. 575, the Court of Appeal considered whether a warrant issued under section 3(1) of the Obscene Publications Act 1959 (O.P.A.) authorised officers to search premises on more than one occasion. During the course of legal argument, section 3(1) was contrasted with section 23(3) of the M.D.A. where the words "at any time or times within one month" might imply authorisation of a number of quite separate searches within that time. The court considered section 23(3) of the M.D.A. 1971 to "fortify, rather than found" their conclusion that the wording of section 3(1) of the O.P.A. 1959 authorised only one search per warrant. (See also *Dickinson* v. *Brown* (1794) 1 Esp. 218; 170 E.R. 334 and section 152(1) of the Licensing Act 1953.)

However, it is unlikely that Parliament intended to give police blanket authorisation to enter premises as often as they wish within the relevant time merely upon the grant of a warrant under section 23(3) of the M.D.A. 1971.

11–12   In the absence of authority to the contrary, the words "time or times" may mean no more than that a justice of the peace is empowered to grant a warrant specifying multiple searches if the evidence given to him on oath justifies such a course. Any other construction would result in the total inability of the court granting the warrant to pre-empt a subsequent entry, search, and seizure within the operational period which is not, on its merits, actually warranted.

By contrast, a search warrant granted under section 8 of P.A.C.E. authorises an entry on one occasion only. If the main or only reason for being on premises is to detect offences under the M.D.A. it is not essential that a warrant be obtained under section 23(3) of the M.D.A. if entry is gained by virtue of another enactment: *Foster* v. *Attarde* (1986) 83 Cr.App.R. 214.

Once a constable is authorised to enter premises by virtue of section 23 of the M.D.A. he may use such force as is reasonably necessary to gain admission and to search the premises and any occupants but, in *King* v. *R.* [1969] 1 A.C. 304, the Privy Council held that a warrant, granted under similar Jamaican legislation, was unlawful if it did not expressly authorise the search of persons as well as premises.

Under section 16 of P.A.C.E. 1984, and the Codes of Practice made under **11–13** the Act, entry to the premises may be effected by the use of force or subterfuge before there is any requirement for a constable to identify himself by producing his warrant card or producing the search warrant as required by section 16(5). Both the Codes of Practice and, by implication, section 23 of the M.D.A., recognise that the use of force or subterfuge is permissible to gain entry. If the law were otherwise, then the whole object of section 16 of P.A.C.E. and section 23 of the M.D.A. 1971 would be frustrated: *Longman* (1989) 88 Cr.App.R. 148, C.A.

> In *Longman*, police officers obtained a warrant to enter L's premises to search for drugs pursuant to section 23 of the M.D.A. 1971. The officers tricked L into opening the door and forced their way into the premises. They stated that they were police officers and that they had a warrant. L shouted to another man whom the police found about to administer cocaine to himself.
>
> *Held*: on appeal, that a warrant was "produced" for the purposes of section 16(5)(*b*), (*c*) of P.A.C.E. 1984 when the occupier of the premises was given an opportunity to inspect it. L obstructed the police under section 23 of the M.D.A. 1971 and, by so doing, he had deprived himself of the opportunity of inspecting the warrant and the warrant card before he was arrested.

Any drugs or relevant documents found may accordingly be seized and retained by the police.

(b) Warrants granted under section 8 of P.A.C.E.

The police also have power to apply to a justice of the peace for a search **11–14** warrant in respect of premises under section 8 of P.A.C.E. Although the granting of a warrant under this section is confined to cases where there is reasonable cause to believe that a "serious arrestable offence" has been committed, nevertheless this may include a major drugs supplier or a person concerned in the unlawful importation/exportation of controlled drugs where substantial gains are suspected to have been made.

Warrants granted under section 8 above may be executed by a constable: P.A.C.E., s.16(1). Again, entry may be effected within one month from the date of its issue: P.A.C.E., s.16(2) but with the qualification that the entry and search must be carried out at a reasonable hour unless the purpose of the search would be frustrated as a result.

(c) Warrants granted under section 28 of the D.T.O.A.

11–15   By section 28(1), a constable (or, in Scotland, the Procurator Fiscal) may, for the purpose of an investigation into drug trafficking, apply to a circuit judge (or, in Scotland, the sheriff) for a warrant in respect of specified premises authorising (by virtue of section 28(2)) a constable to enter and search the premises if an order for the disclosure of material on premises under section 27 of that Act has not been complied with, or certain conditions stipulated in section 28(3) or section 28(4) are fulfilled. Where a constable has entered premises in the execution of a warrant issued under section 28, he may seize and retain any material, other than "items subject to legal privilege" (as defined by section 10 of P.A.C.E.) and "excluded material" (as defined by section 11 of P.A.C.E.) which is likely to be of substantial value to the investigation for the purpose for which the warrant was issued: see section 28(5) of the D.T.O.A.

References in the D.T.O.A. to a "constable" include a person commissioned by the Commissioners of Customs and Excise: see section 28(1) of the D.T.O.A.

(d) Generally

11–16   Although it is obviously desirable that warrants should be correctly drafted, nevertheless an inconsequential error or misspelling is unlikely to vitiate the warrant.

> In *Atkinson* (1976) Crim.L.R. 307 police wished to search the defendant's flat. They thought that the number of the flat was "45" and accordingly obtained a warrant to search "Flat 45." In fact the defendant lived at "Flat 30." Police entered Flat 30 and searched it.
>
> *Held*: the search could not be justified since a highly material particular, concerning the identity of the premises, had been misdescribed.

Following from above, there is abundant authority for the proposition that a general warrant expressing insufficient particulars is illegal at common law: see *Leach* v. *Money* (1765) 19 St.Tr. 1002, *Wilkes* v. *Wood* (1763) 19 St.Tr. 1153 and *Entick* v. *Carrington* (1765) 19 St.Tr. 1030. However, a suggestion that a court had insufficient grounds to justify granting a warrant will not be lightly entertained: see *Wyatt* v. *White* (1860) 5 H. & N. 371.

One object of present legislation seems to be to avoid putting goods into a more sacred category than persons: see Lord Denning M.R. in *Chic Fashions* (*West Wales*) v. *Jones* [1968] 2 Q.B. 299 and *Ghani* v. *Jones* [1970] 1 Q.B. 693.

VII. Seizure of Articles

Where Parliament has given a right to police to search persons and premises in connection with the purposes for which they have been authorised to carry out the search, there exists a corresponding right to seize relevant materials (see sections 8, 18, 32, 54 and 55 of P.A.C.E. and section 23 of the M.D.A.). However, there now exist general powers of seizure, conferred on the police by section 19(1) of P.A.C.E., which are exercisable by a constable who is lawfully on any premises. These powers are to seize anything which: **11-17**

- (i) has been obtained in consequence of the commission of an offence and which is in danger of being concealed, lost, damaged, altered, or destroyed; or
- (ii) is evidence in respect of any offence; or
- (iii) is evidence held by computer in respect of any offence and which may be destroyed, etc., if not seized.

The powers conferred by section 19 are additional to any other powers conferred under P.A.C.E.: section 19(5). Items seized under section 19 may be retained for as long as it is necessary in the circumstances: section 22(1).

In *Ghani* v. *Jones* [1970] 1 Q.B. 693 Lord Denning M.R. said, *obiter*, that seizure was not justified unless the police have reasonable grounds to believe that "the person in possession of it has himself committed the crime, or is an accessory or at any rate, his refusal must be quite unreasonable." But, an unreasonable refusal is not a sufficient reason for seizure under P.A.C.E.

(a) Restoration of documents seized

Where property has been seized by police an application for its restoration may be made to a magistrates' court under section 1 of the Police (Property) Act 1897. The application may be made either "by an officer of police or by a claimant of the property." Sections 21 and 22 of the P.A.C.E. deal with access and copying and retention of documents seized: see also section 22(5) and the Codes of Practice made under section 66 of P.A.C.E.   **11-18**

However, section 22(5) does not apply to customs officers and there is no provision under the Customs and Excise Acts which corresponds to section 1 of the Police (Property) Act 1897.

In *Southampton Justices, ex p. Newman* (1989) 88 Cr.App.R. 202 the applicant had been arrested at home by customs officers and charged with conspiracy to import cannabis. Documents were lawfully seized under sections 17 and 19 of P.A.C.E. The applicant sought the restoration of certain documents, which he maintained were necessary for the preparation of his defence, under section 48 of the Magistrates' Court Act 1980. The Divisional Court refused the application. The words "taken from him" in section 48 of the 1980 Act applied only to property found on a person and not to property taken from the home of an arrested person: see *D'Eyncourt* (1888) 21 Q.B.D. 109 and *Arnell* v. *Harris* [1944] K.B. 60.   **11-19**

However, in *Southampton Justices, ibid.* the Divisional Court suggested that a magistrates' court could, in a case where the defendant had indicated that he required documents to prepare his defence, adjourn the case until the relevant documents had been delivered to the defendant in the interests of justice: *per* MacPherson J. (1989) 88 Cr.App.R. 202, 205.

C. POWERS OF CUSTOMS AND EXCISE

11–20   The powers conferred on customs officials are extensive and deliberately widely drawn in response to the tasks that the Commissioners of Customs and Excise are expected to undertake. Most of the powers are conferred by the C.E.M.A.

Section 1(1) of that Act defines an "officer" as a person commissioned by the Commissioners of Customs and Excise to be an officer. However, there is another class of "officer" which, by section 8(2), includes "any person, whether an officer or not" who is engaged in carrying out an "assigned matter" (see section 1(1)), and shall therefore be deemed to be the "the proper officer." An officer falling within the latter category may be engaged by order of the Commissioners or simply engaged with their concurrence. Whether an officer is a "commissioned" officer or "engaged" under section 8(2), his powers are nevertheless identical: section 8(3).

D. WHO MAY INITIATE A PROSECUTION?

11–21   In *Ealing Justices, ex p. Dixon* [1990] 2 Q.B. 91, the Divisional Court held that a custody officer, in accepting a charge at a police station, did so on behalf of the police force irrespective of which law-enforcement body was in fact responsible for presenting the defendant to the custody officer, so that only the Director of Public Prosecutions might institute proceedings under section 6 of the Prosecution of Offences Act 1985. This meant that a customs officer who had been investigating an offence, arrested somebody without a warrant and took him to a police station to be charged by the custody officer under section 37 of the P.A.C.E. would thereby surrender the prosecution of the proceedings to the Director of Public Prosecutions. Such a conclusion would be inconsistent with section 145(1) of C.E.M.A. provides that no proceedings for an offence under the Customs and Excise Acts should be instituted except by order of the Commissioners.

However, in *Stafford Justices, ex p. Commissioners of Customs & Excise,* [1991] 2 Q.B. 339, the Divisional Court (Lord Justice Watkins and Mr. Justice Nolan) held that *Dixon* was wrongly decided. Proceedings could only be said to have been instituted on behalf of a police force when it was the police who had investigated, arrested, and brought the arrested person to the custody officer. Put shortly, a customs officer in investigating an offence lacked no essential power except that of charging the arrested person: see article 4 of the Police and Criminal Evidence Act 1984 (Application to Customs and Excise) Order (S.I. 1985 No. 1800).

Section 6 of the Prosecution of Offences Act 1985 plainly contemplates **11–22** that persons other than the Director of Public Prosecutions may institute proceedings and prosecute. In *Stafford Justices, ex p. Customs and Excise Commissioners*, the applicant had been arrested in connection with an offence under section 24(1)(*a*) of the D.T.O.A. 1986 and taken by a customs officer to a custody officer at a police station to be charged with that offence. The Divisional Court was prepared to accept that an offence under section 24 of the 1986 Act was an "assigned matter" for the purposes of section 1 and section 145(1) of the C.E.M.A. 1979. Although Parliament had conferred upon custody officers exclusive rights and duties in relation to charging arrested persons (see P.A.C.E. 1984, s.37) there was no reason why others, including customs officers, should not be allowed to take advantage of that charging procedure without surrendering the prosecution of the offence to the Director of Public Prosecutions.

I. POWERS OF SEARCH

The powers of stop and search under the C.E.M.A. are set out in Annex A **11–23** to the Police and Criminal Evidence Act 1984 (Codes of Practice) (No. 2) Order 1990 (S.I. 1990 No. 2580); formerly to be found in the Police and Criminal Evidence Act 1984 (Codes of Practice) (No. 1) Order 1985 (S.I. 1985 No. 1937): see table on p. 196.

There are a large number of activities carried out in respect of certain goods which would entitle an officer to treat the goods as being liable to forfeiture. Controlled drugs unlawfully imported, or intended for export, fall into this category. Once liability to forfeiture arises a number of different powers come into effect.

Thus, by section 161(1) of the C.E.M.A., an officer having a Writ of Assis- **11–24** tance may enter any building or place where there are reasonable grounds to suspect that anything liable to forfeiture is kept or concealed. Entry may be made by day or by night. If the entry is to be made at night, the officer must be accompanied by a constable (section 161(2)). Articles liable to forfeiture may be seized and detained (section 161(1)(*a*)). In the exercise of these powers an officer may break open any window, door or container. He may forcefully remove any impediment (section 161(1)(*b*)).

Additionally, the officer may apply to a justice of the peace for a search warrant, under section 161(3) of the C.E.M.A. (as amended by Schedule 6, para. 6 of P.A.C.E.), which will entitle him to the same powers as if he had a Writ of Assistance. But whereas a Writ of Assistance runs for the duration of that writ and for a period of six months thereafter, a warrant must be executed within one month (see C.E.M.A., s.161(6) and P.A.C.E., Sched. 6, para. 38).

Where a person comes within a category of persons listed in section 164(4), *e.g.* any person who is within the dock area of a port, or who has landed from any ship or aircraft, he may be searched, providing that there are reasonable grounds to suspect that he is carrying any article (not just drugs) with respect to the importation or exportation of prohibited goods. A person who is to be

Power	Object of Search	Extent of Search	Where Exercisable
C.E.M.A. s.163	Goods: (a) on which duty has not been paid; (b) being unlawfully removed, imported or exported; (c) otherwise liable to forfeiture to H.M. Customs and Excise.	Vehicles and vessels	Anywhere
C.E.M.A. s.164	Goods: (a) on which duty has not been paid; (b) the importation or exportation of which is restricted or prohibited by law.	Persons only	At entry to departure from UK; on board or at landing from ships or aircraft; in dock areas or Customs and Excise airports; at entry to, departure from or within approved wharves, transit sheds or free zones; or when travelling to or from any place beyond the N. Ireland boundary.

searched under section 164 may complain to the officer's superior or to a justice of the peace, who will decide whether or not a search is to take place: section 164(2) of the C.E.M.A.

No woman or girl may be searched by a man (section 164(3)) although there is nothing in section 164 to say that a male cannot be searched by a woman!

Any vehicle or vessel may be stopped and searched by an officer, constable, coastguard or a member of the armed forces if there are reasonable grounds to suspect that the vehicle or vessel is carrying, *inter alia*, a controlled drug: section 163.

II. SEARCHING AT WILL

11–25   Many of the powers conferred by the C.E.M.A. do not require an officer to have reasonable grounds to suspect the commission of any offence before he exercises those powers. Thus, by section 27 any officer and "any other officer duly engaged in the prevention of smuggling" may board any ship which is within the limits of a port, or any aircraft at a customs and excise airport, or a vehicle on an approved route, so that he may search it.

It is not clear which categories of person Parliament had in mind when referring to "any other person duly engaged in the prevention of smuggling" but this presumably includes a coastguard or police officers assigned to such a task.

Officers once on board are entitled to free access to every part of the ship, aircraft or vessel and may break open any place or container which is locked and of which the keys are withheld: section 28(1) of the C.E.M.A. Any goods found concealed on board shall be liable to forfeiture: section 28(2).

A commander of an aircraft must allow an officer to board an aircraft and to inspect goods and documents therein: section 33. If an officer or a constable considers that an aircraft is likely to leave the United Kingdom from a place other than a customs and excise airport, then he may take such steps as appear to him to be necessary in order to prevent the flight: section 34. This seems to permit all manner of dramatic measures to be adopted (seemingly with impunity) if the officer sees fit. **11–26**

An officer or constable who has reasonable cause to suspect that signals or messages in connection with a smuggling operation are being made or transmitted from a ship, aircraft, vehicle, house or place, may board or enter, as the case may be, and take such steps as are reasonably necessary to stop and prevent the sending of the signal or message: C.E.M.A., section 84(5).

III. SEIZURE OF ARTICLES AND THE TAKING OF SAMPLES

An officer, constable, coastguard or any member of the armed forces may seize and detain anything liable to forfeiture under the Customs and Excise Acts: C.E.M.A., section 139(1). **11–27**

Samples may be taken of any goods which an officer is empowered to examine under the C.E.M.A.: section 160(1).

IV. DETENTION OF PERSONS

An officer, coastguard, or a member of the armed forces may arrest a person whom he has reasonable grounds to suspect has committed a drugs-related importation or exportation: C.E.M.A., section 138. The power of arrest may be exercised within three years of the offence being committed: section 138(1). **11–28**

E. ILLEGALLY OBTAINED EVIDENCE

It has long been a rule of law, although much criticised, that evidence adduced by unlawful or improper means (save in relation to involuntary confessions) and generally with regard to evidence obtained from the accused **11–29** after the commission of the offence is admissible in evidence: see *Kuruma* [1955] A.C. 197, and *Maqsud Ali* (1966). The principal safeguard has always been the court's inherent discretion to exclude such evidence if its prejudicial effect outweighs its probative value: see *Sang* [1980] A.C. 402 and *Jeffery* v. *Black* [1978] Q.B. 490. A similar discretion has now been given statutory effect by section 78 of P.A.C.E. which enables a court to disallow prosecution evidence if, having regard to the circumstances in which the evidence was obtained, its admissibility "would have such an adverse effect on the fairness of the proceedings." It is not yet clear whether section 78 has altered the earlier position, but it is of interest that the section makes reference to the effect on the fairness of the proceedings. In other words, it would seem that the court is not merely concerned with whether admitting the evidence or not would be unfair to the accused, but also whether the evidence is so grossly prejudicial that it would be unreasonable to admit it. Accordingly, it is submitted that the words quoted were the draftsman's way of rewording the cliché that "justice must not only be done, but also be seen to be done." If, then, a reasonable bystander viewing the proceedings was to be heard to say that the evidence was obtained in circumstances so patently unfair that it would be an affront to our system of justice to admit it, then the judge (fulfilling the role of the bystander) ought to exclude it: but see *Christou and Wright, The Times*, June 1, 1992; *H. M. Advocate* v. *Graham* 1991 S.L.T. 416; *H. M. Advocate* v. *Harper* 1989 S.C.C.R. 472 and *Weir* v. *Jessop* 1992 S.L.T. 533 (a case of entrapment).

F. OBSTRUCTION OF OFFICERS

I. OBSTRUCTION OF POLICE OFFICERS UNDER THE M.D.A.

11–30   Section 23(4) of the M.D.A. provides:

"A person commits an offence if he—
   (a) intentionally obstructs a person in the exercise of his powers under this section; or
   (b) conceals from a person acting in the exercise of his powers under subsection (1) above any such books, documents, stocks or drugs as are mentioned in that subsection; or
   (c) without reasonable excuse (proof of which shall lie on him) fails to produce any such books or documents as are so mentioned where their production is demanded by a person in the exercise of his powers under that subsection."

Subsections (4)(b) and (c) apply only to commercial concerns which carry on business as producers or suppliers of controlled drugs.

Constables or other persons authorised by the Secretary of State may enter the business premises and inspect the companies' paperwork, stock or drugs. Accordingly, an offence will be committed if the relevant items are either concealed or not produced upon demand without a reasonable excuse.

The wording of section 23(4)(b) implies that an accused need only know that the documents, stock or drugs concealed relate to drug transactions and that an officer might wish to see them. However, section 23(4)(c) is absolute in the absence of a reasonable excuse that explains the reason why the documents concerned could not be physically produced when demanded, e.g. destroyed in a fire, or retained by a court for the purposes of pending litigation. The motives of the accused are immaterial. Thus, merely to protect the identity of a confidential client who is lawfully entitled to buy and possess the drugs would not be a defence or a reasonable excuse.

(a) Defining an intentional obstruction

In *Forde (J.)* (1985) 81 Cr.App.R. 19 the Court of Appeal held that an **11–31** offence is committed once an act is done which, when viewed objectively, obstructed the officer in the execution of his powers under section 23 and was intended by an accused to obstruct.

It would therefore appear that the words "intentionally obstructs" have the same meaning as "wilfully obstructs" found in other enactments and notably section 51(3) of the Police Act 1964. In *Hills* v. *Ellis* [1983] Q.B. 680 the Divisional Court, when considering section 51(3) of the Act, asked "what is meant by an 'intention to obstruct'?" and gave the following reply (*per* McCullough J.):

> "I would construe 'wilfully obstructs' as doing deliberate actions with the intention of bringing about a state of affairs which, objectively regarded, amounts to an obstruction ... the fact that the defendant might not have called that state of affairs an obstruction is ... immaterial."

But what is an obstruction? The answer is an act calculated to make it more **11–32** difficult for the police to carry out their duties: see *Rice* v. *Connolly* [1966] 2 Q.B. 414. Thus, to throw drugs away before the police can seize them is a classic example of obstruction under section 23. It is not necessary to prove a "hostile" motive in obstructing the officer: see *Willmott* v. *Atack* [1976] 3 W.L.R. 753 and *Green* v. *Moore* [1982] Q.B. 1044.

> In *Kelly* (November 19, 1984; unreported; 5624883), the Court of Appeal held that an offence is committed under section 23(4)(a) if D knows that the officer is detaining, or trying to detain him, in order to search D for drugs. D's conduct when viewed objectively did obstruct the detention and search. D's conduct, viewed subjectively, was intended to obstruct.

The court in *Kelly* accepted that there may be occasions where the obstruct- **11–33** ing act was performed before the constable had the opportunity to explain what he was doing. However, the existence of such a feature would not automatically excuse a defendant in circumstances where the reasons for the constable's conduct must have been obvious to the defendant.

The term "obstruct" as it appears in section 23 is capable of figurative use and is not limited to physical personal obstruction or restraint. Anything done by an accused with the intention of hindering officers in the exercise of their duty under the warrant issued is capable of bringing the accused within the scope of section 23. The obstruction must, of course, be intentional: *Carmichael* v. *Brannan*, 1986 S.L.T. 5. In that case one defendant swallowed a substance, three defendants jumped from a verandah to avoid arrest, and all of them refused to open the door of the house to which the police sought to gain access.

II. OBSTRUCTION OF CUSTOMS OFFICERS

11–34   By section 16(1) of the C.E.M.A. 1979:

"Any person who—
> (*a*) obstructs [see *George* [1981] Crim.L.R. 185], hinders, molests or assaults any person duly engaged in the performance of any duty or the exercise of any power imposed or conferred on him by or under any enactment relating to an assigned matter, or any person acting in his aid; or
> (*b*) does anything which impedes or is calculated to impede the carrying out of any search for any thing liable to forfeiture under any such enactment or the detention, seizure or removal of any such thing; or
> (*c*) rescues, damages or destroys any thing so liable to forfeiture or does anything calculated to prevent the procuring or giving of evidence as to whether or not any thing is so liable to forfeiture; or
> (*d*) prevents the detention of any person by a person duly engaged or acting as aforesaid or rescues any person so detained,
>
> or who attempts to do any of the aforementioned things, shall be guilty of an offence under this section."

These provisions are really self-explanatory but go a great deal further than section 23 of the M.D.A.

Chapter 12
The Drug Trafficking
Offences Act 1986

A. INTRODUCTION

On July 8, 1986, by virtue of the Drug Trafficking Offences Act 1986 (the **12–01** D.T.O.A.), Parliament introduced sweeping and radical changes in the law to enable the courts to recover the proceeds of drug trafficking. Sections 1(3), 2(1), 24, 34, 38 and 40 came into force on September 30, 1986 (see Drug Trafficking Offences Act 1986 (Commencement No. 1) Order 1986 (S.I. 1986 No. 1488), followed by sections 27 to 29, 31 and 33 (in force on December 30, 1986) and the remainder on January 12, 1987 (see Drug Trafficking Offences Act 1986 (Commencement No. 3) Order 1986 (S.I. 1986 No. 2145).

Previously, the courts were equipped only with the statutory powers of forfeiture; the making of "deprivation" orders or "criminal bankruptcy" orders, and/or the imposition of fines. Save for criminal bankruptcy orders these powers continue to exist, but they are very limited in scope. Thus, by section 27 of the M.D.A. 1971, only those assets which directly relate to an offence committed by the accused, under that Act, may be forfeited: see *Morgan* [1977] Crim.L.R. 488, C.A. Choses in action and intangibles are not usually capable of being forfeited: see *Khan* [1982] 1 W.L.R. 1405, C.A. Drug profits, originally received by the accused but which were then transferred to a third party, could not be seized. The imposition of a substantial fine on the accused, coupled with an order that he pay the costs of the trial (either wholly or in part) is a crude method of recouping drug profits and rightly regarded as bad sentencing policy, being a "back-door" approach. In any event, the bold defendant who simply refused to pay the fine would sometimes prefer to "sit it out" and serve a sentence of imprisonment in default of payment, knowing that the court was powerless to enforce the sale of his assets in order to satisfy the fine or other fiscal orders. It was to meet such weaknesses in the law that the D.T.O.A. 1986 was enacted following recommendations contained in the Home Affairs Committee Fifth Report "*Misuse of Hard Drugs—Interim Report*" H.C. 399, (1985) which had approved the American policy of giving the court "draconian powers" to strip drug dealers of assets acquired during the course of their drug dealing even where their connection with drug trafficking offences is merely "probable."

B. A "DRACONIAN ACT"

12-02   The D.T.O.A. has been appropriately described as a "draconian" piece of legislation and was intended to be so: see *Dickens* (1990) 91 Cr.App.R. 164, *per* Lord Lane C.J. at 167; *Comiskey* (1990) 12 Cr.App.R.(S.) 562, *per* Tucker J. at 568; *Ian Smith* (1989) 89 Cr.App.R. 253, *per* Lord Lane C.J. at 238; and *Robson* (1991) 92 Cr.App.R. 1. This is particularly apparent in respect of the sweeping assumptions which the court can make (all adverse to the defendant) and the number of evidential stages at which the defendant shoulders the burden of proof. The reasons for this approach stem from the scale and nature of the illicit drugs trade, often involving more than one jurisdiction and the laundering of substantial sums of money at home and abroad affecting a number of individuals or corporate bodies, many of whom may be totally innocent parties. Usually it is the defendant who will be in the best position to explain and to account for assets moving in and out of his hands during the relevant period. Parliament has exploited that fact. As Tucker J. observed in *Comiskey* (1990) 12 Cr.App.R.(S.) 562, 567 "the object of the Act is to oblige a defendant to reveal this information so as to enable the court to make an effective order."

Accordingly, the D.T.O.A. imposes an obligation on the defendant to take whatever steps are necessary to satisfy an order made against him upon pain of serving a consecutive sentence in default. Thus:

> "The Act is intended to avoid a situation where a drug dealer serves his sentence with equanimity knowing that on his release substantial funds will be available to enable him to live in comfort ... The Act is designed to oblige him to disclose his assets, or face the risk that if he does not do so the court will make certain assumptions against him, and that he may have to serve an additional sentence of imprisonment if he does not comply with an order"; *per* Tucker J. in *Comiskey, ibid.*

I. THE BROAD APPROACH IN ENGLAND AND WALES

12-03   By section 1 of the D.T.O.A., the moment an accused appears before the Crown Court to be sentenced in respect of a "drugs trafficking offence," the court is obliged to embark upon an inquiry to recover, under a "confiscation order," the proceeds of drug trafficking received by him.

Three points should be borne in mind. First, what is to be confiscated are the *proceeds* of drug trafficking and not merely drug profits. A trafficker who receives £1,000 for the sale of a drug cannot seek to deduct the expenses he incurred in buying and transporting it: *Smith* (1989) 89 Cr.App.R. 25. Broadly speaking his gross receipts are his proceeds. Secondly, the value of a confiscation order will not always signify the extent to which the defendant himself has been engaged in drug trafficking because the Act catches all drug proceeds received by the defendant whether as a result of his drug trafficking *or another's*: see *Smith* (1989) 89 Cr.App.R. 235, and see also *Comiskey* (1990) 12 Cr.App.R. 562 (and note sections 2(1)(*a*) and 1(3)). Thirdly, it is irrelevant whether the drug trafficking in question took place within the jurisdiction of the courts of the United Kingdom, or abroad subject to a "corresponding law": see subsections 38(1) and (3).

The method by which a court may assess the value of the proceeds of drug trafficking is one of the most controversial features of the Act. There will often be cases where an accused can be shown to have received property over a period of years but there exists little or no evidence to prove that the property represents the proceeds of drug trafficking. Accordingly, the Act creates a number of far-reaching assumptions which the court is entitled (but not compelled) to make. Inevitably, in complicated and hotly contested confiscation proceedings, much court time will be spent tracing funds and ascertaining their origin.

II. SUMMARISING THE MECHANICS OF THE ACT

Whenever a defendant appears before the Crown Court to be sentenced in respect of one or more "drug trafficking offences," the court has no alternative but to make a confiscation order, if it can do so, by following the steps set out in section 1 of the D.T.O.A. Section 1(1) reads: **12–04**

> "Subject to subsection (7) below, where a person appears before the Crown Court to be sentenced in respect of one or more drug trafficking offences (and has not previously been sentenced or otherwise dealt with in respect of his conviction for the offence or, as the case may be, any of the offences concerned), the court shall act as follows ... [set out below]."

Note the words *"the court shall act."*

Broadly speaking, the relevant steps (and those which result from an application of section 1) may be briefly summarised as follows: **12–05**

(1)   The court must ask whether the defendant has benefited from drug trafficking: section 1(2) and see §12–20, *infra*.
   (a)   The persuasive burden is on the prosecution to meet the criminal law standard of proof: see *Dickens* [1990] 2 Q.B. 102; *Enwezor* (1991) 93 Cr.App.R. 233 and §§12–40 and 12–52, *infra*.
   (b)   The court may make any of the statutory assumptions contained in section 2(2) and section 2(3). The burden of rebuttal is on the defendant: *Dickens* and *Enwezor, supra* and see *Redbourne, The Times,* June 26, 1992.
(2)   If question (1) is answered affirmatively, then the court must assess the value of the proceeds of drug trafficking received by him: section 1(4) and section 4 and see §12–41; *infra*.
   (a)   The value of the defendant's proceeds represent prima facie the "amount to be recovered" under a confiscation order: section 4(1).
   (b)   The persuasive burden is again on the prosecution to the criminal standard of proof: *Dickens, ibid.*, and *Enwezor, ibid.*
   (c)   The court may apply the statutory assumptions: section 2(2) and section 2(3).

(3) The court may be required to assess the "amount that may be realised" under section 5(3), being the total *value* of realisable property held by the defendant *plus* the total value of gifts made by him and caught by the Act: section 5(3) and section 5(9), see §12–64, *infra*.

(4) If the defendant satisfies the court on a balance of probabilities that the "amount that might be realised" is *less* than the "amount to be recovered" then the court must confiscate the lesser amount: section 4(3). See *Ilsemann* (1990) 12 Cr.App.R.(S.) 398; *Comiskey* (1990) 12 Cr.App.R.(S.) 582; *Carroll* [1991] Crim.L.R. 720. The judge must issue a certificate recording that finding of fact: section 4(2).

(5) If the defendant fails to discharge the burden on him, or fails to raise the issue at all, then the court may make a confiscation order for the full amount determined under steps (1) and (2) above: but see *Comiskey (supra)* and *Keston* (1990) 12 Cr.App.R.(S.) 93 and §12–75, *infra*..

(6) The court must treat the confiscation order as a fine and impose a sentence of imprisonment in default: section 6 and §12–123, *infra*.

(7) In a proper case, the court may vary or discharge the confiscation order: section 14 and see §12–136, *infra*.

The Court of Appeal has advised judges to state the relevant findings at each stage of the proceedings, *per* Neill L.J. in *Johnson* [1991] 2 Q.B. 249, 260.

12–06 When the court makes a confiscation order, it must determine the amount to be recovered from the defendant *before* sentencing him (section 1(4)) and, furthermore, the court is obliged to take account of the order before imposing a fine (section 1(5)(*b*)(i)), or before making an order under section 27 of the M.D.A. 1971 (forfeiture orders) or section 43 of the Powers of the Criminal Courts Act 1973 (as amended) (deprivation orders): see D.T.O.A., ss.1(5)(*b*)(ii) and (iii).

By section 1(5)(*c*), the court is also obliged to leave the confiscation order out of account in deciding the appropriate sentence to be passed on the defendant: but see *Bragason* [1988] Crim.L.R. 778; *Harper* [1989] Crim.L.R. 755; and *Saunders* (1991) 92 Cr.App.R. 6.

Unfortunately, the Act does not make it clear whether the court is prevented from passing a sentence in respect of non-drug-trafficking offences until such an order is made or (at least) until the amount to be recovered from the defendant is ascertained. However, in the absence of express language in the Act to the contrary, it is submitted that the court is not bound to wait until the procedural steps in section 1 are fulfilled before sentencing an offender in respect of non-drug-trafficking offences, if such a course is appropriate.

12–07 Upon the making of a confiscation order, the prosecution may ask the High Court to appoint a receiver to realise assets that are held either by the defendant, or by persons to whom the defendant has directly or indirectly made a "gift" for the purposes of the Act: see section 11 and section 5. Property realised by the receiver may then be applied towards satisfying the order: see section 12 and section 13. Special rules will apply in the case of *any* person (not just the defendant) who is adjudged to be bankrupt but who nevertheless holds "realisable property": see section 15 and section 16. Special rules also apply to companies which are in the process of being wound up but which possess realisable property: section 17.

In order to avoid the risk that a defendant may be tempted to dispose of his assets before a court can confiscate them, the High Court is empowered, upon the application of the prosecutor, to grant a restraint order prohibiting *any* person from dealing with "realisable property" except as directed by the court: sections 7 and 8. Furthermore, a receiver may be appointed to take possession of any realisable property and to manage or to otherwise deal with that property: section 8(6).

Since much realisable property will consist of land or other securities, it is desirable, in cases where a confiscation order has not yet been made, to register a charge on the property to secure the payment of moneys to the Crown. The D.T.O.A. provides the necessary machinery for doing so by virtue of section 9. Accordingly, the High Court may, upon the application of the prosecutor, grant a charging order (*ex parte* if necessary) and may appoint a Receiver to take possession of the property: section 11.

Obviously a defendant may feel aggrieved that the prosecution has detri- **12–08** mentally meddled in his financial affairs, when proceedings do not result in a conviction for a drug trafficking offence. The realisation of his assets means that he was unable to liquidate them and to reinvest the proceeds as he wished. In certain cases the financial loss may be considerable. Third parties, from whose hands property may have been realised by a court under the D.T.O.A., may also be similarly affected. Parliament therefore has taken (at first sight) a robust course and enabled persons so affected to apply to the High Court for an order of compensation to be paid to them: section 19. In reality, the hurdles put in the path of an applicant are considerable. There must be "serious default" on the part of a person concerned in the investigation or prosecution of the offence in question resulting in the loss. As originally drafted, section 19(2)(*a*) also required proof that the proceedings would not have been instituted or continued but for that default. However, this requirement was repealed by Schedule 5 to the Criminal Justice Act 1988. In its place an even greater hurdle has been erected, namely, that "the court shall not order compensation to be paid in any case where it appears to the court that the proceedings would have been instituted or continued if the serious default had not occurred": Schedule 5, C.J.A. 1988. This remarkable proviso seems to debar compensation even in cases where a prosecution is halted by virtue of gross incompetence or bad faith no matter how appalling. However, it is no longer necessary to show that the loss is "substantial." Even when an applicant succeeds in meeting those requirements, it does not follow that he will be fully compensated: the "amount of compensation ... shall be such as the High Court thinks just in all the circumstances of the case": section 19(3).

Finally, the Act creates a number of offences. For example, where A retains, **12–09** or controls, the proceeds of B's drug trafficking, or uses those proceeds to secure funds for B's disposal or to acquire (for B) investment property, then A shall be guilty of the offence of assisting a drug trafficker if A knows or suspects that B is, or has been, a drug trafficker, or has benefited from drug trafficking: section 24.

III. Is a Confiscation Order a Sentence?

12–10   Until the Court of Appeal, of its own motion, answered the question in the affirmative, it was not clear whether a confiscation order could be made the subject of an appeal pursuant to sections 9 and 50(1) of the Criminal Appeal Act 1968 (as amended): see *Johnson* [1991] 2 Q.B. 249. This is because section 1(4) of the D.T.O.A. imposes a mandatory obligation on the court not to sentence or otherwise deal with the offender until the procedural steps of the Act have been complied with. Furthermore, section 1(5)(c) of the D.T.O.A. expressly requires the court to leave the confiscation order "out of account in determining the appropriate sentence." Those two provisions, therefore, seemed to suggest that a confiscation order is not part of the sentence and therefore falls outside the 1968 Act. Section 9 of the Criminal Appeal Act 1968 states that a person "may appeal to the Court of Appeal against any sentence ... passed on him for the offence." At first sight, a confiscation order is not passed on the defendant in respect of the offence, or offences, for which he appeared before the court. It is not a penalty but an order of deprivation. However, by section 50(1) a sentence includes "any order made by a court when dealing with an offender." In *Johnson* (*supra*), the Court of Appeal held that despite the wording of section 1(4) and section 1(5) of the D.T.O.A. a confiscation order does form part of the sentence because first, the powers of the High Court in relation to a confiscation order can only be exercised where the order is not subject to appeal: see section 11(1)(b) and see section 39(13). Secondly, confiscation orders can be made by the Criminal Division of the Court of Appeal: see D.T.O.A., s.6(6). Finally, the court found support in the words of Lord Widgery C.J. in *Hayden* [1975] 1 W.L.R. 852, 854G, when he said that an order for costs comes within the definition of "sentence" in section 50(1) of the Criminal Appeal Act 1968 because "it is an order which is contingent upon there having been a conviction and it is contingent on the person by whom the payment is to be made, having been convicted in that way."

In Scotland the matter is put beyond doubt by section 1(4) of the Criminal Justice (Scotland) Act 1987.

IV. The Scottish Approach

12–11   Most of the provisions of the Drug Trafficking Offences Act do not apply to Scotland: see section 40. A Bill to recover the proceeds of drug trafficking was considered by the Scottish Grand Committee and the First Scottish Standing Committee in 1987. In May of that year, the Criminal Justice (Scotland) Act 1987 received Royal Assent. The Scottish model is also draconian but, unlike the Crown Court in England, the power of the High Court of Justiciary to make a confiscation order is discretionary. The court is not obliged to embark upon an investigation as to the extent of an accused's proceeds of drug trafficking every time the accused is convicted of a drug trafficking offence. Indeed the High Court of Justiciary can only exercise its discretion upon the application of the prosecutor who must make his application prior to sentence or before any part of it has been pronounced (Criminal Justice (Scotland) Act, section 1(1)). Not surprisingly, the Government's view was that relatively few orders will be made in Scotland each year and this view is certainly being confirmed in practice. One merit of the Scottish model is the considerable saving of court time in cases where it is obvious from the outset that the defendant has no assets capable of being realised and where, after investigation by the court, a nil confiscation order is the only realistic order which the court can make. There is also force in the argument that the courts should be primarily concerned with serious cases of drug trafficking. In England, even a solitary incident at the lowest end of the gravity scale is sufficient to trigger off the full rigour of the provisions of the Drug Trafficking Offences Act 1986.

12–12 English courts are obliged to make an order for the total amount which the court assesses to be the value of the defendant's proceeds of drug trafficking (or the value of the accused's realisable property plus the value of the gifts caught by the Act). In Scotland such a figure represents not a mandatory amount to be confiscated, but a ceiling, which the High Court of Justiciary may confiscate. The overriding task of the High Court (if it makes an order) is to require the defendant to pay "such amount as the Court considers appropriate" which does not exceed that ceiling. The discretionary power of the court to determine an "appropriate" amount enables the court to arrive at a decision which does not deprive the defendant of all his assets with the consequential hardship which may descend upon innocent third parties.

V. DELAYING SENTENCING AND SENTENCING CONSIDERATIONS

12–13 Since a court may not proceed to sentence until the court has gone through the procedural steps under that Act, this often means that sentence is adjourned for a considerable period of time in order to enable the parties to prepare and to present evidence and arguments in pursuance of the D.T.O.A. inquiry. Occasionally the D.T.O.A. inquiry is so complicated and protracted that the proceedings take longer to hear than the contested criminal trial itself. In *Smith (Ian)* (1989) 84 Cr.App.R. 235, the appellant was convicted on January 26, 1988 but sentence, and the making of a confiscation order in the sum of £14,000, was not imposed until May 6, after a three-day hearing. Such delays are not uncommon and the defendant can only agonise as to the final result. In *Robson* there was a delay of some four months between conviction and sentence. Although there may be a case for vesting the court with a discretionary power to adjourn sentence until the conclusion of the D.T.O.A. inquiry, it is difficult to see what justification there is for the mandatory position which currently exists under the D.T.O.A. One explanation is that the legislature considered that the court should not be in a position to sentence until all factual matters have been resolved, but this supposes that the sentencer would be entitled to have regard to the evidence placed before him under the D.T.O.A. Section 1(5)(*c*) states that the court should "leave the order out of account in determining the appropriate sentence or other manner of dealing with the defendant." The sentiments expressed in section 1(5)(*c*) are consistent with the general principles of sentencing that an accused is entitled to be sentenced on the basis of what is proved or admitted (to the criminal standard of proof) in respect of the offences for which he falls to be sentenced: see *Ayensu* (1982) 4 Cr.App.R.(S.) 248; *Ralf* (1989) 11 Cr.App.R.(S) 121; *Reeves* (1983) 5 Cr.App.R.(S.) 292; *Bragason* [1988] Crim.L.R. 778; and see the provisions of the Criminal Justice Act 1991 which tend to support that approach.

12–14   However, in *Harper* [1989] Crim.L.R. 755, the Court of Appeal seems to have encroached on this principle in holding that the sentencer may pay some regard to the evidence placed before him under the Drug Trafficking Offences Act if it rebuts an assertion made in mitigation, *e.g.* that the offence represented an isolated incident. In *Saunders* (1991) 92 Cr.App.R. 6, Hutchinson J. said (at p. 10):

> "... it would be absurd to say that if in the course of the Drug Trafficking Offences Act investigation the defendant, for example, admitted extensive drug trafficking, the sentencing judge should entirely disregard that in determining the appropriate sentence. He could and should take it into account in the manner indicated a moment ago."

The Court of Appeal in *Saunders* made two other important observations. The first is that the sentencer should be careful not to take into account factual matters of which the sentencer had not been satisfied beyond reasonable doubt. The second point is that the sentencer should not use the assumptions, made under section 2(3) of the Act, to make a finding "adverse to the defendant in the realm of sentencing which he would not have made applying the ordinary burden of proof" (*per* Hutchinson J. at p. 10).

12–15   The occasions on which sentence may properly take into account matters revealed under the Drug Trafficking Offences Act inquiry will be relatively few in comparison to the large number of cases coming before the courts.

By contrast, in Scotland under the Criminal Justice (Scotland) Act 1987 the court is not obliged to sentence at the conclusion of the inquiry. Instead, the court may sentence the offender without delay and deal with the matter of confiscation at an adjourned date exceeding no more than six months after the date of conviction: section 2(1) of the Criminal Justice (Scotland) Act 1987.

C. PERSONS TO WHOM SECTION 1 OF THE D.T.O.A. APPLIES

12–16   Confiscation orders may only be made against persons who appear before the Crown Court to be sentenced in respect of one or more "drug trafficking offences," a classification which, by section 38(1) of the D.T.O.A. includes:

"(*a*) an offence under section 4(2) or (3) or 5(3) of the Misuse of Drugs Act

1971 (production, supply and possession for supply of controlled drugs);

(*b*) an offence under section 20 of that Act (assisting in or inducing commission outside United Kingdom of offence punishable under a corresponding law);

(*c*) an offence under:

(i) section 50(2) or (3) of the Customs and Excise Management Act 1979 (improper importation):

(ii) section 68(2) of that Act (exportation): or

(iii) section 170 of that Act (fraudulent evasion),

in connection with a prohibition or restriction on importation or exportation having effect by virtue of section 3 of the Misuse of Drugs Act 1971;

(*d*) an offence under section 34 of this Act;

(*e*) an offence under section 1 of the Criminal Law Act 1977 or conspiracy to commit any of the offences in paragraphs (*a*) and (*d*) above;

(*f*) an offence under section 1 of the Criminal Attempts Act 1981 of attempting to commit any of those offences;

(*g*) an offence of inciting another to commit any of those offences, whether under section 19 of the Misuse of Drugs Act 1971 or at common law; and

(*h*) aiding, abetting, counselling or procuring the commission of any of those offences;"

Only the Crown Court is empowered to make a confiscation order under   **12–17**
section 1. Although the section applies in cases where the defendant is committed by the magistrates' court to the Crown Court for sentence pursuant to section 38 of the Magistrates' Courts Act 1980, it does not apply to juveniles who are committed to the Crown Court with a view to being sentenced to youth custody under section 37 of the Magistrates' Courts Act 1980, or where the powers of the court are limited to dealing with the defendant in a way in which a magistrates' court might have dealt with him in connection with the offence charged: (D.T.O.A., s. 1(7)(*b*)). Accordingly, section 1 does not apply to defendants who appeal to the Crown Court against their conviction and/or sentence in the magistrates' court. Furthermore, section 1 has no application where a defendant has been "previously . . . sentenced or otherwise dealt with in respect of his conviction for the offence or . . . any of the offences concerned": section 1(1). Section 1 therefore does not apply to persons who are in breach of a community service order or a suspended sentence of imprisonment.

D. THE MAKING OF A CONFISCATION ORDER

I. General Note

It will be recalled that the court must determine whether the defendant has   **12–18**
benefited from drug trafficking (section 1(2)), and if he has, to determine the

amount to be recovered (see section 1(4) and section 4). Realistically, each element must be examined in the context of the other, since an amount can only be recovered if it represents a benefit of drug-trafficking, and vice versa.

Thus by section 1(3):

> "For the purposes of this Act, a person who has at any time (whether before or after the commencement of this section) received any payment or other reward in connection with drug trafficking carried on by him or another has benefited from drug trafficking."

Accordingly, one cannot divorce the method by which the court must determine whether the defendant has benefited from drug-trafficking, from the procedure laid down in the Act for assessing the value of the defendant's proceeds of that trade.

12–19   Section 1(4) provides that:

> "If the court determines that he has so benefited, the court shall, before sentencing or otherwise dealing with him in respect of the offence or, as the case may be, any of the offences concerned, determine in accordance with section 4 of this Act the amount to be recovered in his case by virtue of this section."·

When one therefore looks at section 4(1), we see that the "amount to be recovered" is to be equated with "the amount the Crown Court assesses to be the value of the defendant's *proceeds of drug trafficking.*"

Note the words in italics. Obviously, there will often be cases where an accused no longer holds capital and/or savings to that extent. The Act does not seek to make him bankrupt in those circumstances but, on the contrary, the Act provides by section 4(3) that the "amount to be recovered" shall therefore be the amount that can be "realised."

II. BENEFIT

(a) Why determine benefit?

12–20   The court must first determine whether the defendant has "benefited" from drug trafficking. If it is obvious that the defendant has obtained no benefit then nothing is to be gained by expending court time and money proceeding any further. The legislature may have originally contemplated that cases in which there was no discernible benefit would be weeded out speedily and expeditiously. Frequently the prosecution indicates to the court, upon conviction, that the defendant has received no benefit and the court is invited to make a nil confiscation order. In the author's experience the Customs and Excise often take a sensible, realistic and robust view in this regard.

In *Dickens* (1990) 91 Cr.App.R. 164 Lord Lane C.J. appears to have had this approach very much in mind when he said (at 168):

> "... the judge has to make a preliminary assessment as to whether it is or is likely to be a 'benefit' case or not. No doubt the evidence from the trial, if there has been one, or from a recital of the facts if there has been a plea,

will be enough for him to form such a preliminary assessment."

However, this approach does not always find favour with the judiciary on **12–21** the grounds that it is for the court to determine whether the accused has benefited from drug trafficking or not and this the court can only do if it is fully informed of the defendant's financial affairs during the relevant period. By section 2(2) of the D.T.O.A. the court may make a number of statutory assumptions (adverse to the defendant) for the purposes of determining whether the defendant has benefited from drug trafficking and not merely for the purpose of assessing his proceeds of drug trafficking. The court cannot begin to consider making any of those statutory assumptions unless it is appraised of the defendant's financial affairs. The objection taken by some courts is that the prosecution frustrates the court's statutory obligation if it fails to submit statements setting out the defendant's finances and matters relevant to drug trafficking under section 3 of the D.T.O.A. There is some force in that complaint but the stark alternative is the prospect of numerous (and perhaps lengthy) inquiries which will result in either nil confiscation orders being made or ones of very low value. The cost expended by law enforcement agencies, the courts and the defence (normally under a legal aid certificate) in pursuing such confiscation orders will be enormous and largely unproductive, as only £1 out of every £7 is collected and this figure does not, of course, take into account the cost of collection: Home Office Working Group on Confiscation (1991).

Under the Scottish legislation, the High Court is not required, as a first step, **12–22** to determine whether the defendant has benefited from drug trafficking. This is because the making of a confiscation order is in any event discretionary (see §12–11, *supra*). The High Court is swiftly directed to assess the value of the defendant's proceeds of drug trafficking in accordance with section 3 of the Criminal Justice (Scotland) Act 1987.

It is submitted that the approach of Lord Lane C.J. referred to above is to be encouraged. It should not be too difficult in the majority of cases to ascertain whether a case may properly be regarded as a "benefit case" which warrants investigation under the D.T.O.A: see the commentary to *Bragason* [1988] Crim.L.R. 778, 779.

(b) Definition of benefit

The phrase "benefited from drug trafficking" is a term which falls to be **12–23** construed in accordance with section 1(3) (*supra*), (see §12–18, *supra* and see section 38(2)). A benefit has the following features:

(i) it must be a payment or other reward;
(ii) it must be received by a person;
(iii) the payment must be received in connection with drug trafficking;
(iv) the drug trafficking must have been carried on by the recipient or another;
(v) the recipient knew that the payment or reward was made "in connection with drug trafficking": *Richards* [1992] 2 All E.R. 572.

(i) *Payment or other reward*

12–24   **Payment does not mean net profit.** In *Smith* (1989) 89 Cr.App.R. 235 Lord Lane C.J. said:

> "... the words 'any payment' ... must mean, indeed it is clear from the wording, any payment in money or in kind. It does not mean ... net profit derived from the payment after the deduction of expenses, whether the expenses are those of purchase, travelling, entertainment or otherwise. The same consideration applies to the words 'other rewards.' "

In other words, the Act is concerned with *proceeds* and not with profit. The appellant contended in *Smith* that the judge erred in evaluating the extent of the appellant's proceeds by aggregating four payments of £2,500 received by him. The appellant contended that each sum received had been invested in purchasing the next consignment for sale so that the money had been "rolled over" by investment. The Court of Appeal noted that there was, in any event, no evidence of money being rolled over in this way but went on to say (*per* Lord Lane C.J.):

> "It seems to us that the section is deliberately worded so as to avoid the necessity, which the appellant's construction of the section would involve, of having to carry out an accountancy exercise which would be quite impossible in the circumstances of this case."

12–25   In *Smith*, counsel for the appellant ingeniously argued that the D.T.O.A. was concerned with profits on the basis, *inter alia*, of section 4(3) which provides that the amount to be confiscated is the "amount that might be realised" at the time the confiscation order is made. Presumably, the submission was that the assets could only have been acquired with the profits, and not with gross proceeds, the bulk of which had been dissipated on expenditure. However, the Court of Appeal rejected that submission on the basis that section 4(3) is a mitigating provision in circumstances where the provisions of section 4(3) have been proved to the court's satisfaction. In any event, the "amount that might be realised" may include assets which were in fact purchased with proceeds lawfully acquired: see *Chrastny (No. 2)* [1991] 1 W.L.R. 1385. The purpose of realising assets (whether lawfully acquired or not) is simply to pay off the confiscation order which represents some, if not all, of the defendant's proceeds of drug trafficking.

The decision of *Smith* has been cited with approval by the Court of Appeal in *Comiskey* (1990) 12 Cr.App.R.(S.) 562, 567. In *McDonald* (1990) 12 Cr.App.R.(S.) 457 the appellant admitted receiving a total of £88,710.30 in respect of numerous drug transactions. He claimed that he spent about £78,840 and thus made a profit of just under £10,000. It was held that notwithstanding the expense incurred, the court would assess the defendant's proceeds at the full amount of £88,710.30.

12–26   **"Other reward."** The payment need not be received as a reward as such (*i.e.* in respect of a role performed by the recipient in a drug trafficking venture) but merely that it was received in connection with drug trafficking carried on by the recipient or another.

In *Osei* [1988] Crim.L.R. 755 the appellant pleaded guilty to the unlawful importation of Class A drugs at Heathrow Airport. The judge made a confiscation order in respect of £2,500 which was found in her possession at the time of her arrest. The appellant claimed that she was a courier (which she was) and that the money was given to her by the organisers of the venture to show to immigration officers to enable her to pass through immigration.

Held: "payment" included not merely the courier's profit or fee but also a benefit of the type described by the appellant. The words "other reward" in sections 1(3), 2(1) and (3) of the D.T.O.A. meant rewards in some form other than payment.

An airline ticket with a view to a free holiday would therefore be some "other reward." The ticket is "property" within the meaning of section 38(1) and, when given to the courier, is a "transfer of property" for the purposes of section 38(10).

It follows that the courts will usually be able to determine that a courier **12–27** travelling from abroad has benefited from drug trafficking in most cases because the evidence frequently reveals that the cost of the courier's airline ticket and hotel expenses have been paid by another. For the purposes of section 2(3), the court may make the assumption that any property transferred to the defendant during the relevant period was a payment or reward received in connection with drug trafficking.

It follows that once it is shown that the defendant received the payment or reward, it is immaterial whether the payment was intended for the defendant's own use or not. In *Osei* (*supra*) there was no evidence that the sum of £2,500 was in the appellant's hands to be disposed of as she would have wished. The cash was intended to satisfy immigration that she had sufficient funds to enable her to obtain leave to enter the United Kingdom. Even if it was arranged that the courier should bank the cash for the ultimate benefit of the instigator, the property is still caught by the wording of sections 1(3), 2(1) and 2(3) of the D.T.O.A.

The value of the payment must be real. **12–28**

In *Johnson* [1991] 2 Q.B. 249 the appellant received a cheque for £6,750 which was credited to her bank account but debited six days later when it was dishonoured on presentation. Nonetheless, the judge included the value of the cheque when assessing the extent of the appellant's proceeds of drug trafficking. The judge was of course entitled to assume that the cheque represented a payment or reward in connection with drug trafficking (section 2(1)(*a*)) but that particular assumption was plainly shown to be incorrect once there was evidence that the cheque was dishonoured and therefore valueless. The appellant had bought a car for £6,000 of which £5,600 had been raised by way of a loan from a finance company. The appellant had paid the deposit of £400 and repaid £900 to the finance company.

Held: her payments/rewards amounted to £1,300 but the balance could not be said to be a payment or reward received "in connection with drug trafficking" because the origin of the money came from the finance company whose funds were in no way tainted.

12–29   **Is the drug itself property?** The courts have not been asked to decide whether the drug is "property" for the purposes of the D.T.O.A. or whether drugs given to the defendant may be said to be a "payment" or "reward" for the purposes of sections 1(3), 2(1) and 2(3) of the Act. The issue is vexed not least as to the value to be placed on the commodity. Is the value to be assessed at the street value in the United Kingdom or in the country of origin? The black market value for an illicit transaction is a dubious basis for valuation. An interesting discussion in respect of these matters appears in the commentary to *Stuart* (1990) 11 Cr.App.R.(S.) 89; see also §12–98, *infra*.

(ii) *"Received" by a person*

12–30   **The "conduit" problem.** In common language, "benefit" connotes some advantage, profit, gain or entitlement to use the money or property in the hands of the recipient. It is clear from section 1(3) that a defendant does not "benefit" unless he has at least "received" the payment or reward: see *Osei* [1988] Crim.L.R. 775; and see §12–26, *supra*. The court may make an assumption that property "*held*" by the defendant during the periods specified in section 2(3) was "received by him" at the earliest time at which he appears to the court to have "held it": section 2(3)(*a*).

It is submitted that the words "received" and "held," as they appear in the Act, import more than just a notional or fleeting exercise of control over payments or rewards coming into the hands of the defendant. Suppose that A, B, C, D and E are all convicted of a drug trafficking offence in respect of which A received £5,000 which he handed to B who in turn gave it to C who banked the money in one account whilst simultaneously transferring £5,000 to D in cash from another account, who then gave the cash to E who placed it in the boot of his car whereupon the police seized the cash from E at the time that all five persons were arrested. In truth only £5,000 moved down the chain from A to E and that sum was recovered by the police. Assuming that each defendant has realisable assets in excess of £5,000, is the court entitled to make a confiscation order against each of the five defendants on the basis that each "received" £5,000? If so, it is a staggering result that an Act, designed to deprive offenders of drug proceeds, can generate and seize £25,000 in this way. If all five defendants appear before the court at the same time, and the £5,000 is before the court, then it is easy for the court to take a realistic course but, logically, a different result should not follow merely because the £5,000 was never found or if only some of the defendants appear before the court. Surprisingly, there is not one reported authority where an appellate court has been invited to resolve this problem but in *Simons* (Croydon Crown Court; unreported) the trial judge ruled that the Act produces the draconian result on the unconvincing ground that *Smith* (1989) 89 Cr.App.R. 235 supports such a conclusion. The decision in *Simons* is to be heard on appeal.

12–31   However, the arguments in support of the contention that each of the defendants, in the above example, has benefited by the sum of £5,000 are powerful on a strict reading of the D.T.O.A. The D.T.O.A. does not define the word "received." Although there exists no definition of "receiving," for the purposes of the Theft Act 1968 (section 22), the authorities decided under that Act establish that "receipt" is proved upon proof of possession of the goods in the sense of control exercised over them by the defendant: see *Watson* [1916] 2 K.B. 385. If possession (*i.e.* control) of the property is sufficient to prove receipt for the purposes of sections 1(3) and 2(1) of the D.T.O.A. then, in the above example, it is difficult to escape the conclusion that A, B, C, D and E have each received the payment of £5,000 and therefore the court is entitled to find that each defendant has benefited by that sum. The absurdity of such a conclusion might be avoided if the evidence established that the sum of £5,000 represented a joint benefit in the hands of A, B, C, D and E. The court may then proceed to assess the respective shares of that benefit between the participants.

> In *Porter* [1990] 1 W.L.R. 1260 P and R pleaded guilty to supplying can- **12–32**
> nabis resin and possessing resin with intent to supply. A confiscation
> order was made, jointly and severally, in the sum of £9,600 against both
> P and R. The venture was joint and they had jointly benefited. However,
> the effect of a joint and several order meant that if either P or R failed to
> pay then the entire burden fell on to the other defendant. Both P and R
> owned a house in joint names which, when sold, left very little to dis-
> charge the confiscation order. The appellant contended that the order
> should not have been made jointly and severally.
>
> *Held*: the appeal would be allowed. Although there had been a joint
> venture, the D.T.O.A. did not contemplate the making of a joint order.
> The terms of section 4(3) envisaged that if the assets of the defendants
> differed, then the amount of the confiscation order could be adjusted to
> reflect their respective shares of the benefit received which, in the circum-
> stances, would result in an order of £4,800 being made against each
> defendant separately.

Accordingly, the court allowed the appeal on the basis that in assessing **12–33** benefit, in accordance with section 1 of the D.T.O.A. the court must, as be- tween co-defendants, determine the respective shares of any joint benefit that they may have received. If the defendants do not give or call evidence as to their respective shares then the court is entitled to assume that they were shar- ing equally. However, the evidence may demonstrate that they shared in vary- ing proportions and a court may assess the proceeds of each defendant on that basis.

It will be appreciated, from *Porter*, that the court is not obliged to hold that the benefit was shared equally, merely that the court may make that assump- tion in the absence of other evidence. Evidence that the defendants benefited in unequal proportions may be derived from evidence that one defendant has greater assets than another (see section 2(1) and note the assumptions which can be made under section 2(3)).

When the decision in *Porter* is examined in the context of the example given above (£5,000 passed from A to E), it will be seen that the problem posed remains largely unresolved but *Porter* does mark the court's ab- horrence to the suggestion that the sentencer is entitled to confiscate against one defendant more than his share of the benefit. In *Porter*, the Court of Appeal explained the machinery which operates in cases where the court can determine the respective shares of each beneficiary. However, in the example given above, A, B, C and D have received no share whatsoever. Their benefit should be assessed at "nil" but, if their benefit is truly nil, then it is artificial to say that they have "benefited" at all. In other words the benefit is not joint but a sole benefit received (ultimately) by E. The "cleanest" solution is to say that A, B, C and D did not "receive" a payment or reward for the purposes of either section 1(3) or section 2. How is this to be achieved unless the word "received" has a meaning going beyond the notion of control/possession? The answer is perhaps to be gleaned from sections 2(3)(a), 38(1), 38(7) and 38(10).

12–34   By section 38(1), "property" includes money. The court may assume that property "held" by the defendant or "transferred to him" during the relevant period was thus "received" by him at the earliest time at which he appears to have "held" it as a payment or reward in connection with drug trafficking carried on by him: section 2(3)(a). Property is "held" by any person if he holds any interest in it: section 38(7).

Again, property is "transferred" by one person to another if the first person "transfers or grants to the other any interest in the property": section 38(10). Accordingly, whether the property is either "held" by the defendant or "transferred to him," the property is not received by him for the purposes of section 2(3), unless he holds or acquires an interest in it. This seems to suggest that a mere transitory acquisition, or the receipt of property without any interest being vested in the defendant, is not sufficient for the purposes of the Act. Such a construction, it is submitted, is neither unworkable nor unreasonable and involves no straining of the provisions. In the ordinary way the court is entitled to assume, under the Act, that property received by the defendant vested him with an interest in it, unless the defendant proves the contrary, on a balance of probabilities: see *Dickens* [1990] 2 Q.B. 102. In that case, the judge concluded that the appellant held an interest in two boats at the material time and consequently their value had to be included both in the proceeds of drug trafficking and in the amount that might be realised at the time of the confiscation order.

In *Porter* the court did not favour a construction of the Act which allows the courts to recover the same figure more than once in circumstances where several defendants participated in the same joint venture: and see *Viner and Long, The Times*, May 25, 1990, C.A.

12–35   The same point seems to emerge from *Chrastny (No. 2)* [1991] 1 W.L.R. 1385 although the result in that case was rather more severe than in *Porter*. In *Chrastny (No. 2)* C was convicted of conspiracy to supply cocaine, and supplying that drug, with a value in excess of £4 million. Her husband had absconded. They controlled assets worth over £2 million. She was ordered to pay a confiscation order in the sum of £2,676,627. The appellant argued that the court should not find that the whole of the property held in joint names, and in their joint possession, was the proceeds of drug trafficking attributable to either defendant and that the value should be apportioned. The court distinguished *Porter* and *Viner and Long, The Times*, May 25, 1990 on the basis that in those cases *all* the defendants were before the court whereas in *Chrastny (No. 2)* the husband had absconded. The appellant exercised

sufficient control of the property to justify a finding that the value of her benefit was just over £2 million. If the appellant's husband were apprehended and
convicted it would not be possible to make an order against him on the basis
of his possession of the same property.

Although the decision appears to be at variance with *Porter*, it is submitted
that they are reconcilable. What must not be overlooked is that in *Chrastny
(No. 2)* the appellant's own benefit was assessed at over £2 million. On that
basis the court was entitled to look to see what assets were realisable at the
time the order was made and to order the confiscation of that sum in accordance with sections 4 and 5 of the Act. *Chrastny (No. 2)* is not authority for the
proposition that the court would be entitled to confiscate the same proceeds
again if her husband were apprehended and convicted.

(iii) *Payment received in connection with drug trafficking*

The payment or reward must have been received in connection with "drug   **12–36**
trafficking" as defined by section 38(1). The term "drug trafficking" is to be
distinguished from "drug trafficking offences": both are separately defined
under section 38(1). Not every "drug trafficking offence" amounts to "drug
trafficking" for the purposes of section 38(1). This includes a conspiracy to
import a controlled drug. Such a conspiracy is a "drug trafficking offence"
but it is not "drug trafficking" under section 38(1). If B visits Jamaica and imports cannabis back into the United Kingdom then the airline ticket and hotel
expenses (paid for by A) are "payments or other rewards" in connection with
drug trafficking carried on by them. However, if B took fright in Jamaica and
decided not to possess, let alone to import, cannabis then it would seem that
neither the ticket nor the hotel expenses would fall within the meaning of section 1(3) because there had not been an activity performed by either A or B
which amounted to "drug trafficking" under the Act: see *Johnson* [1991] 2
Q.B. 249, §12–50, *infra*.

In *Osei* [1988] Crim.L.R. 775 the appellant acted as a courier for the   **12–37**
unlawful importation of Class A drugs. The sum of £2,500 found on her possession was (she claimed) to show to immigration officers to enable her to
obtain leave to enter the United Kingdom. The court held that "payment"
meant any payment whether by way of reward or in some other way connected with drug trafficking. Presumably the appellant had contended that
the sum of £2,500 was wholly divorced from the drugs transaction and that
the object was to fool the immigration officers into believing that she had sufficient funds to enter the country. On the facts in *Osei*, it is difficult to escape
the conclusion that the attempt to circumvent immigration controls was part
and parcel of the fraudulent evasion of the prohibition on importation of a
controlled drug for the purposes of section 170(2) of the Customs and Excise
Management Act 1979. However, the point remains that the payment or
reward must have some connection with drug trafficking even if it was not
exclusively connected with that activity and may (as in *Osei*) have had a dual
purpose. Indeed, section 38(5) of the D.T.O.A. seems to put that beyond
doubt and provides that:

"References in this Act to anything received in connection with drug trafficking include a reference to anything received both in that connection and in some other connection."

Where the payment is traceable to an innocent source, whose funds are not tainted, then the "connection" with drug trafficking is not made out. Indeed if an assumption is made prima facie under sections 2(2) and (3), then proof of an innocent source rebuts the assumption.

(iv) Carried on by the recipient or another

12–38   As has been emphasised already, the primary act is the act of receipt of the payment or reward in the hands of the recipient irrespective as to whether the drug trafficking activity was carried on by him or another. It is therefore unnecessary to establish that the recipient was a party to a conspiracy to commit a drug trafficking offence in respect of which the payment or reward was made: see the wording of section 1(3) and section 2(1)(a). However, by contrast, if the court makes any of the assumptions set out in section 2(3)(a) or (b), the assumption will be made on the basis that the payment or reward was in connection with drug trafficking carried on by the recipient himself. The burden will therefore fall on to the defendant recipient to show, on a balance of probabilities, that the origin of the payment or reward was from a source other than drug trafficking: see Dickens [1990] 2 Q.B. 102; Comiskey (1990) 12 Cr.App.R.(S.) 562; Enwezor (1991) 93 Cr.App.R. 233; and §12–53, infra.

(v) Knowledge of the origin of the proceeds

12–39   In Richards [1992] 2 All E.R. 572 R imported drugs into the United Kingdom concealed in a motor vessel. The co-accused was the prime mover in the venture. He lent £6,000 to R for the purchase of the boat. R denied knowing that, at the time he received the monies, the boat was to be used for smuggling drugs.

Held: it must be shown that the accused knew that the payment or reward was made "in connection with drug trafficking".

The judge made no overt finding of fact as to R's knowledge when he received the £6,000, that the boat was to be used for drug smuggling.

The result is, perhaps, somewhat surprising since, as the respondents pointed out, the 1986 Act provides investigative procedures and therefore the question of knowledge does not arise as it may do if a criminal offence were being created. On the other hand, the reference to "or other reward," as that phrase appears in section 1(3), does tend to suggest that the defendant was aware of the origin of the property, because it is that knowledge which enables the defendant to perceive the payment as a "reward" and not a mere payment or gift.

12–40   **Burden of proof.** The D.T.O.A., for the purposes of section 1(2), does not expressly state upon whom the incidence of proof lies or what is the appropriate standard of proof. However, there is now clear authority that the prosecution has the task of proving both the fact that the defendant has benefited from drug trafficking and the amount of such benefit: see Dickens [1990] 2 Q.B. 102 and Enwezor (1991) 93 Cr.App.R. 233. The evidence upon which that judgment is based will come in part from the trial and in part from statements tendered under section 3 of the Act (*per* Lord Lane C.J. at 107). The burden on the prosecution which, at first sight, appears to be onerous is in fact lightened considerably by the assumptions which the court can make under sections 2(2) and 2(3). Those assumptions can, of course, be rebutted by the defendant on a balance of probabilities but in so far as any of them survive they will, together with other evidence in the case, help the trial judge to determine whether he feels sure that a particular payment or reward was a benefit received by the defendant in connection with drug trafficking for the purposes of section 1(3) and section 2(1) of the Act.

For a more detailed analysis of this topic and the cases of *Dickens* and *Enwezor*, see §12–53.

III. Quantifying the Defendant's Proceeds of Drug Trafficking

Section 2(1) provides that: **12–41**

"For the purpose of this Act—
  (*a*) any payments or other rewards received by a person at any time (whether before or after the commencement of section 1 of this Act) in connection with drug trafficking carried on by him or another are his proceeds of drug trafficking, and
  (*b*) the value of his proceeds of drug trafficking is the aggregate of the values of the payments or other rewards."

(a) Introductory note

The second step is for the court to assess the value of the defendant's pro-   **12–42**
ceeds of drug trafficking. Note the word "value." What has to be recovered prima facie is the value of the defendant's proceeds of drug trafficking (section 4) and not necessarily the value of tangible assets known to exist in the hands of the defendant.

The initial calculation involves aggregating all gross receipts received in connection with drug trafficking and then revaluing the total amount if necessary under section 5(5) to reflect inflation, profitable investment or market fluctuation. The severity of that calculation may be mitigated by the provisions of section 4(3), which provide that the amount to be recovered under the confiscation order is the amount that might be realised *if* that amount is less than the value of the defendant's proceeds of drug trafficking. The court is concerned with "proceeds," not profit, and therefore the expense involved in buying, selling, transporting or distributing the drug is irrelevant and the court can make no deduction in respect of drug proceeds reinvested in another purchase of drugs: see *Smith* (1989) 89 Cr.App.R. 235; *McDonald* (1990) 12 Cr.App.R.(S.) 457; *Comiskey* (1990) 12 Cr.App.R. 562.

A "payment" or "other reward" may be cash but it may also be a benefit in kind, *e.g.* an airline ticket: see *Osei* [1988] Crim.L.R. 775, and §12–26, *supra*. A payment or reward may also be a "gift," a chose in action or another intangible: see section 38(1). It does not matter *when* the payment or reward was received by the defendant. There is not time limit as to how far back the prosecution may scan. Thus, payments made before the commencement of the Act are included. The payment must be actually received by the defendant; presumably an offer to advance a payment or reward cannot be taken into account; and similarly a payment which has been misdirected, (*i.e.* forwarded to another individual in error) cannot feature in the calculation. It does not matter whether the payment is in connection with the defendant's drug trafficking or someone else's: see section 2(1)(*a*).

12-43   The practical effect of section 2(1) may be summarised as follows. If the prosecution can prove that a payment or reward was received by the defendant at any time *and* if it can be proved to be connected with drug trafficking, then such a payment represents the "proceeds" of drug-trafficking for the purposes of the Act. Obviously, there will be many occasions when the prosecution cannot prove the link between a payment and a drug-trafficking offence—however suspicious the circumstances of its receipt may seem. Parliament has therefore permitted the court to make certain "assumptions" concerning the origin of property received by the accused in the circumstances set out in section 2(3) and the court may take into account any statement tendered by the prosecution as to any matters relevant "to the assessment of the value" of the defendant's proceeds of drug trafficking: section 3(1).

Although the Drug Trafficking Offences Act provides that a defendant may also tender a statement to the Crown Court (section 3(4)) it seems that the contents of that statement should be confined to matters relevant to determining "the amount that might be realised" rather than the value of any payments or rewards received by him, assessing the statement is to be conclusive of the matters of which it relates within the terms of section 3(4).

(b) The assumptions

12-44   Section 2(2) provides:

"The Court may, for the purpose of determining whether the defendant has benefited from drug trafficking and, if he has, of assessing the value of his proceeds of drug trafficking, make the following assumptions, except to the extent that any of the assumptions are shown to be incorrect in the defendant's case."

12-45   By section 2(3) those assumptions are:

"(*a*) that any property appearing to the court—
   (i) to have been held by him at any time since his conviction, or
   (ii) to have been transferred to him at any time since the beginning of the period of six years ending when the proceedings were instituted against him,
was received by him, at the earliest time at which he appears to the court to have held it, as a payment or reward in connection with drug trafficking carried on by him,

(*b*) that any expenditure of his since the beginning of that period was met out of payments received by him in connection with drug trafficking carried on by him, and

(*c*) that, for the purpose of valuing any property received or assumed to have been received by him at any time as such a reward, he received the property free of any other interests in it."

Both subsections 2(2) and 2(3) pose difficult problems of construction, but if more thought and a little imagination had been applied to their effect, many of the problems could largely have been avoided. As it is, the courts have been compelled to construe the two subsections in the context of the policy of the Act, and subject to the fact that the making of a confiscation order is a penal sanction.   **12–46**

If the court chooses to make any of the assumptions specified in section 2(3) then (as is apparent from the wording of subsection 2(3)), it will be made on the basis that the defendant has received a payment or reward in connection with drug-trafficking carried on *by him* and by no-one else.

It is plain from the opening words of subsection 2(2) that the court is not *obliged* to make the assumptions in question. Subsection 2(2) is therefore permissive and not mandatory. Although the court must not invoke any of the assumptions capriciously, the circumstances in which the Court of Appeal would be prepared to interfere with the decision of the trial judge in this regard is by no means clear or obvious.

In *Redbourne, The Times*, June 26, 1992, the Court of Appeal was asked "how should a judge decide how to make the assumptions referred to in section 2(3)?" The court observed that there was no express answer to that question in the 1986 Act but it could not have been Parliament's intention that a judge had to be satisfied, on the evidence before him, that the defendant had benefited from drug trafficking *before* he could make any assumptions at all. This conclusion is plainly right having regard to the opening words of section 2(2). However, the judge had to have *some reason to suspect* that the defendant had benefited from drug trafficking before he made this assumption or any of them. It is not clear how a judge should approach this problem. Is the mere fact that the defendant has been convicted of a "drug trafficking offence" a sufficient reason? Presumably not, for if that were so, then the criteria would be fulfilled in every case where the court was obliged to embark upon an enquiry under the Act. Must the reason to suspect exist and relate to each payment or reward that falls to be considered? This approach would be logical. As the Court remarked "it was not necessary or sensible to apply any standard of proof to the question whether there was a reason to suspect that the defendant had benefited from drug trafficking." The question whether the assumptions should be made was a "threshold decision." This means that the judge is entitled to make the assumptions at the start of his enquiry or at any later stage, up to the time when he made his final decision. Accordingly a judge's decision whether to make any of the assumptions, or not, was "an interim one" made on his way to reaching a final decision after a full consideration of the defendants' case.   **12–47**

However, by virtue of subsection 2(2), the trial judge should not make any   **12–48** of the assumptions specified in subsection 2(3) to the extent that "any of the assumptions are shown to be incorrect in the defendant's case."

These words are not easy to understand. At first sight, they seem to imply that the burden of proving an assumption to be incorrect falls on the defendant and indeed this is the construction which has found favour with the courts: see *Dickens* [1990] 2 Q.B. 102. But one reading of subsection 2(2) suggests that this need not necessarily be so if the words "the defendant's case" as they appear in subsection 2(2) are to be treated as being synonymous in meaning with the words "in the case against the defendant." In the ordinary way, a reference to "the defendant's case" may mean one of two things. It may be a reference to the case presented on behalf of the defendant, *e.g.* by calling evidence as part of the defence case. It may also refer to the entire proceedings against a named defendant. We see an example of the latter employed in section 4(1). Accordingly, it is to be regretted that the draftsman did not use plainer language.

12–49   If Parliament intended to place the burden of proof upon the defendant, and no one else, then it would have been very easy for the draftsman simply to have used the words "shown to be incorrect *by the defendant.*" The fact that he did not do so raises the question whether it was Parliament's wish to put a burden of proof upon any particular party at all? This is because the court is *obliged* to follow the steps set out in section 1. Accordingly, unlike any other order or relief, which is made on the application of the party seeking it, the making of a confiscation order (in theory) should normally be initiated by the court: see the opening words in section 1(1). If the evidence in the case—no matter who adduces it—shows an assumption to be incorrect, then the court may not make it.

12–50   In *Johnson* [1991] 2 Q.B. 249 the appellant received a cheque for £6,750 which had been credited into her account. A few days later the bank debited the account on the basis that the cheque was dishonoured on presentation. The court was entitled to make the assumption that the appellant received a payment in connection with drug trafficking but the cheque was plainly of no value, as it was dishonoured, and thus the assumption (if made) would be shown to be incorrect by proof (whoever adduced the evidence) that the cheque had no value. Again, a motor car was bought by the appellant for £6,000 of which £5,600 was obtained by way of a loan from a finance house. The judge was entitled to make the assumption, prima facie, that she held the car and received it as a payment or reward in connection with drug trafficking carried on by her. However, there was no evidence that the money from the finance company was tainted and so the assumption would again be shown to be incorrect in the defendant's case. In both illustrations the evidence appears to have been presented by the prosecution including evidence tendered by them under section 3(1) of the Act.

Unfortunately, it is not apparent, from the wording of the Act, whether the court is duty bound to indicate, during the proceedings, that it proposes to make any of the statutory assumptions or whether it may simply invoke them at the moment of adjudication: and see *Redbourne, supra.*

12–51   Just as the Act does not expressly deal with the *burden* of proof, so it does not deal with the *standard* of proof. However, given that the making of a confiscation order is a penal sanction, and that any assumption made is on the basis that the defendant received a payment or reward in connection with *his* own drug-trafficking, the courts have been swift to decide that the "usual rules" apply, so that a defendant need only prove an issue on the balance of probabilities whereas the Crown must prove any allegation it makes to the criminal standard, namely, that the court feels sure that the allegation is made out: *Dickens* [1990] 2 Q.B. 102; *Enwezor* (1991) 93 Cr.App.R. 233. The D.T.O.A. also fails to provide the Crown Court with any statutory guidance or directions as to the form the hearing should take when following the procedural steps in section 1. However, the practice now established is that the court must conduct a hearing familiar to criminal law practitioners, giving both the prosecution and the defendant an opportunity to call evidence in the traditional, adversarial way and following the customary order of speeches.

In *Redbourne, The Times*, June 26, 1992, the Court of Appeal also con-   **12–52** sidered what the effect of the assumptions would be if they were not rebutted by or on behalf of the defendant. The short answer is that an assumed fact must be treated as being true. There would be little point in making an assumption if such a result were not to follow. The point is reinforced by the wording of section 2(2) which includes a proviso in respect of the converse case where an assumption is shown to be "incorrect" in the defendant's case.

It would seem that, in *Redbourne*, the argument put forward was that any fact, covered by an assumption which was not rebutted, might need further evidence to establish it before the burden on the prosecution would be regarded as satisfied. This argument appears to have been based on two passages in the judgment of Lord Lane C.J. in *Dickens* [1990] 2 Q.B. 102. The first relates to the fact that the prosecution shoulders the persuasive burden, to the criminal standard of proof, although that burden is considerably lightened by the provisions of section 2(2). The second passage states that "In so far as any of [the assumptions] survive they will *together with* any evidence which the judge may accept, assist the judge to decide whether he is satisfied so as to feel sure that the prosecution have made out their case" (emphasis added). The Court of Appeal in *Redbourne* suggested that Lord Lane C.J. had in mind cases where the assumptions cover only part of the prosecution case and therefore other evidence might well be needed to be addressed by the Crown to prove its case. An example, which demonstrates the type of problems Lord Lane C.J. had in mind, is to be found in facts in *Johnson*, cited *supra* (§12–50).

(i) *Definitions*

> For "payment or reward" see §12–24, *supra.*
> For "in connection with drug trafficking" see §12–36, *supra.*

(ii) *Burden of proving the benefit and value of the defendant's proceeds*

Although not expressly clarified by the D.T.O.A., there is now clear auth-   **12–53** ority that the prosecution has the task of proving both the fact that the defendant has benefited from drug trafficking and the extent of that benefit: *Dickens* (1990) 91 Cr.App.R. 164 and *Enwezor (supra).*

Both those cases also make it plain that the standard of proof required is the criminal standard, namely "proof beyond reasonable doubt": *per* Lord Lane C.J. (at 168).

> In *Dickens* the appellant was convicted of conspiracy to import canna-bis. A confiscation order was made in the sum of £129,300. The judge assessed the value of the appellant's proceeds of drug trafficking at £303,432 but he also determined that the amount which might be re-alised under section 4(3) was the sum of £129,300. The judge, in calcu-lating the amount to be included in the confiscation order, took into account the value of two boats lying in Spain. The appellant denied that he had any interest in the boats.
>
> *Held*: that the burden of proving that a particular payment or reward was received by the defendant, in connection with drug trafficking car-ried on by him or another (see sections 1(3) and section 2(1)), rests on the prosecution:
>
> "... the context of the Act and the nature of the penalties which are likely to be imposed, make it clear that the standard of proof required is the criminal standard, namely proof so that the judge feels sure of proof beyond reasonable doubt": *per* Lord Lane C.J.

12–54   The court recognised that, at first sight, the burden on the prosecution was heavy but that in reality this burden was considerably lightened by the assumptions which the court may make under sections 2(2) and (3) of the Act.

The following example demonstrates the relevant principles: suppose D is shown to have received a payment of £1,000 one year prior to proceedings being instituted against him for a drug trafficking offence. The burden rests on the prosecution to prove beyond reasonable doubt, that D received it in connection with drug trafficking carried on by him or another (section 2(1)) and that he therefore benefited to the sum of £1000: section 1(3). Assume there was no direct evidence that D received the money in connection with drug trafficking but the prosecution can show that D was unemployed at the material time with no known sources of legitimate income. On those facts the judge is entitled to find as a fact that the sum was "transferred to [the defen-dant]" during the relevant period (section 2(3)(*a*)(ii)) and that accordingly he "held it" at that moment (see sections 38(7) and 38(10)). That fact alone is enough to enable the court to make the assumption under section 2(3)(*a*)(ii). Accordingly, the judge may (if he wishes) assume that the sum was accord-ingly "received" by the defendant as a payment or reward in connection with drug trafficking carried on by the defendant (section 2(3)(*a*)(ii)).

12–55   Of course the defendant may succeed in rebutting that assumption on a bal-ance of probabilities (*Dickens, supra*) but, if he fails, and the assumption remains intact, the judge must still ask himself the question "am I sure, beyond reasonable doubt, that the payment was received by the defendant in connection with drug trafficking carried on by him or another?"

The judge will not be lightly criticised if he answers the question in the af-firmative on the basis of the assumption made and which remains intact: see *Small* (1988) 88 Cr.App.R. 184. However, in the final analysis, the answer to the question is a matter for the judge. The judge will base his determination partly on the evidence laid before him during the trial and partly from statements tendered under section 3, together with any other evidence put before the court: and see *Redbourne, The Times*, June 26, 1992.

> In *Enwezor* (1991) 93 Cr.App.R. 233 the judge made a confiscation   **12–56**
> order of £20,000. A total of £11,000 had been paid into a building so-
> ciety account in the name of the appellant's sister. The appellant con-
> tended that the payments were made by various people coming from
> Nigeria and not (as alleged) by himself. The trial judge ruled that the pay-
> ments into the account were gifts caught by the Act which represented
> the proceeds of drug trafficking and that the appellant had benefited by
> that amount. The judge said that "it is plain from the general tenor and
> working of the Act that the ordinary criminal burden and standard of
> proof is not applicable." He accordingly made his determination on the
> basis of the civil standard of proof. The judge added that "if the criminal
> standard of proof had applied I would not have found . . . against him."
>   *Held*: on appeal that the judge was entitled to rely on the assumptions
> under sections 2(2) and 2(3) but that the correct standard of proof was
> the criminal standard and that since the judge would have reached a dif-
> ferent conclusion on that basis the appeal would be allowed.

(iii) *Evidential considerations*

The defendant is of course entitled to call evidence during the hearing and   **12–57**
he may seek an adjournment for that purpose. In *Nicholson* (1990) 12
Cr.App.R.(S.) 58 the appellant pleaded guilty to various drug trafficking
offences. Officers found £700 at the appellant's home address. The appellant
wished to call witnesses to show that the money was not the proceeds of drug
trafficking and applied for an adjournment for that purpose. The judge made
remarks which implied that, if the appellant persisted in his request, he might
not get the maximum benefit from his plea of guilty whereupon the appellant
proceeded without calling his witnesses. In the circumstances, the Court of
Appeal held that the judge was putting unfair pressure on the appellant not to
maintain his request for an adjournment and that justice was not seen to be
done.

A curious state of affairs arose in *Jenkins* (1990) 12 Cr.App.R.(S.) 582.
Concern was expressed in the Court of Appeal that the appellant had not been
permitted to give evidence on his own behalf at all in order to rebut assumptions which the trial judge was proposing to make. The transcript of the proceedings in the Crown Court did not make the position clear and therefore the
Court of Appeal assumed in the appellant's favour. If the appellant had in
truth been denied the opportunity to give evidence then this was manifestly irregular and the Court of Appeal in *Jenkins* made that clear. The trial judge also
made an order for £12,000, whereas the prosecution in their statement under
section 3 had only referred to £3,000. Again it appears that the difference in
computation was not fully explored, nor does it seem that the appellant
was given an opportunity to give evidence on that issue. That, as the Court
of Appeal remarked, was "another material irregularity." If the defendant

fails to keep proper records, but he has acquired and spent large sums of money (the origin of which he is not able to explain), then he runs the risk that the court will make findings adverse to him on the basis of the statutory assumptions under sections 2(2) and (3): see *Small* (1989) 88 Cr.App.R. 184.

(iv) *Joint beneficiaries*

12-58   This has already been discussed elsewhere (see §12–30, *supra*). Where two or more defendants have been engaged in a joint enterprise to commit a drug trafficking offence but one defendant is shown to have received more payments during the relevant period than the other, the court must determine the total value of the benefits received jointly and then determine the value of the benefit received by each of the defendants. In the absence of any evidence on the point, the sentencer may (but is not obliged) to assume that the defendants shared equally: see *Porter* [1990] 1 W.L.R. 1260, but contrast that decision with *Chrastny (No. 2)* [1991] 1 W.L.R. 1385.

(v) *Assets held abroad*

12-59   By section 38(3), the D.T.O.A. applies to property whether it is situated in England and Wales or elsewhere.

> In *Hopes* [1989] Crim.L.R. 515 H pleaded guilty to various drug trafficking offences. A confiscation order was made in the sum of £12,000 which the appellant had invested in a house in Wales, having realised that sum from a property in Australia. The appellant declined to call evidence that the sum in question was lawfully obtained.
>
> *Held*: on appeal, the order would be upheld on the basis that the judge was entitled to make an assumption under section 2(3) that the £12,000 represented the proceeds of drug trafficking carried on by him.

It will be noted that the Act applies to all unlawful drug trafficking ventures wherever they are carried out (see section 38(1)) and the Act applies in respect of property held by the defendant anywhere in the world (see section 38(3)). The value of assets held abroad should therefore be included in the determination of the amount which might be realised for the purposes of section 5(3) and section 4(3). The court is concerned with valuations and not with the practicalities of enforcing an order by actually seizing them. The burden will therefore rest on the defendant to liquidate his assets or face the stark alternative of serving a consecutive sentence in default.

The approach adopted in *Hopes* appears to have differed from that in *Bragason* [1988] Crim.L.R. 778; (1988) 10 Cr.App.R.(S.) 258 where the court assessed B's proceeds of drug trafficking at £15,000 but certified that the amount which might be realised from the assets which he held "in the jurisdiction" as nil. It is not clear whether the sentencer thought that it was necessary to assess the value of assets held by the defendant in England and Wales but, if he did, he was clearly in error for the reasons given above (see also section 38(3)).

(vi) Some ramifications of section 2(3)

It will now be evident that the implications of section 2(3) are enormous. **12–60** Even if a defendant is convicted of supplying drugs over a very short period of time, the court is entitled (in appropriate cases) to assume that all property transferred to the defendant over the preceding six years (prior to the moment when proceedings were instituted against him) was a payment or reward made in connection with drug trafficking carried on by the defendant and moreover, that any expenditure made by the defendant over that period, came out of the proceeds of drug trafficking. It may seem harsh that the courts' powers of confiscation run way beyond the limits within which the prosecution is obliged to put its case in relation to any drug trafficking offence for which the defendant appears to be sentenced. However, where property is proved to have been received by an accused and where there is no evidence at all to suggest that when he received it, the accused (or for transferor) were engaged in drug trafficking, then such a lack of evidence may of itself be the best evidence to show that the "assumptions," which the court can make under section 2(2), are incorrect.

Finally, it is important that legal advisers, acting on behalf of defendants accused of drug trafficking offences, should take detailed instructions from their clients in anticipation of proceedings being pursued under the D.T.O.A.

(vii) Periods of time embraced by section 2(3)

It was plainly the intention of Parliament that subsection 2(3) should **12–61** embrace two very different periods of time. Obviously subsection 2(3)(*a*)(ii) relates to the six years ending when the proceedings were "instituted" against the defendant. By section 38(11) proceedings for an offence are instituted in England and Wales:

(*a*) when a justice of the peace issues a summons or warrant under section 1 of the Magistrates Courts Act 1980 in respect of the offence,

(*b*) when a person is charged with the offence after being taken into custody without a warrant,

(*c*) when a bill of indictment is preferred under section 2 of the Administration of Justice (Miscellaneous Provisions) Act 1933 in a case falling within paragraph (b) or subsection (2) of that section;
and where the application of this subsection would result in there being more than one time for the institution of proceedings, they shall be taken to have been instituted at the earliest of those times.

By contrast, section 2(3)(*a*)(i) relates to any property appearing to the court **12–62** "... to have been held by him since his conviction." However, subsection 3(*a*)(i) is so ambiguously drafted that it may be construed to apply either to payments received by the defendant *at any time* in his life and which he continues to hold since his conviction, *or*, it relates only to payments received and held by the defendant *after* his conviction.

The ambiguity arises by virtue of the words "held by him" in subsection 2(3)(*a*)(i). In support of the first construction, the argument is that the draftsman did not (as he did in 2(3)(*a*)(ii)) use the words "transferred to him," or "received by him." Accordingly, it is said that section 2 (3)(*a*)(i) was designed to apply to all property which was received by the defendant, at some time in his life and which he held at the time of his conviction and subsequently. The prosecution may not be able to show when the defendant actually received the property in question, but it may be possible to show when he "held" it and therefore, by section 2(3)(*a*), the court may assume that the property was received "at the earliest time at which he appears to the court to have held it" and, having made the assumption, that it was a payment or reward in connection with drug-trafficking.

12–63   But if section 2(3)(*a*)(i) really does catch property received by the defendant at any time, then why did the draftsmen use the words "at any time *since* his conviction?"

The second interpretation of section 2(3)(*a*)(i) is that the court is only entitled to look to property received and held by the defendant literally *since* his conviction. Any assumption made by the court will be on the basis that the proceeds resulted from the defendant's drug-trafficking. As a matter of common sense it will be far more difficult, if not impossible, to rebut an assumption appertaining to payments received or paid before the six year period. Records relating to a business, etc., which would otherwise support the defendant's contention that it was a payment or reward lawfully earned, may be lost or destroyed. Furthermore, witnesses may no longer be traceable or capable of supporting the legality of a given transaction. Arguably, the statutory assumptions in subsection (3) were therefore intended to embrace only a relatively short period of the defendant's career. Furthermore, the proceeds of drug trafficking may be invested (*e.g.* abroad) and payments made to the defendant after his conviction for a drug-trafficking offence. For a variety of reasons there may be an appreciable delay between conviction and the making of a confiscation order. Since section 2(3)(*a*)(ii) only relates to payments received for a period of six years *ending* when the proceedings were instituted against the defendant, it follows that payments received after conviction would not be caught by that provision. Accordingly, section 2(3)(*a*)(i) was enacted.

It is important to remember that the court *must not* make any of the assumptions in section 2(3) *if* the only offence for which the defendant is to be sentenced is that of assisting a drug trafficker contrary to section 24 of the D.T.O.A.

IV. Assessing the Amount That Might be Realised

(a) Introductory note

12–64   It will be recalled from the above that what is to be recovered by the court, under a confiscation order, is the amount which the Crown Court assesses to be the value of the defendant's proceeds of drug trafficking: section 4(1). This figure represents the ideal. Thus, if a defendant received £10,000 by way of proceeds of drug trafficking then this is what the court would ideally wish to recover by way of a confiscation order.

However, the reality of the situation will often be that the defendant only has assets for a value which is *lower* than the amount which the court assesses to be the value of the defendant's proceeds of drug trafficking. The court may therefore reduce the value of the confiscation order and recover the lesser amount, but only within the terms of sections 4(3), 5(1) and 5(3). It is important to note that the circumstances in which the court can confiscate a lesser amount are very limited and the following points should be borne in mind.

First, there exists no provision under the Act for reducing the amount on grounds of personal hardship. Accordingly, no reduction can be made on the basis that the only realisable asset held by the defendant is the matrimonial home (but see *Keston* (1990) 12 Cr.App.R.(S.) 93 where a contrary impression is given: see §12–75, *infra*). **12–65**

Secondly, the court *must* confiscate the full amount (being the defendant's proceeds of drug trafficking) *unless* it is satisfied that the lesser amount represents the "amount that might be realised" under section 4(3). In those circumstances the court must make an order for the lesser amount. There is no half-way house. **12–66**

"The amount that might be realised" is defined by section 5(3). It is not the same thing as "realisable property" which is separately defined by section 5(1). In the majority of cases the practical effect is that the "amount that might be realised" under section 4 will be the value of the "realisable property," but this need not necessarily be so. In *Carroll* [1991] Crim.L.R. 720 the court determined the value of the defendant's proceeds of drug trafficking at £39,692. His known assets amounted to £16,301 but the court concluded that he had undisclosed assets and made a confiscation order of £30,000. The result implies that the court was satisfied under section 4(3) that the "amount that might be realised" was £30,000 of which in excess of £13,000 represented "hidden assets" (*i.e.* £30,000 – £16,301). By definition, the "amount that might be realised" includes gifts caught by the Act (which did not feature in *Carroll*) and "realisable property" as defined by section 5(1). Accordingly, the court's determination in *Carroll* is only valid if "hidden" assets may properly be included within the definition of "realisable property." This seems unlikely because "realisable property" is a term of art defined by the Act. It is submitted that if the court in *Carroll* was not satisfied that the appellant only had assets worth £16,301, then the requirements of section 4(3) had not been fulfilled and the court would have been entitled to make an order for the full amount. In the ordinary way, it is the defendant who knows the full extent of his "realisable property" and the burden under section 4(3) normally rests on him: see *Comiskey* (1990) 12 Cr.App.R.(S.) 562, *Ilsemann* (1990) 12 Cr.App.R.(S.) 398, and see §12–74, *infra*.

Thirdly, any "realisable property" which forms part of the determination of the "amount that might be realised" under section 5(3) and section 4(3) need not, of itself, have been acquired with the proceeds of drug trafficking because the definition of "realisable property" in section 5(1) includes legitimately acquired property: *Chrastny (No. 2)* [1991] 1 W.L.R. 1385. Thus, if X acquires a motor vehicle, the court has to decide whether it represents the proceeds of drug trafficking. If it does not, then the vehicle must be left out of **12–67** account in determining the value of the defendant's proceeds for the purposes of section 4(1): see, *e.g. Johnson* [1991] 2 Q.B. 249. However, the vehicle (lawfully acquired) will nevertheless be "realisable property" for the purposes of satisfying a confiscation order in respect of any proceeds of drug trafficking that the defendant did receive.

12–68   Fourthly, the burden will normally be on the defendant to satisfy the court of the matters referred to in section 4(3) but it would seem that in appropriate cases, the court may, of its own volition, make a determination under that subsection: see *Keston* (1990) 12 Cr.App.R.(S.) 93; *Comiskey* (1990) 12 Cr.App.R.(S.) 562; *Ilsemann* (1990) 12 Cr.App.R.(S.) 398 and *Carroll* [1991] Crim.L.R. 720; and see §12–85, *infra*. The court is not obliged to determine the extent of the defendant's realisable assets in every case where the court proposes to make a confiscation order. This is because the Act places the burden on the defendant to satisfy the order or serve a consecutive sentence of imprisonment in default of payment: see *Ilsemann* (1990) 12 Cr.App.R. (S.) 398.

(i) *The criteria*

12–69   Section 4(3) provides as follows:

> "If the court is satisfied that the amount that might be realised at the time the confiscation order is made is less than the amount the court assesses to be the value of his proceeds of drug trafficking, the amount to be recovered in the defendant's case under the Confiscation Order shall be the amount appearing to the court to be the amount that might be so realised."

(ii) *Definition of "realisable property"*

12–70   Section 5(1) provides:

> "In this Act, 'realisable property' means, subject to subsection (2) below—
>
> (a) any property held by the defendant; and
> (b) any property held by a person to whom the defendant has directly or indirectly made a gift caught by this Act."

"Realisable property" therefore includes property held by the defendant (section 5(1)(*a*)) but also gifts caught by the Act which are held by any person (section 5(1)(*b*)). Powers of the High Court are exercisable over "realisable property": see sections 8, 9 and 11.

(iii) *Definition of the "amount that might be realised"*

12–71   Section 5(3) provides:

> "For the purposes of sections 3 and 4 of this Act the amount that might be realised at the time a confiscation order is made against the defendant is:
>
> (*a*) the total of the values at that time of all the realisable property held by the defendant less
> (*b*) where there are obligations having priority at that time the total amounts payable in pursuance of such obligations,
>
> together with the total of the values at that time of all gifts caught by this Act."

Thus section 5(3) is concerned with *values* not limited to the value of realisable property. Significantly, the draftsmen did not refer to "realisable property" in section 4 and this omission is deliberate. The Act contemplates a situation in which the defendant made gifts "caught" by the Act (as defined by section 5(9)), the *value* of which may be assessed for the purposes of section 5(3) and section 4, but which fall outside the strict definition of "realisable property" as set out in section 5(1).

The points referred to above were graphically demonstrated in *Dickens*   **12–72**
[1990] 2 Q.B. 102. The appellant had been convicted of conspiracy to import cannabis and a confiscation order was made for £129,300 on the basis that the amount which "might be realised" was only £129,300. Included in that sum was the value of a Range Rover motor vehicle. That vehicle had been acquired by D which he gave to his wife. D had therefore made a gift to her and it was a gift caught by section 5(9). However D's wife sold the vehicle to a solicitor, for value, who bought it in good faith. The Range Rover was therefore not a gift to him and it was not "realisable property" within the meaning of section 5(1). Accordingly, the appellant contended that the "amount that might be realised" should have been reduced by the value of the Range Rover.

This argument would have been valid if the phrase "amount that might be   **12–73**
realised" as it appears in section 4 is the same thing as "realisable property." However, the Court of Appeal referred to the fact that "realisable property" and "amount that might be realised" were separately defined under the Act and meant two very different things. Lord Lane C.J. said (at 111):

> "... the phrase 'realisable property' does not appear in section 4 of the Act and in particular does not appear in section 4(3). If Parliament had wished the confiscation order to be confined to the defendant's 'realisable property' as defined by section 5(1), then it would undoubtedly have said so in section 4(3), which it did not. We have no doubt that that was deliberate and was designed to ensure that drug traffickers could not protect the assets they had acquired through drug trafficking by 'giving' those assets to others."

Accordingly, the judge was entitled to look at the *value* of the gift made by D to his wife. That gift was caught by the Act (section 5(9)) and its value fell within the definition of "the amount that might be realised" (section 5(3)) for the purposes of section 4(3). The fact that the gift to the wife could no longer be physically realised was irrelevant.

It will be appreciated that the determination made by the court, as to whether a particular transaction is a gift or not, has serious implications if the property is in the hands of a third party who took the property within notice of its origin. Where the property is not only a gift but is "realisable" within the meaning of section 5(1), then the ramifications for the third party are potentially stark since he may be faced with an order from the High Court for the property to be delivered up to a Receiver appointed under section 11 of the Act. It is by no means clear whether third parties have a right to be heard (or to be legally represented) at the Crown Court in respect of that part of the drug trafficking investigation which affects them. The answer is probably in the negative but there have been cases where the trial judge has permitted third parties to make representatives.

(iv) *Who raises the issue under section 4(3)?*

12–74   In theory the court need only make two determinations before making a confiscation order. First, whether the defendant has benefited from drug trafficking and secondly, to assess the value of the defendant's proceeds of drug trafficking. In practice, the court will often need to go on and assess the amount that might actually be realised under section 4(3). However, the opening words, "If the court is satisfied . . ." poses the question as to whether the court, of its own motion, should initiate the third stage or whether it is the defendant who must take the initiative and satisfy the court on a balance of probabilities that a lesser amount should be confiscated.

12–75   In *Johnson* (1991) 2 Q.B. 249, Neill L.J. said (at 259):

> "It is only necessary to make a calculation in accordance with section 4(3) of the 1986 Act if it appears that the amount that might be realised at the time that the confiscation order is made is less than the amount the court assesses to be the value of the defendant's proceeds of drug trafficking. In the present case it is accepted on behalf of the appellant that her proceeds were not less than £1,300."

Those last few words imply that it is for the defendant to initiate a determination under section 4(3). However, in *Keston* (1990) 12 Cr.App.R.(S.) 93: (wrongly referred to as "*Preston*" in [1990] Crim.L.R. 528) the appellant had conceded that the sum of £17,000 was an appropriate sum for a confiscation order. It was also agreed that the sole realisable asset of the appellant was the matrimonial home where he lived with his wife and child. These facts were not made known to the trial judge. In the Court of Appeal, Pill J. said that had those facts been made known to the judge he might have taken a different course and, that having been referred to section 4(3), he might have made a very much lower confiscation order or possibly no order at all: "There were other courses which he might have taken."

With respect, the judgment in *Keston* is not easy to understand. It can be read as implying that in every case the court should determine "the amount that might be realised" under section 4(3). However, the judgment does not, in terms, go that far and such a statement would be at variance with *Johnson, Comiskey* (1990) 12 Cr.App.R.(S.) 562, *Ilsemann* (1990) 12 Cr.App.R.(S.) 398 and *Carroll* [1991] Crim.L.R. 720. In any event there exists no discretion in the D.T.O.A. to reduce the amount, which might be recovered by a confiscation order, on the grounds of personal hardship.

12–76   It is not apparent from the report in *Keston* what the court had in mind when referring to "other courses" which the judge might have taken. By section 1(5), the court must leave the order out of account in determining the appropriate sentence or other manner of dealing with the defendant. If the court in *Keston* had in mind the possibility of combining a fine with a confiscation order then such a course, although technically possible, would be highly unusual because the confiscation order is the means by which the defendant is deprived of his assets and that sum may be sufficiently great to exhaust the defendant's means to pay a fine: see *Hedley* (1990) 90 Cr.App.R. 70.

In *Dickens* [1990] 2 Q.B. 102 the Court of Appeal explained the mechanics of the Act in some detail, but determining the "amount that might be realised" was not a stage which the court analysed in terms of the burden of proof or the requisite standard applicable or upon whom the burden was carried. The court did remark that determining the "amount that might be realised" *may* overlap with the determination of the defendant's proceeds of drug trafficking and, indeed, Lord Lane C.J. said (at 105):

> "The provisions are intentionally draconian. Since the amount of those proceeds and the size of his realisable assets at the time of conviction are likely to be peculiarly within the defendant's knowledge, it is not surprising perhaps if essential burdens are cast upon him . . . ."

In *Comiskey* (1990) 12 Cr.App.R.(S.) 562 the judge assessed the appellant's proceeds of drug trafficking at £250,000. In the judgment of the Court of Appeal, Tucker J. asked whether there was anything *to cause the judge* to be satisfied that the amount that might be realised was less than the value of the defendant's proceeds of drug trafficking in circumstances where the appellant did not give evidence during the D.T.O.A. enquiry or call evidence. **12–77**

Tucker J. said (at 567):

> "On whom is the duty laid of satisfying the court that the amount that might be realised is less than the assessed value of the proceeds? There can be no doubt that the defendant is in an incomparably better position to do so since he (or she) alone knows what has become of the proceeds . . . there is no obligation on the Crown to satisfy the court under section 4(3) . . . ."

So, the burden is certainly not on the Crown to satisfy the court under section 4(3) but, the mere fact that the defendant is normally in a better position to shoulder the burden does not therefore preclude the court, of its own motion, following the steps in section 4(3). This line of reasoning seems to be supported by another passage in the judgment of Tucker J. in *Comiskey* when he said (at 567): **12–78**

> "The only remaining question is whether the court itself ought to conclude as a matter of common sense that the amount that might be realised must be less than the value of the proceeds by reason of the expenses that must necessarily have been involved in the operation . . . draconian though the provisions of the Act may be, the court . . . cannot ignore the fact that some expenses must have been incurred."

The Court of Appeal therefore reduced the amount of the order from £250,000 to £200,000.

Much of the reasoning in *Comiskey* is sound and the guidance helpful but the passage cited above is, with respect, of questionable validity if the Act is strictly construed. When the court referred to expenses involved in "the operation," it is not entirely clear what "operation" the court had in mind. If that was intended to be a reference to the drug trafficking activities carried on by the defendant, in respect of which payments were received and invested, then **12–79** allowing for expenses incurred is just the sort of accounting exercise which the Court of Appeal in *Smith* [1989] 1 W.L.R. 765, and *Comiskey* itself, said should not take place. If, by "operation," the Court was referring to expenses incurred in acquiring realisable property (*e.g.* conveyancing fees; stamp duty, etc.) then, again, it is difficult to see how such an exercise (even on a common sense basis) is consistent with the draconian provisions of the Act. However, that said, there is no doubt that there is much force in the suggestion that section 4(3) envisages that either the defendant or the court itself may carry out a determination under section 4(3). Each case must depend on its own facts as to who should take the initiative: see §12–101, *infra.*

12–80   In *Ilsemann* (1990) 12 Cr.App.R. (S.) 398 the Court of Appeal again made it plain that the court is not *obliged* to make a determination under section 4(3) unless the defendant raises the issue evidentially.

> In *Ilsemann*, the trial judge made a confiscation order in the sum of £396,385 as representing the defendant's proceeds of drug trafficking. The prosecution submitted a schedule showing that the realisable assets *known to the prosecution* were only £214,637. The appellant agreed both figures. He did not give, or call, evidence and argued that the court could only confiscate those assets known to exist and which the prosecution could prove existed.
>
> *Held*: on appeal, that it was for the defendant to satisfy the court that the lesser figure was all that was realisable. The appellant had not sought to challenge the larger figure.

12–81   As Lord Lane C.J. in *Dickens* [1990] 2 Q.B. 102 remarked, the extent of the defendant's realisable assets is likely to be peculiarly within the defendant's knowledge and (*per* Tucker J. in *Comiskey*) "the object of the Act is to oblige a defendant to reveal this information so as to enable the court to make an effective order." It is therefore usually not enough for the defendant merely to sit back and rely on the facts put forward by the prosecution. If the prosecution in *Ilsemann* had admitted that the lower figure represented the extent of the defendant's assets as being the "amount that might be realised" then it is submitted that the court, armed with that admission, can say that it is satisfied that the requirements of section 4(3) have been satisfied even if the defendant did not formally give evidence in support of that admission. The latter course would be unnecessary. However, in *Ilsemann*, the issue as to whether the defendant had hidden assets was very much at large. Similarly, in *Carroll* [1991] Crim.L.R. 72, the judge made a confiscation order for £30,000. The appellant's proceeds of drug trafficking were assessed at £39,692 but the prosecution could only prove assets worth £16,301. The judge heard evidence from the appellant but concluded that he had undisclosed assets. He made a confiscation order for £30,000. The Court of Appeal held that the judge was correct in his determination. The appellant had failed to discharge the burden on him to satisfy the court that the "amount that might be realised" was less than the "value of his proceeds."

12–82   The authorities therefore seem to show that, under the Act, either the defendant or the court may take the initiative to make a determination under section 4(3) and section 5(3). Each case depends on its own facts. What has not been conclusively decided is whether the defendant carries merely an *evidential* burden under section 4(3) or whether he must go on and discharge the *persuasive* burden as well.

In an interesting commentary to *Robson* [1991] Crim.L.R. 222 the learned commentator said:

> "If the prosecution are trying to establish that the defendant has an interest in a property, in order to allow the court to make assumptions for the purpose of assessing the value of his proceeds of drug trafficking *Dickens* [1990] Crim.L.R. 603 establishes that the prosecution must prove the existence of his interest to the criminal standard; but if the defendant is attempting to establish that some other party has an interest in a house of which he appears to be the owner, in order to reduce "the amount that might be realised" under section 5(4)(*a*)(ii) it seems that the burden of proof will be on the defendant (see *Ilsemann* (1990) 12 Cr.App.R. (S.) 398) presumably to the civil standard."

It is respectfully submitted that this analysis is not complete in that *Dickens*   **12–83** is authority for the proposition that the prosecution need only adduce prima facie evidence that the defendant "held" an interest in property for the purposes of the Act. Once that is done the court may then make any of the assumptions under section 2(2) and (3). What the prosecution *is* required to prove, to the criminal standard, is that the property held by the defendant, at the material time, was a payment or reward carried out in connection with drug trafficking carried on by him or another: section 2(1) (and, if appropriate, section 2(3)).

(v) *Standard of proof*

None of the cases, cited above, has expressly stated the standard of proof   **12–84** which the defendant must discharge but it is plain that the standard is the civil standard. Not one authority suggests a contrary proposition.

(vi) *Evidential or persuasive burden under section 4(3)?*

This is not a straightforward issue. Although it is usually the defendant   **12–85** who shoulders the burden of satisfying the court of the matters set out in section 4(3), the court may of its own motion initiate such a determination: see *Comiskey* (1990) 12 Cr.App.R.(S.) 562; *Keston* (1990) 12 Cr.App.R.(S.) 93 and *Ilsemann* [1991] Crim.L.R. 141, §12–78, *supra*.

In *Ilsemann*, the court was not prepared to accept that the appellant had no hidden assets and therefore, on the facts of that particular case, the appellant's only course would have been to have given evidence in support of his contention that the lesser figure was appropriate.

It follows that the defendant has at least an *evidential* burden but, once raised, does he also have the *persuasive* burden?

The prosecution in *Ilsemann* could only prove realisable assets of £214,637. The appellant did not give evidence. Had he gone into the witness box and merely said that he had no hidden assets, would the court then be obliged to accept that blanket assertion in the absence of any evidence to the contrary? Again, can the court speculate as to the extent of the defendant's hidden assets (as seems to have occurred in *Carroll* [1991] Crim.L.R. 720) and arbitrarily stipulate an amount for the purposes of section 4 as being the amount which may be recovered? Does the burden fall on the defendant to show that a transfer of property was not a gift but was a disposal for full value? (See *Enwezor* (1991) 93 Cr.App.R. 233.)

12–86   In endeavouring to answer these questions it is, perhaps, not very helpful to analyse the problem merely in terms of whether the defendant carries an evidential or persuasive burden. This is because the D.T.O.A. operates in a way which is unique in the criminal law by virtue of the assumptions which the court can make (adverse to the defendant's interests), in the context of the mandatory steps which the court is obliged to follow under the Act. Prima facie the court is obliged to recover the amount which the court assesses to be the value of the defendant's proceeds of drug trafficking having regard to any assumptions which the court may make under section 2. The court need not proceed to determine the "amount that might be realised" under section 4(3) *unless* the defendant raises the issue and this he can only realistically do by giving evidence. Ultimately, the court must satisfy itself of the matters set out in section 4(3), on all the available evidence, before it is entitled to substitute the lesser figure.

In other words, once the court has determined the amount to be recovered under a confiscation order (being the proceeds of the defendant's drug trafficking), the presumption is that the defendant has sufficient assets to satisfy the order and that this presumption can only be displaced if the court is satisfied to the contrary under section 4(3). The result in *Ilsemann, supra* consistent with that view although a rather more liberal approach appears to have been taken in *Carroll* (*supra*) and *Comiskey* (1990) 12 Cr.App.R.(S.) 562 where some "allowance" was made in the final determination of the amount to be confiscated.

As has been said already (see §12–64), the basis for making any such allowance is questionable in the face of the presumption described above.

12–87   In practice the net effect is that the defendant will generally have the task of discharging not only the evidential burden but also the persuasive burden because, in reality, how else is he to satisfy the court of the relevant matters in section 4(3)? On first principles, evidence of any witness (including therefore a defendant) which is unchallenged, is to be accepted as representing the truth of the matter testified on pain of punishment for perjury if the evidence subsequently transpires to be false. In *Johnson* [1991] 2 Q.B. 249, the Court of Appeal seems to have followed this approach: see *McDonald* (1990) 12 Cr.App.R.(S.) 457.

The approach suggested above would result in little or no prejudice to the prosecution because where the court makes a confiscation order and later discovers that assets are available to the court which were originally unknown, then the court may vary the order under section 47 of the Supreme Court Act 1981 within the relevant time limit: see *Miller* (1990) 92 Cr.App.R. 191 and the provisions of the Criminal Justice (International Co-operation) Act 1990, s.16.

12–88   In *Dickens* [1990] 2 Q.B. 102 a witness, called by the prosecution, testifies that D had claimed owning two boats which were lying in southern Spain and showed the witness photographs of those two boats. D denied any interest in them. On appeal, the appellant argued that the prosecution should have made further enquiries as to the existence or non-existence of these boats, and that in the absence of such enquiries, the burden of disproving the alleged connection no longer rested on the defendant. The court rejected that argument. There was evidence on which the judge was entitled to conclude, as he did, that the boats were held by the appellant and that their values must be included in the proceeds of drug trafficking and in the amount that might be realised at the time of the confiscation order.

The appellant's argument seems to have been advanced on the basis that he had discharged the evidential burden and that the task of discharging the persuasive burden shifted to the prosecution. The Court of Appeal, without actually deciding the point, resolved the argument by concluding that the trial judge was entitled to find as he did on the basis of the evidence already put before him. Certainly the defendant is not to be denied the right to give evidence: see *Jenkins* (1990) 12 Cr.App.R.(S.) 582.

Where co-defendants are involved, who shared a joint benefit and may even own assets jointly, the provisions of section 4(3) highlight the importance of quantifying the extent of a particular defendant's benefit and then tailoring the confiscation order to his actual means: see: *Porter* [1990] 1 W.L.R. 1260 and *Robson* (1991) 92 Cr.App.R. 1.

(b) Quantifying the amount that might be realised

The "amount that might be realised" is defined by section 5(3) as follows:

"For the purposes of sections 3 and 4 of this Act the amount that might be realised at the time a confiscation order is made against the defendant is—   **12-89**
  (a) the total of the values at that time of all the realisable property held by the defendant less
  (b) where there are obligations having priority at that time the total amounts payable in pursuance of such obligations,
together with the total of the values at that time of all gifts caught by this Act."

It will be seen that the calculation therefore involves the sum of the value of   **12-90**
"realisable property" (defined by section 5(1)) *plus* the value of gifts caught by the Act (see section 5(9)) but excluding the total value of payments made in pursuance of obligations "having priority." Such obligations are specified in section 5(7) as follows:

"For the purposes of subsection (3) above, an obligation has priority at any time if it is an obligation of the defendant to—
  (a) pay an amount due in respect of a fine, or other order of a court, imposed or made on conviction of any offence, where the fine was imposed or order made before the confiscation order, or
  (b) pay any sum which would be included among the preferential debts (within the meaning given by section 386 of the Insolvency Act 1986) in the defendant's bankruptcy commencing on the date

of the confiscation order or winding up under an order of the court made on that date."

(i) "Obligations having priority": sections 5(3) and 5(7)

12–91   In *McDonald* (1990) 12 Cr.App.R.(S.) 457 the appellant's proceeds of drug trafficking were assessed at £88,710,30. His realisable assets amounted to £870 cash and a flat in Bath worth £50,000 as its marketable value. However, the flat was subject to an outstanding mortgage of £18,000. The trial judge declined to deduct the mortgage on the basis that the debt was not an obligation having priority under section 5(3) and section 5(7). It was correctly conceded in the Court of Appeal that the judge erred in that regard. However, two loans that were provided by relatives towards payment of the deposit when purchasing the flat, were to be disregarded in computing the amount under section 5. Although not apparent from the report these loans may have been found to have been informal in nature which did fall with the category of an "obligation having priority" within the meaning of section 5(7).

(ii) *Valuation and re-valuations*

12–92   Provisions dealing with the re-valuation of property and gifts to take account of changes in the value of money, successful investment and so on, are to be found in sections 5(4), 5(5) and 5(6) as follows:

"5(4) Subject to the following provisions of this section, for the purposes of this Act the value of property (other than cash) in relation to any person holding the property—
  (a) where any other person holds an interest in the property, is—
    (i) the market value of the first mentioned person's beneficial interest in the property less
    (ii) the amount required to discharge any incumbrance (other than a charging order) on that interest, and
  (b) in any other case, is its market value.
  (5) Subject to subsection (10) below, references in this Act, to the value at any time (referred to in subsection (6) below as "the material time") of a gift caught by this Act or of any payment or reward are references to—
    (a) the value of the gift, payment or reward to the recipient when he received it adjusted to take account of subsequent changes in the value of money, or
  (b) where subsection (6) below applies, the value there mentioned, whichever is the greater.
  (6) Subject to subsection (10) below, if at the material time the recipient holds—
    (a) the property which he received (not being cash) or
    (b) property which, in whole or in part, directly or indirectly represents in his hands the property which he received,
the value referred to in subsection (5)(b) above is the value to him at the material time of the property mentioned in paragraph (a) above or, as the case may be, of the property mentioned in paragraph (b) above so far as it so

represents the property which he received, but disregarding in either case any charging order."

The obvious importance of putting before the court up-to-date and accurate information regarding values and expenses cannot be too strongly emphasised if a fair order is to be made: *Lemmon* [1991] Crim.L.R. 791.   **12–93**

It is not necessary that the assets must be proved to be the proceeds of drug trafficking for the purposes of section 4(3) and section 5(3) except in the case of gifts made more than six years prior to the institution of proceedings against him (see section 5(1)(*b*) and section 38(ii)): see *Chrastny (No. 2)* [1991] 1 W.L.R. 1385.

An interesting exercise in valuation appeared in *Chapman, The Times,*   **12–94** November 18, 1991. In that case a confiscation order was made against C in the sum of £3,120,015.36. The problem concerned the value of a house bought by C's wife to whom C had made a gift of £58,000. The wife bought the house for £78,000 and used the gift as part payment. The balance of £20,000 she obtained by way of mortgage. By the date of the confiscation order the house was worth £150,000. The trial judge assessed the updated value of the wife's gift as £58,000/£78,000 × £150,000 = £111,538. On appeal, C contended that the judge erroneously failed to take into account the mortgage debt of £20,353.32 outstanding at the time of the order. By section 5(4), where any person (other than the defendant) holds an interest in property then the value is the market value *less* the amount required to discharge an incumbrance: section 5(4)(*a*). With some reservation, the Court of Appeal held that the appropriate formula was (£150,000 − £20,353.32) × 58/78 = £96,403. Effect must be given to section 5(4) and bearing in mind that the provisions of the Act were penal, they should be construed, if there was any doubt, in favour of the appellant.

(iii) *Establishing an interest in property*

As has been said, "the amount that might be realised," as defined by section   **12–95** 5(3), includes "realisable property," being property held by the defendant or a person to whom the defendant has made a gift caught by the Act (sections 5(1) and (9)). Property is held by any person if he holds any interest in it (section 37(7)) and, again, property is transferred by one person to another if the first person transfers or grants to the other any interests in the property (section 38(10)). It follows that the court must be satisfied that the defendant held an interest in property at the relevant time for the purposes of determining the benefit (and the extent of that benefit) pursuant to sections 1(2), 4(1), 2(1) and 2(3) as well as determining the "amount that might be realised" under section 4(3). It is for the prosecution to put before the court prima facie evidence that property has been held by the defendant before the court may make any of the assumptions under section 2(3) of the D.T.O.A.: *Dickens* [1990] 2 Q.B. 102.

Deciding whether the defendant held an interest in property may sometimes be a difficult matter which can only be resolved by an application of the civil law. There is no doubt that realisable property also includes a beneficial interest created under a resulting or constructive trust: see *Robson* (1991) 92

Cr.App.R. 1.

12-96   In that case R pleaded guilty to several drug trafficking offences. The trial judge assessed R's benefit as £8,750 but determined the full extent of R's proceeds of drug trafficking at £18,361, being the amount that might also be realised under a confiscation order. The judge accordingly made an order in that sum. In calculating the sum of £18,361 the judge took into account the sum of £1,490 found at R's house. The judge also had to resolve whether a house in Cambridge was also realisable property. He found that it was and that the appellant had a 60 per cent. interest and his mother had a 40 per cent. interest in that house. The house was worth £72,500 at the time the order was made. It had been bought in 1987 for £39,500 in the mother's name. She had paid the deposit of £2,500 as well as the legal costs and expenses. She also contributed £3,000 towards improvements. R lived in the house from September 1987 until November 1988 together with a number of lodgers who had paid a total of £3,000 to R but which was used by the mother to discharge the mortgage. The mother never lived in the house and R paid outgoings on the property. R referred to the house as "his house."

12-97   The Court of Appeal held that on those facts there was neither a constructive nor resulting trust which vested in R a beneficial interest in the house because the evidence did not disclose a common intention that R should acquire such an interest and there was no finding that R acted to his detriment. Furthermore, the evidence did not show that R had made a contribution to the cost of capital acquisition for there to be a resulting trust. The outgoings were not referable to the purchase of the property and the appellant's assertion that the house was "his" afforded no proper basis for inferring a common intention that R held a beneficial interest. The Court was referred to *Eves* v. *Eves* [1975] 1 W.L.R. 1338 and *Grant* v. *Edwards* [1986] Ch. 638. In both of those cases the court concluded that a beneficial interest was conferred in circumstances where the beneficiary had acted to her detriment. Accordingly, in *Robson*, the court reduced the confiscation order to £1,490.

(iv) *Value of the drugs*

12-98   In theory, at least, it is open to argument whether drugs seized by police or Customs and Excise can properly be regarded as "property" for the purposes of the D.T.O.A. which may therefore be taken into account when determining the extent of the benefit received by a defendant in accordance with sections 2 and 4 as well as determining the assets that might be realised for the purposes of sections 4(3) and 5(3). In practice the courts will seize the drugs under section 27 of the M.D.A. but this step cannot be taken until proceedings under the D.T.O.A. have been concluded (see section 1(4) of the D.T.O.A.). There is already clear authority for the proposition that proceeds which have been invested in buying drugs, which have then been sold and the proceeds of that sale rolled over into yet another purchase of drugs, all count towards the determination of the benefit received: *Smith* (1989) 89 Cr.App.R. 235. If the proceeds of the sale can be included, they why should the value of drugs seized (and therefore not yet sold) not also be taken into account? In cases where there is evidence that the defendant expended a known sum of money on the purchase of drugs, then the court is entitled to assume that the expenditure was made out of payments received by him in connection with drug trafficking carried on by him (D.T.O.A., s.2(3)(*b*)). However, as the wording of section 2(3)(*b*) makes plain, that assumption only applies in connection with expenditure made by the defendant. If the drug in question was bought by another, then section 2(3)(*b*) has no application. By section 2(1) "proceeds of drug trafficking" are defined as "payments or other rewards" received in connection with that activity.

It is true that by section 2(3)(*a*), the court may assume that property either **12–99** "held" by the defendant or "transferred" to him during the relevant period was received by him in connection with drug trafficking carried on by him, but only on the basis that the property is assumed to have been a "payment or reward" received in that regard. Accordingly, even if the drugs may therefore be said to fall within the definition of "property" (see subsections 38(1), (7) and (10)), it is submitted that drugs intended for re-sale, and not received as a *payment* or *reward*, cannot come within the scope of section 2(1) or 2(3)(*a*) and must therefore be left out of account when determining the extent of the defendant's benefit.

Logically, there is no valid reason why the drugs themselves should not be **12–100** regarded as "property" as defined by section 38(1). However the real difficulty is quantifying the appropriate value. Most drugs are relatively cheap to cultivate, manufacture or to buy in the country of origin. The value of the drug, for the purposes of sentencing, is the so-called "street-value," being the price paid for the drug at street level in the United Kingdom (*e.g.* per gramme or per tablet). The street-value will usually bear no relation to the value of that drug at the moment the defendant received it. In any event it is inconceivable to think that the drug (even if it is "property") could truly be regarded as "realisable" or had more than a "nil" value given the illicit nature of the substance or the unlawful activity contemplated by the defendant. Not all controlled drugs and illegal *per se*. Indeed many have a legitimate purpose in proper hands including heroin, cocaine, amphetamine and many Class B and C drugs which are legitimately used clinically to relieve pain or to tranquillise. There will therefore be cases where drugs seized in the hands of a drug trafficker could be used legitimately and have a commercial value of the legitimate market. Such cases are, however, likely to be very rare and the valuation too cumbersome and difficult to justify the exercise. The better course is to ignore the value of the drugs seized in all but the most exceptional cases (but see the commentary to *Stuart* [1989] Crim.L.R. 599).

(v) *Actual value of property*

There is authority for the proposition that the combined effect of sections **12–101** 5(1) and 5(3) is to suggest that what the court has to have regard to in determining the "amount that might be realised" is the actual property held by the defendant or by a person to whom he has given it: *Comiskey* (1990) 12 Cr.App.R.(S.) 562, 568.

If by "actual property" the Court of Appeal meant no more than actual values assessed in accordance with the express provisions of the Act then the judgment is without complaint. However, in *Comiskey* the court went on to say that:

"... the court cannot close its eyes to the obvious and cannot ignore the fact that some expenses must have been incurred. There can be no question of carrying out an accounting exercise, but it does not seem to us that some acknowledgement ought to be made of the realities of the situation."

The court, in the light of those remarks, reduced the order from £250,000 to £200,000. The intention of the court was laudable but unhappily the provisions of the Act, strictly construed and applied, do not permit such an exercise. It is not plain from the judgment what expenses the court had in mind or even what the activity or operation was that incurred expense. Given that the court could not carry out an accounting exercise, it is not clear upon what basis the discount of £50,000 was made—presumably it was (at best) an informed estimate or (more likely) a guess.

12–102   Where property is ascertained, the obvious importance of putting before the court up-to-date information as to value cannot be too strongly emphasised if an erroneous and over optimistic valuation is to be avoided: *Lemmon* [1991] Crim.L.R. 791. It is not clear whether the prosecution or the defendant has the burden of proving the correct value of the property. If the defendant contends that the "amount that might be realised" under section 4(3) is less than the value of property alleged by the prosecution, then it seems that it is for the defendant to prove the lower valuation: see *Ilsemann* (1990) 12 Cr.App.R.(S.) 398; *Comiskey* (1990) 12 Cr.App.R.(S.) 562; *Carroll* [1991] Crim.L.R. 720.

(vi) *Increase in realisable property*

12–103   If the judge makes a confiscation order on the basis that the amount that might be realised is less than the amount assessed to be the value of his proceeds of drug trafficking then, on the application of either the prosecutor or the receiver, an application may be made to the High Court for a certificate of the amount that might actually be realised.

E. EVIDENCE

12–104   The judge is entitled to rely on the evidence given during the trial. The prosecution is not obliged to call or recall that evidence again during the drug trafficking investigation: *Jenkins* (1990) 12 Cr.App.R.(S.) 582. The prosecution may rely and call evidence in respect of any statement or notice served by them in accordance with section 3 of the D.T.O.A. As the Court of Appeal in *Comiskey* (1990) 12 Cr.App.R.(S.) 562 remarked:

"Section 3 of the Act provides convenient and effective machinery for ascertaining matters relevant to the courts' determination of the amount to be paid under a confiscation order. It is very desirable that those responsible for the prosecution of offences should make full use of this."

The court also pointed out the desirability, in appropriate cases, of inviting the defendant to indicate to what extent he accepts the Crown's allegations or, if he does not do so, to indicate any matters he proposes to rely on (see section 3(2)). However, a statement made out of court by a person not called as a witness cannot be admitted except in accordance with established principles of admissibility at common law or under statute: see *Chrastny (No. 2)* [1991] 1 W.L.R. 1385.

I. STATEMENTS TENDERED

Putting the relevant party to "strict proof" of their case will often result in the contents of any statement tendered to the other side not being admitted for a variety of reasons, *e.g.* the statement infringes the hearsay rule. Where, for example, a prosecutor is in possession of information alleging that on certain dates valuable property was given to the accused, he may seek to embody those allegations in a statement which he can then serve on the defence by way of section 9 of the Criminal Justice Act 1967, in the hope that the statement will be accepted. In fact, if put to strict proof, the prosecutor might find that he cannot prove the contents at all. **12–105**

To meet this problem and for the purposes of the D.T.O.A., Parliament has endeavoured to make life a little easier for the prosecutor by imposing certain obligations on the defendant in order to see if a certain amount of "common ground" can be established. Thus, by section 3(1) of the D.T.O.A., where: **12–106**

"(*a*) there is tendered to the Crown Court by the prosecutor a statement as to any matters relevant to the determination whether the defendant has benefited from drug trafficking or to the assessment of the value of his proceeds of drug trafficking, and

(*b*) the defendant accepts to any extent any allegation in the statement, the court may, for the purposes of that determination and assessment, treat his acceptance as conclusive of the matters to which it relates."

There is nothing in section 3(1) that is either controversial or out of the ordinary. But where a defendant declines to accept, to any extent, any obligation in the statement then one looks to section 3(2) which provides:

"Where—
(*a*) a statement is tendered under subsection (1)(*a*) above, and
(*b*) the court is satisfied that a copy of that statement has been served on the defendant,
the court may require the defendant to indicate to what extent he accepts each allegation in the statement and, so far as he does not accept any such allegation, to indicate any matters he proposes to rely on."

Section 3(2) now asks the court to adopt an inquisitorial role. The defendant may therefore be asked to state those matters (if any) which he proposes to rely on to refute an allegation contained in the statement tendered. The penalty, for a failure to comply with section 3(2), is set out in section 3(3) which provides as follows: **12–107**

"If the defendant fails in any respect to comply, with a requirement under subsection (2) above he may be treated for the purposes of this section as accepting every allegation in the statement apart from—

(*a*) any allegation in respect of which he has complied with the requirement, and

(*b*) any allegation that he has benefited from drug trafficking or that any payment or other reward was 'received by him in connection with drug trafficking' carried on by him or another."

Although it is obvious from the wording of section 3(3)(*b*) that the legislature was not prepared to go so far as to say that a defendant's non-compliance with the requirements of subsection 2 should be construed as an admission that he either benefited from drug trafficking, or that any payment or reward received by him represents the proceeds of that activity, the reality of the situation is that once the prosecution has established that the defendant has received property, it is open to the court to see if it may assume that the payment was received in connection with drug trafficking by virtue of section 2(2) and (3). The burden of showing that assumption to be incorrect may very well fall upon the defendant: section 2(2).

12–108   Suppose that a defendant indicates to the court that he does not accept a particular allegation in a statement tendered and served on him under section 3(2), and suppose that the defendant indicates to the court a number of matters upon which he proposes to rely. Is the court then bound to accept that he has complied with section 3(2) or, may the court (believing that the accused could indicate a great deal more) treat him as having failed to meet the requirements of that subsection? Although any court must be very slow to conclude that an accused has failed to comply with section 3(2), nevertheless, where a defendant is clearly demonstrated to be obstructive or less than forthcoming, there exists no good reason why the court should be prevented from treating his conduct as a constructive failure to meet the requirements of subsection 3(2).

II. STATEMENT TENDERED BY THE DEFENCE

12–109   Section 3(4) provides that where:

"(*a*) there is tendered to the Crown Court by the defendant a statement as to any matters relevant to determining the amount that might be realised at the time the confiscation order is made, and

(*b*) the prosecutor accepts to any extent any allegation in the statement, the court may, for the purposes of that determination, treat the acceptance by the prosecutor as conclusive of the matters to which it relates."

It will be seen that subsection 3(4) is limited purely to matters relevant to determining the amount that "might be realised" at the time the confiscation order is made. Unlike sections 3(1) to 3(3) it is not expressed to include matters that are relevant to determining whether the defendant has benefited from drug trafficking or assessing the value of his proceeds as a result.

So far as both the prosecution and the defence are concerned, an allegation may be accepted or matters may be indicated or relied upon in rebuttal, for the purposes of section 3, either "(*a*) orally before the court, or (*b*) in writing in accordance with Crown Court Rules": section 3(5).

III. USE OF ADMISSIONS IN THE TRIAL FOR THE OFFENCE

Section 3(6) provides an accused with a crucial safeguard, namely that: 12–110

"No acceptance by the defendant under this section that any payment or other reward was received by him in connection with drug trafficking carried on by him or another shall be admissible in evidence in any proceedings for an offence."

Thus where, for example, a defendant is accused of supplying drugs over a period of two weeks but he accepts (for the purposes of proceedings under the D.T.O.A.) that he has received property in connection with drug trafficking over the preceding six years, it is not open to the prosecutor to use that admission to initiate fresh proceedings, or to support the charge alleged, or to support an application to add a count alleging the supplying of drugs over the longer period to which the admission relates: and see §12–165, *infra*.

Section 5(1) provides:

"In this Act, "realisable property" means, subject to subsection (2) below:
   (*a*) any property held by the defendant and
   (*b*) any property held by a person to whom the defendant has directly or indirectly made a gift caught by this Act."

In *Re T. (Restraint Order), The Times*, May 19, 1992, the Court of Appeal   12–111
held that section 3 of the D.T.O.A. enabled the Crown Court to make orders which were or might be akin to disclosure orders (and see *Re O. (Restraint Order)* [1991] 2 Q.B. 520). Section 3(6) was designed to prevent the defendant from refusing to answer an allegation that an asset was received as a payment or reward for drug trafficking on the ground of self-incrimination. Self-incrimination should therefore be no ground for failing to comply with a Crown Court order under section 3.

However, by section 5(2) property is not realisable if: 12–112

"(*a*) an order under section 43 of the Powers of Criminal Courts Act 1973 (deprivation orders),
  (*b*) an order under section 27 of the Misuse of Drugs Act 1971 (forfeiture orders) or,
  (*c*) an order under section 223 or 436 of the Criminal Procedure (Scotland) Act 1975 forfeiture of property),
   is in force in respect of the property."

Section 5(2) enacts the obvious in that property already seized by an order of the Court, albeit under a different enactment, can hardly be seized twice and made the subject of a confiscation order.

Property is said to be "held" by any person if he holds any interest in it (section 38(7)) and includes "a reference to property vested in his trustee in bankruptcy; permanent or interim trustee within the meaning of the Bankruptcy (Scotland) Act 1985 or liquidator": see section 38(8).

For the purposes of section 5(1)(*a*), it is immaterial whether the property was received by the defendant in connection with drug trafficking or not: see *Chrastny (No. 2)* [1991] 1 W.L.R. 1385. This makes good sense since the object of the D.T.O.A., at this stage of the proceedings is to assess the extent of the defendant's assets and thereby enable the court to re-coup ill-gotten gains even if some or all of those gains had originally been squandered.

IV. GIFTS

12–113   Different considerations apply in relation to "gifts" as is apparent from the wording of section 5(9), particularly section 5(9)(*b*).

Section 5(9) reads:

> "A gift (including a gift made before the commencement of section 1 of this Act) is caught by this Act if:
>
> (*a*) it was made by the defendant at any time since the beginning of the period of six years ending when the proceedings were instituted against him, or
>
> (*b*) it was made by the defendant at any time and was a gift of property:
>
> (i)   received by the defendant in connection with drug trafficking carried on by him or another, or
>
> (ii) which in whole or in part directly or indirectly represented in the defendant's hands property received by him in that connection."

It is therefore plain that where it can be shown that the defendant made a gift at *any time* in his career then it will be caught by the Act *if* it was received by him in connection with, or represents the proceeds of, drug trafficking. No such qualifications or restrictions operate in respect of gifts made by the defendants during the six-year period ending when proceedings were instituted against him: see section 5(9)(*a*). Accordingly, it is submitted that all gifts made by the defendant during the relevant six-year period are caught by the Act and it is immaterial whether they represent the proceeds of drug trafficking or not.

12–114   It is tempting to construe section 5(9) in conjunction with the assumptions the court may make pursuant to sections 2(2) and (3), but such an approach is liable only to mislead, not least because section 2 and section 5 are concerned with two very different stages in the determination of a confiscation order. Section 5 applies only after the court has assessed the value of the defendant's proceeds of drug trafficking by making, if necessary, any of the statutory assumptions for that purpose.

The Act makes no provision for the incidence of the burden or standard of proof for the purposes of section 5(9)(*b*).

A gift is expressly caught by the Act if it is made by the defendant, but it is not clear what the position would be if the gift was in fact made by a person other than the defendant, *e.g.* by his wife. Presumably where a person can be demonstrated to have acted on behalf of the defendant, then the courts would have little difficulty in holding that the acts performed were in reality those of the defendant himself.

In the ordinary way a "gift" of property relates to a transfer of property, to another, free of any consideration. But the Act anticipates cases where the defendant transfers property to another for a consideration far less than the actual value of the property. Accordingly, section 5(10) provides: **12–115**

"For the purposes of this Act—

(a) the circumstances in which the defendant is to be treated as making a gift include those where he transfers property to another person directly or indirectly for a consideration the value of which is significantly less than the value of the consideration provided by the defendant, and

(b) in those circumstances, the preceding provisions of this section shall apply as if the defendant had made a gift of such share in the property as bears to the whole property the same proportion as the difference between the values referred to in paragraph (a) above bears to the value of the consideration provided by the defendant."

It follows that where property is sold to another for a consideration which substantially reflects its true value then the property sold is not realisable. Instead, the court will look to the payment received by the defendant, as a result of the sale, and confiscate that sum, or the property it represents, if it has been converted. Obviously, if the defendant does not invest or re-invest the proceeds of sale but chooses to squander the proceeds instead, then the extent of the defendant's "realisable property" is diminished as a result.

By section 38(1), property is transferred by one person to another "if the first person transfers or grants to the other any interest in the property."

(a) Valuing the property

The value of property, other than cash, is based on the market value of the property less any debt payable in connection with it, *e.g.* a mortgage. Thus, section 5(4) provides: **12–116**

"Subject to the following provisions of this section, for the purposes of this Act the value of property (other than cash) in relation to any person holding the property:

(a) where any other person holds an interest in the property, is:

(i) the market value of the first mentioned person's beneficial interest in the property less

(ii) the amount required to discharge any incumbrance (other than a charging order) on that interest, and

(b) in any other case, is its market value."

The D.T.O.A. makes special provision in connection with the valuation of gifts. Obviously, a gift of property made by a defendant in, for example,

1978, will now be worth a great deal more once inflation is taken into account. Accordingly, section 5(5) provides for an adjustment of the value of a gift as follows:

> "Subject to subsection (10) below, references in this Act to the value at any time (referred to in subsection (6) below as "the material time") of a gift caught by this Act or of any payment or reward are references to:
>
>   (*a*) the value of the gift, payment or reward to the recipient when he received it adjusted to take account of subsequent changes in the value of money, or
>   (*b*) where subsection (6) below applies, the value there mentioned, whichever is the greater."

12–117   Section 5(6) is concerned with the value of the gift as assessed by the recipient himself. For example, if an antique vase (being the proceeds of drug trafficking) is sold to the recipient for £1,200 when, in fact, according to expert opinion it was only worth £800, the Act takes the higher figure as representing the value of the gift. Section 5(6) reads as follows:

> "Subject to subsection (10) below, if at the material time the recipient holds:
>
>   (*a*) the property which he received (not being cash), or
>   (*b*) property which, in whole or in part, directly or indirectly represents in his hands the property which he received,
> the value referred to in subsection (5)(*b*) above is the value to him at the material time of the property mentioned in paragraph (*a*) above or, as the case may be, of the property mentioned in paragraph (*b*) above so far as it so represents the property which he received, but disregarding in either case any charging order."

12–118   As we have seen, the defendant may transfer property for a consideration significantly less than its actual value. The D.T.O.A. will treat that transfer as a gift: section 5(10)(*a*). Obviously the property, once in the hands of the recipient may increase in value. Therefore, by section 5(10)(*b*) the value of the property so transferred is calculated as follows:

> "In those circumstances, the preceding provisions of this section shall apply as if the defendant had made a gift of such share in the property as bears to the whole property the same proportion as the difference between the values referred to in paragraph (*a*) above bears to the value of the consideration provided by the defendant."

Suppose for example that D transfers property to X for a consideration of £1,000. The property was actually worth £10,000. By section 5(10)(*b*) the original value of the gift transferred was £9,000 in the ratio of 1:9. If, when the confiscation order is made, the property is then worth £100,000, the value of the gift is in the proportion of 1:9, *i.e.* £90,000.

(b) Knowledge that a gift represents drug proceeds

The D.T.O.A. did not seek to punish those who acquired gifts knowing **12–119** that they represented the proceeds of drug trafficking. However, sections 14(3), (5) and (6) of the Criminal Justice (International Co-operation) Act 1990 provide:

"(3) A person is guilty of an offence if, knowing or having reasonable grounds to suspect that any property is, or in whole or in part directly or indirectly represents, another person's proceeds of drug trafficking, he acquires that property for no, or for inadequate, consideration."

"(5) For the purposes of subsection (3) above consideration given for any property is inadequate if its value is significantly less than the value of that property, and there shall not be treated as consideration the provision for any person of services or goods which are of assistance to him in drug trafficking.

(6) A person guilty of an offence under this section is liable—

(a) on summary conviction, to imprisonment for a term not exceeding six months or a fine not exceeding the statutory maximum or both:

(b) on conviction on indictment, to imprisonment for a term not exceeding fourteen years or a fine or both."

Sections 14(3) and 14(5) give legislative force to Article 3(1)(c) of the 1988 **12–120** Vienna Convention against Illicit Traffic in Narcotic Drugs and Psychotropic Substances.

An offence under section 14(3) is a "drug trafficking offence" for the purposes of the D.T.O.A. (see paragraph 4(4) of Schedule 4 to the Criminal Justice (International Co-operation) Act 1990). However, the offence does not entitle the courts to make any of the assumptions in section 2 of the D.T.O.A. (see paragraph 4(2) of Schedule 4 to the Criminal Justice (International Co-operation) Act 1990). The reason for this appears to be that a distinction should be drawn (as a matter of policy) between so-called "money laundering" offences and more serious drug trafficking offences (note the remarks of the Minister of State, Home Office, H.L., Vol. 514, col. 592).

Subsections 14(3) and 14(5) must be read together. One object of these provisions is clearly to catch gifts and bargains which the recipient knew, or had reasonable cause to suspect, to represent the proceeds of another's drug trafficking. But the provisions are designed to *exclude* persons who provide goods or services (notwithstanding that they knew, or had reasonable cause to suspect, that the payment came from the proceeds of drug trafficking (see the Minister of State, Home Office, H.L., Vol. 514, col. 887)), providing that those goods or services were not supplied to assist in drug trafficking. Accordingly, if such goods or services were therefore provided for adequate consideration, then no offence would be committed on the wording of subsection 14(3). However, where goods (*e.g.* motor vessel parts) were sold to another so as to be of assistance to him in drug trafficking, then subsection 14(5) creates a fiction and deems any payment not be consideration at all and thus the supplier falls foul of subsection 14(3).

(i) *"Are of assistance to him"*

12–121   No attention appears to have been given as to whether an accused must have *intended* that the goods or services would in fact be utilised to assist another in drug trafficking. The draftsman's use of the word "are" (as opposed to "had been") seems to introduce a rather speculative element into the offence.

(ii) *"Having reasonable grounds to suspect"*

The test here is objective.

F. ENFORCING A CONFISCATION ORDER

12–122   Broadly stated, there are two ways in which a confiscation order may be enforced. The first method is by treating such an order as a fine: a defendant who is tempted not to pay the fine faces the prospect of a consecutive sentence of imprisonment in default. The second method is by the appointment of a Receiver who will (if necessary) seize, realise and manage the defendant's realisable property.

I. TREATING THE CONFISCATION ORDER AS A FINE

12–123   Section 6(1) of the D.T.O.A. clearly sets out the general principles to be applied:

> "Where the Crown Court orders the defendant to pay any amount under section 1 of this Act, sections 31(1) to (3C) and 32(1) and (2) of the Powers of Criminal Courts Act 1973 (powers of Crown Court in relation to fines and enforcement of Crown Court fines) shall have effect as if—
> (a) that amount were a fine imposed on him by the Crown Court, and
> (b) [repealed by Schedule 16 to the Criminal Justice Act 1988]."

The penalties to be imposed in default are currently as follows:

Not exceeding £50	5 days
Over £50, not exceeding £100	7 days
Over £100, not exceeding £400	14 days
Over £400, not exceeding £1,000	30 days
Over £1,000, not exceeding £2,000	45 days
Over £2,000, not exceeding £5,000	3 months
Over £5,000, not exceeding £10,000	6 months
Over £10,000, not exceeding £20,000	12 months
Over £20,000, not exceeding £50,000	18 months
Over £50,000, not exceeding £100,000	2 years
Over £100,000, not exceeding £250,000	3 years
Over £250,000, not exceeding £1 million	5 years
Over £1 million	10 years

12–124   Even where monies had actually been taken from the defendant at the time of his arrest, it was a mandatory requirement of section 6 of the D.T.O.A. that a term of imprisonment be imposed in default of payment of the sums confiscated: *Popple and others, The Times*, May 21, 1992. This is because Customs and Excise officers, for example, did not have power to pay money in satisfaction of a confiscation order without first obtaining the defendant's consent or applying to a magistrates' court for a distress warrant.

By section 6(2) of the D.T.O.A., a term of imprisonment (or detention) ordered to be served in default of payment, shall run *after* the defendant has served any sentences of imprisonment which were imposed in respect of the offences for which he appeared at the Crown Court.   **12–125**

Thus, section 6(2) provides:

"Where:
  (*a*) a warrant of commitment is issued for a default in payment of an amount ordered to be paid under section 1 of this Act in respect of an offence or offences, and
  (*b*) at the time the warrant is issued, the defendant is liable to serve a term of custody in respect of the offence or offences,
the term of imprisonment or of detention under section 9 of the Criminal Justice Act 1982 (detention of persons aged 17 to 20 for default) to be served in default of payment of the amount shall not begin to run until after the term mentioned in paragraph (b) above."

By section 6(3) of the D.T.O.A.:   **12–126**

"The reference in subsection (2) above to the term of custody which the defendant is liable to serve in respect of the offence or offences is a reference to the term of imprisonment, youth custody or detention under section 4 or 9 of the said Act of 1982 which he is liable to serve in respect of the offence or offences; and for the purposes of this subsection:
  (*a*) consecutive terms and terms which are wholly or partly concurrent shall be treated as a single term, and
  (*b*) there shall be disregarded:
    (i) any sentence suspended under section 22(1) of the said Act of 1973 which has not taken effect at the time the warrant is issued,
    (ii) in the case of a sentence of imprisonment passed with an order under section 47(1) of the Criminal Law Act 1977, any part of the sentence which the defendant has not at that time been required to serve in prison, and
    (iii) any term of imprisonment or detention fixed under section 31(2) of the said Act of 1973 for which a warrant of commitment has not been issued at that time."

One interesting point is whether the words "offence or offences" in section 6(2) refers only to "drug trafficking offences." Suppose D appears before the Crown Court to be sentenced in respect of an offence of supplying drugs over a period of one month (count 1) and an offence of robbery (count 2). He is sentenced to three years' imprisonment on count 1 and six years' imprisonment on count 2; both sentences to run concurrently. A confiscation order is made in the sum of £12,000. By section 6(1), a term of 12 months' imprisonment is ordered to be served in default. D does default. Does the term of 12 months' imprisonment run after the sentence in respect of count 1 is served (being a "drug trafficking offence"), or, after the total sentence of six years' imprisonment, in respect of both offences, is served?

The point is not free from difficulty but when section 6(2) and (3) speak of the "offence or offences" this can only be a reference to the offence or offences in respect of which the confiscation order is made under section 1, *i.e.* "drug trafficking offences" (and see section 6(2)(*a*)). Accordingly, it is submitted that a sentence in default must run consecutively to any term of imprisonment imposed in respect of the drug trafficking offence or offences.

II. COMMITTING A DEFAULTER INTO CUSTODY

12–127   The plain purpose of the D.T.O.A. was that a person convicted of a drug trafficking offence should be deprived of the proceeds to the extent that they were realisable. Committing a defendant to prison by way of a "warrant of commitment" under section 6(2) is a course of last resort. The magistrates (who may issue such a warrant) should therefore consider all other methods of enforcing payment prior to the issue of a warrant: see *Harrow Justices, ex p. D.P.P.* [1991] 1 W.L.R. 395.

The practical consequences flowing from the defendant's commitment to prison are three-fold. First, the period to be served in default will relieve the defendant of the requirement to satisfy that proportion of the order which remains outstanding. The defendant therefore effectively "serves" his way out of paying the order and so defeats the primary purpose of the Act. Secondly, a warrant, once issued, cannot be withdrawn by the magistrates' court: *Newport Pagnell Justices, ex p. Smith* (1988) 152 J.P. 475. Thirdly, proceedings for the purposes of the D.T.O.A. are "concluded" upon the defendant serving a term of imprisonment in default: section 38(12) as amended by Schedule 5, paragraph 16 of the Criminal Justice Act 1988. Powers conferred on the High Court in respect of the making of a restraint or charging order, or the realisation of property by the appointment of a receiver, are only exercisable where proceedings are not concluded (see D.T.O.A., ss.7 to 13).

12–128   In *Harrow Justices, ex p. D.P.P.* (*supra*) the Divisional Court suggested that the magistrates should keep in mind a number of points when exercising their discretion whether or not to issue a warrant of commitment, including that:

(1) The object of the confiscation order was to divest the defaulter of money or other realisable assets.

(2) It was not a matter of choice for the defaulter to buy his way out of such an order by serving the term of imprisonment imposed in default.

(3) The mere fact of a confiscation order was evidence that when it was made there were realisable assets available to meet the requirements of the order.

(4) Even if at the date when justices had to consider the question of enforcement, the value of realisable assets was less than at the date of the confiscation order, it was open to the defaulter to apply for a certificate of inadequacy under section 14 of the D.T.O.A. which would lead to a reduction in the amount of the original order.

(5) Given the *inter partes* nature of the procedure leading to a confiscation order, the prosecution would probably have had information available which would be relevant for the justices' consideration. More compellingly, the prosecution would have had a legitimate interest in being heard before the justices came to a decision.

(6) Given the purposes of the D.T.O.A., it was incumbent on justices to consider all methods of enforcement short of issuing a warrant of commitment in a D.T.O.A. case before doing so.

On the facts of that particular case, the court granted *certiorari* to quash a **12–129** decision to commit D to prison, in circumstances where magistrates had made no enquiry into D's means but merely relied on the fact that he was at the time serving a prison sentence.

III. Confiscation Where Defendant Dies or Absconds

As the law presently stands, where a defendant either dies or absconds **12–130** before a confiscation order is made, the court seems to be powerless to make a confiscation order. An indication of the sort of problems that can arise where a defendant absconds were demonstrated in *Chrastny (No. 2)* (1991) Cr.App.R. 406. In that case the court had to determine whether property held jointly between husband and wife (both of whom had been jointly charged with a drug trafficking offence) was "realisable" for the purposes of section 4(3), in circumstances where the wife had been convicted but where the husband had absconded. The court answered that question affirmatively. If the husband were to be apprehended, tried and convicted then the court could not include in any confiscation order against him, property realised to satisfy the order payable by his wife because the property was no longer under his control: *per* Glidewell L.J. at 414. The Home Office Working Group on Confiscation has identified three situations to which different considerations may well apply but which fall outside the ambit of the D.T.O.A. namely (1) death after conviction but before a confiscation order is made; (2) defendant absconds after conviction but before the order is made; and (3) the defendant either dies or absconds before conviction. Since this work is primarily concerned with an analysis of current law, it is not proposed to examine these situations here but the reader should be aware of their significance and should read the Report of the Home Office Working Group (a copy of which may be obtained from C7 Division, Home Office, 50 Queen Anne's Gate, London, SW1H 9AT).

IV. Appointment and Powers of a Receiver

12–131 In summary, once a confiscation order has been made which is not subject to appeal and which has not been satisfied, the High Court may, on the application of the prosecutor, appoint a receiver to realise any realisable property (section 11(5)) with a view to satisfying the confiscation order (section 13(2)) and to apply the property so realised on the defendant's behalf towards the satisfaction of the order (section 12(1)). A reasonable opportunity must be given for persons holding any interest in the property to make representations to the court (section 11(8)). Sums remaining in the hands of the receiver after the satisfaction of a confiscation order must be distributed among the holders of property in such proportions as the court shall direct (section 12(2)).

12–132 The material powers conferred on a receiver are set out in section 11 of the Act which provides:

"(1) Where:

    (*a*) in proceedings instituted for a drug trafficking offence, a confiscation order is made,

    (*b*) the order is not subject to appeal, and

    (*c*) the proceedings have not been concluded,

the High Court may, on an application by the prosecutor, exercise the powers conferred by subsections (2) and (6) below.

(2) The court may appoint a receiver in respect of realisable property.

(3) [set out at §12–168.]

(4) The court may order any person having possession of realisable property to give possession of it to any such receiver.

(5) The court may empower any such receiver to realise any realisable property in such manner as the court may direct.

(6) The court may order any person holding an interest in realisable property to make such payment to the receiver in respect of any beneficial interest held by the defendant or, as the case may be, the recipient of a gift caught by this Act as the court may direct and the court may, on the payment being made, by order transfer, grant or extinguish any interest in the property.

(7) Subsections (4) to (6) above do not apply to property for the time being subject to a charge under section 9 of this Act.

(8) The court shall not in respect of any property exercise the powers conferred by subsection (3)(*a*), (5) or (6) above unless a reasonable opportunity has been given for persons holding any interest in the property to make representations to the court."

12–133 It must be noted that by section 11(1)(*b*) a receiver cannot be appointed if the order is subject to appeal. An order is expressed, pursuant to section 38(13) as amended by Schedule 5 to the Criminal Justice Act 1988, to be subject to appeal:

"... until (disregarding any power of a court to grant leave to appeal out of time) there is no further possibility of an appeal on which the order could be varied or set aside."

Again, by section 11(1)(c), a receiver can only be appointed if "proceedings have not been concluded." By section 38(12) proceedings in England and Wales for an offence are concluded on the occurrence of one of the events set out in that section (as amended by Schedule 5 to the Criminal Justice Act 1988).

The Powers of the High Court or the receiver must be exercised within the framework set out in section 13 which (insofar as it is material) provides: **12–134**

"(2) Subject to the following provisions of this section, the powers shall be exercised with a view to making available for satisfying the confiscation order or, as the case may be, any confiscation order that may be made in the defendant's case the value for the time being of realisable property, held by any person by the realisation of such property.

(3) In the case of realisable property held by a person to whom the defendant has directly or indirectly made a gift caught by this Act, the powers shall be exercised with a view to realising no more than the value for the time being of the gift.

(4) The powers shall be exercised with a view to allowing any person other than the defendant or the recipient of any such gift to retain or recover the value of any property held by him.

(5) An order may be made or other action taken in respect of a debt owed by the Crown.

(6) In exercising those powers, no account shall be taken of any obligations of the defendant or of the recipient of any such gift which conflict with the obligation to satisfy the confiscation order."

It will be seen that the principal object is to satisfy the confiscation order notwithstanding any obligation which the defendant or the recipient may have which conflicts with the satisfaction of the order.

V. The Application of Proceeds of Realisation

The application of proceeds of realisation and other sums is explained in section 12 (as amended) which provides: **12–135**

"(1) Subject to subsection (2) below, the following sums in the hands of a receiver appointed under section 8 or 11 of this Act or in pursuance of a charging order, that is:

    (a) the proceeds of the enforcement of any charge imposed under section 9 of this Act,

    (b) the proceeds of the realisation, other than by the enforcement of such a charge, of any property under section 8 or 11 of this Act, and

    (c) any other sums, being property held by the defendant,

shall first be applied in payment of such expenses incurred by a person acting as an insolvency practitioner as are payable under section 17A(2) of this Act and then shall after such payments (if any) as the High Court may direct have been made out of those sums, be applied on the defendant's behalf towards the satisfaction of the confiscation order.

(2) If, after the amount payable under the confiscation order has been fully paid, any such sums remain in the hands of such a receiver, the receiver shall distribute those sums:

    (*a*) among such of those who held property which has been realised under this Act, and

    (*b*) in such proportions,

as the High Court may direct after giving a reasonable opportunity for such persons to make representations to the court."

The provisions of section 12 are largely self-explanatory. Expenses incurred by the receiver will be met out of realised property.

G. VARIATION OF A CONFISCATION ORDER

I. VARIATION BY THE DEFENDANT

12–136   A variation of a confiscation order is to be carefully distinguished from an appeal against the making of an order. Where a defendant complains that the court erred in the determination of the order, *e.g.* in the assessment of his proceeds of drug trafficking, then his appropriate course is to appeal against the making of the order because such an order is a sentence for the purposes of sections 9 and 11 of the Criminal Appeal Act 1968: see *Johnson* [1991] 2 Q.B.

However, a variation of a confiscation order under the D.T.O.A. is confined to a reduction in the amount of the order in cases where the defendant's realisable property is inadequate to satisfy the making of an order. Thus section 14(1) provides:

> "If, on an application by the defendant in respect of a confiscation order, the High Court is satisfied that the realisable property is inadequate for the payment of any amount remaining to be recovered under the order the court shall issue a certificate to that effect, giving the court's reasons."

12–137   Note that the High Court can do no more than to issue a Certificate and to give its reasons for so doing. It cannot vary the order under section 14. Clearly if the defendant has been adjudged bankrupt then the court must take into account the extent to which his property will be distributed amongst his creditors. The court must also guard against the manipulative defendant who has taken steps to prevent the court seizing his assets. To this end, section 14(2) provides:

> "For the purposes of subsection (1) above:
>
>   (*a*) in the case of realisable property held by a person who has been adjudged bankrupt or whose estate has been sequestrated the court shall take into account the extent to which any property held by him may be distributed among creditors, and
>
>   (*b*) the court may disregard any inadequacy in the realisable property which appears to the court to be attributable wholly or partly to anything done by the defendant for the purpose of preserving any

property held by a person to whom the defendant had directly or indirectly made a gift caught by this Act from any risk of realisation under this Act."

By section 14(3), where a Certificate has been issued under subsection **12–138** 14(1), the defendant "may apply to the Crown Court for the amount to be recovered under the order to be reduced." The powers of the Crown Court are expressed, by section 14(4) to be as follows:

"The Crown Court shall, on an application under section (3) above:
  (a) substitute for the amount to be recovered under the order such lesser amount as the court thinks just in all the circumstances of the case, and
  (b) substitute for the term of imprisonment or of detention fixed under subsection (2) of section 31 of the Powers of Criminal Courts Act 1973 in respect of the amount to be recovered under the order a shorter term determined in accordance with that section (as it has effect by virtue of section 6 of this Act) in respect of the lesser amount."

It would seem that the Crown Court is obliged to substitute a lesser amount although the actual figure is entirely a matter for the court to decide. Even if the High Court were to quantify the amount by which the realisable property is inadequate to satisfy the order, the Crown Court is not obliged to vary the order to that extent but must substitute a lesser amount "as the court thinks just in all the circumstances of the case."

Nothing in section 14 requires the prosecution to be put on notice of an application under that section which, may therefore be made *ex parte*. However, it is difficult to imagine many applications proceeding on that basis and it is submitted that the appropriate course is for the prosecutor to be notified.

II. VARIATION BY THE PROSECUTION

Where, at the time the confiscation order is made, the court was satisfied **12–139** that the amount that might be realised was less than the amount assessed to be the value of the defendant's proceeds of drug trafficking, and so made a confiscation order for the lesser amount under section 4(3), the prosecutor is entitled to apply to the High Court for a variation of the original order if it subsequently transpires that the defendant's realisable assets were greater than first thought. This increase may arise in two ways: first, by virtue of previously hidden assets being discovered or secondly, by virtue of changes in the value of the property in question.

As originally drafted, the D.T.O.A. did not enable the prosecution to apply for a variation of the original order in such circumstances or at all. By an ingenious route, the prosecution in *Miller* (1990) 92 Cr.App.R. 191 successfully applied for a variation of the order by invoking the provisions of section 47 of the Supreme Court Act 1981 in circumstances where further assets held by the defendant at the time the order was made, were discovered. This route might not be appropriate in all cases and, in any event, the procedure is subject to time limits (normally 28 days): see also *Onwuka* (1992) 95 Cr.App.R. 47.

12–140 In 1990, Parliament enacted the Criminal Justice (International Co-operation) Act 1990 and took the opportunity to amend the law. Parliament did not, technically speaking, amend the D.T.O.A. itself but, by section 16 of the 1990 Act, the prosecution is now entitled to apply for a variation in the limited circumstances specified below:

"(1) This section has effect where by virtue of section 4(3) of the Drug Trafficking Offences Act 1986 (insufficient realisable property), the amount which a person is ordered to pay by a confiscation order is less than the amount assessed to be the value of his proceeds of drug trafficking.

(2) If, on an application made in accordance with subsection (3) below, the High Court is satisfied that the amount that might be realised in the case of the person in question is greater than the amount taken into account in making the confiscation order (whether it was greater than was thought when the order was made or has subsequently increased) the court shall issue a certificate to that effect, giving the court's reasons.

(3) An application under subsection (2) above may be made either by the prosecutor or by a receiver appointed under the said Act of 1986 in relation to the realisable property of the person in question.

(4) Where a certificate has been issued under subsection (2) above the prosecutor may apply to the Crown Court for an increase in the amount to be recovered under the confiscation order; and on that application the court may—

(*a*) substitute for that amount such amount (not exceeding the amount assessed as the value referred to in subsection (1) above) as appears to the court to be appropriate having regard to the amount now shown to be realisable; and

(*b*) increase the term of imprisonment or detention fixed in respect of the confiscation order under subsection (2) of section 31 of the Powers of Criminal Courts Act 1973 (imprisonment in default of payment) if the effect of the substitution is to increase the maximum period applicable in relation to the order under subsection (3A) of that section."

Similar amendments were made to the Scottish Law by section 17 of the 1990 Act (see section 1(1)(*b*) of the Criminal Justice (Scotland) Act 1987).

12–141 It will be seen from the wording of section 16 that the High Court is not itself empowered to vary the order. It can do no more than to certify that the facts set out in section 16(2) exist and to leave it to the Crown Court to substitute an amount that is "appropriate" (section 16(4)(*a*)) and to increase the default period accordingly (section 16(4)(*b*)).

It should also be noted that section 16 of the 1990 Act does not apply to property which comes into the possession of the defendant after the order is made. Furthermore, an application made under section 16 is subject to a ceiling, namely, the amount which the Crown Court assessed to be the proceeds of the defendant's drug trafficking. That figure will often be calculated on the basis of what was believed to be the defendant's financial position, over the relevant period, at the time the original order was made. The Home Office Working Group on Confiscation suggests that the Crown Court should be empowered to make a fresh order on the basis of a reassessment of the extent of the defendant's benefit.

Under both section 14 of the D.T.O.A. and section 16 of the Criminal Jus-   **12–142**
tice (International Co-operation) Act 1990, it is necessary to go to the High Court first and not straight to the Crown Court. It is not clear why the legislature thought this route to be desirable or necessary. An initial reaction is that the provisions were intended to confer upon the High Court a supervisory role and thus safeguard the interests of persons likely to be affected by a successful application, but the terms of sections 14 and 16 impose a mandatory obligation on the High Court to issue a certificate upon making the requisite findings of fact for the purposes of section 14(1) and section 16(2). Neither of these two sections gives any indication or guidance as to the burden or standard of proof. The normal rule is that "he who asserts must prove" but it is not clear whether a different approach should be adopted in the light of the decisions of *Dickens* [1990] 2 Q.B. 102; *Ilsemann* (1990) 12 Cr.App.R.(S.) 398 and *Comiskey* (1990) 12 Cr.App.R.(S.) 562; *Carroll* [1991] Crim.L.R. 720.

H. RESTRAINT AND CHARGING ORDERS

I. INTRODUCTION

The primary objective of the D.T.O.A. is the recovery of the proceeds of   **12–143**
drug trafficking. Stiff terms of imprisonment are imposed upon defaulters. However, committal to prison is not only a course of last resort, it is also self-defeating because the period served in default will relieve the defendant of the requirement to satisfy that proportion of the order which remains outstanding, and accordingly he may enjoy the benefit of his assets upon release: see *Harrow Justices, ex p. D.P.P.* [1991] 1 W.L.R. 395. Once a defendant serves a sentence in default, the proceedings for the purpose of the Act are "concluded" (section 38(12) of the D.T.O.A. as amended by Criminal Justice Act 1988, Sched. 5, para. 16) and accordingly the powers conferred on the High Court in respect of realisable property cease.

Under the D.T.O.A. the courts do not have to wait to see if the convicted   **12–144**
defendant will default before taking action to realise his property. The High Court (or a receiver appointed by that Court) may order any person having possession of "realisable property" to deliver it up to a receiver (section 11(4)), who may realise that property as directed by the Court (section 11(5)).

Once a person learns that proceedings for a drug trafficking offence may be instituted against him then the temptation to disprove, or to conceal, his assets will be very strong.

In civil law, an injunction may be granted to restrain the defendant from   **12–145**
disposing of assets to defeat the interests of the plaintiff should he be successful in the action: *Mareva Compania Naviera S.A.* v. *International Bulk*

Carriers S.A. [1980] 1 All E.R. 213, C.A. Restraint orders made under the D.T.O.A. (see s.8), are intended to achieve a similar result. They have been described as closely analogous to the Mareva injunction. Indeed Lord Donaldson M.R. has graphically described the statutory jurisdiction as the "Drugs Act Mareva": *Re Peters* [1988] 3 All E.R. 46, 51e.

The broad scheme involved in making protective orders is to prevent a defendant from rendering any confiscation order nugatory by disposing of his assets prior to conviction. This point is reinforced by section 13(2) which provides that powers exercisable by the High Court or receiver (including powers under section 8) shall be exercised with a view to satisfying the confiscation order by realising the value of realisable property held by any person.

12–146   To make the disposal of property more difficult, the Act empowers the High Court to make a charging order on realisable property for securing payment to the Crown: section 9. The effect of a charging order is the same as a general equitable charge and enforceable in the same courts: section 10(4). The law in relation to equitable charges, overriding and minor interests, overreaching and the effect on third parties is highly technical and bound up in the rules affecting the registration of charges for the purposes of the Land Charges Act 1972 and the Land Registration Act 1925.

12–147   In the ordinary way, proceedings under sections 8 and 9 of the D.T.O.A. are exercisable where proceedings have actually been instituted against the defendant for a drug trafficking offence (see section 7(1), *infra*) but section 7(2) (as amended by Criminal Justice Act 1988, Sched. 5, para. 2) makes it clear that those powers are also exercisable where a person is "to be charged" with such an offence either by the laying of an information or otherwise:

"(1) The powers conferred on the High Court by sections 8(1) and 9(1) of this Act are exercisable where:
    (*a*) proceedings have been instituted in England and Wales against the defendant for a drug trafficking offence,
    (*b*) the proceedings have not been concluded, and
    (*c*) the court is satisfied that there is reasonable cause to believe that the defendant has benefited from drug trafficking.
(2) Those powers are also exercisable where the court is satisfied:
    (*a*) that, [whether by the laying of an information or otherwise, a person is to be charged with] a drug trafficking offence, and
    (*b*) that there is reasonable cause to believe that he has benefited from drug trafficking, [...]
(4) Where the court has made an order under sections 8(1) or 9(1) of this Act by virtue of subsection (2) above, the court shall discharge the order if the [...] proceedings [in respect of the offence are not instituted (whether by the laying of an information or otherwise)] within such time as the court considers reasonable."

12–148   Given that applications under sections 8 and 9 may be made *ex parte* (and prior to charge), the property of a prospective defendant (and innocent third parties affected by the orders) can be hit by surprise. The harshness of the Act, as originally drafted, has been ameliorated by amendments made by Schedule 5 to the Criminal Justice Act 1988 which now permits an application for the discharge of variation of a restraint or charging order by persons affected by such orders. Notice is to be given to persons affected by a charging order: section 9(3)(*c*) (see paragraph 4 of Schedule 5 to the Criminal Justice Act, 1988). A similar provision exists in respect of a restraint order (see section 8(4), *Re R. (Restraint Order)* [1990] 2 Q.B. 307 and R.S.C., Ord. 115).

It should be carefully noted that an application for a restraint order cannot be made (and the powers exercisable thereunder shall not have effect) in relation to property subject to a charging order made under section 9. The reason for this is that the powers of the High Court, and the receiver appointed by the Court to manage or otherwise deal with the property are extensive: see section 8(6) and sections 11(3), (4), (5) and (6).

II. RESTRAINT ORDERS

Effect of a restraint order. It has been said (§12–145, *supra*) that a restraint   **12–149**
order is closely analogous to a Mareva injunction in civil proceedings and designed to prevent a person (not just the defendant) dealing with, or disposing of property, which may be made the subject of a confiscation order when the defendant appears before the Crown Court to be sentenced in respect of one or more drug trafficking offences: see *Re Peters* [1988] 3 All E.R. 46.

A restraint order has the effect of freezing all the realisable property from the moment the order is made. It prohibits any person from "dealing" with any realisable property (see section 8(1)). Accordingly, the defendant is prevented from petitioning for his own bankruptcy. It also prevents him from making an application to the County Court for an interim order (under section 252 of the Insolvency Act 1986) preventing the institution of proceedings against him, or his property, where the defendant intends to make a proposal to his creditors for a composition in satisfaction of his debts or a scheme or arrangements of his affairs which involves the realisable property caught by the restraint order: *Re M., The Times*, April 17, 1991, and see sections 15(2) and (3) of the D.T.O.A.

It should also be noted that restraint orders are normally coupled with a   **12–150**
disclosure order as a means of identifying and ascertaining the whereabouts and value of assets affected by the restraint order. Disclosure orders are dealt with below (see §12–163, *infra*): *Re O. (Restraint Order)* [1991] 1 All E.R. 330 and *Re T. (Restraint Order), The Times*, May 19, 1992. Such orders should be coupled with a condition to give effect to the common law rule against self-incrimination.

Section 8(1) provides as follows:

"The High Court may by order (in this Act referred to as a 'restraint order') prohibit any person from dealing with any realisable property, subject to such conditions and exceptions as may be specified in the order."

Section 8 is of no effect in relation to any property for the time being subject to a charge under section 9: see section 8(3).

(a) When may a restraint order be made

12–151   The powers are exercisable by the High Court or by a receiver appointed by the Court under section 8(6) where proceedings have actually been instituted against a defendant or, where a person is to be charged with a drug trafficking offence: section 7(2) (as amended by Schedule 5 of the Criminal Justice Act 1988). In either case it will be seen that there must exist reasonable cause to believe that the accused has benefited from drug trafficking: see sections 7(1)(*c*) and 7(2)(*b*). The court is obliged to discharge the order if the proceedings in respect of the offence are not instituted within a reasonable time: section 7(4) as amended by paragraph 2(b) of Schedule 5 to the Criminal Justice Act 1988. For sections 7(1), (2) and (4) see §12–147, *supra*.

(b) Applying for an order

12–152   Section 8(4) is largely self-explanatory:

"A restraint order:
  (*a*) may be made only on an application by the prosecutor,
  (*b*) may be made on an *ex parte* application to a judge in chambers, and
  (*c*) shall provide for notice to be given to persons affected by the order."
Note also, R.S.C., Ord. 115.

The importance of giving notice was emphasised in *Re R. (Restraint Order)* [1990] 2 Q.B. 307. Otton J., delivering the judgment of the Divisional Court, said "it is, in my view, incumbent on the commissioners, or any other body which is exercising the powers granted under the restraint procedure, to consider carefully who should be informed."

In that case, the applicants were landlords who let industrial premises to T who installed plant and machinery. T fell in arrears with his rent and was subsequently charged with a drug trafficking offence. The landlords attempted to distrain on the plant and machinery unaware of the existence of a restraint order, under section 8. They organised an auction but cancelled it upon being informed of the order. They incurred costs and a loss of rent as a result of the delay in being able to forfeit the lease. Notwithstanding that a restraint order was analogous to a Mareva injunction, the court had no jurisdiction either under the D.T.O.A., or its inherent jurisdiction, to grant an indemnity as against the Customs and Excise Commissioners for the loss and costs incurred.

(c) Property affected by the order

12–153   Section 8(2) provides:

"A restraint order may apply:
  (*a*) to all realisable property held by a specified person, whether the property is described in the order or not, and
  (*b*) to realisable property held by a specified person, being property

transferred to him after the making of the order."

The order therefore relates only to property that is "realisable" within the meaning of section 5(1) and (2) of the D.T.O.A. Accordingly, gifts caught by the Act (see section 5(9)) are included. The order must specify the person holding the property. This is clearly important because notice must be given to the persons so specified: (section 8(4)(c)).

For clarity it is desirable that the order should particularise the property affected by the order but this is not strictly speaking essential. Thus the order may be drafted in the following form:

> "The Defendants be restrained whether by themselves, their servants or agents or otherwise until further order for removing from the jurisdiction of the Court or from otherwise disposing of, diminishing or otherwise in any way dealing with money, goods, property or other assets whatever within or without the jurisdiction. . . . That all the defendants be restrained from in any way howsoever dealing with [   ] . . . That [Mr. X] be restrained in any way howsoever from dealing with bank account number [   ] held at the [Bank] . . ."

"Realisable property" includes property whether it is situated in England **12–154** and Wales or abroad: see section 38(3), and accordingly the restraint order may similarly embrace property within or without the jurisdiction (see the draft order above).

(d) Prohibit "dealing with" realisable property

The purpose of a restraint order is to prohibit persons affected by the order **12–155** from "dealing with" any realisable property subject to such conditions and exceptions as may be specified in the order: section 8(1). By section 8(7), "dealing with property," held by any person, includes:

> "(a) where a debt is owed to that person, making a payment in reduction of the amount of the debt, and
> (b) removing the property from Great Britain."

The purpose of section 8(7)(a) is to preserve the value of property. It will be seen that section 8(7) is merely inclusory, and it does not offer a comprehensive definition of the phrase "dealing with" as it appears in section 8(1). Conventional restraint orders include a prohibition against the "disposing of" or "diminishing of" assets within or without the jurisdiction and it is plain that both activities describe an act of "dealing" for the purposes of section 8(1). Less clear, perhaps, are accountancy exercises used to determine the financial position or standing of an individual or corporate body. In *Re K. (Restraint Order)* [1990] 2 Q.B. 298, F made large payments into two deposit accounts. She also obtained an overdraft from the bank on condition that the bank had a right to "combine and consolidate" all her accounts. F gave her two brothers a mandate over the overdraft account. F and her two brothers were charged with a drug trafficking offence but only one brother was convicted. There was a credit balance in her deposit accounts of £639,541.87 but an overdrawn balance of £337,585.59 on the overdraft account. The Crown Prosecution Service sought and obtained a restraint order in respect of the sums then held in the two deposit accounts. The Bank of India applied to the High Court for a variation of that order so as to permit the accounts to be combined and consolidated. The balance remaining therefore would be £301,956.28.

12–156　　During the course of argument, the bank made two concessions: first, that the monies deposited in the two deposit accounts were a gift from the convicted brother; and secondly, that all monies deposited were the proceeds of drug trafficking. Nevertheless, the bank contended, (1) that the right of a bank to combine and to consolidate accounts arose by operation of law and not by agreement and was a right *sui generis*; (2) that the D.T.O.A. does not extinguish or diminish the inherent right of the bank to combine accounts; (3) the right to combine accounts is a means of establishing the true indebtedness of the customer to the bank and the bank to the customer; it is merely an accounting procedure.

Otton J. upheld the submissions of the bank. There is a presumption that a statute does not alter vested rights. Nothing in the D.T.O.A., so ruled Otton J., alters vested rights or extinguishes or diminishes them. Otton J. referred to section 13(4) which provides that powers under, *inter alia*, section 8 shall be exercised with a view to allowing any person other than the defendant (or the recipient of a gift caught by the D.T.O.A.) to retain or recover the value of property held by him. This would appear to cover a lien.

As stated above, the purpose of section 8(7)(*a*) is to preserve the value of property. However, section 8(7)(*a*) does not impose a complete embargo on the payment of debts to third parties because the court under section 8(1) may permit payments in certain circumstances. The circumstances in which the value of realisable property may be diminished by the courts permitting payments to be made to innocent third parties, *e.g.* in respect of expenses, are not easy to categorise.

12–157　　In *Re Peters* [1988] 3 All E.R. 46, a strongly constituted Court of Appeal (Civil Division) held that the jurisdiction to make or to vary a restraint order under the D.T.O.A. was analogous to that under the Mareva jurisdiction; its purpose being to strike a balance before trial between preserving a defendant's assets to satisfy a possible confiscation order if he were convicted, and meeting his reasonable requirements meanwhile. In other words, the primary objective of the order is to prevent an accused rendering any confiscation order nugatory by disposing of his assets before conviction, but the defendant is entitled to maintain himself and his family, within reasonable limits, from the resources available to him. In striking a balance between the interests of the Court, and the defendant, the Court will have regard to all the circumstances of the case. In *Re Peters* (*supra*), the Court of Appeal said that the *anticipatory* discharge of liabilities which could be expected to arise only after he had been acquitted or convicted was wholly contrary to section 13(2) and the underlying purpose of the protective provisions of the Act. By "anticipatory discharge of liabilities", the Court seems to have had in mind expenditure which a defendant would wish to make at some time in the future but which would go beyond his reasonable requirements. This would, therefore, include items of expenditure on luxury goods, the provision of a holiday and so on. Mann L.J. said (at 52): "In my experience a restraint order does not, and properly does not, prevent the meeting of ordinary and reasonable expenditure."

In *Re Peters* McNeill J. varied a restraint order to enable P to comply with a **12–158** consent order, made in matrimonial proceedings, that the defendant pay to his son (a minor) £25,000 in respect of school fees and maintenance until he reached the age of 18. The lump sum to the son was in settlement of the claim for periodical payments, lump sum and property adjustment orders. P's assets were assessed at £95,000 and his proceeds of drug trafficking were said to be about £540,000. On appeal, the Court of Appeal ruled in favour of the Commissioners of Customs and Excise. The sum of £25,000 amounted to a discharge of future liabilities and not consonant with the purpose of section 13(2). In so far as there was a conflict between the court order in the divorce proceedings, and the restraint order, it should have been resolved in favour of the restraint order. It is not clear whether the Commissioners had agreed that the payment of the £25,000 would be a "gift caught by the Act" as defined by section 5(9). Counsel for the son contended that it was not a gift at all, and in this respect the Court of Appeal agreed, because the payment was in satisfaction of future liabilities.

Again, it is not clear in *Re Peters* above, whether the Commissioners con- **12–159** tended that the Court, in exercising its powers (*inter alia* under section 8) should ignore any obligations of the defendant in the terms of section 13(6) which provides:

"In exercising those powers, no account shall be taken of any obligations of the defendant or of the recipient of any such gift which conflict with the obligation to satisfy the confiscation order."

The Court of Appeal, in considering section 13(6), was inclined to accept the contention of the son that section 13(6) presupposed the existence of a confiscation order. Although convicted of a drug trafficking offence, the father had yet to be sentenced, or a confiscation order made, at the date judgment in *Re Peters* was delivered.

(e) Legal expenses

In *Re P.; Re W., The Times*, April 11, 1990, C.A. the Court of Appeal con- **12–160** sidered variations of restraint orders to allow the payment of legal expenses. It will be seen that the combined effect of R.S.C., Ord. 115, r. 4(1) and section 8(1), (see above) is to exempt both legal and living expenses of the defendant from property subject to a restraint order. Indeed, in *Re Peters* (1988) 3 All E.R. 46, Nolan J. had previously varied a restraint order on those grounds. However, in *Re P.; Re W.* the question arose as to whether the judge was correct to order that the solicitors' legal costs should be taxed at the conclusion of the trial on an indemnity basis. The Court had no difficulty in holding that such a course was not wrong in principle, even if taxation could result in some delay in pronouncing sentence. The decision on the point is plainly right being consonant with the purpose expressed in section 13(2).

In *Re P.; Re W. (supra)*, the applicants also submitted that the restraint order should have contained a maximum figure for legal costs. This was normal practice in the case of Mareva applications: see *PCW (Underwriting Agencies) Ltd.* v. *Dixon* [1983] 2 All E.R. 158.

The Court of Appeal did not find this matter straightforward, and indeed, suggested that in future cases, judges might think it desirable to include such a maximum figure for legal expenses. However, the judge had a discretion in the matter and the Court of Appeal would not lightly interfere with the exercise of that discretion.

12–161　　In *Customs & Excise Commissioners* v. *Norris* [1991] 2 Q.B. 293, the question of legal costs arose again but on this occasion the question was whether the applicant should be allowed access to funds held by him in order to prosecute the appeal. Having regard to section 8(1), R.S.C., Ord. 115, r. 4(1), and the authorities discussed above, it is hardly surprising that the Court of Appeal (Civil Division) answered the question affirmatively. The principal argument of the Commissioners was that the full value of the defendant's realisable property would be diminished if the application succeeded (contrary to section 13(2)), and that the defendant's appeal could be funded, either by the defendant's family (as was the case at trial) or by legal aid. The Court of Appeal swiftly rejected both alternatives. First there was no obligation on the family to fund the appeal, nor should they be forced to do so, and secondly, it would be an odd position if the court forced somebody to qualify for legal aid who would not otherwise qualify.

(f) Variation of a restraint order

12–162　　Section 8(5), as amended by paragraph 3 of Schedule 5 to the Criminal Justice Act 1988 provides as follows:

> "A restraint order:
> (a) may be discharged or varied in relation to any property, and
> (b) shall be discharged when proceedings for the offences are concluded.
> (5A) [An application for the discharge or variation of a restraint order may be made by any person affected by it.]"

Many of the cases concerning the considerations to be examined by the High Court have been discussed: see *Re Peters* [1988] Q.B. 871, *Re P.; Re W., The Times*, April 11, 1990.

III. DISCLOSURE ORDERS

12–163　　Nothing is expressly stated in either the D.T.O.A. or the corresponding provisions in the C.J.A. 1988, which empowers the High Court to compel a defendant to swear on affidavit disclosing the nature, whereabouts and value of assets held by persons affected by the restraint order. However, disclosure orders are normally sought in all cases in which restraint orders are made. In *Re O. (Disclosure Order)* [1991] 1 All E.R. 330 the appellants were required to swear an affidavit in the following terms:

"... disclosing the full value of any salary, money, goods or other assets whatsoever within and without the jurisdiction identifying with full particularity the nature of all such assets, their whereabouts and whether the same be held in their own names or jointly with some other person or persons or by nominees or otherwise howsoever on their behalf ..."

In *Re O.* (*Disclosure Order*), *supra* the question was raised whether the court has any jurisdiction to make such an order. A similar question arose in *A. J. Bekhor & Co. Ltd.* v. *Bilton* [1981] 2 W.L.R. 565 in the context of Mareva injunctions where orders for the disclosure of assets are frequently made. The Court of Appeal (Civil Division) in *Bekhor* upheld the validity of disclosure orders as being inherent in the power granted by what is now section 37 of the Supreme Court Act 1981 "to make all such ancillary orders as appear to the court to be just and convenient to ensure that the exercise of the Mareva jurisdiction is effective for its purpose," *per* Ackner L.J. at 576. In *Re O.*, the same Court held that the High Court must have been intended to have power to render effective a restraint order. The decision in *Re O.* was concerned with section 77 of the C.J.A. 1988 but the Court remarked that the jurisdiction to make restraint orders under the D.T.O.A. is mirrored by that under the C.J.A. 1988 and (*obiter*) that "a decision in relation to one Act will apply equally to the other," *per* Lord Donaldson M.R. at 527. See also *Re T.* (*Restraint Order*), *The Times*, May 19, 1992 in which *Re O.* was followed in the context or orders made under section 8 of the D.T.O.A. **12–164**

For the reasons set out below, a disclosure order should contain an appropriate condition to give effect to the rule against self-incrimination: see *Re O.* (*Disclosure Order*), *supra*.

The reader should be aware of the provisions of section 14 of the Criminal Justice (International Co-operation) Act 1990. By that section a person is guilty of an offence if he conceals or disguises any property or converts or transfers that property, or removes it from the jurisdiction, being property which in whole or in part represents the proceeds of drug trafficking for the purpose of avoiding, *inter alia*, the making or enforcement of a confiscation order.

(a) Rule against self-incrimination

Section 3(6) of the D.T.O.A. expressly provides that acceptance by the defendant of any allegation, made by the prosecution in a section 3 statement, that the defendant received a payment or reward in connection with drug trafficking, shall not be admissible in criminal proceedings for an offence. This is consistent with the common law rule against self-incrimination. Thus, no man shall be compelled to comply with an order which might to incriminate him: see *Lamb* v. *Munster* (1982) 10 W.B.D. 110. In *Re O.* (*Disclosure Order*) [1991] 1 All E.R. 330 it was held that nothing in section 77 of the C.J.A. 1988 (and therefore section 8 of the D.T.O.A.) abrogates the common law rule. Although this might tend to frustrate the purpose of a disclosure order, the solution was to impose conditions on the use which may be made of the affidavits sworn in compliance with the order. The Court of Appeal **12–165** suggested that an "appropriate condition," which should be inserted in all disclosure orders, would read:

> "No disclosure made in compliance with this order shall be used as evidence in the prosecution of an offence alleged to have been committed by the person required to make that disclosure or by any spouse of that person": *per* Lord Donaldson M.R. at 336.

The Court suggested that such a condition was "preferable" to the giving of an undertaking merely limiting the class of person to whom the disclosed information could be given and the purposes for which it could be used: *per* Lord Donaldson M.R. at 336, and see *Re T., The Times*, May 19, 1992.

12–166   The use of a condition against self-incrimination, in the context of restraint orders made under section 77 of the C.J.A. 1988 and the corresponding provisions of the D.T.O.A., relates to a "special case" where although technically civil, the proceedings were ultimately bound up with criminal proceedings. Accordingly, the use of such a condition is not appropriate in the context of a civil action and the order cannot be used as a substitute for the privilege against self-incrimination: see *A. T. & T. Istel Ltd.* v. *Tully, The Times*, November 18, 1991; *Re O. (Disclosure Order) (supra)*; *Att.-Gen.* v. *Times Newspapers Ltd* [1991] 2 W.L.R. 994 distinguished: and *Rank Film Distributors Ltd.* v. *Video Information Centre* [1982] A.C. 380.

IV. APPOINTMENT OF A RECEIVER

12–167   Clearly, it will often be desirable, particularly in complicated cases where assets are not easily seized, to employ the services of a receiver. Accordingly, section 8(6) provides:

> "Where the High Court has made a restraint order, the court may at any time appoint a receiver:
> (*a*) to take possession of any realisable property, and
> (*b*) in accordance with the court's directions, to manage or otherwise deal with any property in respect of which he is appointed,
> subject to such exceptions and conditions as may be specified by the court; and may require any person having possession of property in respect of which a receiver is appointed under this section to give possession of it to the receiver."

12–168   In cases where a receiver has been appointed under this section, the court must exercise its powers in accordance with the provisions of section 11 (Realisation of Property); section 12 (Application of Proceeds of Realisation) and section 13 (Exercise of Powers of High Court or Receiver). Each of those sections has been quoted above (in so far as they are material) save for section 11(3) which provides:

> "The court may empower a receiver appointed under subsection (2) above, under section 8 of this Act or in pursuance of a charging order:
> (*a*) to enforce any charge imposed under section 9 of this Act on realisable property or on interest or dividends payable in respect of

such property, and

(*b*) in relation to any realisable property other than property for the time being subject to a charge under section 9 of this Act, to take possession of the property subject to such conditions or exceptions as may be specified by the court."

(a) Protection of receivers

Section 18 provides: **12–169**

"(1) Where a receiver appointed under section 8 or 11 of this Act or in pursuance of a charging order takes any action:

(*a*) in relation to property which is not realisable property, being action which he would be entitled to take if it were such property,

(*b*) believing, and having reasonable grounds for believing, that he is entitled to take that action in relation to that property,

he shall not be liable to any person in respect of any loss or damage resulting from his action except in so far as the loss or damage is caused by his negligence.

(2) Any amount due in respect of the remuneration and expenses of a receiver so appointed shall, if no sum is available to be applied in payment of it under section 12(3)(*a*) of this Act, be paid by the prosecutor or, in a case where proceedings for a drug trafficking offence are not instituted, by the person on whose application the receiver was appointed."

(b) A defendant cannot appoint a receiver

In *Re M., The Times*, April 17, 1991, Otton J. described as "unthinkable" **12–170** the fact that an application could be entertained by the High Court for an appointment of a receiver by or on behalf of the defendant to preserve assets intended for the satisfaction of a confiscation order. Otton J. ruled that an appointment of a receiver could only be made by the prosecutor given that an application for a restraint order could, similarly, only be made by the prosecutor.

(c) Consent of the receiver needed to sell

Where a person has an interest in property, but wishes to take possession or **12–171** to sell that property, the consent of the receiver or the Court should be obtained. In *Re M., The Times*, May 20, 1991, a restraint order was made against M whose property included a restaurant. Valuers had advised the receiver that the restaurant should be sold as soon as possible. However, two mortgagees had interests in that property and they expressed a wish to take possession and to sell the property. The Divisional Court held that because the property was under the Court's restraint the mortgagees were affected by that restraint and accordingly the mortgagees could not attempt to take possession or to sell without the consent of the Receiver or the Court.

V. Charging Orders

12–172   Where a person is about to be charged, or has been charged, in connection with a drug trafficking offence, the High Court upon the application of the prosecutor (*ex parte* if necessary), may make a charging order under section 9 in respect of certain assets (chiefly land, securities and trusts) held by, or on behalf of that person. The powers exercisable by the Court under section 9 comply with the requirements of sections 11, 12 and 13 cited above.

By section 9(2) a "charging order" is defined as:

"...an order made under this section imposing on any such realisable property as may be specified in the order a charge for securing the payment of money to the Crown."

12–173   Not all assets may be the subject of a charging order. Indeed by section 9(4) and subject to subsection (6), a charge may be imposed by a charging order only on:

"(*a*) any interest in realisable property, being an interest held beneficially by the defendant or by a person to whom the defendant has directly or indirectly made a gift caught by this Act
   (i) in any asset of a kind mentioned in subsection (5) below, or
   (ii) under any trust, or
(*b*) any interest in realisable property held by a person as trustee of a trust if the interest is in such an asset or is an interest under another trust and a charge may by virtue of paragraph (*a*) above be imposed by a charging order on the whole beneficial interest under the first-mentioned trust."

12–174   The assets referred to in subsection 9(4) are expressed by section 9(5) to be:

"(*a*) land in England and Wales, or
(*b*) securities of any of the following kinds:
   (i) government stock,
   (ii) stock of any body (other than a building society) incorporated within England and Wales,
   (iii) stock of any body incorporated outside England and Wales or of any country or territory outside the United Kingdom, being stock registered in a register of the unit holders or kept at any place within England and Wales,
   (iv) units of any unit trust in respect of which a register of the unit holders is kept at any place within England and Wales."

The Secretary of State may amend this list: see section 10(6).

12–175   Section 9(6) allows the High Court to extend the charge to include any interest or dividend payable in respect of the assets listed in section 9(5)(*b*), *supra*.

The High Court may discharge or vary the charging order and it must do so if either the proceedings for the offence are concluded or if the value of the amount secured by the charge is paid into court: section 9(7). Where a charging order has been protected by an entry registered under the Land Charges Act 1972 or the Land Registration Act 1925 an order, discharging the charging order under section 9(7), may direct that the registered entry be cancelled: section 10(5).

VI. Compensation

Where persons hold realisable property in connection with proceedings **12–176** instituted against any person which do not result in his conviction, it is open to them to apply for compensation under section 19 which, by subsection (1) as amended by Schedule 5 to the Criminal Justice Act 1988 provides:

"(1) If proceedings are instituted against a person for a drug trafficking offence or offences and either:
  (a) the proceedings do not result in his conviction for any drug trafficking offence, or
  (b) where he is convicted of one or more drug trafficking offences;
    (i) the conviction or convictions concerned are quashed [...]
    (ii) he is pardoned by Her Majesty in respect of the conviction or convictions concerned,
the High Court may, on an application by a person who held property which was realisable property, order compensation to be paid to the applicant [if, having regard to all the circumstances, it considers it appropriate to make such an order.]"

However, quite considerable hurdles are placed in the path of the party **12–177** seeking compensation under this section. Thus, by section 19(2) and 19(2A), as amended by Schedule 5 to the C.J.A. 1988:

"(2) The High Court shall not order compensation to be paid in any case unless the court is satisfied:
  (a) that there has been some serious default on the part of a person concerned in the investigation or prosecution of the offence or offences concerned, being a person mentioned in subsection (4) below, [...]
  (b) that the applicant has suffered [...] loss in consequence of anything done in relation to the property by or in pursuance of—
    (i) an order of the High Court under sections 8 to 11 of this Act, or
    (ii) [Repealed by Criminal Justice (Scotland) Act 1987 s.70(2) and Sched. 2.]
(2A) The Court shall not order compensation to be paid in any case where it appears to the Court that the proceedings would have been instituted or continued if the serious default had not occurred."

The persons, mentioned in section 19(2)(a), are listed in section 19(4): **12–178**

"Compensation payable under this section shall be paid:
  (a) where the person in default was or was acting as a member of a police force out of the police fund out of which the expenses of that police force are met,
  (b) where the person in default was a member of the Crown

Prosecution Service or acting on behalf of the service, by the Director of Prosecutions, and

(c) where the person in default was an officer within the meaning of the Customs and Excise Management Act 1979 by the Commissioners of Customs and Excise."

By subsection (3) the amount of compensation payable under section 19 "shall be such as the High Court thinks just in all the circumstances of the case."

12–179   Given the wording of section 19(2) it follows that very few cases are likely to succeed under this section. Proving some serious default on the part of a person concerned in the investigation or prosecution, is difficult enough but establishing that the proceedings would not have been instituted or continued had it not been for that default, is unlikely to be successful in all but the rarest and clearest of cases. It is no longer necessary to prove that the loss was "substantial": see Schedule 5 to the Criminal Justice Act 1988.

I. OFFENCES UNDER THE ACT

I. ASSISTING DRUG TRAFFICKERS

12–180   By section 24(1) and (2):

"(1) Subject to subsection (3) below, if a person enters into or is otherwise concerned in an arrangement whereby:

(a) the retention or control by or on behalf of another (call him "A") of A's proceeds of drug trafficking is facilitated (whether by concealment, removal from the jurisdiction, transfer to nominees or otherwise), or

(b) A's proceeds of drug trafficking:
   (i) are used to secure that funds are placed at A's disposal, or
   (ii) are used for A's benefit to acquire property by way of investment,

knowing or suspecting that A is a person who carries on or has carried on drug trafficking or has benefited from drug trafficking, he is guilty of an offence.

(2) In this section, references to any person's proceeds of drug trafficking include a reference to any property which in whole or in part directly or indirectly represented in his hands his proceeds of drug trafficking."

12–181   The offence is designed to prohibit the "laundering" of drug money. It is triable either way and punishable on conviction on indictment, to imprisonment for a term not exceeding 14 years or to a fine or to both (section 24(5)(a)) and, on summary conviction, to a term of imprisonment not exceeding six months or to a fine not exceeding the statutory maximum or to both (section 24(5)(b)). An offence under section 24 is expressed, by subsection 24(6), to fall within Part II of Schedule 1 to the Criminal Justice Act 1982 so that offenders will not be eligible for early release. It is also a "serious arrestable offence" for the purposes of section 116 of the Police and Criminal Evidence Act 1984: see section 36.

The *mens rea* of the offence is either knowing or suspecting that "A" is a   **12–182** person who carried on, or has carried on drug trafficking, or has benefited from someone else's drug trafficking. The burden of proving those matters rests on the prosecution, and see *Colle* (1992) 95 Cr.App.R. 67. However, it would seem that it is not necessary for the prosecution to prove that the defendant knew or suspected that he had in fact entered into, or was otherwise concerned in, any of the arrangements specified in subsection 24(1). The prosecution need do no more than to prove, as a fact, that the defendant entered into or was concerned in an arrangement as defined by section 24(1)(*a*) or (*b*). Thus where D provides a false reference in the name of B, (being an alias for A), the fact that D did not know the reference was to be used by A to conceal A's proceeds of drug trafficking is irrelevant. By providing a false reference D became concerned in an arrangement (albeit organised by others). Section 24(1) does not preface the phrase "enters into" or "concerned" with the word "knowingly."

To reinforce the point, section 24(4) provides statutory defences but the   **12–183** legislature has shifted the burden of proof to the accused to prove, by section 24(4), (and see *Colle, supra*):

"(*a*) that he did not know or suspect that the arrangement related to any person's proceeds of drug trafficking, or
(*b*) that he did not know or suspect that by the arrangement the retention or control by or on behalf of A of any property was facilitated or, as the case may be that by the arrangement any property was used as mentioned in subsection (1) above, or
(*c*) that:
　(i)　he intended to disclose to a constable such a suspicion, belief or matter as is mentioned in subsection (3) above in relation to the arrangement, but
　(ii)　there is reasonable excuse for his failure to make disclosure in accordance with subsection (3)(*b*) above."

Not only does the Act prohibit the laundering of drug monies, it also seeks   **12–184** to encourage the relaying of information concerning the movement of monies to the police, even if that information was originally given to a party who was contractually bound to treat it as confidential.

Thus, section 24(3) provides:

"Where a person discloses to a constable a suspicion or belief that any funds or investments are derived from or used in connection with drug trafficking or any matter on which such a suspicion or belief is based:
　(*a*)　the disclosure shall not be treated as a breach of any restriction upon the disclosure of information imposed by contract, and
　(*b*)　if he does any act in contravention of subsection (1) above and the disclosure relates to the arrangement concerned, he does not commit an offence under this section if the disclosure is made in accordance with this paragraph that is:

> (i)   it is made before he does the act concerned, being an act done with the consent of the constable, or
> (ii) it is made after he does the act, but is made on his initiative and as soon as it is reasonable for him to make it."

Accordingly, a banker who holds money on behalf of A, suspecting that A has benefited from drug trafficking will not be in breach of contract if he discloses his suspicion to a constable (section 24(3)(*a*) and he will be protected by the provisions of subsection 24(3)(*b*)(i) or 24(3)(*b*)(ii)). Solicitors representing alleged drug traffickers may find that they are put in a similarly difficult position.

12–185   It should be noted that the expression "drug trafficking" is a term of art defined by section 38(1) as amended by Schedule 4, paragraph 4 to the Criminal Justice (International Co-operation) Act 1990 to mean:

> "... doing or being concerned in any of the following, whether in England and Wales or elsewhere:
> (*a*) producing or supplying a controlled drug where the production or supply contravenes section 4(1) of the Misuse of Drugs Act 1971 or a corresponding law;
> (*b*) transporting or storing a controlled drug where possession of the drug contravenes section 5(1) of that Act or a corresponding law;
> (*c*) importing or exporting a controlled drug where the importation or exportation is prohibited by section 3(1) of that Act or a corresponding law;
> [(*d*) manufacturing or supplying a scheduled substance within the meaning of section 12 of the Criminal Justice (International Co-operation) Act 1990 where the manufacture or supply is an offence under that section;]
> and includes a person doing the following, whether in England and Wales or elsewhere, that is entering into or being otherwise concerned in an arrangement whereby:
> (i)   the retention or control by or on behalf of another person of the other person's proceeds of drug trafficking is facilitated, or
> (ii) the proceeds of drug trafficking by another person are used to secure that funds are placed at the other person's disposal or are used for the other person's benefit to acquire property by way of investment."

Accordingly, "drug trafficking" is to be carefully distinguished from a "drug trafficking offence" which is also defined in section 38(1) as amended by Schedule 4, paragraph 4 to the Criminal Justice (International Co-operation) Act 1990.

II. Proceeds of Drug Trafficking Offences

12–186   Three separate offences were created in the Criminal Justice (International Co-operation) Act 1990, s.14 to give legislative effect to the provisions of Article 3 of the 1988 Vienna Convention against Illicit Traffic in Narcotic

Drugs and Psychotropic Substances.

It will be seen that the first offence is concerned with the activities of the drug trafficker who seeks to avoid prosecution or the making of a confiscation order, by concealing or transferring his proceeds (section 14(1)). The second offence relates to the same activity but committed by a person other than the trafficker himself (section 14(2)). The third offence is aimed at the recipient of gifts knowing or having reasonable grounds to suspect that the gift represents the proceeds of another's drug trafficking (sections 14(3) and (5)).

Offences under section 14 of the Criminal Justice (International Co-operation) Act 1990 are "drug trafficking offences" for the purposes of the D.T.O.A. 1986, and section 27 of the M.D.A. 1971 (as amended by section 70 of the Criminal Justice Act 1988). However, an offence under section 14 does not entitle the courts to make any of the "assumptions" under section 2(2) of the D.T.O.A. 1986: (see Sched. 4, para. 4(2)). This is to preserve the distinction between money-laundering offences and more serious drug trafficking offences (see the Minister of State, Home Office, H.L., Vol. 514, col. 902).   **12–187**

A conviction for an offence under section 14 puts the offender in the category of prisoners in respect of whom the Secretary of State has no power of early release (see Criminal Justice (International Co-operation) Act s.31(1) and Sched. 4, para. 3 amending Part II of Schedule 1 to the Criminal Justice Act 1982; and the Minister of State, Home Office, H.L., Vol. 514, col. 902).

(a) Section 14(1)

"A person is guilty of an offence if he—   **12–188**

    (*a*) conceals or disguises any property which is, or in whole or in part directly or indirectly represents, his proceeds of drug trafficking; or

    (*b*) converts or transfers that property or removes it from the jurisdiction."

Section 24 of the D.T.O.A. 1986 makes it an offence for another to assist a drug trafficker to retain the benefit of the latter's drug trafficking. Section 14(1) of the 1990 Act fills a gap in section 24 so as to make the drug trafficker himself guilty of an offence if he attempts to avoid the events referred to in section 14(1).

(b) Section 14(2)

"A person is guilty of an offence if, knowing or having reasonable grounds   **12–189**
to suspect that any property is, or in whole or in part directly or indirectly represents, another person's proceeds of drug trafficking, he—

    (*a*) conceals or disguises that property; or

    (*b*) converts or transfers that property or removes it from the jurisdiction,

for the purpose of assisting any person to avoid prosecution for a drug trafficking offence or the making or enforcement of a confiscation order."

Section 14(2) applies to the acts of persons other than the drug trafficker. Depending on the facts of a given case, there may be an overlap between the scope of section 14(2) and section 24 of the D.T.O.A. 1986.

(c) Sections 14(3)–(5)

12–190   "(3) A person is guilty of an offence if, knowing or having reasonable grounds to suspect that any property is, or in whole or in part directly or indirectly represents, another person's proceeds of drug trafficking, he acquires that property for no, or for inadequate consideration.

(4) In subsections (1)(*a*) and (2)(*a*) above the references to concealing or disguising any property include references to concealing or disguising its nature, source, location, disposition, movement or ownership or any rights with respect to it.

(5) For the purposes of subsection (3) above consideration given for any property is inadequate if its value is significantly less than the value of that property, and there shall not be treated as consideration the provision for any person of services or goods which are of assistance to him in drug trafficking."

12–191   Both subsection (3) and subsection (5) must be read together. One object of these provisions is clearly to catch gifts and bargains which the recipient knew, or had reasonable cause to suspect, represents the proceeds of another's drug trafficking. But the provisions are designed to *exclude* persons who provide goods or services (notwithstanding that they knew, or had reasonable cause to suspect, that the payment came from the proceeds of drug trafficking (see the Minister of State, Home Office, H.L., Vol. 514, col. 887), providing that those goods or services were not supplied to assist in drug trafficking. Accordingly, if such goods or services were provided for adequate consideration, then no offence would be committed on the wording of subsection (3). However, where goods (*e.g.* motor vessel parts) were sold to another so as to be of assistance to him in drug trafficking, then subsection (5) creates a fiction and deems any payment not to be consideration at all and thus the supplier falls foul of subsection (3).

12–192   "**Are of assistance to him.**" No attention appears to have been given as to whether an accused must have *intended* that the goods or services would in fact be utilised to assist another in drug trafficking. The draftsman's use of the word "are" (as opposed to "had been") seems to introduce a speculative element into the offence.

"**Having reasonable grounds to suspect.**" The test here is objective.

III. OFFENCE OF PREJUDICING AN INVESTIGATION

12–193   Section 31(1) of the D.T.O.A. provides:

"Where, in relation to an investigation into drug trafficking, an order under section 27 of this Act has been made or has been applied for and has not been refused or a warrant under section 28 of this Act has been issued, a person who, knowing or suspecting that the investigation is taking place, makes any disclosure which is likely to prejudice the investigation is guilty of an offence."

Section 27 (considered at §12–196, *infra*) is concerned with the making of material available to a constable or an officer of customs and excise relevant to an investigation into drug trafficking.

An offence under section 31 can only be committed if an order under section 27 has been made or applied for, or a warrant (authorising a search) under section 28 has been issued. The prosecution must prove that the accused knew or suspected that the investigation was taking place, but it is not necessary for the prosecution to prove either that he knew or suspected that any of the steps mentioned in section 31(1) had in fact been taken, or that he knew or suspected that the disclosure was likely to prejudice the investigation.

By section 31(2): **12–194**

"In proceedings against a person for an offence under this section, it is a defence to prove:
- (*a*) that he did not know or suspect that the disclosure was likely to prejudice the investigation, or
- (*b*) that he had lawful authority or reasonable excuse for making the disclosure."

An offence under section 31 is triable either way and punishable on indictment to imprisonment for a term not exceeding five years or to a fine or to both (section 31(3)(*a*)) and, on summary conviction, to a term of imprisonment not exceeding six months or to a fine not exceeding the statutory maximum or both (section 31(3)(*b*)). The offence is not a "drug trafficking offence" within the meaning of section 38(1) but it is an arrestable offence for the purposes of P.A.C.E.

IV. INVESTIGATIONS INTO DRUG TRAFFICKING

Notwithstanding the fact that the police or the customs and excise may **12–195** have insufficient evidence to arrest or charge an individual in connection with a drug trafficking offence, nevertheless, by section 27(1) a constable may for the purpose of an investigation into drug trafficking, apply to a circuit judge for an order under section 27(2) requiring the person who appears to be in possession of particular material, or material of a particular description to *either* produce it to a constable for him to take away, *or* to give a constable access to it for a period of seven days unless a longer or shorter period is deemed to be appropriate by order of the court: section 27(3).

(a) Sections 27(1), (2) and (3) of the D.T.O.A.

As amended by section 70(2) and Schedule 2 to the Criminal Justice (Scot- **12–196** land) Act 1987, these sections provide as follows:

"(1) A constable may, for the purpose of an investigation into drug trafficking, apply to a circuit judge for an order under subsection (2) below in relation to particular material or material of a particular description.

(2) If on such an application the judge is satisfied that the conditions in subsection (4) below are fulfilled, he may make an order that the person who appears to him to be in possession of the material to which the application relates shall:

(*a*) produce it to a constable for him to take away, or

(*b*) give a constable access to it,

within such period as the order may specify.

This subsection is subject to section 30(11) of this Act.

(3) The period to be specified in an order under subsection (2) above shall be seven days unless it appears to the judge that a longer or shorter period would be appropriate in the particular circumstances of the application."

Section 30(11) of the Act is concerned with the disclosure of information held by government departments. Accordingly, by section 30(11) an order granted under section 27(2) may require an officer of the department (whether named in the order or not) to comply with the order, and "such an order shall be served as if the proceedings were civil proceedings against the defendant."

(b) Section 27(4)

12–197   No order may be made under section 27(1) unless the conditions in subsection (4) are fulfilled. These are:

"(*a*) that there are reasonable grounds for suspecting that a specified person has carried on or has benefited from drug trafficking,

(*b*) that there are reasonable grounds for suspecting that the material to which the application relates:

(i)   is likely to be of substantial value (whether by itself or together with other material) to the investigation for the purpose of which the application is made, and

(ii) does not consist of or include items subject to legal privilege or excluded material, and

(*c*) that there are reasonable grounds for believing that it is in the public interest, having regard:

(i)   to the benefit likely to accrue to the investigation if the material is obtained, and

(ii) to the circumstances under which the person in possession of the material holds it,

that the material should be produced or that access to it should be given."

12–198   It will be noted that the order may be made against any individual (named in the order) who appears to be in possession of the material to which the application relates: see section 27(2). It is not necessary to show that he is suspected of having benefited from drug trafficking or that he is suspected of having committed any offence. An order of a circuit judge under section 27 will have effect as if it were an order of the Crown Court (section 27(7)).

However, the section expressly refers to a "circuit judge" and not "the Crown Court." Accordingly, a recorder, or an assistant recorder has no jurisdiction to make an order under section 27: see *Central Criminal Court, ex p. Francis and Francis* [1989] A.C. 346.

By section 27(9)(*a*) an order under subsection (2) shall "not confer any right to production of, or access to, items subject to legal privilege or excluded material." "Items subject to legal privilege" and "excluded material" have the same meanings as in P.A.C.E.: see section 29(2) of the D.T.O.A.

(c) Section 10 of P.A.C.E.: "legal privilege"

By section 10 of P.A.C.E.:   **12–199**

"(1) Subject to subsection (2) below, in this Act 'items subject to legal privilege' means:

(*a*) communications between a professional legal adviser and his client or any person representing his client made in connection with the giving of legal advice to the client;

(*b*) communications between a professional legal adviser and his client or any person representing his client or between such an adviser or his client or any such representative and any other person made in connection with or in contemplation of legal proceedings and for the purposes of such proceedings; and

(*c*) items enclosed with or referred to in such communications and made:

　(i)　in connection with the giving of legal advice; or

　(ii)　in connection with or in contemplation of legal proceedings and for the purposes of such proceedings,

when they are in the possession of a person who is entitled to possession of them.

(2) Items held with the intention of furthering a criminal purpose are not items subject to legal privilege."

(d) Section 11 of P.A.C.E.: "excluded material"

So far as "excluded material" is concerned, section 11 of P.A.C.E. reads: **12–200**

"(1) Subject to the following provisions of this section, in this Act 'excluded material' means:

(*a*) personal records which a person has acquired or created in the course of any trade, business, profession or other occupation or for the purposes of any paid or unpaid office and which he holds in confidence;

(*b*) human tissue or tissue fluid which has been taken for the purposes of diagnosis or medical treatment and which a person holds in confidence;

(*c*) journalistic material which a person holds in confidence and which consists:

　(i)　of documents; or

    (ii) of records other than documents.

    (2) A person holds material other than journalistic material in confidence for the purposes of this section if he holds it subject:

        (*a*) to an express or implied undertaking to hold it in confidence; or

        (*b*) to a restriction on disclosure or an obligation of secrecy contained in any enactment, including an enactment contained in an Act passed after this Act.

    (3) A person holds journalistic material in confidence for the purposes of this section if:

        (*a*) he holds it subject to such an undertaking, restriction or obligation; and

        (*b*) it has been continuously held (by one or more persons) subject to such an undertaking, restriction or obligation since it was first acquired or created for the purposes of journalism."

(e) Section 13 of P.A.C.E.: "journalistic material"

12–201   By section 13 of P.A.C.E. "journalistic material" means:

"(1) Subject to subsection (2) below, ... material acquired or created for the purposes of journalism.

(2) Material is only journalistic material for the purposes of this Act if it is in the possession of a person who acquired or created it for the purposes of journalism.

(3) A person who receives material from someone who intends that the recipient shall use it for the purposes of journalism is to be taken to have acquired it for those purposes."

V. Privilege and the Position of the Solicitor

12–202   In *Central Criminal Court, ex p. Francis and Francis* [1989] A.C. 346 an order was made under section 27 of the D.T.O.A. against a firm of solicitors, requiring them to give the police access to material in their possession relating to the affairs of one of their clients, Mrs. G, who was acquiring property with the proceeds of drug trafficking on the part of D.

    The solicitors contended that the material was subject to legal privilege and therefore the order should not have been made. It will be recalled that an order under section 27(2) shall not confer any right to production of, or access to, "items subject to legal privilege" (section 27(*a*)) as defined by section 29(2) and section 10 of P.A.C.E. However, by section 10(2), "items held with the intention of furthering a criminal purpose are not items subject to legal privilege."

12–203   The case was argued on three important assumptions: (1) that D intended to further a criminal purpose of concealing his proceeds of drug trafficking by acquiring property for Mrs. G; (2) that Mrs. G was innocent of complicity; (3) that the solicitors acted with propriety and with no suspicion of any illegality affecting the transaction.

    The House of Lords had to rule on the proper construction of section 10(2).

The key question was "to whose intention does subsection (2) refer?" Does the intention have to rest with the *holder* of the material (*e.g.* the solicitor) or with the client (Mrs. G), or, is it enough that the intention is that of a third party who has not in fact received any legal advice (*e.g.* D)? By a majority (Lord Bridge and Lord Oliver dissenting), the House of Lords concluded that the "intention of furthering a criminal purpose" cannot be restricted to the intention of the person who actually has the items in his possession. In other words, it is enough to show that the client or even a third party had the necessary intention. Accordingly, the validity of the order was upheld.

The basis upon which the majority arrived at their conclusion is persuasive but not free of difficulty for the reasons given principally by Lord Bridge.

(a) Solicitor and client

In order to understand the various opinions expressed in *Francis'* case, it is **12–204** important to have regard to the common law rule laid down in *Cox* (1884) 14 Q.B.D. 153 which held that the protection of legal professional privilege excludes communications made by a client to his solicitor with the intention of furthering a criminal purpose and that the "client must either conspire with his solicitor or deceive him": *per* Stephen J. at 168. This neat phrase embraces the situation of a solicitor, acting in good faith, who is unaware of any illegality intended by the client. Put shortly, the majority held that section 10(1) and (2) reflected the common law position. Lord Bridge and Lord Oliver disagreed. Lord Bridge saw no sound basis for making the assumption that in section 10, Parliament set out to reproduce in the form of a statutory code, every aspect of the common law relating to legal professional privilege, and that if "true codification had been intended, something more elaborate would clearly be required" (at 781 b/c). Indeed, Lord Oliver could see good reason why Parliament, would wish to restrict the denial of legal privilege on the basis that a solicitor should not be put in a position where the correctness of his decision depends on an intention of which he knows nothing (at 794 g/h).

(b) Solicitor, client and the third party

In *Francis'* case (*supra*), it was assumed that both the client and the solicitor **12–205** acted in good faith. The question therefore arose as to whether it could properly be said that, at common law, a criminal intent on the part of a stranger destroys what is, after all, the privilege of the client. Neither Lord Bridge [1988] 3 All E.R. 775, H.L. (at 785 f–h) nor Lord Oliver (at 793 g/h) could find any authority in the common law to answer that question affirmatively. In their opinion if the majority is right then "it is breaking new ground" (*per* Lord Oliver, at 793 h). However, Lord Goff relied on a passage in the judgment delivered by Stephen J. in *Cox* when he said that:

> "The reason on which the rule is said to rest cannot include the case of communications ... intended to further any criminal purpose, for the protection of such communications cannot possibly be otherwise than injurious to the interests of justice .... "

Lord Goff regarded as immaterial to that exception, whether it is the client himself, or a third party who is using the client as his innocent tool, who has the criminal intention (at 799 f–j). The Divisional Court, in *Francis*' case [1988] 1 All E.R. 677, also seems to have had in contemplation the client who is "the innocent instrument or beneficiary of the third party's criminal purpose" (*per* Lloyd L.J. at 682).

12–206   An order under D.T.O.A., s. 27(2) will override any obligation as to secrecy or other restrictions upon the disclosure of information imposed by statute or otherwise (section 27(9)(*b*)), and may be made in relation to material in the possession of an authorised government department (section 27(9)(*c*)).

Where the material to which an application under section 27(2) relates, consists of information contained in a computer, then the data must be produced in a form in which it can be taken away and in which it is both visible and legible: section 27(8).

Where an order is made under section 27(2)(*b*) then the constable may order any person who appears to the court to be entitled to grant entry to the premises, to allow a constable to enter the premises to obtain access to the material.

VI. AUTHORITY FOR SEARCH

12–207   By D.T.O.A., s. 28(1) a constable may apply to a circuit judge for a warrant in relation to specified premises, authorising (by virtue of subsection (2)) a constable to enter and search premises if the court is satisfied that:

(*a*)   an order made under section 27 has not been complied with, *or*
(*b*)   the conditions in subsection (3) are fulfilled; *or*
(*c*)   the conditions in subsection (4) are fulfilled.

12–208   By section 28(3) the conditions referred to in subsection (2)(*b*) are:

"(*a*) that there are reasonable grounds for suspecting that a specified person has carried on or has benefited from drug trafficking, and
(*b*)   that the conditions in section 27(4)(*b*) and (*c*) of this Act are fulfilled in relation to any material on the premises, and
(*c*)   that it would not be appropriate to make an order under that section in relation to the material because:
(i)   it is not practicable to communicate with any person entitled to produce the material, or
(ii)   it is not practicable to communicate with any person entitled to grant access to the material or entitled to grant entry to the premises on which the material is situated, or
(iii)   the investigation for the purposes of which the application is made might be seriously prejudiced unless a constable could ensure immediate access to the material."

12–209   Again, by section 28(4) the conditions referred to in subsection 28(2)(*c*) are:

"(*a*) that there are reasonable grounds for suspecting that a specified person has carried on or has benefited from drug trafficking, and

(*b*) that there are reasonable grounds for suspecting that there is on the premises material relating to the specified person or to drug trafficking which is likely to be of substantial value (whether by itself or together with other material) to the investigation for the purpose of which the application is made, but that the material cannot at the time of the application be particularised, and

(*c*) that:

    (i) it is not practicable to communicate with any person entitled to grant entry to the premises, or

    (ii) entry to the premises will not be granted unless a warrant is produced, or

    (iii) the investigation for the purpose of which the application is made might be seriously prejudiced unless a constable arriving at the premises could secure immediate entry to them."

A constable who enters premises in the execution of a warrant issued under **12–210** section 28 may seize and retain any material other than items subject to "legal privilege" and "excluded material" (see section 29(2) of the Act and sections 10, 11 and 13 of P.A.C.E.) which is likely to be of "substantial value" to the investigation for the purposes of which the warrant was issued: see section 28(5).

VII. Disclosure of Information Held by Government Departments

By section 30(1) the High Court may, on the application of the prosecutor, **12–211** order material in the possession of an authorised government department to be produced to the court within a period specified by the court. The material must first have been submitted to an officer of the relevant department either by the defendant or by a person who has at any time held realisable property (section 30(1)(*a*)); secondly, the material must have been made by an officer of that department in relation to the defendant or such a person (section 30(1)(*b*)); or thirdly, the material is correspondence which passed between an officer of the relevant department and the defendant or such a person (section 30(1)(*c*)).

No order may be made under section 30(1) unless the conditions specified in section 7(1) or section 7(2) are satisfied (section 30(2): see §12–147 for conditions), and no material may be produced under section 30(1) unless it appears to the High Court that the material is likely to contain information that would facilitate the exercise of the powers conferred on the court by virtue of sections 8 to 11 of the Act or, alternatively, on a receiver appointed under section 8 or 11 of the Act or in pursuance of a charging order: see section 30(4).

The court may order the disclosure of the material produced by the relevant **12–212** government department to any member of the police force (section 30(8)(*a*));

the Crown Prosecution Service (section 30(8)(*b*)), or an officer within the meaning of the Customs and Excise Management Act 1979 (section 30(8)(*c*)).

However, the court must not disclose any part of the material unless a reasonable opportunity has been given for an officer of the department to make representations to the court *and* it appears to the court that the material is likely to be of substantial value in exercising "functions" relating to drug trafficking: see section 30(7).

The expression "authorised government department," as it appears in section 30, means a government department which is an authorised department for the purposes of the Crown Proceedings Act 1947: see section 38(1).

J. DRUG CASH IMPORTED OR EXPORTED

I. INTRODUCTION

12–213   In recent years it has been the experience of the Customs and Excise that large sums of cash are being exported and imported into the United Kingdom. There currently exists no exchange control regulations in this country so that cash imported may be changed into foreign currency which is then exported. Subject to a device, which is discussed below, neither the officers of Customs and Excise nor the police, have any powers to seize the cash to investigate its origins if there are reasonable grounds for suspecting that the cash directly or indirectly represents the proceeds of someone's drug trafficking. As a result of complaints expressed in evidence by American and British law enforcement officers to the Home Affairs Select Committee (see the 7th Report 1989, Vol. I; para. 87) Parliament enacted Part III of the Criminal Justice (International Co-operation) Act 1990, ss.25–29.

12–214   The Metropolitan Police also complained that the abolition of exchange controls has been exploited by drug traffickers (see para. 87 of the 7th Report). The Home Affairs Committee has therefore recommended that the law be changed to:

   (i)   require anyone importing or exporting cash over a limit set by H.M. Customs to declare it;

  (ii)   make illegal the import or export of proceeds of drug trafficking or other serious crimes and;

 (iii)   allow customs officers to retain cash entering or leaving the country which they know or suspect arises from the proceeds of such crime.

This approach has found favour with the Customs and Excise with the consequent assumption of the powers which may be required by Article 5 of the 1988 Vienna Convention (see para. 88 of the 7th Report). These recommendations have not become law. It is debatable whether such proposals would run contrary to existing laws concerning the free movement of capital and the E.C. Capital Liberalisation Directive. The Home Affairs Committee has suggested that requiring a declaration of cash over a pre-set limit would not require primary legislation but could be achieved by an order issued under section 1 of the Import, Export and Customs Powers (Defence) Act 1939.

II. SUMMARY OF THE POSITION

The effect of these provisions is draconian. The general scheme is as fol- **12–215**
lows. Where a customs officer, or a constable, has reasonable grounds for suspecting that the "cash" imported or exported (being £10,000 or more)
directly or indirectly represents the proceeds of drug trafficking, the officer
may seize that cash (section 25(1) of the Criminal Justice (International Co-
operation) Act) and detain it for up to 48 hours without the need to make any
application to a court. After 48 hours, the officer must either return the cash
or apply to a justice of the peace (or in Scotland the sheriff) for an order permitting its continued detention on the grounds set out in section 25(2). The
order cannot endure longer than three months (section 25(3)), but further
orders can be made by the court provided the total period of detention does
not exceed two years from the date of the first order (section 25(3)). It should
be noted that these powers may be exercised even if no criminal proceedings
have been instituted (or even contemplated) against any person for a drug
trafficking offence in connection with the money seized. Where proceedings
are instituted (section 25(6)), or where application is made to forfeit the
money on the basis that it represents drug proceeds (section 26(1)), the cash is
not to be released until the relevant proceedings have been concluded (and so
overrides the two-year restriction set out in section 25(3)). If forfeiture is
applied for, the prosecutor need only prove that the cash represents the proceeds of drug trafficking to the civil standard. This is at variance with the position under the D.T.O.A.: see *Dickens* [1990] 2 Q.B. 102 and *Enwezor*
(1991) 93 Cr.App.R. 233.

The person from whom the cash seized, or any person on whose behalf the **12–216**
cash being exported or imported, may apply to the magistrates' court (or in
Scotland the sheriff) for the money to be released on the basis that there are no
grounds for its detention, or its detention is not justified (section 25(5) of the
Criminal Justice (International Co-operation) Act). Clearly in this instance
the burden is on the applicant (presumably to the civil standard).

Notice must be given to persons affected by the order (section 28(1)).

The money must be held in an interest-bearing account, (payable to the
Crown if forfeited or to the person entitled to possession if released), unless
the money was released within 48 hours of its seizure: section 27.

It should be noted that "exported" has an extended meaning and includes
cash "being brought to any place in the United Kingdom for the purpose of
being exported": section 29(1).

III. THE PREVIOUS POSITION

Reference has already been made to the reasons why Part III of the Act **12–217**
1990 was enacted. However, in several cases, the Commissioners of Customs
and Excise have achieved a similar result (seizure, detention and forfeiture) by
an ingenious if not complicated route through the C.E.M.A. 1979. Under the

1979 Act, a number of offences and events entitle the Commissioners to seize the goods in question which are then *liable* to forfeiture. Under the 1979 Act "goods" includes "money."

Thus, to take an example, section 78(2) of the C.E.M.A. 1979 provides:

"Any person entering or leaving the United Kingdom shall answer such questions as the proper officer may put to him with respect to his baggage and any thing contained therein or carried with him, and shall, if required by the proper officer, produce that baggage and any such thing for examination at such place as the Commissioner may direct."

12–218   Note the words "shall answer" in section 78(2). The consequences of a failure to comply with section 78(2) appear in section 167(1) of the C.E.M.A. which provides that:

"If any person either knowingly or recklessly—
(a) makes or signs, or causes to be made or signed, or delivers or causes to be delivered to the Commissioners or an officer, any declaration, notice, certificate or other document whatsoever; or
(b) makes any statement in answer to any question put to him by an officer which he is required by or under any enactment to answer, being a document or statement produced or made for any purpose of any assigned matter, which is untrue in any material particular, he shall be guilty of an offence under this subsection and may be detained; and any goods in relation to which the document or statement was made shall be liable to forfeiture."

12–219   Accordingly, if an officer asks a passenger at the airport the question "are you taking anything out of England?" or "do you have anything which you have obtained in the United Kingdom?" and the passenger replies in the negative, then the argument is that section 167(1) of the C.E.M.A. is contravened if in truth the passenger is exporting £50,000 which he obtained in the United Kingdom. Identifying the "assigned matter" (defined by section 1 of the C.E.M.A. 1979), for the purposes of section 167(1) may prove difficult, but it has been argued to include the investigation of an offence under section 24 of the D.T.O.A. (assisting a drug trafficker). By section 139(1) of the C.E.M.A. 1979 the Commissioners may seize or detain "anything liable to forfeiture" and invoke condemnation proceedings for the forfeiture of the cash under section 139(6) and Schedule 3 to the C.E.M.A. 1979. The validity of this route has not been the subject of any reported decision of a superior court and a number of difficult issues arise. The relationship between section 78 and section 167(1) is not clear. There is an obligation to answer questions put to a person entering or leaving the United Kingdom in respect of his baggage and "anything" carried with him, but must the question be directed to goods which are "prohibited, restricted or dutiable" under the 1979 Act or may the questions be general? It is startling that a person who answers the question "are you taking goods out of England?" negatively, commits an offence under section 167(1) if he knows he has in his pockets a wallet containing £300. Is an officer of Customs and Excise entitled to seize the £300? Furthermore, is forfeiture contingent upon a conviction or is it enough to prove that an offence has been committed albeit that the offender was not in fact prosecuted?

IV. GENERAL POWER OF SEIZURE AND DETENTION

Section 25(1) of the Criminal Justice (International Co-operation) Act **12–220**
1990 provides:

"A customs officer or constable may seize and, in accordance with this section, detain any cash which is being imported into or exported from the United Kingdom if its amount is not less than the prescribed sum and he has reasonable grounds for suspecting that it directly or indirectly represents any person's proceeds of, or is intended by any person for use in, drug trafficking."

V. PERIOD OF DETENTION AND CONTINUED DETENTION

Section 25(2) of the 1990 Act provides: **12–221**

"Cash seized by virtue of this section shall not be detained for more than forty-eight hours unless its continued detention is authorised by an order made by a justice of the peace or in Scotland the sheriff: and no such order shall be made unless the justice or, as the case may be, the sheriff is satisfied—

    (*a*) that there are reasonable grounds for the suspicion mentioned in subsection (1) above; and

    (*b*) that continued detention of the cash is justified while its origin or derivation is further investigated or consideration is given to the institution (whether in the United Kingdom or elsewhere) of criminal proceedings against any person for an offence with which the cash is connected."

(a) Further applications for continued detention

Section 25(3) of the Act provides: **12–222**

"Any order under subsection (2) above shall authorise the continued detention of the cash to which it relates for such period, not exceeding three months beginning with the date of the order, as may be specified in the order; and a magistrates court or in Scotland the sheriff, if satisfied as to the matters mentioned in that subsection, may thereafter from time to time by order authorise the further detention of the cash but so that—

    (*a*) no period of detention specified in such an order shall exceed three months beginning with the date of the order; and

    (*b*) the total period of detention shall not exceed two years from the date of the order under subsection (2) above."

(b) Making the application

12–223   By section 25(4) of the 1990 Act:

"Any application for an order under subsections (2) or (3) above shall be made by the Commissioners of Customs and Excise or a constable if made to a justice or magistrates' court and by a procurator fiscal if made to the sheriff."

(c) Application for release

12–224   Either the prosecutor or an interested party may apply for the money to be released in the circumstances set out in section 25(5) of the Act below:

"At any time while cash is detained by virtue of the foregoing provisions of this section—

(a) a magistrates' court or in Scotland the sheriff may direct its release if satisfied—
(i) on an application made by the person from whom it was seized or a person by or on whose behalf it was being imported or exported, that there are no, or are no longer, any such grounds for its detention as are mentioned in subsection (2) above; or
(ii) on an application made by any other person, that detention of the cash is not for that or any other reason justified; and

(b) a customs officer or constable, or in Scotland a procurator fiscal, may release the cash if satisfied that its detention is no longer justified but shall first notify the justice, magistrates' court or sheriff under whose order it is being detained."

(d) When the money must not be released

12–225   There are two relevant circumstances as set out in section 25(6) below:

"If at a time when any cash is being detained by virtue of the foregoing provisions of this section—

(a) an application for its forfeiture is made under section 26 below; or
(b) proceedings are instituted (whether in the United Kingdom or elsewhere) against any person for an offence with which the cash is connected,

the cash shall not be released until any proceedings pursuant to the application or, as the case may be, the proceedings for that offence have been concluded."

(e) Forfeiture under the Criminal Justice (International Co-operation) Act

12–226   Section 26 provides:

"(1) A magistrates' court or in Scotland the sheriff may order the forfeiture of any cash which has been seized under section 25 above if satisfied, on an application made while the cash is detained under that section, that the cash directly or indirectly represents any person's proceeds of, or is intended by any person for use in, drug trafficking.

(2) Any application under this section to a magistrates' court shall be made by the Commissioners of Customs and Excise or a constable and to the sheriff by a procurator fiscal.

(3) The standard of proof in proceedings on an application under this section shall be that applicable to civil proceedings; and an order may be made under this section whether or not proceedings are brought against any person for an offence with which the cash in question is connected."

VI. Interpretation

Section 29(1) of the 1990 Act provides: **12–227**

"In this Part of this Act—

'cash' includes coins and notes in any currency;

'customs officer' means an officer commissioned by the Commissioners of Customs and Excise under section 6(3) of the Customs and Excise Management Act 1979;

'drug trafficking' has the same meaning as in the Drug Trafficking Offences Act 1986 or, as respects Scotland, in Part I of the Criminal Justice (Scotland) Act 1987;

'exported,' in relation to any cash, includes its being brought to any place in the United Kingdom for the purpose of being exported;

'the proceeds of drug trafficking' has the same meaning as in the said Acts of 1986 and 1987 respectively and includes proceeds received by any person as well as after the coming into force of this part of this Act."

Chapter 13
Powers of Forfeiture

A. STATUTORY POWERS (OTHER THAN UNDER THE D.T.O.A.)

I. GENERAL NOTE

13–01   In England and Wales, where the court is concerned to recover the proceeds of drug trafficking from any person convicted of a drug trafficking offence, the appropriate machinery is that laid down in the Drug Trafficking Offences Act 1986; and see *Stuart* (1990) 11 Cr.App.R.(S) 89. Much of that Act does not extend to Scotland and therefore decisions made under the Drug Trafficking Offences Act 1986 are not binding on Scottish courts (and see the Criminal Justice (Scotland) Act 1987).

II. FORFEITURE UNDER THE C.E.M.A. 1979

13–02   Reference has already been made to the fact that under the Customs & Excise Management Act 1979, the Commissioners have broad powers of forfeiture in relation to many activities embraced by the Customs and Excise Acts (see Chapter 2). Anything liable to forfeiture under those Acts may be seized or detained by any officer, constable, member of Her Majesty's armed forces, or a coastguard (section 139(1) of the C.E.M.A.) and dealt with in accordance with section 139 of and Schedule 3 to the 1979 Act.

Thus, goods improperly imported may be forfeited under section 49(1). By section 88 ships, aircraft and vehicles which are constructed, altered or fitted in any manner for the purpose of concealing "goods" (including stores and baggage: section 1(1)) may be forfeited. A ship under 250 tons may be forfeited if any part of its cargo is thrown overboard, or is staved, or destroyed to prevent seizure (section 89). A ship over 250 tons (section 142) may have other penalties imposed under section 143: see *Att.-Gen.* v. *Hunter* [1949] 2 K.B. 111.

Forfeiture proceedings under the Customs and Excise Acts are *in rem*: see *Denton* v. *John Lister Ltd.* [1971] 3 All E.R. 669.

III. FORFEITURE UNDER THE M.D.A. 1971

Section 27 of the Misuse of Drugs Act 1971 as amended by the Criminal **13–03**
Justice Act 1988, s.70, and the Criminal Justice (International Co-operation)
Act 1990, provides:

"(1) Subject to subsection (2) below, the court by or before which a person
is convicted of an offence under this Act or a drug trafficking offence, as
defined in section 38(1) of the Drug Trafficking Offences Act 1986 or an
offence to which section 1 of the Criminal Justice (Scotland) Act 1987
relates, may order anything shown to the satisfaction of the court to relate
to the offence, to be forfeited and either destroyed or dealt with in such
other manner as the court may order.

(2) The court shall not order anything to be forfeited under this section,
where a person claiming to be the owner of or otherwise interested in it
applies to be heard by the court, unless an opportunity has been given to
him to show cause why the order should not be made."

An order under section 27 must be made within 28 days after passing sentence and cannot be varied, or rescinded, or made after that period: see *Menocal* [1980] A.C. 598.

Section 27 will only apply to things shown "to relate to the offence." As **13–04**
originally drafted, any property sought to be forfeited under section 27 had to
relate to an offence created under the M.D.A. 1971 alone. Accordingly, a
conspiracy to contravene an offence under that Act was excluded because the
M.D.A. 1971 created no statutory conspiracies: *Cuthbertson* [1981] A.C.
470. The ambit of section 27 has been widened considerably to include a
"drug trafficking offence" as defined by section 38(1) of the D.T.O.A. 1986
or section 1 of the Criminal Justice (Scotland) Act 1987. A "drug trafficking
offence" includes an offence of conspiring, inciting or attempting to commit
specified offences under the M.D.A.

However, only tangible things—capable of being destroyed—can be forfeited under section 27 of the M.D.A. and not choses in action: see *Cuthbertson (supra)* and *Beard* [1974] 1 W.L.R. 1549. In other words, the property
sought to be forfeited must relate to the transaction which is covered by an
appropriate charge or count on the indictment. In *Cuthbertson*, T and C had
transferred a considerable portion of their shares in the profits to various
bank accounts in Switzerland and France. Assets representing their proceeds
of drug trafficking were traced and amounted to about £¾m. The judge made
a forfeiture order under section 27 for that amount. The House of Lords held
that it was necessary to connect the specific thing sought to be forfeited with
the particular substantive offence to which it related. As Lord Diplock
observed (at 406f/g), orders of forfeiture under section 27 were not intended
by Parliament to serve "as a means of stripping the drug trafficker of the total
profits of their unlawful enterprises."

The decision in *Cuthbertson* has been criticised in academic circles (see **13–05**
[1980] Stat.L.R. 166 and [1981] Stat.L.R. 64) but it is submitted that Lord
Scarman correctly described section 27 as being concerned "not with resti-
tution, compensation or the redress of illegal enrichment but with forfeiture":

Cuthbertson [1981] A.C. 470, 486; and note by contrast the sweeping effect of the D.T.O.A.

However, where money is seized by police *in specie*, *e.g.* in the form of banknotes, and then put into a bank account by police for safe keeping, the money so seized is sufficiently tangible for the purposes of section 27. The relevant moment is the moment of seizure: see *Marland* (1985) 82 Cr.App.R. 134.

(a) The tangible item must relate to the offence

13–06   In *Cuthbertson*, the House of Lords emphasised the importance of ensuring that the tangible items relate to the offence. In *Haggard* v. *Mason* [1976] 1 W.L.R. 187, the Court of Appeal quashed an order under section 27 which related to the sum of £146 found in the defendant's possession. He had been convicted of offering to supply another with LSD. The £146 represented the remaining proceeds of M's illegal dealings which were not the subject of a separate charge. Accordingly, the money did not "relate" to the offences. Similar considerations resulted in a forfeiture order being quashed in the case of *Ribeyre* (1982) 4 Cr.App.R.(S.) 165, where R admitted that £700 was the proceeds of drug sales but the receipt of the money was not reflected by a suitable count on the indictment (R having pleaded guilty to possessing cocaine with intent to supply it) and the £700 did not relate to that purpose. Judges in other cases have fallen into the same trap: see *Morgan* [1977] Crim.L.R. 488; *Cox* [1987] Crim.L.R. 141; *Llewellyn* (1985) 7 Cr.App.R.(S.) 225; *Boothe* (1987) 9 Cr.App.R.(S.) 8; *Simms* (1987) 9 Cr.App.R.(S.) 417; *O'Farrell* (1988) 10 Cr.App.R.(S.) 74; *Askew* [1987] Crim.L.R. 584; and *Neville* [1987] Crim.L.R. 585.

In *Maidstone Crown Court, ex p. Gill* [1986] 1 W.L.R. 1405, a forfeiture order under section 27 had to be quashed in respect of a motor car which related to a charge to which the accused had pleaded not guilty and the matter was "left on the file."

(b) Orders made against non-defendants

13–07   Section 27(2) gives the owner of goods, or an interested party in it, the right to have the opportunity of being heard before an order is made.

Where the evidence is that such parties were put on notice, or should have been, that the item in question was going to be used for some illegal purpose, then it might be proper for a judge to make a forfeiture order: *Maidstone Crown Court, ex p. Gill*, but see *Churcher* (1986) 8 Cr.App.R.(S.) 94, *infra*.

(c) Opportunity to give evidence

13–08   In *Churcher* (1986) 8 Cr.App.R.(S.) 94, the Court of Appeal observed that the court was under a duty to give the defendant a proper opportunity to put material before it, in order to demonstrate that the requirements of the section were not fulfilled. The facts in *Churcher* related to two sums of money found in the possession of the appellant. He pleaded guilty to a variety of drug trafficking offences. On similar facts a court today would endeavour to confiscate such moneys under the D.T.O.A.

IV. FORFEITURE UNDER THE P.C.C.A. 1973

Section 43(1) and 43(1A) of the Powers of Criminal Courts Act 1973, as amended by section 69 of the Criminal Justice Act 1988, provides: **13–09**

"(1) Subject to the following provisions of this section, where a person is convicted of an offence and—
> (a) the court by or before which he is convicted is satisfied that any property under his control at the time when he was apprehended for the offence or when a summons in respect of it was issued—
>> (i) has been used for the purpose of committing, or facilitating the commission of, any offence, or
>> (ii) was intended by him to be used for that purpose; or
> (b) the offence, or an offence which the court has taken into consideration in determining his sentence, consists of unlawful possession of property which—
>> (i) has been lawfully seized from him; or
>> (ii) was in his possession or under his control at the time when he was apprehended for the offence of which he has been convicted or when a summons in respect of that offence was issued,

the court may make an order under this section in respect of that property, and may do so whether or not it also deals with the offender in respect of the offence in any other way and without regard to any restrictions on forfeiture in an enactment contained in an Act passed before the Criminal Justice Act 1988.

(1A) In considering whether to make such an order in respect of any property a court shall have regard—
> (a) to the value of the property; and
> (b) to the likely financial and other effects on the offender of the making of the order (taken together with any other order that the court contemplates making)."

In *Boothe* (1987) 9 Cr.App.R.(S.) 8, B was convicted of possessing a drug intending to supply it and unlawfully possessing a drug. Officers, by chance, stopped B's motor car and found packages of cocaine. £1,489 was found in his possession. B was not a regular full-time dealer.   **13–10**

Held: (1) the forfeiture of his motor car under section 43 of the Powers of Criminal Courts Act 1973 was valid.

Held: (2) the forfeiture of the money under M.D.A., s.27 must be quashed.

It was contended in *Boothe* that the motor car was not essential for the commission of the offence (see what is now section 43(1)(a)(i), and *Lidster* [1976] Crim.L.R. 80). The court had no difficulty in concluding that the use of the car was an "integral part" of the offence as it was being used to transport packages of cocaine: but see *Brown* (February 28, 1974; unreported).

It follows from the above that a tenuous connection between the item and the commission of the offence is not enough: see *Jones* (October 10, 1985; unreported).

If, as in *Boothe*, money found in the possession of the accused cannot be forfeited under section 27 of the M.D.A., the court may be able to justify an order under section 43(1)(*a*)(ii) if it can be shown, for example, that the money was intended to be used by the defendant to increase his stock-in-trade (*i.e.* to buy additional drugs in order to supply them) and provided that the defendant either pleads guilty, or is convicted of an offence which reflects his intention. However, the matter is not clear: see *Tarpy* (February 8, 1985; unreported).

13–11   It should be noted that section 43(1) of the Powers of Criminal Courts Act 1973 is confined to property used or facilitating the commission of an offence (or intended to be so used) by the person convicted. It does not apply in cases where someone other than the defendant intended to (or did) use the property: *Slater* [1986] 1 W.L.R. 1340; but see *Coleville-Scott* [1990] 1 W.L.R. 958.

If, during the course of the trial or plea in mitigation, the defence make it plain that the prosecution case on possession is not accepted, it is essential that the trial judge holds an inquiry and (if necessary) hears evidence: see *Braker* (March 19, 1985; unreported).

Forfeiture orders, under section 43, should not be used as a method of ordering that the proceeds of sale be used to meet a compensation order which is not otherwise enforceable: see *Jarvis* (February 5, 1985; unreported).

Chapter 14
Sentencing

A. MAXIMUM SENTENCES FOR OFFENCES UNDER THE M.D.A. 1971

By section 25 of the M.D.A., the maximum sentences which may be imposed in respect of any of the offences under the Act are set out in Schedule 4, as amended by the following enactments: **14–01**

- (*a*) sections 27 and 28 of, and Schedule 5 to the Criminal Law Act 1977;
- (*b*) sections 32(2) and 32(3) of, and Schedule 7 to the Magistrates' Courts Act 1980;
- (*c*) section 46 of the Criminal Justice Act 1982;
- (*d*) the Controlled Drugs (Penalties) Act 1985.

For ease of reference, Schedule 4 to the M.D.A. is set out at the end of this Chapter.

In the ordinary way, by section 32(2) of the Magistrates' Courts Act 1980, offences triable either way, and which are not specified in Schedule 1 to that Act, carry a maximum fine on summary conviction in the "prescribed sum," *i.e.* £2,000 (see S.I. 1984 No. 447).

For reasons which are not entirely easy to understand, section 32(5) of the 1980 Act provides that section 32(2) does not apply (on summary conviction) in respect of an offence under section 5(2) of the M.D.A. if that offence involves a Class B or Class C drug. Moreover, section 32(2) does not apply to an offence under sections 4(2), 4(3), 5(3), 8, 12(6) or section 13(3) if the controlled drug involved falls within Class C. Accordingly, the appropriate penalties are set out in Schedule 5 to the Criminal Law Act 1977 as amended by Schedule 7 to the 1980 Act.

The maximum penalty of £400, in respect of an offence contrary to section 17(3) of the M.D.A., is set at level 3 of the "standard scale": see section 46(1) of the Criminal Justice Act 1982 and S.I. 1984 No. 447.

The Controlled Drugs (Penalties) Act 1985 increased, from 14 years' imprisonment to life imprisonment, the maximum sentences in respect of offences under sections 4(2), 4(3) or 5(3) of the M.D.A. which involve a Class A drug.

B. MAXIMUM SENTENCES FOR OFFENCES UNDER THE C.E.M.A. 1979

14–02   By Schedule 1 to the C.E.M.A., where a person is convicted of an offence contrary to section 50 (unlawful importation) or section 68 (unlawful exportation) or section 170 (fraudulent evasion), and where the offence involves a Class A or Class B drug, then he shall be liable, on *summary conviction* to either:

    (i)   a penalty of the "prescribed sum" (*i.e.* £2,000: see S.I. 1984 No. 447); or
    (ii) of three times the value of the goods, whichever is the greater; or
    (iii) to imprisonment for a term not exceeding six months; or
    (iv) to both.

On conviction *on indictment*, he shall be liable to either:

    (i)   a penalty "of any amount"; or
    (ii) imprisonment for a term not exceeding 14 years in the case of Class B drugs; or
    (iii) life imprisonment where the goods are a Class A drug (see the Controlled Drugs (Penalties) Act 1985; or
    (iv) to both.

14–03   Cases involving a Class C drug attract lesser penalties, namely (*per* paragraph 2 of Schedule 1 to the C.E.M.A. 1979):

    "(*a*) on summary conviction in Great Britain, to a penalty of three times the value of the goods or £500, whichever is the greater, or to imprisonment for a term not exceeding three months, or to both;
    (*b*) on summary conviction in Northern Ireland, to a penalty of three times the value of the goods or £100, whichever is the greater, or to imprisonment for a term not exceeding six months, or to both;
    (*c*) on conviction on indictment, to a penalty of any amount, or to imprisonment for a term not exceeding five years, or to both."

14–04   Persons convicted of an importation/exportation offence can no longer expect "early release" from their sentences under section 32 of the Criminal Justice Act 1982, since such an offence falls into the category of "excluded offences" as specified in Part III of Schedule 1 to that Act. Moreover, parole will no longer be available for prisoners sentenced to five years, or more, in respect of an offence of drug trafficking. The decision of the Home Secretary in this respect has not been effectively challenged: see *Re Findlay* [1985] A.C. 318.

I. VALUATION

14–05   It may seem strange that the court can order three times the value of drugs in the context of an illicit trade. How is the value to be assessed? The answer, which is not entirely satisfactory, is that the court may look to the "black market" value of the drugs as well as the legitimate value. This answer is the combined product of section 171(3) of the C.E.M.A. 1979 and the decision of the Divisional Court in *Byrne* v. *Low* [1972] 3 All E.R. 526.

Section 171(3) reads as follows:

> "Where a penalty for an offence under any enactment relating to an assigned matter is required to be fixed by reference to the value of any goods, that value shall be taken as the price which those goods might reasonably be expected to have fetched, after payment of any duty or tax chargeable thereon, if they had been sold in the open market at or about the date of the commission of the offence for which the penalty is imposed."

Accordingly, the value is the value of the drugs "if they had been sold in the open market." If one construes the words "open market" literally, then section 171(3) can have no application since drugs unlawfully imported cannot "openly" be marketed. If sold, their price can only be at the black market value.

This problem was considered in *Byrne* v. *Low* [1972] 3 All E.R. 526.   **14–06**

> B unlawfully imported prohibited goods, namely indecent articles. The invoice price of the goods was approximately £2,235. The magistrates sentenced B to a fine of £3,000 which was varied, on appeal to quarter sessions, to £100 on the basis that since the importation was prohibited there was no "open market" for them.

The Divisional Court allowed the appeal. Lord Widgery C.J. held (at 529) that a court is not "restricted by the distinction between the so-called black market and white market." He said (at 529a/b): "What is being sought is the price which a willing seller would accept from a willing buyer for those goods as landed at the port or airport at which they were originally landed."

The court thought that the invoice price could be a very good guide to the open market value "and may well be the conclusive and only guide."

II. Assessing the Street Value

Of course, drug transactions are rarely committed to paper in intelligible   **14–07** form. Accordingly, evidence of the value of a given substance will normally be given to the court by an expert, normally a police officer who has had many years' experience in dealing with drug offences. His information will be obtained from a variety of sources: prisoners or suspects may speak of the value; the officer may have been personally engaged in undercover drug operations during the course of which he has negotiated a price, or he may refer to records kept by the National Drugs Intelligence Unit (the N.D.I.U.) at New Scotland Yard, which collates information concerning drug activities nationwide. The tables produced by the Unit are elaborate and frequently updated. Values are expressed by region and will reflect a variety of important factors including the purity of the drug.

In *Afzal*, *The Times*, June 25, 1991, the Court of Appeal remarked that prosecuting counsel should take great care to ensure that correct figures in respect of the street value of the drug were placed before the court. Accordingly, where the appellants thought they were importing heroin of reasonable quality which in fact had a purity as low as 1 per cent. then the court would be entitled to have regard to what the appellants thought they had done but that some reduction was required because the *actus reus* was not as serious as in cases where the level of purity was higher with greater devastating consequences.

The case of *Afzal* highlights the importance which the court attaches to the street value of a controlled drug. Although prosecuting counsel shoulders the responsibility of exercising care in putting before the court a correct figure, the source of his information will tend to come from an officer (who may or may not be experienced in drug cases).

14-08 Two points should be borne in mind. The street value of a drug should not be slavishly followed by the courts as being the only relevant criterion for the purposes of applying the sentencing guidelines expressed in *Aramah* (1983) 76 Cr.App.R. 190 and *Bilinski* (1988) 86 Cr.App.R. 146. Street values vary as monetary values and market forces vary.

> In *Patel* [1987] Crim.L.R. 839 the appellant was sentenced to 12 years' imprisonment for his part in a conspiracy to supply 1.99 kilogrammes of heroin of 55 per cent. purity estimated at trial to be worth £750,000. On appeal, P called a representative of "Release" and the respondents called a representative of the N.D.I.U. as well as an officer to give evidence concerning the appropriate street value. The witnesses agreed that heroin (40 per cent. to 50 per cent. purity) was sold in $\frac{1}{8}$ gramme wraps at £10 each. The total value was therefore £160,000.
>
> *Held*: on appeal, the sentence would be reduced to 10 years' imprisonment.

The court remarked that the use of street values as an aid to sentencing was to be regarded with caution but so long as it was relied upon as a rough yardstick, there was no reason why the courts should not measure the length of sentence to some degree by it. The case of *Patel* reinforces the observations made in *Afzal (supra)* as to the importance of putting before the court reliable figures and information. Consult also Kay, "*Aramah* and Street Value of Drugs" [1987] Crim.L.R. 814.

The reader is invited to read §§ 10–43, *et seq.* in relation to expert evidence.

III. Is the Street Value Admissible Evidence?

14-09 Objection has often been taken to the admissibility of evidence as to street values, usually on the basis that the hearsay rule is infringed and that the evidence cannot be properly tested. Sometimes the objection is that the nature and quality of the drug in question cannot equate with the valuation given. For example, at the moment of importation, herbal cannabis may be heavily intermixed with seeds and stalk which is extracted by the time the final product is sold at street level. The valuation tends to be no more than an elementary calculation: namely, multiplying the gross weight of the consignment (including the extraneous matter), by the so-called street value, expressed per gramme or ounce.

Thus, in the case of herbal cannabis, the court is unlikely to know whether the street value cited is based on the assumption that extraneous material, such as seeds and stalk, has been excluded or not.

However, the principle seems to be well established that evidence may be   **14–10** given as to street value. In *Bryan*, decided on November 8, 1984 (3923B84; unreported), the Court of Appeal held that the evidence of a Drug Squad officer with experience of street dealing is admissible as to the fact of what happens on the street. He was therefore entitled to give evidence of the street value of drugs. However, this was not a matter for a pharmacist who would probably have less information concerning black market prices than a Drug Squad officer. Wood J. said:

> "The view of this court is that police officers with their experience of dealing with these problems, being on the streets and with their knowledge and meeting those having a drug problem and those pushing drugs, have a very wide experience and can give evidence of fact of what takes place on many occasions on the streets."

Expert evidence concerning the value of goods, chattels and property is not new in English law: see *English Exporters (London) Ltd.* v. *Eldonwall Ltd.* [1973] 1 Ch. 415, and the reader is invited to read §10–43, *et seq.* in relation to expert evidence.

C. SENTENCING GUIDELINES

Sentencing attitudes quickly change and it would be idle to pretend that the   **14–11** authorities do not reflect attitude "swings" over the years. Thus, in *Pandit* [1974] Crim.L.R. 60, a 35-year-old man, with no previous convictions, was sentenced to 18 months' imprisonment after he pleaded guilty to the importation of 27.5 grammes of cannabis for his own use. His sentence was upheld on appeal. Again, in *Daher* (1969) 53 Cr.App.R. 490, a sentence of three years' imprisonment was upheld where D unlawfully imported approximately five kilogrammes of cannabis resin in the false bottom of a suitcase. The defendant was then aged 19, of good character and had been recruited as a drugs runner in the Lebanon. Such cases are rightly to be regarded as being out of line with current sentencing policy over the last few years. In order to achieve a consistent approach to sentencing in drug cases, guidelines were given by the Court of Appeal in *Aramah* (1983) 76 Cr.App.R. 190. By contrast, in Scotland, there is no tariff in sentencing: see *Kenmure* v. *Lowe*, 1990 S.C.C.R. 367 and Robert Shiels, "Controlled Drugs and Assistance to the Authorities" 1991 S.L.T. 187.

D. GENERAL PRINCIPLES

14–12   The most important consideration in applying sentencing guidelines in cases of unlawful drug smuggling has been said to be the defendant's position in the drug smuggling venture: see *Hussain, The Times*, June 27, 1990. As a general proposition, the observations of the Court of Appeal are obviously correct but these should not, of course, be seen as watering down the substantial credit to be given in appropriate cases in respect of pleas of guilty or co-operation with the authorities.

When sentencing for an offence of being knowingly concerned in the fraudulent evasion of the prohibition on the importation of a controlled drug, it is not always appropriate to assess the seriousness of the offence by reference solely to the quantity of drugs involved. Some regard should be given to the method of importation, the degree of organisation and the difficulty of detection: *Kouadio, The Times*, February 21, 1991. The street value of the drug should also be taken into account (see *infra*). It is not valid mitigation that the defendant was in transit to another country and that the drug was not intended for distribution in the United Kingdom: see *Gasper* (1988) 10 Cr.App.R.(S.) 173, §14–31, *infra*.

Similarly, where a defendant produces a controlled drug by experimental means in this country, the trial judge is entitled to take into account the fact that the purpose of the experiment was to produce the drug on a large scale in another country: see *Couzens, The Times*, April 17, 1992. The fact that production of the drug would be lawful by the laws of that other country is irrelevant if the drug is to be unlawfully distributed elsewhere.

So far as mitigation is concerned, it was said in *Aramah* (1983) 76 Cr.App.R. 190 that a confession of guilt coupled with considerable assistance to the police could properly be marked by a substantial reduction in what would otherwise be the proper sentence: see §14–50.

E. THE DECISION IN *ARAMAH*

I. CLASS A DRUGS

14–13   The Court of Appeal took as its example heroin but described all Class A drugs as the most dangerous of all the addictive drugs, being easy to handle, involving enormous profits, attracting the worst type of criminal and causing heroin addicts to obtain supplies of the drug (costing hundreds of pounds sterling a week) to satisfy "the terrible craving." Lord Lane C.J. remarked:

> "It is not difficult to understand why in some parts of the world, traffickers in heroin in any substantial quantity were sentenced to death and executed. Consequently, anything which the courts of this country can do by way of deterrent sentences on those found guilty of crimes involving Class A drugs should be done."

The attitude of the British courts towards sentencing in respect of drug trafficking offences is not dissimilar to that of the Australian courts. In *McCarthy* v. *The Queen* (1988) 38 A.Crim.R. 407 it was held that those who deal in heroin in substantial quantities must expect to be treated harshly. It is not relevant to argue that the sentence imposed results in a release date similar to that which would apply had life imprisonment been imposed: *Wong* (1988) 39 A.Crim.R. 1 (New South Wales Court of Criminal Appeal).

The guidelines regarding Class A drugs are summarised below. It should be noted that the sentences stated in relation to the importation of heroin reflect the guidance given in *Bilinski* (1988) 86 Cr.App.R. 146 which "raised" the starting figures in (i) and (ii) *infra*, from those expressed in *Aramah* (*i.e.* from seven years to 10 years; and from 12 years to 14 years).

(a) Importation of heroin, etc.

(i)	Amounts valued over £1 million	14 years	**14–14**
(ii)	Amounts valued over £100,000	10 to 14 years or more	
(iii)	An "appreciable" amount	normally 4 years.	

(b) Supplying heroin

"The sentence will largely depend on the degree of involvement, the amount of trafficking and the value of drug being handled," (*per* Lord Lane C.J.: *Aramah* (1983) 76 Cr.App.R. 190, 192). A sentence of less than three years would seldom be justified. The nearer the source of supply the defendant was shown to be, the heavier would be the sentence.   **14–15**

(c) Simple possession of heroin

"It is at this level that the circumstances of the individual offender become of much greater importance. Indeed the possible variety of considerations is so wide, including often those of a medical nature, that it is impossible to lay down any practical guidelines ... The maximum penalty for simple possession of Class A drugs is seven years' imprisonment and a fine, and there will be very many cases where deprivation of liberty is both appropriate and expedient." (*per* Lord Lane C.J., *Aramah*, *supra*, 193.)   **14–16**

II. Class B Drugs

Cannabis was singled out by the Court of Appeal as being the drug most likely to be exercising the minds of the courts.   **14–17**

(a)	*Importation*	
	Massive quantities	10 years
	Over 20 kgs	3 to 6 years
	Up to 20 kgs	18 months to 3 years

(b) *Supply*

Massive quantities ....10 years

Other cases ....1 to 4 years

(c) *Possession*

Small amounts/personal use ....Fines

Persistent flouting ....Possible custodial

III. Is *ARAMAH* OUT OF DATE?

14–18   Judicial concern had been expressed that the level of sentencing for serious drug offences was too low and this was particularly true after Parliament passed the Controlled Drugs (Penalties) Act 1985, which increased from 14 years' to life imprisonment, sentences in respect of the supply and importation/exportation of Class A drugs. Therefore some revision of the guidelines in *Aramah* (*supra*) was required to take account of the higher ceiling in respect of such drugs. In any event, in *Gilmore, The Times*, May 21, 1986 the Court of Appeal felt that "the time had come" when it was necessary to move up the level of sentencing for such offences. May L.J. expressed the same view in *Ansari* (1985) 7 Cr.App.R.(S.) 312, C.A. and again in *Obliyaei* (October 14, 1985; unreported; 2267C85) although, in both cases, the Court of Appeal felt constrained to apply the guidelines in *Aramah*.

Such expressions of judicial opinion have not gone unheeded for in *Bilinski* (1988) 86 Cr.App.R. 146, Lord Lane C.J. looked again at *Aramah*, but only in so far as it applied to Class A drugs, and advised that, (*a*) where the street value of the consignment was in the order of £100,000 or more, the starting point should no longer be seven years but 10 years, and (*b*) where the street value of the consignment was £1 million or more the starting point should be increased from 12 years' imprisonment to 14 years. Accordingly, B, having pleaded guilty to importing 3.035 kilogrammes of heroin of 90 per cent. purity, had his sentence of 12 years' imprisonment reduced to eight years.

14–19   The court in *Bilinski* made no other changes to the guidelines in *Aramah*. However, at the time *Bilinski* was decided, confusion had arisen as to whether the sentences suggested in *Aramah*, in so far as they related to drugs in Class B and Class C, were too low: see, for example, *Beaumont* [1987] Crim.L.R. 786, a case concerning the supply of cannabis. Since that time, a line of cases has repeated that the sentencing guidelines expressed in *Aramah* (1983) 76 Cr.App.R. 190 remain the same, notwithstanding increased penalties in respect of Class A drugs under the Controlled Drugs (Penalties) Act 1985: see *Daly* (1988) 9 Cr.App.R.(S.) 519 and *Fleming* (1989) 89 Cr.App.R. 225.

There is some evidence that the Court of Appeal will depart from the guidelines in *Aramah* if it is appropriate to do so. Thus, in *Brown* (June 16, 1986; unreported; 769B86; Rose J.) a sentence of five years' imprisonment was upheld where B possessed less than one kilogramme of cannabis resin intending to supply it. B had previous convictions for drug possession and supplying. Rose J. remarked that *Aramah* laid down guidelines only and that a deterrent sentence was appropriate in the circumstances.

F. THE VALUE OF CITING SENTENCING DECISIONS

Aramah (1983) 76 Cr.App.R. 190 represents something of a landmark in　**14–20**
our law because it marks the first of a line of cases which offer guidance to
sentencers in respect of a number of different areas of the law. In one sense
everything said in these cases should be treated as *obiter*, but it is, of course,
very persuasive and should do much to produce consistent sentencing in this
country. However, as the Court of Appeal has remarked on several occasions,
decisions such as *Aramah* provide guidance only and must not be seen as laying down rigid rules to be applied strictly in every case: see *Nicholas*, *The
Times*, April 23, 1986, *per* Lord Lane C.J. and *Brown* (June 16, 1986; unreported; 769B86).

For this reason, the extent to which "guideline" cases and other sentencing
authorities may properly be cited has yet to be satisfactorily resolved. The
author once heard Lord Widgery C.J. severely castigate counsel for sentencing such authorities to the court on the grounds that each case had to be
decided on its own facts. In *De Havilland* (1983) 5 Cr.App.R.(S.) 109 (at
114), Dunn L.J. fired "a warning shot" regarding the increasing practice of
citing sentencing decisions of the Court of Appeal when he said:

> "...the appropriate sentence is a matter for the discretion of the sentenc-
> ing judge. It follows that decisions on sentencing are not binding author-
> ities ... Indeed they could not be, since the circumstances of the offence
> and of the offender present an almost infinite variety from case to case ...
> Occasionally this Court suggests guidelines for sentences ... But the sen-
> tencer retains his discretion within the guidelines, or even to depart from
> them if the particular circumstances of the case justify departure."

By contrast, in *McEvilly*, *The Times*, November 4, 1986, C.A., Lord Lane　**14–21**
C.J. expressed the view that public money expended on unnecessary sentencing appeals might have been avoided if *Current Sentencing Practice* (Sweet &
Maxwell, looseleaf edition) had been drawn to the trial judge's attention. It is
submitted that there can be nothing improper in the citation of "guideline"
cases but the value in citing other sentencing cases must be a matter of professional judgment.

G. SENTENCING EXAMPLES

I. HEROIN

(a) Importations

In *Tim-Loy* [1974] Crim.L.R. 59 T, aged 37 years, imported heroin　**14–22**
worth £150,000. No previous convictions. Sentenced to 10 years' imprisonment.
　Held: Appeal dismissed.

In *Poh* [1982] Crim.L.R. 132, two appellants aged 64 years and 58 years imported 32 kilogrammes of heroin in two cars. Total value of the heroin was about £5 million. The appellants contended that they were not the prime movers. They were sentenced to 14 years' imprisonment, the maximum sentence at that time.

Held: Appeal dismissed. They had allowed themselves to become involved in the moving of drugs on an enormous scale and therefore they had forfeited any rights to humanitarian consideration.

14–23 *Meah* (1990) 12 Cr.App.R.(S.) 461, M1, aged 27, imported 136 grammes of heroin (37 per cent. purity) worth £17,000. M2, aged 26, imported 57 grammes of heroin (40 per cent. purity) worth £6,806. The drug was intended for personal consumption: see *Newton* hearing. Previous convictions of both irrelevant; M1's sentence of six years reduced to three years. M2's sentence of four years reduced to two years.

> "... it is not right to say that [importation] must be treated simply as a case of possession ... if the quantity is substantial, the result may well be immediate imprisonment for a substantial period": *per* Jupp J. at 464.

Olumide (1988) 9 Cr.App.R.(S.) 364. Sentence of seven years upheld for importing 140.9 grammes of heroin with a street value of £11,000. Defendant 36 years of age with previous conviction for unlawfully importing five kilogrammes of cannabis into the United Kingdom in 1981.

Kamis (January 31, 1992; unreported; Maidstone Crown Court). Turkish lorry driver sentenced to 14 years' imprisonment, for knowingly importing 65.5 kilogrammes of heroin (street value £8.6 million) concealed in two tyres. Defendant pleaded guilty; he was of good character and middle-aged; he anticipated receiving £21,000 reward and readily admitted his guilt to customs officers.

(b) Supplying/possession with intent

14–24 In *Ashraf* [1982] Crim.L.R. 132, H stopped in a car and found to be in possession of 52 grammes of heroin, worth £5,200, which he had obtained from A. A was found in possession of 45 grammes of heroin. H admitted being concerned with drug deals. H sentenced to 10 years; A sentenced to seven years.

Held: Beginners or not, anyone who trades in dangerous drugs, particularly heroin, must expect very severe sentences when caught. The sentences could not be criticised.

14–25 The court will of course take into account the period of time the defendant has been engaged in supplying heroin, the purity of the drug involved and the volume of business.

In *France* (1984) 6 Cr.App.R.(S.) 283 F was a modest supplier of heroin over a few weeks and sold drugs to finance his own habit. Sentenced to four years' imprisonment.

Held: sentence upheld.

In *Gee* (1984) 6 Cr.App.R.(S.) 86. A sentence of six years was reduced to four years where G sold heroin to feed his own addiction and not for profit. He supplied on a small scale on a social basis.

Hutton (1988) 9 Cr.App.R.(S.) 484; conspiracy to supply heroin. A supplied H on two occasions with two or three grammes of heroin (£300). Both pleaded guilty. Sentences from six years, in the case of A, to four years; and in the case of H, from four years to three years.

(c) Possession

Eliot (1988) 10 Cr.App.R.(S.) 454; 30 months upheld for possession of　　**14–26**
10.7 grammes of heroin (purity unknown); guilty plea; E admitted buying 12 grammes for £600.

II. LSD

(a) Importation and supply

In *Humphrey* (1981) 3 Cr.App.R.(S.) 63, the Court of Appeal held that a　　**14–27**
sentence of three years' imprisonment, imposed on a man of good character who had unlawfully imported sufficient LSD for 1,999 doses, was neither manifestly excessive nor wrong in principle. This was so despite his good character, his determination to rehabilitate himself and his expression of remorse.

Again, in *McCullough* (1982) 4 Cr.App.R.(S.) 363, a sentence of six years' imprisonment was upheld for conspiracy to supply LSD. He was found to be in possession of enough LSD to make 8,000 doses and planned to import and to sell LSD on a substantial scale. Two thousand doses had already been sold.

III. MORPHINE

(a) Importation

Cases involving the importation of morphine are relatively uncommon　　**14–28**
since it is not a substance popular with drug users. However, in *Ahmad* (1980) 2 Cr.App.R.(S.) 19, C.A. a sentence of seven years' imprisonment was upheld for the importation of 991 grammes of morphine even though the appellant was a man of previous good character who acted as a courier. This case must now be viewed in the light of the guidelines in *Aramah* (1983) 76 Cr.App.R. 190 and *Bilinski* (1988) 86 Cr.App.R. 146.

IV. COCAINE

(a) Importation

14–29   Although *Aramah* focused its attention on heroin cases, in fact no distinction is to be made between the types of Class A drugs: see *Martinez* (1984) 6 Cr.App.R.(S.) 364 where the court drew attention to the dangers of cocaine. M, a man of good character, was sentenced to four years' imprisonment for the importation of 23.7 grammes of cocaine, worth £3,000. *Held*: appeal dismissed.

> In *Parada* (1984) 6 Cr.App.R.(S.) 219, six years' imprisonment was imposed on two couriers, aged 25 and 26, who imported cocaine worth £500,000.
> *Held*: appeal dismissed.
>
> In *Taan* (1982) 4 Cr.App.R.(S.) 17, a 12-year sentence of imprisonment was upheld for being concerned in the importation of £2.5 million worth of cocaine. T was involved in the organisation of the trade having booked and paid for the tickets of two co-defendants.
> No assistance of any sort had been given to the Customs and Excise.

14–30   In *Suermondt* (1982) 4 Cr.App.R.(S.) 5, 10 years' imprisonment was upheld for the unlawful importation of about 10 kilogrammes of cocaine transported in three consignments. S bought the drug in Peru and intended to sell it in England. Value: £1,400,000. S was aged 32; had been a deep sea diver for six years whereupon he had been injured. Fined $600 in Australia for the unlawful importation of heroin; visited Peru on business; pleaded guilty; gave information concerning a corrupt airline official.

> *Radjabi-Tori* (1990) 12 Cr.App.R.(S.) 375. Nine years upheld for importing 989 grammes of cocaine (85 per cent.), sent by post. 40 years of age with no convictions. Street value £120,000; deliberate importation for his own profit.
>
> *Lawson* (1987) 9 Cr.App.R.(S.) 52. Six years upheld for importation of 98 grammes of cocaine (70 per cent.); guilty plea. L of good character; a courier but a determined smuggler.

14–31   *Gasper* (1988) 10 Cr.App.R.(S.) 173; 10 years upheld for the unlawful importation of four kilogrammes of cocaine (£927,000) carried in a body belt; appellant pleaded guilty; and see *Vrana* (December 18, 1991; unreported; 90/4023/82).

> *Jara* [1988] Crim.L.R. 551; D and J imported cocaine; H (retailer) and C (book-keeper) convicted of supplying cocaine and possession with intent to supply cocaine. D, 20 years; J, 18 years; H, 10 years; C, five years. On appeal sentences reduced: D and J, 12 years; H, eight years; C, four years. D gave information which led to arrest of H and others.

Vivancos [1988] Crim.L.R. 629. Six years upheld for unlawfully importing 399 grammes of cocaine (42 per cent.; worth £30,000). Initially denied knowledge, subsequently admitted packet contained cocaine; purported to co-operate in trapping the organiser but organiser not found. Co-operation not long or detailed and did not result in apprehension. V did the least that could be expected in the circumstances.

The Court of Appeal in *Mariotti* (December 12, 1984; unreported; 6203B83) made it plain that only severe punishment could be expected if cocaine was imported for whatever reason. Accordingly, a mother who wished to bring her family to England and therefore imported £12,000 worth of cocaine, had her appeal against a six-year sentence dismissed.

(b) Supplying

In *Aramah* it was said that a sentence of less than three years is seldom justi- **14–32**
fied in cases involving the supplying of Class A drugs.

> In *Davies* (1982) 4 Cr.App.R.(S.) 302, D pleaded guilty to possessing 6.5 grammes of cocaine with intent to supply and bought 10 grammes from M-P. M-P was convicted of possessing 20 grammes of cocaine with intent to supply. D sentenced to 15 months' imprisonment. M-P sentenced to four years' imprisonment. M-P had 14 previous convictions. *Held*: appeals dismissed.

Marshall-Price was clearly more heavily implicated than Davies. Police raided Marshall-Price's flat which was plainly a safe house for drug trafficking. The doors and windows were lined with steel. The court observed that "it is inevitable that people supplying hard drugs will be sent to prison and, as a general rule, the sentence of imprisonment is to be measured in terms of years and not months" (*per* Griffiths L.J. at 302).

> In *Longley-Knight* (1988) 10 Cr.App.R.(S.) 147; 28 months' detention reduced to 22 months (giving two months' credit in respect of time spent in custody pending sentence) for the unlawful importation of 197.42 grammes of cocaine (worth £30,000). Female appellant aged 16; travelled with accomplice aged 18. An adult would expect seven years; appellant played a lesser role than her accomplice.

> *Samuels* (1990) 12 Cr.App.R.(S.) 118. Seven years reduced to five for possessing with intent to supply 13.96 grammes of cocaine (52 per cent.). Sold cocaine on five occasions; profit between £300 to £400 on each sale; contested trial.
> > "The starting point for this type of offence should in general now be five years at least, both for supplying and for possession with intent to supply": *per* Lord Lane C.J., and see *Satvir Singh* (1988) 10 Cr.App.R.(S.) 402.

(c) Importation or possession for personal use

14–33   Clearly the fact that the drugs were intended for personal consumption is a mitigating factor but offenders, even if they are of previous good character, are in great danger of receiving an immediate custodial sentence. Where the amount involved is appreciable then such a result is almost inevitable. Thus, in *Keech (Walter)* (1984) 6 Cr.App.R.(S.) 402, K, a famous television personality, pleaded guilty to the unlawful importation of 36.7 grammes of cocaine (worth £4,500) which was contained in a shaving cream can. K obviously knew the risks involved and took careful steps to evade the prohibition on importation. His appeal, against an immediate sentence of nine months' imprisonment, was dismissed.

However, in *Diamond* (1985) 7 Cr.App.R.(S.) 152, a sentence of eight months' imprisonment, of which six months were ordered to be suspended, plus the imposition of a £4,000 fine, was upheld where D, aged 34 years and of good character, was convicted of possessing cocaine.

V. CANNABIS

(a) Importation

14–34   In *Price* (1985) 7 Cr.App.R.(S.) 190, a sentence of seven years' imprisonment was reduced to five years in connection with the importation of 60.80 kilogrammes of cannabis. The quantity was substantial and clearly fell within the three- to six-year tariff suggested by the Court of Appeal in *Aramah*.

Again, in *Abdut* (1981) 3 Cr.App.R.(S.) 100, a sentence of five years was reduced to three years' imprisonment in respect of a man of good character, aged 43 years, who imported 43.65 kilogrammes of herbal cannabis. The court had regard to the fact that what was being imported was not a Class A drug; that the appellant was a man of good character; a model prisoner who would be unable to have any visits from his family because they resided in Ghana as he normally did.

> *Daly* [1988] Crim.L.R. 258; five years reduced to two years in the case of Daly for the unlawful importation of 15 kilogrammes of herbal cannabis. In the case of Whyte, four years' imprisonment was reduced to two-and-a-half years for the unlawful importation of 12 kilogrammes of herbal cannabis. Both defendants pleaded guilty. Whyte's offence was more sophisticated: and see *Watson* (1988) 10 Cr.App.R.(S.) 256.

14–35   The court will obviously analyse the role played by the defendant in a smuggling venture. Thus, in *Chisti* (1981) 3 Cr.App.R.(S.) 99, the Court of Appeal reduced from nine years to six years a sentence of imprisonment imposed on the appellant for the importation of one-third of a ton of cannabis with a street value of over £600,000. The appellant was a Pakistani, 47 years of age, of previous good character who was not the principal in the transaction.

In *Forsythe* (1980) 2 Cr.App.R.(S.) 15 S, aged 60 years and of previous good character, suggested to his father a scheme for unlawfully importing into the United Kingdom cannabis packed into furniture. Some 152.7 kilogrammes had been imported in this way. In 1980, the value to the importer was about £78,000 and some £200,000 at street level. He was sentenced to 10 years' imprisonment.

Held: this sentence would be reduced to five years' imprisonment.

The court accepted in *Forsythe* the appellant's contention that the original sentence was out of accord with sentences imposed in other cases which clearly it was.

A partly suspended sentence of imprisonment is not appropriate for either a courier or an organiser of a drug smuggling venture. The policy of the court is to deter other couriers and not simply to punish the individual: see *Dawson* (1982) 4 Cr.App.R.(S.) 360.

(b) Possession with intent to supply

Elder (1990) 12 Cr.App.R.(S.) 337; two-and-a-half years' imprisonment **14–36** reduced to 21 months. Pleaded guilty to possessing 22 deals weighing 31 grammes to sell at £5 each. E had 10 previous convictions but was operating at the very bottom end of the market: and see *Sanderman* (1989) 11 Cr.App.R.(S.) 165.

Finkhouse (1990) 12 Cr.App.R.(S.) 17. Two years reduced to 15 months with nine months to serve. Pleaded guilty to possessing 23 deals weighing $\frac{1}{8}$oz. each of cannabis worth £300. Had supplied $\frac{5}{8}$ozs. of cannabis over three to four weeks; aged 23; no previous convictions.

Cook (1990) 12 Cr.App.R.(S.) 374. Three years reduced to two years for possessing with intent to supply 631 grammes of cannabis resin. C was 26 years of age with numerous convictions: see also *MacDonald* (1983) 5 Cr.App.R.(S.) 22.

Hudson v. *H.M. Advocate*, 1990 S.C.C.R. 200. Four years' imprisonment upheld for the unlawful possession of 426.8 grammes of cannabis resin with intent to supply contrary to section 5(3) of the M.D.A. The drug was intended for friends and not commercial supply.

(c) Importation of cannabis oil

Aramah (1983) 76 Cr.App.R. 190 was applied in *Briggs* (June 12, 1984; **14–37** unreported; 392B84). A sentence of five years' imprisonment was held to be correct for the unlawful importation of 3¼ kilogrammes of cannabis oil. An estimate of its street value was given as £50,000. It was not possible to accurately equate the oil with an amount of cannabis resin of equivalent strength. The court had to look at the case on broader lines.

(d) Importation and possession of cannabis for personal use

14–38   In *Atherton* (June 14, 1984; unreported; 1271C84) a sentence of nine months' imprisonment was upheld on appeal, in respect of a consignment of 1.13 kilogrammes of cannabis which was sent to D in a parcel for D's own use.

Ordinarily, possession of a very small amount of cannabis for the defendant's personal use would not result in a custodial sentence but a continuous or persistent flouting of the law might justify a short custodial sentence: see *Aramah* (*supra*); *Osbourne* (1982) 4 Cr.App.R.(S.) 262; *Jones* (1981) 3 Cr.App.R.(S.) 5 and *Robertson-Coupar* [1982] Crim.L.R. 536.

VI. THE COURTS' ATTITUDE TOWARDS COURIERS

14–39   In *Aramah* (1983) 76 Cr.App.R. 190, the Court of Appeal remarked that the good character of a courier, as he usually was, is of less importance than the good character of a defendant in other cases. In the judgment of the court, the reason why this should be is that drug-smuggling organisers deliberately recruit persons who will exercise the sympathy of the court. Thus, students and the sick and the elderly were (and are) often employed as couriers. They are vulnerable to suggestion and vulnerable to the offer of quick profit. The court was concerned that such smugglers would also believe that the courts might be moved to misplaced sympathy in their cases. Similar considerations had been voiced a year earlier by Lawton L.J. in *Hamouda* (1982) 4 Cr.App.R.(S.) 137; see also *Anderson* [1981] Crim.L.R. 270.

It is a fact that many couriers are extremely vulnerable. Many of them are foreigners, often astonishingly uneducated, poor, naive and frequently have never travelled beyond their own region let alone to another country. They are therefore easy targets for the smuggler. Furthermore, they are expendable. They are easy targets for the officers of Customs and Excise who quickly spot a bewildered, nervous and sometimes plainly inept visitor. By imposing deterrent sentences on couriers, the courts in this country, and elsewhere, hope that the "word will be spread" and so deter others from acting as couriers. But achieving success in that way perhaps depends on the making of too many assumptions which, given the vulnerability of the type of person being considered, cannot realistically be made. Having said that, the courts are undoubtedly put in a very difficult position.

VII. NEWTON HEARINGS/FACTUAL BASIS FOR SENTENCE

14–40   It has to be remembered that a courier may not always know precisely what he is carrying. He may be told that it is something prohibited from importation into England but he does not always appreciate what the substance is, *e.g.* cannabis or heroin. Although narcotics are expensive to buy in the United Kingdom, drugs such as heroin and cannabis are astonishingly cheap to buy in the producing country and it would be idle to suppose that some organisers do not think it tactically advantageous to keep the courier "in the dark" as to the precise substance he will be asked to carry. After all, how much does the organiser really stand to lose, compared to the vast profits which he may expect to make, sooner or later? For the purposes of a charge under the C.E.M.A. it does not matter what the defendant believes the goods to be so long as he knew them to be prohibited from importation: see *Hussain* [1969] 2 Q.B. 567, and *Hennessey* (1978) 68 Cr.App.R. 419. Again, for the purposes of a charge under the M.D.A., his ignorance (subject to section 28 of the Act) as to the quality of the thing, will afford him no defence. But a mistaken belief that the offending drug is of a different kind from that which he had been told it was is a mitigating factor: see *Ghandi* (1986) 8 Cr.App.R.(S.) 391, and similarly, a mistaken belief that the goods imported were of a totally different character, *e.g.* pornographic videos, is also a mitigating factor: see *Ellis* (1987) 84 Cr.App.R. 235, 248.

However, in *Bilinski* (1988) 86 Cr.App.R. 146, B pleaded guilty to im- **14–41** porting 3.036 kilogrammes of heroin. He claimed that he believed the packages contained cannabis although a book found in his possession seemed to relate to the topic of heroin. He was sentenced to 12 years' imprisonment. The trial judge had taken the view that the appellant's view was irrelevant and therefore declined to hear evidence about it in accordance with the principles set out in *Newton* (1982) 4 Cr.App.R.(S.)388. The Court of Appeal held that the appellant's belief was relevant to sentence and that the man who believed he was importing cannabis was less culpable than the man who knew it to be heroin. However, to what extent such a belief mitigated the sentence would depend on the facts in each case including the degree of care exercised by a defendant. In *Bilinski* the mitigating effect of B's belief (if held) was small but the appeal was allowed on that and other grounds.

If a defendant's story is patently false then the judge is entitled to reject it without hearing evidence: see *Hawkins* (1985) 7 Cr.App.R.(S.) 351 and *Bilinski* (*ibid.*). The decision of *Mackenzie* (1985) 7 Cr.App.R.(S.) 441, which suggested a contrary proposition, may no longer be good law.

Furthermore, the calling of evidence if disbelieved, or if it only repeated an **14–42** absurd and spurious explanation given by a defendant, may considerably nullify any discount to be gained from a plea of guilty: see *Walton* [1987] Crim.L.R. 512; *Stevens* (1986) 8 Cr.App.R.(S.) 297; *Jauncey* (1986) 8 Cr.App.R.(S.) 401 and *Mackenzie* (*supra*).

If the trial judge does accept the defendant's explanation, the next question is to what extent is the sentencer bound to sentence the defendant on the basis of his explanation? This is particularly important on the question of the value of the goods involved, or believed to be involved, because the guidelines in *Aramah* are based substantially on the street value of drugs. Suppose a smuggler believed that he was importing one kilogramme of cannabis worth £1,500 whereas he imported one kilogramme of heroin worth £200,000. If he were truly to be sentenced accordingly to his belief then the sentence he might expect to receive is a maximum of 18 months' imprisonment, and not (if his belief were otherwise) a sentence of 10 years' imprisonment or more.

The answer seems to be simply this: a mistaken belief as to the type of goods **14–43** imported or handled is only a mitigating *consideration*. It does not entitle the defendant to be sentenced on that basis as such at all. The relevant value is therefore the street price of the drug involved. The defendant's error merely entitles him to a discount which, depending on the facts of the case (including the degree of care exercised by him), may be substantial or it may be negligible: see *Bilinski* (*supra*).

Not every contentious issue raised during mitigation is a suitable matter for inquiry by the trial judge. So where a defendant with many previous convictions alleges that he has changed his lifestyle and reformed himself, a Newton hearing is not appropriate: *Odey* (1984) 6 Cr.App.R.(S.) 318, C.A. But where a defendant claims that he imported a large quantity of drugs for his own consumption then this is just the sort of case where a judge should hold a Newton hearing unless the suggestion is so absurd that it can be rejected out of hand: *Meah* (1991) 92 Cr.App.R. 254. In that case Meah unlawfully imported 150 packets of heroin (136 grammes of 37 per cent. purity worth £16,930) of which almost 70 packets had been swallowed. Marlow unlawfully imported 71 packets of heroin (worth £6,806) of which 32 packets had been swallowed. In each case the appellants claimed that the drugs were intended for personal consumption. In neither case did the judge hold a Newton hearing. In reducing Meah's sentence from six years to three years, and Marlow's sentence from four years to two years, the Court of Appeal held that in having declined to hold a Newton hearing, the judge had to sentence on the basis that he had accepted that these large quantities of the drugs were intended for personal consumption. Jupp J. added (at 257):

> "If a judge does think it right to sentence on the basis that drugs have been brought in for a man's personal consumption, it will still be a serious offence and, if the quantity is substantial, the result may well be immediate imprisonment for a substantial period."

The reader should also be mindful of the observations of the Court of Appeal in *Mohun* [1992] Crim.L.R. 598.

VIII. BURDEN AND STANDARD OF PROOF

14–44   The defence version must be accepted unless the judge, or the jury, is sure that it is wrong and the Court of Appeal will not interfere with the finding unless, for example, no reasonable tribunal could have reached that result: see *Ahmed* [1985] Crim.L.R. 250, C.A. (Parker L.J.).

Curiously, in *Hall* (October 19, 1984; unreported; 3013C84), Lincoln J. remarked that where the sentence is likely to be the same whichever version is accepted, it is undesirable that the trial judge should be seen to be adopting the prosecution version. If Lincoln J. meant no more than that the benefit of the doubt should be resolved in favour of the accused, then clearly there can be no complaint, but any tribunal which is required to resolve conflicting versions should not be slow to express frankly the version it accepts or rejects. This is so even where the judge considers that the sentence is likely to be the same.

(a) Personal circumstances of the defendant

There is a substantial deterrent element to sentences imposed in respect of **14–45**
drug trafficking offences. The personal considerations of an accused are secondary: see *Aramah* (1983) 76 Cr.App.R. 190. A graphic example of just
how "secondary" these considerations can be appears in *Stark* [1992]
Crim.L.R. 384. A sentence of four years' imprisonment was upheld for the
unlawful importation of heroin worth £2,500. The appellant, who had been
H.I.V. positive, developed AIDS. His life expectancy was said to be no better
than 12 months. The appellant said he wished to die in dignity. The Court of
Appeal dismissed the appeal. There was a risk that the appellant would resort
again to drug trafficking but, in any event, the court said "It is not for the
court to manipulate the sentence to achieve a desirable social end": *per*
Jowitt J.

The result in *Stark* is supported by other authority: see *Herasymenko* (unreported) and *Aramah, ibid.* However, the approach of the courts is not
entirely consistent in this regard. In *Saunders* (1992; unreported) the Court of
Appeal reduced the sentence on the appellant convicted of offences of dishonesty (in relation to the "Guinness Affair") having regard to the appellant's
physical and mental condition.

It is no mitigation to say that a certain drug (*e.g.* cannabis) is part of one's
religion: see *Daudi* (1982) 4 Cr.App.R.(S.) 306.

(b) No challenge by prosecution

Where an explanation is put forward by the defendant which the pros- **14–46**
ecution then choose not to challenge, the judge may consider it appropriate to
sentence on that basis. Thus in *Lawless* [1981] Crim.L.R. 845, L pleaded
guilty to possessing 960 grammes of cannabis resin with intent to supply. He
claimed that he bought the drug on behalf of a syndicate of five or six persons,
and not with a view to resale. The prosecution did not challenge this version.
The Court of Appeal reduced his sentence of two years' imprisonment so as to
allow his immediate release (after having served nearly 12 months), on the
grounds that the case could not be safely treated as a commercial venture.

Of course, if the trial judge feels uneasy about the matter he may, of his own
volition, assess the defendant's version in accordance with the principles set
out in *Newton, supra.*

(c) Acceptance of pleas

When a defendant pleads guilty to "lesser counts" he is entitled to be sen- **14–47**
tenced on that basis. So where, in *Lawrence* (1981) 3 Cr.App.R.(S.) 49 the
appellant pleaded guilty to one count of cultivating cannabis plants and two
counts of possessing cannabis resin, but pleaded not guilty to a further count
of possessing a controlled drug with intent to supply (these being accepted by
the court), the judge was bound to deal with the appellant purely on the basis
that the drugs were for his own consumption.

In England and Wales, it would seem to be settled that a court may proceed to try an accused for an offence alleging possession of a controlled drug, with intent to supply it, contrary to section 5(3) of the M.D.A. notwithstanding the fact that the accused has already entered a plea of guilty to simple possession of the same drug contrary to section 5(2): see *Bebbington* (1978) 67 Cr.App.R. 285, C.A. If an accused is convicted of the section 5(3) offence, no separate penalty should be imposed for the lesser offence.

In one sense, an admission by the accused to simple possession merely assists the prosecution to prove an essential element of an offence charged under section 5(3). If the prosecution, or the court, anticipate the basis upon which a plea to simple possession is to be tendered (usually that the drug was intended for personal consumption) and that basis is not acceptable to the prosecution, or to the court, then the court need not accept such a plea, but proceed to try the accused on both counts.

The Scottish approach, however, is very different. There, an accused cannot be found guilty of more than one offence arising out of the same *species facti*: *Kyle* v. *H.M. Advocate*, 1988 S.L.T. 601. Accordingly, the Crown cannot competently pursue a charge of possession with intent to supply, in circumstances where the accused had entered a plea of guilty to simple possession so that the jury were not put in charge of the latter count and therefore had no means of knowing upon what basis that plea had been accepted: *Mattison* v. *H.M. Advocate*, 1992 S.L.T. 197.

(d) Specimen counts, etc.

14–48   Frequently the evidence in the case paints a picture of a defendant who is more heavily implicated in drug dealing than the specimen counts on the indictment actually demonstrate. In such cases there can be no objection if, having evaluated the evidence put before the jury, the judge comes to the view that the defendant should be sentenced in a way which marks that greater degree of involvement: see *Ghanderi* (October 16, 1984; unreported; 1291B83).

However, the above is very different to cases where the prosecution either fails to include sufficient or appropriate counts on the indictment to reflect the extent of an accused's involvement, or where there are sufficient counts but the defendant either pleads guilty to, or is convicted of, only some of them. In these circumstances the courts are bound to sentence on the basis of the facts of the particular offence or offences.

14–49   In *Ayensu* (1982) 4 Cr.App.R.(S.) 248, the appellants pleaded guilty to one count of unlawfully importing 46.87 grammes of cannabis. Their passports showed that they had made frequent trips between Ghana and the United Kingdom. They admitted to customs officers that they had smuggled cannabis into the United Kingdom on other occasions. A count alleging a conspiracy to import drugs was not proceeded with. Their counsel submitted that the plea represented the whole of their admissions.

The Court of Appeal held that it was the task of the Crown Court to sentence on the basis of the particular offence. The court could not take into account matters which were hotly contested or the alleged admissions given to the customs officers.

Ayensu is in accord with the decision of *O'Conner* (1981) 3 Cr.App.R.(S.) 225 but not, it would seem, with *Russen* (1981) 3 Cr.App.R.(S.) 134 where the court remarked that:

> "... the court is perfectly entitled to look at a man's statement in order to discover if the incident in question is an isolated incident or not. When it appears perfectly clear from the statement that the event in question is not an isolated incident, the court is entitled to take that into account when sentencing."

It is submitted that *Ayensu* and *O'Conner* are to be preferred.

(e) Assistance to law enforcement

This has long since been regarded as a powerful mitigating factor: see *Aramah* (1983) 76 Cr.App.R. 140. An immediate confession of guilt coupled with considerable assistance to the police or customs should therefore be marked by a substantial reduction in what would otherwise be the "proper sentence": see *Afzal, The Times*, October 14, 1989. In *Yaman* (January 14, 1992; unreported), the Court of Appeal reduced the appellant's sentence in respect of a conspiracy to supply three kilogrammes of heroin from 13 years' to 10 years' imprisonment after he had given "quite considerable assistance to police." Glidewell L.J. remarked "that fact does earn him the support of those concerned to stamp out this terrible trade."   **14-50**

The court will therefore take into account the extent of the assistance given and it should not overlook the degree of danger which can attach to such assistance being given.   **14-51**

In *Sivan* (1988) 87 Cr.App.R. 407 the court gave guidance as to how the facts of any assistance given should be furnished to the court in cases where the defendant was an informer:

> "First, it was ... advisable that there should be before the court a letter from a senior officer ... unconnected with the case, who had examined all the facts and was able to certify that the facts were as reported by the officers conducting the investigation, that is, facts relating to the assistance rendered by the defendant.
>
> Second, ... there had to be a statement in writing from the officer in charge of the investigation setting out those facts.
>
> Third, it was advisable in the more important cases that the officer in charge of the investigation should be available to give evidence if necessary, whether in court or in the judge's room as the situation might demand."

See also: *Debbag* (1991) 12 Cr.App.R.(S.) 733, and Robert Shiels, "Controlled Drugs and Assistance to the Authorities" 1991 S.L.T. 187.

(f) Social supplying

14–52 Many cases have considered the extent to which a supply of drugs to a small circle of friends of other drug users is a mitigating factor.

In *Bennett* (1981) 3 Cr.App.R.(S.) 68, the court implicitly regarded such a feature as amounting to some mitigation: see also *Smith* (1980) 2 Cr.App.R.(S.) 18 where a sentence of 12 months was upheld for an offence of possessing cannabis with intent to supply a small circle of friends for modest profit.

> In *Spinks* [1987] Crim.L.R. 786, a 23-year-old male of previous good character pleaded guilty to one offence of heroin. He and a friend agreed to buy £10 worth of heroin which they both duly consumed. Sentenced originally to 12 months' imprisonment.
>
> *Held*: too severe; sentence reduced to effect immediate release, *i.e.* equivalent to a sentence of about three months.

Although every case involving the supply of a controlled drug is a serious matter, the court will give credit for the absence of a commercial motive.

> In *Daudi* (1982) 4 Cr.App.R.(S.) 306, sentences of three months' detention and six months' imprisonment were upheld on two appellants who purchased £600 worth of cannabis on behalf of 50 members of a Rastafarian sect who had each contributed £12.

The court remarked that it would be "a denial of justice" for the court to say "because you are a Rastafarian you are entitled to be treated entirely differently from other members of the community if you chose to break the law": (*per* Griffiths L.J. at 307).

In *French* (May 12, 1986; unreported; 7476C85) sentences of three-and-a-half years' imprisonment and two-and-a-half years' were said to have erred on the side of leniency in respect of two appellants who had supplied drugs to fellow students even though they had pleaded guilty and had been frank with police.

14–53 The presence of a commercial motive, even if the drugs were to be supplied to friends, is an aggravating feature. In *Bowman-Powell* (1985) 7 Cr.App.R.(S.) 85, a sentence of four years' imprisonment was upheld in respect of the possession of 12 doses of LSD which the appellant intended to supply to friends.

The fact that a person supplies other drug users or addicts is something of a "double-edged sword." In *Guiney* (1985) 7 Cr.App.R.(S.) 200 a sentence of six years' imprisonment was reduced to four years where G had supplied other addicts with heroin. G was a "small-time supplier." See also *Hyams* (1983) 5 Cr.App.R.(S.) 312 and *Gee* (1984) 6 Cr.App.R.(S.) 86.

(g) Importing drugs intending to re-export them

14–54 There is in fact no mitigation at all in the argument that the drugs were merely in transit to another country, or were not intended for distribution in the United Kingdom: see *Mbelu* (1981) 3 Cr.App.R.(S.) 157 and *Winter* [1973] Crim.L.R. 63, C.A.

The drug trade is an international business carried on to the detriment of citizens of all civilised countries. Accordingly, this country owes a duty to other civilised countries to deter the trade: *per* Griffiths L.J. in *Otjen* (1981) 3 Cr.App.R.(S.) 186, and see *Chukwu* (May 10, 1984; unreported; 1433C84).

(h) Is police entrapment mitigation?

In *Sang* [1980] A.C. 402, the House of Lords held that although a trial **14–55** judge had no discretion, except in the case of confessions, to refuse to admit evidence merely because it had been improperly obtained, nevertheless, it could be a significant factor in mitigation. Lord Fraser of Tullybelton said (at 446 A/B.):

> "The degree of guilt may be modified by the inducement and that can appropriately be reflected in the sentence: see *Birtles* [1969] 1 W.L.R. 1047 and *Browning* v. *J.W.H. Watson (Rochester) Ltd.* where Lord Goddard C.J. pointed out that the court could even grant an absolute discharge in such circumstances."

Consequently in *Petfield* (unreported; 407E86) Kennedy J. accepted that there had been police entrapment which led to P and C possessing 1.78 kilogrammes of cannabis and 27.62 grammes of amphetamine, with intent to supply it. The judge took account of it and sentenced P and C to 21 months' imprisonment and 12 months' imprisonment respectively.

Each case will of course depend on its own facts. It is well known that many **14–56** drug operations, particularly elaborately planned ventures, come to light and are successfully prosecuted as a result of police or Customs and Excise "undercover" work. This may include an officer posing as an interested purchaser of narcotics in order to ascertain who the suppliers, or importers, are in a distribution network. Such work is sometimes dangerous and without it many serious cases would go undetected. Is it therefore to be said that, in every case, entrapment is a significant mitigating factor?

In *Underhill* (1979) 1 Cr.App.R.(S.) 270, it is submitted that the Court of Appeal took a realistic view. The appellant was encouraged to sell a quantity of drug to a police officer who, on one view of the facts, instigated the offence. But the court declined to treat this feature as mitigation on the grounds that the appellant was, in any event, ready to sell the drugs to anybody who was willing to pay the price. The court suggested that one would have to inquire whether the offence, or one like it, would have been committed notwithstanding the involvement of police and, secondly, whether investigating officers "crossed the line" between legitimate infiltration of criminal activities and conduct which could "fairly be condemned as illegitimate instigation."

> In *Beaumont* [1987] Crim.L.R. 786 B pleaded guilty to being concerned in the supply of cannabis. Undercover agents asked B if she knew anyone who would supply them with cannabis. B suggested her father and took the agents to meet him whereupon he produced a quantity of cannabis

and was arrested along with B. B was sentenced to two years' imprisonment. The judge ignored the entrapment aspect. B was also pregnant.

Held: the trial judge was wrong to ignore entrapment and the sentence would be reduced to 12 months of which six months would be suspended.

14–57 It is not clear from the report whether B was a person of previous good character or not, or whether the prosecution alleged that she had been concerned in the supply of cannabis on other occasions. Clearly, where a person of good character is entrapped, and there is no reason to believe that the offence would have been committed but for the instigation of the officers, or agents, then the entrapment must be quite substantial mitigation. However, on the facts of *Beaumont*, it is obvious that the appellant's father was ready and willing to sell cannabis and B undoubtedly acted in concert with him. Unfortunately, it is not apparent from the report whether the court applied the principles expressed in *Underhill* (1979) 1 Cr.App.R.(S.) 270 and therefore *Beaumont*, as reported, should be treated with caution: see also *Chapman* (1989) 11 Cr.App.R.(S.) 222 and *Mackey* [1992] Crim.L.R. 602.

IX. PENALTIES: SCHEDULE 4 TO THE M.D.A.

SCHEDULE 4

(as amended by the Criminal Law Act 1977, the Magistrates' Court Act 1980, the Criminal Justice Act 1982 and the Controlled Drug (Penalties) Act 1985)

Section	Offence	Mode	Class A	Class B	Class C	General
s.4(2)	Production	S	6 months or [£2000] or both	6 months or [£2000] or both	3 months or [£500] or both	—
		I	Life or a fine or both	14 years or a fine or both	5 years or a fine or both	—
s.4(3)	Supplying	S	6 months or [£2000] or both	6 months or [£2000] or both	3 months or [£500] or both	—
		I	Life or a fine or both	14 years or a fine or both	5 years or a fine or both	—
s.5(2)	Possession	S	6 months or [£2000] or both	3 months or £500 or both	3 months or £200 or both	—
		I	7 years or a fine or both	5 years or a fine or both	2 years or a fine or both	—
s.5(3)	Possession with intent to supply	S	6 months or [£2000] or both	6 months or [£2000] or both	3 months or £500 or both	—
		I	Life or a fine or both	14 years or a fine or both	5 years or a fine or both	—
s.6(2)	Cultivation	S	—	—	—	6 months or [£2000] or both
		I	—	—	—	14 years or a fine or both
s.8	Occupier	S	6 months or [£2000] or both	6 months or [£2000] or both	3 months or £500 or both	—
		I	14 years or a fine or both	14 years or a fine or both	5 years or a fine or both	—

Section	Offence	Mode	Class A	Class B	Class C	General
s.9	Opium	S	—	—	—	6 months or [£2000] or both
		I	—	—	—	14 years or a fine or both
s.9A	Supply articles	S	—	—	—	6 months or level 5
s.11(2)	Safe custody	S	—	—	—	6 months or [£2000] or both
		I	—	—	—	2 years or a fine or both
s.12(6)	Practitioner prescribing	S	6 months or [£2000] or both	6 months or [£2000] or both	3 months or £500 or both	—
		I	14 years or a fine or both	14 years or a fine or both	5 years or a fine or both	—
s.13(3)	Practitioner prescribing	S	6 months or [£2000] or both	6 months or [£2000] or both	3 months or £500 or both	—
		I	14 years or a fine or both	14 years or a fine or both	5 years or a fine or both	—
s.17(3)	Information relating to supply	S	—	—	—	level 3
		I	—	—	—	—
s.17(4)	Giving false information	S	—	—	—	6 months or [£2000] or both
		I	—	—	—	2 years or a fine or both
s.18(1)	Regulation contravention	S	—	—	—	6 months or [£2000] or both
		I	—	—	—	2 years or a fine or both

Section	Offence	Mode	Class A	Class B	Class C	General
s.18(2)	Licence contravention	S	—	—	—	6 months or [£2000] or both
		I	—	—	—	2 years or a fine or both
s.18(3)	False information	S	—	—	—	6 months or [£2000] or both
		I	—	—	—	2 years or a fine or both
s.18(4)	Obtaining licence falsely	S	—	—	—	6 months or [£2000] or both
		I	—	—	—	2 years or a fine or both
s.20	Assisting an offence under corresponding law	S	—	—	—	6 months or [£2000] or both
		I	—	—	—	14 years or a fine or both
s.23(4)	Obstruction	S	—	—	—	6 months or [£2000] or both
		I	—	—	—	2 years or a fine or both

Key
S = Summary trial
I = Trial on indictment
[.] = Fine being the "prescribed sum."

Chapter 15
A General Guide to Drug Misuse

15–01   Frequently the courts are asked to draw inferences of fact from "the surrounding circumstances" of the case. Yet, in a high proportion of cases involving drugs, the relevant circumstances will display a way of life that is often totally alien to the majority of the population. Therefore, without some knowledge of drug misuse, it is no easy matter to find, let alone accurately interpret, the necessary hallmarks that point the way to the truth. It is important to remember that many of the reasons for drug-taking, coupled with the methods of drug use and abuse, are as various as they are personal and liable to change as quickly as fashion and personal techniques bend with current market forces, medical and public influences or other social or delinquent trends.

Accordingly, this Chapter is included to provide a few basic facts and principles applicable to the types of drugs under consideration, the methods of their misuse and their consequential effects. The information is provided for *guidance* only and is therefore necessarily descriptive. Astonishingly, courts often find themselves trying drug cases with little or no scientific help. The importance of adducing sound expert evidence (except in obviously straightforward cases) cannot be too strongly emphasised.

Having regard to the above, little is to be gained by describing every controlled drug. Instead, the main categories have been defined by their "type," *e.g.* opiates, hallucinogenics and so on. Within each category or "type," only the most popularly abused drugs are described. Nevertheless they serve as useful examples of other drugs of the same class.

A. TYPES OF DRUG

I. OPIATES

15–02   These are some of the most dangerous drugs abused. They include heroin, opium, morphine, DF 118, methadone (physeptone), dipipanone (diconal), and pethidine. All were developed as pain relievers of varying degrees of strength. All share the fact that they are physically and psychologically addictive. Tolerance can develop alarmingly and it is not uncommon to find heroin addicts who consume up to half a gramme of heroin per day in order to fight off the effects of withdrawal.

(a) Heroin

Towards the end of the nineteenth century, diamorphine hydrochloride, a 15–03 derivative of morphine, was synthetically produced to serve as a powerful pain reliever. Termed "heroin" in 1899 (from the Greek, "hero"), the drug was recognised as having the ability to inflate the personality. Today, heroin is widely abused for that very reason.

All heroin must be imported, the majority of which now comes from Pakistan. In its purified form the drug will be a white powder, otherwise it will assume a brown or beige appearance. When put into soluble form, it is then capable of being injected (*i.e.* "mainlined"), but this practice has several very dangerous aspects. First, a host of diseases including hepatitis and AIDS may be transmitted by the use of unclean needles. Secondly, heroin is often "cut" with an inert substance in order to reduce the level of purity. Depending on the integrity of the dealer, many substances are used to dilute the drug, *e.g.* lactose or paracetamol. There have been rare instances of despicable dealers adulterating the drug with patently harmful materials such as Vim, Plaster of Paris and talcum powder, which devastate the arteries and damage various organs. Since 1988 the addition of phenbarbitone to heroin has become more frequent. This makes the treatment of heroin abuse more difficult. The reasons for "cutting" the drug are dealt with elsewhere, (see §15–31, *infra*). (It is worth noting that as heroin has become more plentiful and a greater number of "suppliers" are competing on the black market, the practice of cutting the drug with bad substances seems to be declining.) Thirdly, the rate of absorption is instantaneous but tolerance may develop more quickly.

The perils of injecting the substance have caused other methods of consumption to increase in popularity, particularly smoking the drug, colloquially referred to as "chasing the dragon." This involves putting heroin onto a piece of silver foil which is held over a small flame. The vapour/smoke is inhaled through a tube, *e.g.* a milk-shake straw or a roll of paper. Occasionally, heroin is inhaled or "snorted." The rate of absorption is slower by reason of the mucous membranes which restrict the penetration of the drug into the blood-stream. 15–04

Over the last 10 years the price of heroin, in real terms, has fallen, while its purity has increased from between 20 per cent. to 50 per cent. with an average of about 39 per cent. "Fixes" can be bought in "deals" costing as little as £5 or £10 representing approximately one-eighth of a gramme. A "deal" or "fold" is often a strip of paper measuring approximately four inches square, wrapped to form a sachet. Since heroin is being imported in ever greater quantities it is now easier for a user to acquire "bulk purchases" at a much reduced price, an important point to bear in mind when considering an allegation of possession with intent to supply the drug contrary to section 5(3) of the M.D.A. Per kilogramme, heroin may cost between £20,000 and £40,000, depending on purity (50 per cent. to 90 per cent.) Most heroin had been of Turkish or Iranian origin, but this picture is shifting with international events. Over 500kg. of heroin was seized in 1991.

According to the B.B.C. Drugwatch Survey 1985, most users will receive their first supply from a friend and then resort to a known dealer for a constant supply.

(b) Opium

15–05   The unripe seed capsules of the opium poppy (*Papaver somniferum* L) are cut to release a brown liquid. Once dried and removed from the capsules, the result is a narcotic used as a sedative and intoxicant. Opium may be raw, prepared or medicinal. (See: definitions in Part IV of Schedule 2.)

(c) Morphine

15–06   There are many alkaloids of the opium poppy of which morphine is the most valuable. Aptly named "morphine" after "Morpheus," the God of Dreams and the Son of Sleep, it is highly addictive both physically and psychologically. Tolerance also develops. It is not a popular drug with drug abusers since it produces very unpleasant side-effects.

(d) Methadone and DF 118

15–07   One widely used technique in the treatment of heroin addiction is the substitution of methadone (physeptone) or DF 118 (dihydrocodeine) for heroin. The advantages are that these drugs block the effects of withdrawal and cause less dependence than heroin. It follows that by adopting a course of substitution, using drugs that are progressively less addictive, the addict is hopefully "weaned" off his or her addiction. The technique is not without its critics because it would *not* be correct to describe either methadone or DF 118 as a "safe" drug. Both are synthetic pain relievers but are also addictive. The effects and side-effects of DF 118 are less severe than those of methadone. For that reason DF 118 is a Class B controlled drug while methadone is Class A.

(e) Dipipanone (Diconal)

15–08   This is another narcotic pain reliever capable of causing morphine-type dependence. Diconals ("dikes") contain dipipanone and cyclizine hydrochloride (an antihistamine). Only the former is controlled by the M.D.A. 1971 (Class A).

II. Psychotropic/Hallucinogenic Drugs

15–09   All such drugs are very potent and include LSD, "angel dust," DMT (dimethyltryptamine) and psilocin (from the so-called "magic mushroom"). All produce mind-bending, psychedelic effects and loosely mimic psychosis. They are not thought to be addictive but mentally disturbing experiences may be encountered causing, in extreme cases, actual mental breakdown.

(a) Lysergic Acid Diethylamide (LSD)

First synthesised in 1938 in the Sandoz Laboratories in Basle, LSD is one of **15–10**
the most powerful hallucinogens known to man. It has been used, clinically,
to treat acute alcoholics. Psychotherapists originally expressed considerable
interest in the drug, but tests produced few favourable results and interest in it
fell away when it was realised that the artificial effect of LSD on the mind differed from schizophrenia and so could not be used by psychiatrists to effectively understand, let alone treat, that type of mental disorder. LSD was
extensively abused in the 1960s and the 1970s. There are strong indications
that the drug is again increasing in popularity. The drug is difficult to detect
being colourless, tasteless and odourless, but a minute quantity produces a
colossal effect. Tracing the "factories" has proved to be a monumental task
involving a great deal of police time. Impregnated onto "dots" of paper, small
tablets, or lumps of sugar, LSD is usually taken by mouth but can also be
"snorted" or injected. Effects of the drug are unpredictable. Many cases have
been reported of users engaging in bizarre conduct as they enacted their experiences, including attempts to "fly," with occasionally fatal results. Perhaps
the most invidious aspect of the drug is its ability to cause "flashbacks" or
"ghosts," even months after the last dose in which the user resumes his psychotropic experiences.

The number of LSD seizures has increased during 1990 and 1991 (approximately 300,000 doses in 1990). Cases have been reported involving LSD papers inserted into capsules. The concentration of LSD in paper units averages
between 50 µg and 60 µg. Its street value ranges between £2 and £6 per unit.

(b) Psilocin

The mushroom, *psilocybe mexicana*, had been used by the Aztecs in some **15–11**
of their religious ceremonies. Today, it is better known as the "magic mushroom." The active constituent is *psilocin* which was first synthesised by Hoff-
man in the 1950s. The mushroom itself is probably not controlled. When
picked and chewed, the effect is mildly hallucinogenic. If the drug is extracted
then it is classified as a Class A substance.

III. COCAINE

In recent years, cocaine has come to be labelled as the "rich man's speed." **15–12**
This is not new. Cocaine has always been expensive to abuse. What is new is
the extent to which the drug has swollen in popularity in the last few years: see
Martinez (1984) 6 Cr.App.R.(S.) 364. Cocaine has been with us for over 100
years, being an alkaloid obtained from the leaves of the coca plant, which
grows in abundance in South America, particularly Bolivia. When the leaves
are dried and then chewed with powdered lime, the substance stimulates the
nervous system and reduces the desire to eat. For centuries, the leaves have
been used in this way by the natives of the Andes.

Formerly used as a local anaesthetic (particularly by dentists), cocaine had been used in many preparations including chewing gum and "Coca-Cola," hence the name, although cocaine has long since been removed from the product. Although the drug was abused by certain elements of the Victorian middle-classes, it was last significantly abused in Britain in the 1920s. Today, cocaine is used to a very limited extent in practical medicine by reason of its dangers and addictive quality. Both coca and cocaine are controlled by the M.D.A. as Class A drugs.

All cocaine is imported, mainly from South America, and usually takes the form of a white powder. The drug is administered by running a "line" of the substance along a flat surface, *e.g.* a sheet of glass/mirror and then sniffed through a tube of rolled up paper. The once popular method of injecting cocaine under the skin has declined.

In 1991 some 1000 kilogrammes of cocaine (including "crack") were seized. Cocaine may appear in a *salt* form (cocaine hydrochloride) or in *base* form and indeed these two forms also exist in respect of heroin and amphetamine. The distinction between the *base* and *salt* forms is emphasised below. At street level, the average purity of the salt is between 35 per cent. and 39 per cent., and the cost per gramme is between £50 and £90. A kilogramme of cocaine (97 per cent. pure) might cost up to £30,000.

(a) Crack cocaine

15-13   "Crack" is not new but its production has been simplified in recent years. "Crack" is still cocaine but it is "free base cocaine" and not a salt.

The base form of a drug appears as a wax or an oil. It may be converted into a *salt* by treating it with an acid. If hydrochloric acid is applied to cocaine then the base can be converted into *cocaine hydrochloride* (or diamorphine hydrochloride, if applied to heroin). Cocaine base is normally referred to merely as "cocaine." It is controlled in Part I, paragraph 1 of Schedule 2 to the 1971 Act. The *salt* is controlled by paragraph 4 of that Part to the Schedule.

Similarly, the *salt* form of a drug may be converted into *base* by using alkali (*e.g.* sodium bicarbonate or ammonia). This cycle (i.e. salt—base—salt—base) may be repeated and indeed this may assist purification.

Cocaine *base* is waxy, melts and vapourises readily and is therefore preferable for smoking. It is insoluble in water and therefore unsuitable for injecting.

By contrast, the *salt* of cocaine appears as crystals. It does not vaporise easily but it is soluble in water and may therefore be injected.

It follows from the above that *base* cocaine is required if it is to be smoked. "Crack" is merely a dried form of base cocaine. If base cocaine is not available then the salt must be converted into base. One method is to mix the salt with alkali and water. Ether may be added to the mixture. The cocaine base dissolves in ether but ether repels water. Accordingly the ether layer is removed and the water discarded. The ether evaporates and the free base cocaine remains. This process is highly dangerous because ether is inflammable.

A second method is to mix the salt of cocaine with an alkali (*e.g.* baking powder) and water. The mixture is boiled and the base melts and separates. The water is removed. Alternatively, if baking powder and salt is moistened with water and heated in a microwave oven, "crack" may be produced.

Converting a drug from salt to base or vice versa is an act of production for the purposes of section 4 of the 1971 Act: see *Russell* (1992) 94 Cr.App.R. 351; *Greensmith* [1983] 1 W.L.R. 1124 and Chapter 6.

Crack may retail at about £25 per rock.

IV. AMPHETAMINES

These are stimulants used in medicinal preparations for a wide range of **15–14** purposes, including the alleviation of depression, treating alcoholism, slimming aids or simply to maintain a state of alertness. Their effects are not dissimilar to adrenalin. Subsequently the user will experience a mood "trough" and other possible effects, *e.g.* nausea, dizziness and weakness.

Abusers may administer amphetamines by injection but they are mainly taken by mouth or sniffed. The effect of the drug is enhanced by injection but tolerance will develop more quickly. The M.D.A. has controlled many amphetamines including amphetamine sulphate, methyl phenidate (Ritalin), dexamphetamine (Dexedrine) and chlorphentermine (used as a slimming drug).

The popularity of amphetamine has risen considerably in recent years. The street level purity is typically 6 per cent. or less and retails between £10 and £15 per gramme. Caffeine and glucose are popular cutting agents but other agents include aspirin and boric acid. Amphetamine often appears in tablet or capsule form. Relatively little *methylamphetamine* ("ice") has been seized. Methylamphetamine is a hydrochloride salt suitable for smoking. It is a Class B drug.

(a) Ecstasy

"Ecstasy" (M.D.M.A.) is a Class A drug, being a derivative of amphetamine. **15–15** It is normally sold in capsule or tablet form and retails between £10 and £20 per unit. In 1990 there was evidence that M.D.M.A. was declining in popularity as it competed with an increased consumption of LSD. However, 1991 has seen a substantial increase in the consumption of M.D.M.A. Reports suggest that up to half-a-million people have used the drug, a significant number of whom have not abused drugs before. In at least one European country this drug has been lawfully employed under strictly controlled conditions for the purposes of psychotherapy. The doses given are low and only occasionally repeated over a long time scale.

Reports in the press have occasionally described serious side effects of the drug but such reports must be viewed with caution because there have been a disturbing number of cases where Ecstasy has been mixed with other drugs such as LSD. Occasionally, the substance may be described as "ecstasy" when in fact it is a mixture of amphetamine and ketamine ("Special K": controlled under the Medicines Act 1968). Ketamine is said to be a dangerous drug. Ecstasy is sometimes described as a "designer drug" which perhaps suggests that its abuse represents a fashion which may soon pass without causing a long-term social problem. In 1991 some 250,000 doses were seized.

V. Mood Enhancers/Cannabis

15–16   All narcotics will have an effect on mood but cannabis is renowned for creating effects of relaxation, timelessness, changes of perspective and apparent "happiness" or "distress." There is much evidence that cannabis will accentuate pre-existing moods of happiness or tension which may, in turn, be linked to the prevailing environment. It is probable that the drug is not addictive and the evidence of physical or mental harm resulting from its use is equivocal.

In certain African countries, and in the West Indies, cannabis is regularly used and may even form part of the sub-culture. Some people use it as a medicine, *e.g.* for colds, some will fry their fish in the oil, others will smoke the herb or make tea from it, or sprinkle the herb into soups. Others even bake with it. Its use in the United Kingdom is, on average, less exotic, being principally smoked.

15–17   Cannabis is grown in many parts of the world, *e.g.* Morocco, Thailand and India. The active constituent of cannabis is T.H.C. (tetrahydracannabinol). Extracted in its purest form, *i.e.* pure T.H.C., the drug is controlled as a Class A drug. Not all of the plant contains T.H.C., therefore not all of it will be controlled. Section 37(1) of the M.D.A. [as amended by section 52 of the Criminal Law Act 1977] defined "cannabis" as meaning:

"any plant of the genus *Cannabis* or any part of any such plant ... except that it does not include cannabis resin or any of the following products after separation from the rest of the plant, namely—
(*a*) mature stalks of any such plant
(*b*) fibre produced from mature stalk or any such plant
(*c*) seed of any such plant."

Although it is not illegal to possess the seeds, it is an offence to sow them in order to cultivate the plant: see section 6 M.D.A.

The most popular forms of cannabis are:

(i)   *cannabis oil*: very potent;
(ii) *cannabis resin*: less concentrated than oil and extracted from the leaves;
(iii) *herbal cannabis*: weaker than resin; produced from the dried leaves, flowering and fruiting tops of the plant.

When smoked, cannabis produces a sweet, distinctive smell.

VI. Sedatives (Hypnosedatives)/Barbiturates

15–18   These drugs are the opposite of amphetamines. They all depress the operation of the brain. In large doses they will act as sleeping drugs (hypnotics); in small doses they will tranquilise. The drugs may be a *barbiturate* (*e.g.*

barbitone or phenobarbitone) or *non-barbiturate* for example, chloral hydrate (known as a "Mickey Finn" when combined with alcohol), chlormethiazole (Heminevrin), or methaqualone. In 1971, methaqualone (a sedative) was classified as a Class C drug but all barbiturates escaped control, notwithstanding abundant evidence of widespread abuse and psychological dependence. However, the real peril of methaqualone was not in its use as a sedative, but as a powerful hypnotic when combined with diphenhydramine (an antihistamine). If taken with alcohol the effects are pronounced. "Mandrax" was the trade name of a substance that contained both these drugs. It has now been withdrawn in the light of widespread abuse as an hypnotic.

(a) Barbituric acid

Barbituric acid was discovered on St. Barbara's Day in 1869. Since then the   **15–19** acid has been combined to form several salts and esters (*i.e.* the barbiturates). Barbitone, barbitone sodium and phenobarbitone are long term sedatives. All substances containing 5,5 disubstituted barbituric acid are now controlled (Class B). As from April 1, 1986 other sedatives are controlled, including:

(a) Glutethimide (Doriden) (Class B).
(b) Ethchlorvynol (Class C).
(c) Nitrazepam (Mogadon) (Class C).
(d) Methyprylone (Noludar) (Class C).

(b) Tranquilisers

Some of these drugs are also subject to control, including (as from April 1,   **15–20** 1986):

(a) Chlordiazepoxide (Librium) (Class C).
(b) Clobazam (Frisium) (Class C).
(c) Clonazepam (Rivotril) (Class C).
(d) Diazepam (Valium) (Class C).
(e) Flurazepam (Dalmane) (Class C).
(f) Meprobamate (Equanil) (Class C).
(g) Oxazepam (Serenid-D) (Class C).
(h) Temazepam (Normison) (Class C).
(i) Triazolam (Halcion) (Class C).

All sedatives are highly addictive, particularly psychologically, and tolerance is liable to develop. When combined regularly with alcohol there is a marked increase in the risk of overdosing, since alcohol is also a depressant. To a person *physically* dependant on a sedative, the symptoms of the sudden withdrawal can be most unpleasant, including fear, sickness and delirium.

VII. SLIMMING DRUGS

Certain drugs are designed to encourage the loss of appetite or to "burn up   **15–21** energy." They may ostensibly accentuate the level of one's "awareness." The effects are therefore similar to amphetamine and indeed many slimming drugs contain amphetamine as an active ingredient. We have seen that amphetamine is controlled (Class B) and examples of other "slimmers" are:

    (a)   Phenmetrazine (Class B).
    (b)   Dexamphetamine (Class B).
    (c)   Benzphetamine (Class C).
    (d)   Chlorphentermine (Class C).

[Dexamphetamine is omitted from paragraph 1(*a*) of Part II of Schedule 2 to the M.D.A., but it is still included in Part II by virtue of paragraph 2, being a stereoisomeric form of amphetamine: see S.I. 1985 No. 1995.]

VIII. Solvents

15–22   In the last few years an alarming number of individuals, predominantly teenagers, have indulged in the highly dangerous practice of "sniffing" solvents, *e.g.* glues. The glue is often put into a bag, the top of which is shaped to cover the nose and mouth. The vapours released are then inhaled. Many other toxic substances are abused, ranging from typewriter correction fluid to nail varnish remover. It is the relative ease and inexpense involved in obtaining these substances which find favour with the teenage abuser, rather than the "satisfaction" derived from the abuse.

In attempting to control the abuse of solvents, Parliament has been faced with a major practical problem. One option would be to control the chemical ingredient concerned under the M.D.A. but this would adversely affect commerce and the everyday lives of millions of non-abusers. The alternative was to restrict the supply of certain solvents to persons likely to be affected. Parliament opted for the latter course which led to the passing of the Intoxicating Substances (Supply) Act 1985.

B. THE CONSUMPTION FACTORS

I. Administration

15–23   By section 37(2) M.D.A. 1971 the misuse of a drug involves:

"... misusing it by taking it; and the reference ... to the taking of a drug is a reference to the taking of it by a human being by way of any form of self-administration, whether or not involving assistance by another."

Drugs are principally taken by injection, by mouth and by inhalation into the lungs or the nostrils. Injections may be *intravenous*, *e.g.* heroin, *intramuscular*, *e.g.* heroin, if slow absorption is intended (rarely done and dangerous) or *subcutaneous* (under the skin) *e.g.* cocaine. Different methods of administration determine different rates of absorption of the drug into the bloodstream. Intravenous injection produces a near-instant effect. Other methods are much slower.

II. DOSAGE

Assessing the amount of the drug to administer involves a very complex   15–24
interaction between first, the rate of absorption; secondly, the rate at which
the drug is destroyed/eliminated by the body; and thirdly, the desired effect.
Dosage will also depend on many personal factors including the level of personal tolerance to the drug. An addict may consume heroin at a rate which
might well kill a normal individual.

III. DRUG METABOLISM

The body keeps certain drugs inactive until a chemical conversion has   15–25
taken place or until it can be excreted. In this way, the body keeps certain substances "in storage" until needed or eliminated from the body altogether.

IV. DESTRUCTION AND DISPOSAL

If the level of absorption exceeds the rate at which the body gets rid of the   15–26
drug then there will be a build up of that drug in the body. Depending on the
drug and the amount consumed, it may be a matter of hours or months,
before the drug is totally removed or destroyed by the body.

V. ADDICTION

Dependence may be *physical*, in which event tolerance develops. The body   15–27
therefore needs the drug in order to prevent the effects of withdrawal if the
regular administration of the substance is suddenly halted or interrupted.
Alternatively, dependence may be *psychological*, resulting in a "craving" for
the drug. Curing both forms of addiction is very difficult. Indeed treatment
can only be successful if the addict displays a determined resolve to rid himself
of the habit.

VI. SYNERGISTICS: THE DRUG COCKTAIL

A combination of several drugs may have no more effect than if only one   15–28
drug had been taken. Where the effect of any combination is greater than if
only one drug had been taken, the drugs are said to act *synergistically*. If the
effect produced is less, then they are said to act *antagonistically*. Sometimes
addicts will mix a "cocktail" in order to mimic the effects of a substance that
they would prefer to use, *e.g.* heroin, but which may be in short supply.
Alternatively, the cocktail may be intended to produce a totally different experience, may be the product of an "experiment," or is intended to defeat certain side effects, *e.g.* depression, sickness or trembling.

It should come as no surprise to find that drug dealers have jumped on the
band-wagon and now retail ready-made cocktails. Nevertheless, this is a
fairly recent development but a most disturbing one. Heroin, imported from

Pakistan for example, has occasionally been found to contain phenobarbitone and methaqualone. The amount of heroin in the product may be no higher than 30–35 per cent. but, given the presence of the other drugs, the effect is largely similar to heroin of greater purity. The user may be totally unaware of the additives. If tolerance develops the user will therefore be unwittingly addicted to the additive(s) as well as to the heroin. He will be deterred from buying elsewhere since other supplies may not contain, say, phenobarbitone (to which he is now addicted), and will experience withdrawal symptoms in consequence. Furthermore, the user wishing to cure his addiction will find the task far more difficult, since treatment must now attack addiction to more than one substance.

It follows that dealers peddling this type of concoction can only expect the courts to administer harsh penalties.

VII. OTHER "DRUG" TERMS

15–29   It will be seen from the various Schedules to the M.D.A. and the current Regulations that drugs are specified as "controlled" in paragraph 1 of Parts I, II or III of Schedule 2 to the M.D.A. However, the Schedules also refer to the "stereoisomeric forms," "esters," the "ethers" and the "salts" of various controlled drugs. These terms are not defined by the M.D.A., being terms of science. Without a reasonable knowledge of chemistry, merely defining these terms is not very helpful. Nevertheless, if only to serve as an indication, here they are:

Isomers consist of at least two compounds which are structurally different but molecularly identical. Since they differ structurally, the compounds will have different chemical and physical properties. However, where the structures of the compounds are asymmetrically similar then they may be optically *stereoisomeric*: their chemical and physical properties are the same.

Esters are combinations of alcohol and acid forming organic chemicals. They often produce an appealing fragrance.

Common ether is made up of carbon, hydrogen and oxygen, but *ethers* is a generic term embracing compounds made by the interaction of alcohols and acids.

Expressed very generally, a *salt* is the resultant combination of a metal atom with other non-metal atoms, *e.g.* chloride and sulphate.

C. THE TOOLS OF "THE TRADE" AND OTHER HALLMARKS

15–30   Proving possession of a drug is relatively easy. Proving allegations of supplying, possession with intent to supply, permitting premises to be used for smoking cannabis, etc., frequently involves asking the courts to draw safe inferences from the surrounding circumstances. When assessing the relevance and the significance of certain facts, the following points should be borne in mind:

(i) The quantity bought by a drug user will depend on his means and the state of the black market.

(ii) A bulk purchase will be very much cheaper. A large quantity of drug divided up into several small "lots," "doses," "deals" or "folds," *may* indicate an intent to supply but, may either have been acquired in that form or may have been divided up by the user in order to regulate his intake.

(iii) The *place* where the drug was found is clearly relevant and may be highly significant. Thus a large quantity of drug that would still be consistent with personal use, might well be inconsistent with that purpose if the drug had been found in the suspect's pocket at a public house, place of work, or at school.

(iv) Unexplained "profits" in the hands of a suspect is frequently a powerful indication that clinches allegations of supplying. "Following the money" is therefore an invaluable line of enquiry which is frequently neglected. However, it is an item that must also be examined with care, for it is only too easy to make false assumptions. Where large "profits" received by the defendant are totally unaccounted for and not consistent with the known legitimate activities of the individual concerned, then that fact will clearly be relevant to charges of supplying or trafficking in controlled drugs. Again, where the cost of buying the drug, said to be for personal use, exceeds the user's income, then that fact will also be relevant to an allegation of supply or possession with intent to supply because it may indicate that small quantities were sold by the user in order to feed his addiction.

Of course, monies may have been acquired by other illegal activities, *e.g.* theft, prostitution, in which case the suspect will be most reluctant to admit those offences which may explain the existence of large sums of money in his possession which have not been invested with a financial institution. Secondly, there is always the possibility of the "hidden income," *i.e.* credit, that would substantially account for the difference. Many drug suppliers sell drugs on credit. It is sometimes their way of ensuring a continuity of trade with the recipient of the drug. Again, arrears of rent and other debts must be put into the calculation since one might discover that had it not been for the drug-habit the bills would otherwise have been paid.

(v) Scales used for measuring minute quantities, *e.g.* milligrammes and grammes, may be equivocal if the suspect is a user of drugs who, typically, must measure his own supply in such small amounts.   **15–31**

(vi) Razor blades, panes of glass or mirrors bearing traces of the drug, straws, tubes or rolls of paper, squares of silver foil, hubble-bubble pipes, may all be consistent with personal use but may also be consistent with supplying (save for the pipe) if other features are present, *e.g.* a very large quantity of drug.

(vii) Cutting agents. These are used to dilute certain drugs, especially heroin. The existence of a large quantity of drug coupled with a separate finding of a familiar cutting agent may be indicative of supply. Such a view may be reinforced if the drug is also found to be mixed with that agent. There are three reasons why the drug may be cut. First, to maximise profits if cut for the purpose of supply. Secondly, to reduce the purity, from the addict's point of view, if a lesser dose is required, or in order to enforce an "economy" by padding out the quantity, and thirdly, with a view to adding another active substance to achieve a desired effect. In recent years the practice of cutting the drug with "rubbish," *i.e.* a harmful additive such as cleaning powder, seems to be on the decline. This is probably not because suppliers have become more scrupulous, but simply because it makes good commercial sense given that there is now much more heroin on the black market, sold by many more dealers. Since competition is tougher, there is a disincentive to supply "bad" heroin.

15–32   (viii) The existence of a large number of strips of paper (perhaps torn from a magazine), or a number of small plastic "bank bags," may also suggest supplying.

(ix) An exceptionally large number of casual acquaintances visiting the suspect's home for apparently unsociably short periods of time, may indicate supplying if other tools of the trade, etc., are found at the address.

(x) Abbreviated records or calculations for which no reasonable explanation is given may suggest supply but might also be a record of sums owed to various drug creditors. This is another feature which must be examined with particular care.

(xi) A suspect, found in possession of a drug, who is not himself a user of that drug. Such a finding of fact is totally inconsistent with personal use and therefore the suspect is either holding the drug on behalf of another, *e.g.* as a mere bailee, or is an outright supplier.

D. THE STATUTORY BODIES

I. THE ADVISORY COUNCIL

15–33   The Advisory Council created by section 1 of the M.D.A., is entrusted with the responsibility of keeping under review the situation in the United Kingdom with respect to drugs which are being abused, or are likely to be abused, or may have harmful effects sufficient to constitute "a social problem." It must therefore monitor the current situation, promote research (section 1(2)(e)) and, above all, advise the government on measures:

(i)   which ought to be taken to prevent drug misuse;
(ii) to deal with resultant social problems;
(iii) to restrict/supervise the supply of dangerous drugs;
(iv) to facilitate treatment;
(v)   to promote co-operation between the community and the professions;
(vi) to educate the public.

15–34   It is apparent that the Advisory Council needs to pool the knowledge of many different disciplines. Accordingly, the Council consists of at least 20 members, including practitioners from the field of medicine, dentistry, veterinary medicine and pharmacy. Other members must have wide and recent experience of social problems connected with drug misuse.

It has already been noted how important it is that the law should be as certain as possible while being flexible enough to adjust to social and medical opinion. With every change of Government there may also be a change of policy or direction. Nevertheless, continuity is substantially maintained through the Advisory Council by virtue of section 31(3) of the M.D.A. which provides:

> "The Secretary of State shall not make any regulations under this Act except after consultation with the Advisory Council."

Again, the Advisory Council must be consulted before draft Orders in Council, intended to amend the classes of controlled drugs in Schedule 2 of the M.D.A., are laid before Parliament; see section 2(5), or before an Order is made under section 7(4) (restricting the use of certain drugs to research purposes only; or prohibiting a practitioner, pharmacist, etc., from manufacturing, supplying or administering certain drugs other than by licence): see section 7(5).

II. TRIBUNALS

Where a practitioner is suspected of being in breach of certain provisions of the M.D.A., or is, in fact, in breach of any of them, the Secretary of State may contemplate issuing a *direction* to that practitioner not to prescribe, administer or supply drugs specified in the direction. In order to investigate the matter, the Secretary of State should refer the case to a tribunal who shall report on it to the Secretary of State: section 14(1) of the M.D.A. If the tribunal finds the case "proved" it may indicate, in its report, the controlled drugs which it considers should be specified in the direction: section 14(4).   **15–35**

The tribunal consists of five persons. The chairman, who is a barrister or solicitor of at least seven years' standing, is appointed by the Lord Chancellor. The remaining members are all drawn from the practitioner's profession. Proceedings are normally heard in private unless the respondent, *i.e.* the practitioner, successfully applies to the tribunal for a public hearing: see Schedule 3 of the M.D.A.

The Lord Chancellor may regulate the rules of procedure to be followed and the rules of evidence to be observed. All parties may be legally represented.

III. ADVISORY BODIES

If the tribunal finds the case proved, and the Secretary of State notifies the respondent of his intention to give a direction prohibiting the respondent prescribing, administering or supplying certain drugs, then the respondent may within 28 days make representations in reply. If representations are made the case is then referred by the Secretary of State to an advisory body consisting of three persons chaired by a Queen's Counsel appointed by the Lord Chancellor. The respondent may be legally represented. The task of the advisory bodies, as the name implies, to advise the Secretary of State: see section 14(6) and section 14(7) of the M.D.A. Their findings are not binding on the Secretary of State.   **15–36**

IV. PROFESSIONAL PANEL

15–37   The above procedure can be protracted. The Secretary of State may consider that prompt and decisive measures are required. Accordingly, by section 15(1), where the Secretary of State considers that a practitioner has been prescribing irresponsibly, hence the need for rapid action, he may give temporary directions to the practitioner. In order to protect the interests and rights of the respondent, the Secretary of State *must* first refer the case to a professional panel which in turn, must afford the respondent the right to be heard. The Secretary of State may not give temporary directions unless the panel confirms that the information available "affords reasonable grounds" for thinking that the respondent has been prescribing controlled drugs irresponsibly: see sections 15(2)(*a*) and *b*).

The panel consists of a chairman and two members all of whom are drawn from the ranks of the respondent's profession. The respondent is entitled to be legally represented.

Appendix
Schedule 2 to the Misuse of Drugs Act 1971

[As amended by S.I. 1973 No. 771, S.I. 1975 No. 421, S.I. 1977 No. 1243, S.I. 1979 No. 299, S.I. 1983 No. 765, S.I. 1984 No. 859, S.I. 1985 No. 1995, S.I. 1986 No. 2230, S.I. 1989 No. 1340, S.I. 1990 No. 2589.]

CONTROLLED DRUGS

PART I

CLASS A DRUGS

"1. The following substances and products, namely:—

(*a*) Acetorphine
Alfentanil
Allylprodine
Alphacetylmethadol
Alphameprodine
Alphamethadol
Alphaprodine
Anileridine

Benzethidine
Benzylmorphine
(3-benzylmorphine)
Betacetylmethadol
Betameprodine
Betamethadol
Bezitramide
Bufotenine

Cannabinol, except where contained in cannabis or cannabis resin
Cannabinol derivatives

Carfentanil
Clonitazene
Coca leaf
Cocaine

Desomorphine
Dextromoramide
Diamorphine
Diampromide
Diethylthiambutene
Difenoxin (1-(3-cyano-3, 3-diphenylpropyl) -4-phenylpiperidine-4- carboxylic acid)
Dihydrocodeinone O-carboxymethyloxime
Dihydromorphine
Dimenoxadole
Dimepheptanol
Dimethylthiambutene
Dioxaphetyl butyrate
Diphenoxylate

Dipipanone
Drotebanol (3, 4-dimethoxy-17-
  methylmorphinan-6β, 14-diol)

Ecgonine, and any derivative of
  ecgonine which is convertible
  to ecgonine or to cocaine
Ethylmethylthiambutene
Eticyclidine
Etonitazene
Etorphine
Etoxeridine

Fentanyl
Furethidine

Hydrocodone
Hydromorphinol
Hydromorphone
Hydroxypethidine

Isomethadone

Ketobemidone

Levomethorphan
Levomoramide
Levophenacylmorphan
Levorphanol
Lofentanil
Lysergamide
Lysergide and other N-alkyl
  derivatives of lysergamide

Mescaline
Metazocine
Methadone
Methadyl acetate
Methyldesorphine
Methyldihydromorphine
  (6-methyldihydromorphine)
Metopon
Morpheridine
Morphine
Morphine methobromide,
  morphine N-oxide and other
  pentavalent nitrogen morphine
  derivatives
Myrophine

[Nicodicodine
  (6-nicotinoyldihydrocodeine)]

Nicomorphine
  (3,6-dinicotinoylmorphine)
Noracymethadol
Norlevorphanol
Normethadone
Normorphine
Norpipanone

Opium, whether raw, prepared or
  medicinal
Oxycodone
Oxymorphone

Pethidine
Phenadoxone
Phenampromide
Phenazocine
Phencyclidine
Phenomorphan
Phenoperidine
Piminodine
Piritramide
Poppy-straw and concentrate of
  poppy-straw
Proheptazine
Properidine (1-methyl-4-
  phenyl-piperidine-4-carboxylic
  acid isopropyl ester)
Psilocin

Racemethorphan
Racemoramide
Racemorphan
Rolicyclidine

Sufentanil

Tenocylidine
Thebacon
Thebaine
Tilidate
Trimeperidine

4-Bromo-2,5-dimethoxy-
  α-methylphenethylamine
4-Cyano-2-dimethylamino-4,
  4-diphenylbutane
4-Cyano-l-methyl-4-
  phenylpiperidine
4-Methyl-aminorex
N,N-Diethyltryptamine

N,N-Dimethyltryptamine	2-Methyl-3-morpholino-1,
2,5-Dimethoxy-α,	1-diphenylpropanecarboxylic
4-dimethylphenethylamine	acid 4-methyl-aminorex
1-Methyl-4-phenylpiperidine	4-Phenylpiperidine-4-carboxylic
-4-carboxylic acid	acid ethyl ester

(b) any compound (not being a compound for the time being specified in sub-paragraph (a) above) structurally derived from tryptamine or from a ring-hydroxy tryptamine by substitution at the nitrogen atom of the sidechain with one or more alkyl substituents but no other substituent;

(c) any compound (not being methoxyphenamine or a compound for the time being specified in sub-paragraph (a) above) structurally derived from phenethylamine, an N-alkylphenethylamine, α-methylphenethylamine, an N-alkyl-α-methylphenethylamine, α-ethylphenethylamine, or an N-alkyl-α-ethylphenethylamine by substitution in the ring to any extent with alkyl, alkoxy, alkylenedioxy or halide substituents, whether or not further substituted in the ring by one or more other univalent substituents.

(d) any compound (not being a compound for the time being specified in sub-paragraph (a) above) structurally derived from fentanyl by modification in any of the following ways, that is to say,

(i) by replacement of the phenyl portion of the phenethyl group by any heteromonocycle whether or not further substituted in the heterocycle;

(ii) by substitution in the phenethyl group with alkyl, alkenyl, alkoxy, hydroxy, halogeno, haloalkyl, amino or nitro groups;

(iii) by substitution in the piperidine ring with alkyl or alkenyl groups;

(iv) by substitution in the aniline ring with alkyl, alkoxy, alkylenedioxy, halogeno or haloalkyl groups;

(v) by substitution at the 4-position of the piperidine ring with any alkoxycarbonyl or acyloxy group;

(vi) by replacement of the N-propionyl group by another acyl group;

(e) any compound (not being a compound for the time being specified in sub-paragraph (a) above) structurally derived from pethidine by modification in any of the following ways, that is to say,

(i) by replacement of the 1-methyl group by an acyl, alkyl whether or not unsaturated, benzyl or phenethyl group, whether or not further substituted;

(ii) by substitution in the piperidine ring with alkyl or alkenyl groups or with a propano bridge, whether or not further substituted;

(iii) by substitution in the 4-phenyl ring with alkyl, alkoxy, aryloxy, halogeno or haloalkyl groups;

(iv) by replacement of the 4-ethoxycarbonyl by any other alkoxycarbonyl or any alkoxyalkyl or acyloxy group;

(v) by formation of an N-oxide or of a quaternary base.

2. Any stereoisomeric form of a substance for the time being specified in paragraph 1 above not being dextromethorphan or dextrorphan.

3. Any ester or ether of a substance for the time being specified in paragraph 1 or 2 above (*not being a substance for the time being specified in Part II of this Schedule*).

4. Any salt of a substance for the time being specified in any of paragraphs 1 to 3 above.

5. Any preparation or other product containing a substance or product for the time being specified in any of paragraphs 1 to 4 above.

6. Any preparation designed for administration by injection which includes a substance or product for the time being specified in any of paragraphs 1 to 3 of Part II of this Schedule."

[Drotebanol and section 3 were inserted by S.I. 1973 No. 771.
Nicodicodine was omitted by S.I. 1973 No. 771.
Difenoxin and 4-Bromo-2,5-dimethoxy,α-methylphenethylamine were inserted by S.I. 1975 No. 421. Section 1(*a*) was inserted by the same order.
Sections 1(*b*) and 1(*c*) were inserted by S.I. 1977 No. 1243.
Phencyclidine was inserted by S.I. 1979 No. 299.
Sufentanil was inserted by S.I. 1983 No. 765.
Alfentanil, eticyclidine, rolicyclidine and tilidate were inserted by S.I. 1984 No. 859.
Tenocyclidine was inserted by S.I. 1985 No. 1995.
Carfentanil, lofentanil and sections 1(*d*) and 1(*e*) were inserted by S.I. 1986 No. 2230.
4-Methyl-aminorex and 2-Methyl-3-morpholino-1,1-diphenylpropanecarboxylic acid 4-methyl-aminorex were inserted by S.I. 1990 No. 2589.]

PART II

CLASS B DRUGS

"1. The following substances and products, namely:—

(*a*) Acetyldihydrocodeine
Amphetamine

Cannabis and cannabis resin
Codeine

[Dexamphetamine]
Dihydrocodeine

Ethylmorphine
  (3-ethylmorphine)

Glutethimide

Lefetamine

Mecloqualone

Methaqualone
Methylamphetamine
Methylphenidate
Methylphenobarbitone

Nicocodine
Nicodicodine
  (6-nicotinoyldihydrocodeine)
Norcodeine

Pentazocine
Phenmetrazine
Pholcodine
Propiram

(*b*) any 5,5 disubstituted barbituric acid.

2. Any stereoisomeric form of a substance for the time being specified in paragraph 1 of this part of this Schedule.

3. Any salt of a substance for the time being specified in any of paragraphs 1 or 2 of this Part of this Schedule.

4. Any preparation or other product containing a substance or product for the time being specified in any of paragraphs 1 to 3 of this Part of this Schedule, not being a preparation falling within paragraph 6 of Part I of this Schedule."

[Nicodicodine and propiram were inserted by S.I. 1973 No. 771.
Section 1(*a*) was inserted by S.I. 1984 No. 859, as were mecloqualone, methaqualone, methylphenobarbitone and any 5,5 disubstituted barbituric acid.
Dexamphetamine was omitted by S.I. 1985 No. 1995.
Glutethimide, lefetamine, pentazocine were inserted by S.I. 1985 No. 1995.]

PART III

CLASS C DRUGS

"1. The following substances, namely:—

Alprazolam

Benzphetamine
Bromazepam
Buprenorphine

Camazepam
Cathine
Cathinone
Chlordiazepoxide
Chlorphentermine
Clobazam
Clonazepam
Clorazepic acid
Clotiazepam
Cloxazolam

Delorazepam
Dextropropoxyphene
Diazepam
Diethylpropion

Estazolam
Ethchlorvynol
Ethinamate
Ethyl loflazepate

[Fencamfamin]
Fenethylline
Fenproporex
Fludiazepam
Flunitrazepam
Flurazepam

Halazepam
Haloxazolam

Ketazolam

Loprazolam
Lorazepam
Lormetazepam

Mazindol
Medazepam
Medozolam
Mefenorex
Mephentermine
Meprobamate
[Methaqualone]
Methyprylone

Nimetazepam
Nitrazepam

341

Nordazepam

Oxazepam

Oxazolam

[Pemoline]

Phendimetrazine

[Phentermine]

Pinazepam

Pipradrol

Prazepam

[Prolintane]

Propylhexedrine

Pyrovalerone

Temazepam

Tetrazepam

Triazolam

N-Ethylamphetamine

2. Any stereoisomeric form of a substance for the time being specified in paragraph 1 of this part of this Schedule (*not being phenylpropanolamine*)

3. Any salt of a substance for the time being specified in any of paragraph 1 or 2 of this Part of this Schedule.

4. Any preparation or other product containing a substance for the time being specified in any of paragraphs 1 to 3 of this Part of this Schedule."

[Fencamfamin, phentermine, prolintane and pemoline were omitted by S.I. 1973 No. 771.

Dextropropoxyphene was inserted by S.I. 1985 No. 765.

Diethylpropion was inserted by S.I. 1984 No. 859.

Methaqualone was omitted by S.I. 1984 No. 859.

Alprazolam, bromazepam, camazepam, chlordiazepoxide, clobazam, clonazepam, clorazepic acid, clotiazepam, cloxazolam, delorazepam, diazepam, estazolam, ethchorvynol, ethinamate, ethyl loflazepale, fludiazepam, flunitrazepam, flurazepam, halazepam, haloxazolam, ketazolam, loprazolam, lorazepam, lormetazepam, mazindol, medazepam, meprobamate, methyprylone, nimetazepam, nitroazepam, nordazepam, oxazepam, oxazolam, pinazepam, prazepam, temazepam, tetrazepam and triazolam were all inserted by S.I. 1985 No. 1995.

Phentermine was reinserted by S.I. 1985 No. 1955.

Cathine, cathinone, fenethylline, fenproporex, mefenorex, propylhexedrine, pyrovalerone, N-Ethylamphetamine and the italicised material in section 2 were inserted by S.I. 1986 No. 2230.

Fencamfamin was reinserted by S.I. 1986 No. 2230.

Buprenorphine was inserted by S.I. 1989 No. 1340.

Medozolam was inserted by S.I. 1990 No. 2589.]

INDEX